International

Also by Martin Wight

The Development of the Legislative Council 1606–1945 (1946).

Power Politics (1946).

The Gold Coast Legislative Council (1947).

Attitude to Africa, with W. Arthur Lewis, Michael Scott and
Colin Legum (1951).

British Colonial Constitutions 1947 (1952).

Diplomatic Investigations, edited and contributed to, with
Herbert Butterfield (1966).

Systems of States, edited by Hedley Bull (1977).

Power Politics, edited by Hedley Bull and Carsten Holbraad (1978).

International Theory
The Three Traditions

Martin Wight

Edited by
Gabriele Wight and Brian Porter

With an introductory essay by
Hedley Bull

Leicester University Press, London
for
The Royal Institute of International Affairs, London

Leicester University Press
(a division of Pinter Publishers Ltd)
25 Floral Street, Covent Garden, London, WC2E 9DS

First published in Great Britain in 1991; paperback edition 1994

British Library Cataloguing in Publication Data

A CIP catalogue record for this book is available from The British Library

ISBN 0 7185 1412 2 (hbk)
       0 7185 1744 X (pbk)

Extract from 'East Coker' from *Four Quartets* reprinted by permission of Faber and Faber Ltd from *Collected Poems 1909-1962* by T.S. Eliot

The Royal Institute of International Affairs is an independent body which promotes the rigorous study of international questions and does not express opinions of its own. The opinions expressed in this publication are the responsibility of the authors.

Typeset by Mayhew Typesetting, Rhayader, Powys
Printed and bound in Great Britain

Contents

Preface

Martin Wight first formulated his international theory during a course of lectures he gave at the London School of Economics in the 1950s. Brian Porter and I have aimed at reproducing them in a form as true to the original as possible. There are no additions and few omissions. No doubt my husband would have revised and altered the material had he lived to do so. Indeed, some of the themes were developed, modified or touched upon especially in, for instance, the chapters on 'Western Values in International Relations' and 'The Balance of Power' in *Diplomatic Investigations* (1966) and in *Systems of States* (1977) respectively. All the same, we decided to publish these lectures not least because references are made to their main ideas and line of argument in current publications and also lecture courses and seminars in International Relations Departments.

Some ten years ago Hedley Bull first planned to edit the manuscript with me. His trust in the value of the undertaking and the enthusiasm he showed when we began the work have been the mainspring of my effort to tackle the task after his untimely death. Mary Bull's active help and support since, played no little part in this. I am grateful to her for letting me use Hedley's thoughtful analysis of the lectures as an introduction.

Brian Porter valiantly stepped into the breach Hedley Bull had left. For his guiding hand and patience stretched over several years I cannot express my thanks adequately. He undertook to read the entire text and rephrased where necessary obscure passages. Collating several versions of an introduction as well as of conclusions he gave the whole a final coherence. I am most grateful.

But my daughter Barbara had imposed the first order upon the large amount of material and transcribed it from the shorthand of the lecture notes into the smooth, logical and easily readable first copy of the book. I would not have managed the task so well, if at all. My greatest thanks go to her. She has given invaluable time, wit and care to the project.

My sincere thanks to the staff of the LSE library without whose help I would never have been able to unearth many pamphlets and long out-of-print publications. Pauline Wickham of Chatham House gave me encouragement, moral and practical support over all these years of gestation. She also exerted on us a certain pressure, from time to time, necessary to complete the book. I shall always be grateful to her. Last but not least my thanks to Alison Jones whose good humour and expertise sustained me more than I can say while she initiated me into the labyrinth of the simplest of computer models. No less know-how was shown by Matthew Akester and Anthony Smith when helping me over the last hurdle, the indexing. It was crucial to meet deadlines! Their calm and that of my long-suffering family was soothing and essential to me.

Alas, it was John Vincent, the other mentor, after Hedley Bull, to whom I should have handed the 'final version' for comment and approval. His sudden death cuts deep.

G.W.
Speldhurst, Kent

When in 1986 Gabriele Wight invited me to assist her in editing these lectures on 'International Theory', I felt both honoured to be asked to participate, and excited at the prospect of seeing a long-harboured wish fulfilled: the appearance in print of the lectures I had attended and been enthralled by when a student of Martin's at the London School of Economics in the 1950s. Martin Wight exercised a profound influence on all who came to know him, but it was in these lectures that his unrivalled qualities as a teacher — immense erudition, humane judgement, pungent expression, and an aura of great moral authority — were displayed at their clearest and brightest. Indeed, the lectures not only attracted many students whose specific academic concerns lay outside theoretical approaches, but very soon became famous, if only by report, throughout the International Relations profession. They appeared to bring almost everything that went on in the world of politics, and particularly international politics, and which otherwise seemed chaotic, into sharp focus, so that one began to see the philosophical springs to nearly all political outlook and behaviour.

The task of editing these lectures was a daunting one. Gabriele and Barbara Wight undertook the arduous work both of producing a text from Martin's notes, preserved on hundreds of small sheets of paper in his impeccable hand, and of tracing and verifying the innumerable references. My own role, helped by memories of the lectures, and the notes I took at the time, was the more congenial one of checking that this text was as accurate a representation of the lectures as could be achieved. For the most part, Martin's notes were sufficiently detailed and well-structured for their meaning to be clear, and although on occasion the sense was with difficulty wrung from a few puzzling words, in only one or two instances did we find ourselves at a loss. Again, in only a few cases were references not traced or the labour involved in tracing them would have been out of all proportion to their value. In such instances we ask the reader's indulgence.

The other main editorial task was the refinement of the text we now had before us. Had Martin Wight, who was a perfectionist in the preparation of material for publication, himself turned these lectures into a book, he would undoubtedly have made many changes and excisions. We, however, have approached this problem conservatively, making small changes only in the interests of clarity, and in nearly every case leaving in, rather than taking out, material that appeared to be of marginal value. If the argument has been slowed thereby, the reader will at least be compensated by a rich quarry of example and illustration. The few deletions we judged it right to make were almost exclusively of references to minor political events or issues, topical at the time the lectures were delivered in the 1950s but now largely forgotten. On the other hand we felt it no part of our task to bring the illustrative material up to date, and simply limited ourselves to a few brief editors' references to more recent happenings that seemed especially relevant to the argument.

When Martin Wight first drafted these lectures, he gave the names Realist, Rationalist and Revolutionist to his three traditions. At some point he preferred calling them the Machiavellian, Grotian and Kantian traditions of politics. As he was continually revising these lectures, but not all at once, in some the earlier terms are employed, and in others the later. We decided that to turn all into one or the other for the sake of uniformity would be unjustifiable, and so we have left them as we found them.

The reader should also bear in mind that although these lectures have now been put into book form, they are still basically lectures, designed to stimulate, even provoke, youthful minds. It is this quality, which made them so exciting to listen to, which accounts for the occasional over-emphasis, or dramatic searching after superlatives, to which Hedley Bull refers in his Introduction.

Because these lectures have been much more heard about than heard, few scholars have been in a position to write about them. I attempted a study in 1975 and sent a copy to Hedley Bull. My paper was later published as 'Patterns of Thought and Practice: Martin Wight's "International Theory"' in *Reason of States*, edited by Michael Donelan (1978). Meanwhile Hedley Bull's own magisterial assessment appeared as the second Martin Wight Memorial Lecture, delivered at the London School of Economics on 29th January 1976. This, we both agreed, with but little adaptation, would make an ideal introduction to the present volume, and to this suggestion Mary Bull generously gave her consent.

At every stage in the long process of editing, we have made the many problems which we encountered the subject of consultation and agreement. It was a piece of happy fortune that Gabriele Wight and I should dwell in the same county. The many visits I made to Speldhurst, and the hospitality I received from the Wight family, have added to a sense of satisfaction at helping to make Martin's work more widely known the pleasantest of memories.

B.E.P.
Seasalter, Kent

Martin Wight and the theory of international relations *

Hedley Bull

It was Professor Manning who urged me to attend the lectures on International Theory being given by Martin Wight, then reader in the Department of International Relations at the London School of Economics and Political Science. These lectures made a profound impression on me, as they did on all who heard them. Ever since that time I have felt in the shadow of Martin Wight's thought — humbled by it, a constant borrower from it, always hoping to transcend it but never able to escape from it. Until 1961, when he moved to the University of Sussex, I was his junior colleague. After that time I was able to keep in touch with his work through the meetings of the British Committee on the Theory of International Politics, for which many of his best papers were written. Since Martin Wight's death in 1972 I have become more intimately acquainted with his ideas than ever before, through being involved in the editing of his unpublished manuscripts.

Let me say a little about this. Wight was a perfectionist who published very little of his work. His writings on International Relations comprise one sixty-eight page pamphlet, published in 1946 by Chatham House for one shilling and long out of print, and half a dozen chapters in books and articles, some of the latter placed in obscure journals as if in the hope that no one would notice them. He was one of those scholars — today, alas, so rare — who (to use a phrase of Albert Wohlstetter's) believe in a high ratio of thought to publication.

It has seemed to me a task of great importance to bring more of his work to the light of day. That the work he left should be published at all was not self-evident. Some of it is unfinished. Some may never have been intended for publication. If it was his judgment that the

* This paper was first delivered as the second Martin Wight Memorial lecture on 29 January 1976 at the London School of Economics and published in *Brit. J. International Studies* 2 (1976), 101–16.

work did not meet the very high standards he set himself for publication, should his judgment not be respected? For myself, what has weighed most is not the desire to add lustre to Martin Wight's name, but my belief in the importance of the material itself and in the need to make it available to others, so that the lines of inquiry he opened up can be taken further. Especially, perhaps, there is a need to make Martin Wight's ideas more widely available in their original form, rather than through the second-hand accounts of others, such as myself, who have been influenced by him. Fortunately the notes — detailed and immaculate in his beautiful handwriting — of the lectures on International Theory which impressed me so deeply when I arrived at the London School of Economics, and are the most profound of his contributions to International Relations, have been preserved.

In this discussion of some of Martin Wight's own ideas, I shall not attempt to provide a survey of his life and thought as a whole. I have sought to provide the sketch of one in the introduction to his *Systems of States*.[1] I want instead to focus on one part of Martin Wight's legacy, *viz.* his ideas on the Theory of International Relations. First, I propose briefly to state what some of these ideas were. Secondly, I shall consider some questions that have long puzzled students of his work about the interpretation and assessment of these ideas. And thirdly I shall ask what can be learnt from Martin Wight's example.

When in the 1950s Wight was developing his lecture course at the London School of Economics the scientific or behaviourist movement towards what was called 'A Theory of International Relations' was gathering strength in the United States. This movement had its roots in dissatisfaction with what was taken to be the crude and obsolete methodology of existing general works about International Relations, especially those of Realist writers such as E.H. Carr, George F. Kennan and Hans Morgenthau, which formed the staple academic diet of the time. The hope that inspired the behaviourists was that by developing a more refined and up-to-date methodology it would be possible to arrive at a rigorously scientific body of knowledge that would help explain the past, predict the future and provide a firm basis for political action.

Wight's interest in the Theory of International Relations may also have owed something to dissatisfaction with the writings of the Realists, with which his own essay on *Power Politics* had close affinities, although his was a dissatisfaction with their substance rather than with their methodology. But the kind of theory to which he was drawn was utterly different from that which was intended by the behaviourists. He saw the Theory of International Relations — or, as he called it, International Theory — as a study in political philosophy or political speculation pursued by way of an examination of the main

---

1. Martin Wight, *Systems of States* (Leicester, 1977).

traditions of thought about International Relations in the past. Whereas the behaviourist school sought a kind of theory that approximated to science his was the kind that approximated to philosophy. Whereas they began by rejecting the literature of the past, even the immediate past — and it was the latter they had in mind when they spoke, rather absurdly, of 'traditionalists' — he began with the resolve to rediscover, to assemble and to categorize all that had been said and thought on the subject throughout the ages. While the behaviourists sought to exclude moral questions as lying beyond the scope of scientific treatment, Wight placed these questions at the centre of his inquiry. Where they hoped to arrive at 'A Theory of International Relations' that would put an end to disagreement and uncertainty, Wight saw as the outcome of his studies simply an account of the debate among contending theories and doctrines, of which no resolution could be expected.

Wight's attitude towards the behaviourists was the source of one of my own disagreements with him. I felt that they represented a significant challenge and that it was important to understand them and engage in debate with them. The correct strategy, it appeared to me, was to sit at their feet, to study their position until one could state their own arguments better than they could and then — when they were least suspecting — to turn on them and slaughter them in an academic Massacre of Glencoe. Wight entertained none of these bloody thoughts. He made no serious effort to study the behaviourists and in effect ignored them. What this reflected, of course, was the much greater sense of confidence and security he had about his own position. The idea that an approach to Theory as unhistorical and unphilosophical as this might provide a serious basis for understanding world politics simply never entered his head.

At the heart of Martin Wight's Theory course was the debate between three groups of thinkers: the Machiavellians, the Grotians and the Kantians — or, as he sometimes called them (less happily, I think) the Realists, the Rationalists and the Revolutionists. The Machiavellians he thought of crudely as 'the blood and iron and immorality men,' the Grotians as 'the law and order and keep your word men,' and the Kantians as 'the subversion and liberation and missionary men.' Each pattern or tradition of thought embodied a description of the nature of international politics and also a set of prescriptions as to how men should conduct themselves in it.

For the Machiavellians — who included such figures as Hobbes, Hegel, Frederick the Great, Clémenceau, the twentieth-century Realists such as Carr and Morgenthau — the true description of international politics was that it was international anarchy, a war of all against all or relationship of pure conflict among sovereign states. To the central question of the Theory of International Relations — 'What is the nature of international society?' — the Machiavellians give the answer: there is no international society; what purports to be international society — the system of international law, the mechanism of

diplomacy or today the United Nations — is fictitious. The prescriptions advanced by the Machiavellians were simply such as were
advanced by Machiavelli in *The Prince*: it was for each state or ruler
to pursue its own interest: the question of morality in international
politics, at least in the sense of moral rules which restrained states in
their relations with one another, did not arise.

For the Grotians — among whom Wight included the classical international lawyers together with Locke, Burke, Castlereagh, Gladstone,
Franklin Roosevelt, Churchill — international politics had to be
described not as international anarchy but as international intercourse,
a relationship chiefly among states to be sure, but one in which there
was not only conflict but also co-operation. To the central question of
Theory of International Relations the Grotians returned the answer
that states, although not subject to a common superior, nevertheless
formed a society — a society that was no fiction, and whose workings
could be observed in institutions such as diplomacy, international law,
the balance of power and the concert of great powers. States in their
dealings with one another were not free of moral and legal restraints:
the prescription of the Grotians was that states were bound by the
rules of this international society they composed and in whose conti-
nuance they had a stake.

The Kantians rejected both the Machiavellian view that international
politics was about conflict among states, and the view of the Grotians
that it was about a mixture of conflict and co-operation among states.
For the Kantians it was only at a superficial and transient level that
international politics was about relations among states at all; at a
deeper level it was about relations among the human beings of which
states were composed. The ultimate reality was the community of
mankind, which existed potentially, even if it did not exist actually,
and was destined to sweep the system of states into limbo. The
Kantians, like the Grotians, appealed to international morality, but
what they understood by this was not the rules that required states to
behave as good members of the society of states, but the revolutionary
imperatives that required all men to work for human brotherhood. In
the Kantian doctrine the world was divided between the elect, who
were faithful to this vision of the community of mankind or *civitas
maxima* and the damned, the heretics, who stood in its way.

This Kantian pattern of thought, according to Wight, was embodied
in the three successive waves of Revolutionist ideology that had
divided modern international society on horizontal rather than vertical
lines: that of the Protestant Reformation, that of the French Revolution and that of the Communist Revolution of our own times. But it
was also embodied, he thought, in the Counter-Revolutionist
ideologies to which each of these affirmations of horizontal solidarity
gave rise: that of the Catholic Counter-Reformation, that of International Legitimism and that of Dullesian Anti-Communism.

Having identified these three patterns of thought Wight then went
on to trace the distinctive doctrines that each of them put forward

concerning war, diplomacy, power, national interest, the obligation of treaties, the obligation of an individual to bear arms, the conduct of foreign policy and the relations between civilized states and so-called barbarians. It is impossible to summarize what Martin Wight had to say about the three traditions without in some measure vulgarizing it. The impact of his lectures was produced not only by the grandeur of the design but also by the detailed historical embroidery, worked out with great subtlety, humanity and wit and with staggering erudition. In the hands of a lesser scholar the three-fold categorization would have served to simplify and distort the complexity of international thought. But Wight himself was the first to warn against the danger of reifying the concepts he had suggested. He insisted that the Machiavellian, Grotian and Kantian traditions were merely paradigms, to which no actual thinker did more than approximate: not even Machiavelli, for example, was in the strict sense a Machiavellian. Wight recognized that the exercise of classifying international theories requires that we have more pigeon-holes than three and so he suggested various ways in which each of the three traditions could be further subdivided: the Machiavellian tradition into its aggressive and its defensive form, the Grotian tradition into its Realist and idealist form, the Kantian tradition into its evolutionary and its revolutionary forms, its imperialist and its cosmopolitanist forms, its historically backward-looking and its forward-looking or progressivist forms. He was always experimenting with new ways of formulating and describing the three traditions and in some versions of his lectures he suggested a fourth category of what he called Inverted Revolutionists, the pacifist stream of thought represented by the early Christians and by Tolstoy and Gandhi. He was aware that particular international thinkers in many cases straddle his categories: thus he explored, for example, the tension in Bismarck's thought between a Machiavellian perspective and a Grotian one, the tension in Woodrow Wilson between a Grotian perspective and a Kantian one, and the tension in Stalin between a Kantian perspective and a Machiavellian one. He saw the three traditions as forming a spectrum, within which at some points one pattern of thought merged with another, as infra-red becomes ultra-violet.

There are three questions about Wight's ideas on International Theory that I want to consider. First, as between the Machiavellian, the Grotian and the Kantian perspectives where did Martin Wight himself stand? This was a question that earnest students would put to him plaintively at the end of a lecture. Wight used to delight in keeping students guessing on this issue and went out of his way to give them as little material as possible for speculating about it. In one of his lectures he quoted the following conversation of the earl of Shaftesbury: 'People differ in their discourse and profession about these matters, but men of sense are really but of one religion . . . "Pray my lord, what religion is that which men of sense agree in?"

"Madam," says the earl immediately, "men of sense never tell it."[2]

Of course, if we had to put Martin Wight into one or another of his own three pigeon-holes there is no doubt that we should have to consider him a Grotian. Indeed, in one of the early versions of his lecture course he did actually say that he regarded the Grotians or Rationalists as 'the great central stream of European thought,' and that he would regard it as the ideal to be a Grotian, while partaking of the realism of the Machiavellians, without their cynicism, and of the idealism of the Kantians, without their fanaticism. He displayed his leaning toward the Grotians when, in one of the chapters he wrote in *Diplomatic Investigations*, he gave an account of the Grotian tradition under the heading 'Western Values in International Relations,' claiming that this tradition was especially representative of values of Western civilization because of its explicit connection with the political philosophy of constitutional government, and also because of its quality as a *via media* between extremes.[3] He was attracted towards the Grotian pattern of thought, I think, because he saw it as more faithful than either of the others to the complexity of international politics. He saw the Grotian approach to international morality, for example, as founded upon the recognition that the moral problems of foreign policy are complex, as against the view of the Kantians that these problems are simple, and the view of the Machiavellians that they are non-existent. The Grotian tradition, he thought, was better able to accommodate complexity because it was itself a compromise that made concessions to both the Machiavellian and the Kantian points of view. The Grotian idea of the just war, for example, was a compromise between the Kantian idea of the holy war or crusade and the Machiavellian idea of war as the *ultima ratio regum*. The Grotian idea that power in international society should be balanced and contained was a compromise between the Kantian demand that it should be abolished and the view of the Machiavellians that it was the object of the struggle. The view of the Grotians that the relations of the advanced countries with so-called barbarians should be based on the principle of trusteeship was a compromise between the Kantian notion that they should be based on liberation and assimilation, and the Machiavellian contention that they should be based on exploitation.

Nevertheless, it would be wrong to force Martin Wight into the Grotian pigeon-hole. It is a truer view of him to regard him as standing outside the three traditions, feeling the attraction of each of them but unable to come to rest within any one of them, and embodying in his own life and thought the tension among them. As a young man Wight took up the position of an Inverted Revolutionist or pacifist. *Power*

---

2. G. Burnet, *History of his Own Time*, vol. i, bk. II, ch. I.
3. See H. Butterfield and M. Wight (eds), *Diplomatic Investigations* (London, 1966), pp. 89–131.

Politics, which he published at the age of thirty-three, is generally thought to embody a Machiavellian or Realist point of view and can certainly be linked more readily to the Machiavellian tradition than to the Grotian. As he grew older, it appears to me, the Grotian elements in his thinking became stronger: they are much more prominent in his contributions to *Diplomatic Investigations*, published in 1966, than in his earlier writings and reach their highest point in the essays on states systems which he wrote in the last years of his life. As one of the factors causing him to move closer to the Grotian perspective after he came to the London School of Economics, I should not myself discount the influence upon him of Professor Manning, despite the great contrasts in their respective approaches to the subject. Certainly the idea of international society occupied a central place in Manning's thinking and it emerges, I suggest, from the volume of essays presented to him, to which Martin Wight contributed along with others among Manning's former colleagues and students, that there were certain common elements in the outlook of all those who worked in the Department at that time, no less noticeable in Wight's contribution than in the others.[4]

But Wight was too well aware of the vulnerability of the Grotian position ever to commit himself to it fully. He understood that it is the perspective of the international establishment. The speeches of Gladstone in the last century and of Franklin Roosevelt in this century proclaimed that their respective countries should seek in their foreign policies to conform to the common moral standards and sense of common interest of international society as a whole and in so doing they provided us with some of the most memorable statements of the Grotian idea. But what Wight asks us to notice about these two statesmen is that each of them, at the time he spoke, was the leader of the most powerful country in the world. The comfortable Grotian phrases do not come so readily to the lips of the oppressed, the desperate or the dissatisfied. In his lectures, as in his contribution to *The World in March 1939*, Wight expounds with remarkable detachment the critique put forward of Anglo–French Grotian legalism by Hitler in *Mein Kampf*: that Britain and France, the sated imperial powers, were like successful burglars now trying to settle down as country gentlemen, making intermittent appearances on the magistrate's bench.[5] Wight asks us to reflect on the fundamental truth lying behind Hitler's tedious phrases: that Britain and France had got where they were by struggle, that they could not contract out of the struggle at a moment that happened to suit them, still less could they justify themselves in attempting to contract out of it by appealing to moral principles which they had ignored when

---

4. See A.M. James (ed.), *The Bases of International Order. Essays Presented to C.A.W. Manning* (London, 1973).
5. See Arnold Toynbee (ed.), *The World in March 1939* (London, 1952).

they were committed to the struggle.

If Wight could recognize the force of the Machiavellian critique of Grotian doctrines he is at first sight less capable of regarding sympathetically the Kantian critique of them. There was much about the Kantians — 'The Political Missionaries or Fanatics', as he called them in his early drafts of his lectures — that repelled him. He notes how Kantians begin by repudiating all intellectual authorities, and any methodology save the principles of pure thought, but then become enslaved to sacred books; the Jacobins to Rousseau, the Communists to Marx. He saw it as the central paradox of the successive waves of Revolutionist and counter-Revolutionist doctrine that they aim at uniting and integrating the family of nations but in practice divide it more deeply than it was divided before. He held that these internal schisms of Western international society reflected the importation of attitudes which had previously prevailed in the external schism of Western international society and Islam. Just as in the Peloponnesian War the conflict between democratic and olig-archical factions imported into relations among Greeks the attitudes that previously had characterized the struggle between Hellenism and Medism, so in modern international history the various horizontal conflicts we have witnessed between the faithful and the heretical reproduce and reflect the earlier struggle between the Christian and the Infidel. The view that the Turk is Antichrist gives place to the view that the Pope — or some secular equivalent of him — is Antichrist; the epitaph of this historical connection between the internal and the external schisms of international society being the strange doctrine of Luther that Antichrist is the Pope and the Turk combined: the Pope his spirit and soul and the Turk his flesh and body.

Wight's in some respects negative attitude towards the Kantian tradition reflected his religious views. He saw the Revolutionist and counter-Revolutionist doctrines of modern times as perversions of the New Testament, secularized debasements of the story of the Messiah — just as he saw Hitler's National Socialism as a perversion of the Old Testament, the self-appointment of a new Chosen People. Wight was also repelled by progressivist doctrines of International Relations, which are found principally, although not I think exclusively, within the Kantian tradition and above all in Kant himself. One of Wight's most persistent themes is that in international politics by contrast with domestic politics progress has not taken place in modern times; that international politics is incompatible with progressivist theory; that in progressivist theories the conviction precedes the evidence; that 'it is not a good argument for a theory of international politics that we shall be driven to despair if we do not accept it.'

Wight's rejection of the belief in progress reflects, once again, not only his study of the evidence but his religious views. For him secular pessimism was the counterpart of theological optimism. 'Hope,' as he once wrote, 'is not a political virtue; it is a theological virtue.'[6] Wight's lack of hope about the future of the secular world was, I think, so total, so crushing that only a deeply religious person could have sustained it. This lack of hope is most dramatically expressed in his invocation of de Maistre's 'occult and terrible law of the violent destruction of the human species.'[7] It is expressed also in his thesis that war is inevitable, even though particular wars are avoidable: a view he had the fortitude to contemplate because he was able to persuade himself that at the theological level this did not matter.[8] 'For what matters,' he said in a broadcast in 1948, 'is not whether there is going to *be* another war or not, but that it should be recognised, if it comes, as an act of God's *Justice*, and if it is averted, as an act of God's *Mercy*.'[9]

Yet there are moments when Wight seems as much drawn towards the Kantian tradition as towards the Machiavellian or the Grotian. He argues, in a long discussion of Kant's *Perpetual Peace*, that the progressivist argument from despair, while not intellectually speaking a 'good' argument, is nevertheless not a contemptible or dishonourable one: the optimism of a man who, like Kant, has looked into the abyss, but who says 'No, looking down makes me giddy: I can only go on climbing if I look upward' — such an optimism grounded in utter despair merits respect. Wight also sees that the belief in progress is not the deepest element in the Kantian tradition. The deepest element — the element that must draw us to it — is the moral passion to abolish suffering and sin: the moral passion of Kant's hymn to duty, of Ivan Karamazov's cry that eternal harmony is not worth the tears of one tortured child, of Lenin's burning faith that suffering is not an essential part of life. Wight traces with care the distinction between the evolutionary Kantians, who believe that suffering is the cause of sin, and that if suffering can be abolished, sin can be abolished – and the revolutionary Kantians, such as Marx and Lenin, who believe that sin is the cause of suffering, and that suffering can be eradicated only if sin is first eradicated.

While Wight in his maturity was personally more drawn to the Grotian tradition than to either the Machiavellian or the Kantian, the essence of his teaching was that the truth about international politics had to be sought not in any one of these patterns of thought but in the debate among them. The three elements of international politics which they emphasized — the element of international anarchy stressed by the Machiavellians, the element of international inter-course, stressed by the Grotians and the element of the community of mankind, stressed by the Kantians — are all present. Wight's argument

---

6. 'Christian Commentary', talk on the BBC Home Service, 29 Oct. 1948.
7. *Diplomatic Investigations*, op. cit., pp. 33–4.
8. For Wight's discussion of the inevitability of war see 'War and International Politics', *The Listener*, 13 Oct. 1953.
9. See 'Christian Commentary', op. cit.

was that any attempt to describe the subject in terms of one of the cardinal elements to the exclusion of the others, was bound to break down.

There is a second question about what Martin Wight had to say that I wish to consider. Is it true? Can one really categorize the history of thought about international politics in this way? And if one can, does an account of the debate among the three traditions really advance our understanding of international politics in the twentieth century?

I believe myself that Wight tried to make too much of the debate among the three traditions. Much that has been said about International Relations in the past cannot be related significantly to these traditions at all. Wight was, I believe, too ambitious in attributing to the Machiavellians, the Grotians and the Kantians distinctive views not only about war, peace, diplomacy, intervention and other matters of International Relations but about human psychology, about irony and tragedy, about methodology and epistemology. There is a point at which the debate Wight is describing ceases to be one that has actually taken place, and becomes one that he has invented; at this point his work is not an exercise in the history of ideas, so much as the exposition of an imaginary philosophical conversation, in the manner of Plato's dialogues.

I have already mentioned that Wight insisted that the three traditions were only to be taken as paradigms and that he was always urging us not to take what he said about them too seriously. But one has to take it seriously, or not at all. In all of Wight's work there is an instinct for the dramatic, a searching after superlatives — the *classic* expression of a point of view, the *earliest* statement of it, its *noblest* epitaph — that is the source of tantalizing hypotheses and is what made his teaching so exciting. But one has to keep reminding oneself that the truth might be less dramatic, the superlatives not applicable, the hypotheses not fully tested. Again, in all his work there is an instinctive assumption — the legacy of Toynbee's impact upon him as a young man — that there is some rhythm or pattern in the history of ideas which is there, waiting to be uncovered. But we have to recognize the possibility that in some cases the rhythm or pattern may not be there at all. The defence he was inclined to put up — that he is merely putting forward suggestive paradigms or ideal types — will not do. It makes his position impregnable, but only at the price of making it equivocal.

But if the account of the three traditions will not bear all the weight that Martin Wight sought to place upon it there is no doubt that it has a firm basis in reality. Anyone who seeks to write the history of thought about International Relations that Martin Wight himself was so superbly equipped to undertake will find it essential to build on the foundations which he laid. His analysis of the three traditions, moreover, was profoundly original. There is one passage in Gierke's account of the natural law tradition in which the germ of the idea is stated, but I have seen no evidence that Wight was aware of this passage and in any case it does not entail the great structure of ideas which, when fully grown in his mind, it became.[10]

That his account of these past traditions of thought contributes directly to our understanding of contemporary international politics there can be no doubt. In form his course was an exercise in the history of ideas, but in substance it was a statement about the world, including the world today. It presented the issues of contemporary international politics in historical and philosophical depth — requiring us, when confronted with some description of present events or some attitude taken up towards them, to view it as part of a series of recurrent descriptions or attitudes of the same kind, to identify the premises that lay behind it and to seek out the best of the arguments that had been presented, down the ages, for it and against it.

Wight's approach, it appears to me, provides an antidote to the narrow and introverted character of the professional academic debate about International Relations, the in-breeding and self-absorption of the journals and the textbooks, opening it out to wider intellectual horizons. It is striking that several of the current fashions within that professional debate have as their point of departure the discovery of some aspect of the subject which his own exposition of it has always embraced. The idea, for example, that international politics is not just a matter of relations between states, but also a matter of so-called 'transnational' relations among the individuals and groups that states compose, is one to which Martin Wight's exposition affords a central place; it is the core of the Kantian tradition. The notion which is central to the studies of models of future world order, now rising to a flood in Princeton and elsewhere, that it is necessary to look beyond the framework of the system of sovereign states and to contemplate alternative forms of universal political organization — is one with which Wight was always concerned; one has only to think of his protest against 'the intellectual prejudice imposed by the sovereign state', his doctrine (derived from Toynbee) that the idea of the normalcy of the system of states is an optical illusion, and his attempt — in the essays on states systems — to explore the geographical and chronological boundaries of the modern states system, and to suggest some of the issues with which a general historical account of the main forms of universal political organization — today, virtually uncharted territory — would have to be concerned. The recent revival of interest, in the Western world, in Marxist, or Marxist–Leninist accounts of world politics, and the important neo-Marxist analyses of imperialism and neo-colonialism, fall into place quite naturally in Wight's presentation of the subject — even though it is true that he was not much interested in the economic dimension of the subject,

---

10. See Otto von Gierke, *Natural Law and the Theory of Society 1500 to 1860* (trans. Ernest Barker) (Beacon Press, Boston, 1957), p. 85. (This is a reissue of the translation published by Cambridge University Press, 1934.)

and that his failure to deal with the history of thought about economic aspects of International Relations is one of the points at which he is vulnerable to criticism. Above all, perhaps, the rediscovery of moral questions by the political science profession, the realization that International Relations is about ends as well as means — which is the only meaning we can give to what is now so portentously called 'the post-behavioural revolution' — merely takes us back to the point at which Wight began his inquiry.

Wight's approach also provided an antidote to the self-importance and self-pity that underlie the belief of each generation that its own problems are unique. 'One of the main purposes of university education,' he wrote in his lecture notes, 'is to escape from the *Zeitgeist*, from the mean, narrow, provincial spirit which is constantly assuring us that we are at the summit of human achievement, that we stand on the edge of unprecedented prosperity or unparalleled catastrophe, that the next summit conference is going to be the most fateful in history . . . It is a liberation of the spirit to acquire perspective, to recognise that every generation is confronted by problems of the utmost subjective urgency, but that an objective grading is probably impossible; to learn that the same moral predicaments and the same ideas have been explored before.'

Is there not a danger in following these injunctions that when confronted by some genuinely unprecedented situation we may fail to recognize it? Does not world politics in the twentieth century reflect developments — too obvious to enumerate — which it is correct to regard as without precedent, and is it not a delusion to imagine that these developments can be understood by the seeking out of historical parallels rather than by immersing ourselves in the study of what is recent and new, in all its individuality?

There is such a danger as this but it is not inherent in Wight's position. He did not maintain that every international political situation has an exact historical precedent or that fundamental change does not occur. Indeed, the conception of history as a storehouse of precedents that can be discovered and then applied as practical maxims of statecraft to contemporary political issues is one which he strongly attacked. He regarded this approach to history as the methodological gimmick of the Machiavellians — prominent in the writings of Carr and Morgenthau, as it had been earlier in those of the Social Darwinists, traceable back to the view of Bolingbroke that 'history is philosophy teaching by examples', and resting ultimately on Machiavelli's own assumption that laws of politics could be derived from history because history took the form of mechanically recurring cycles.

There is a third question I want to consider. In what sense did Martin Wight think that theoretical inquiry in International Relations is possible? Wight's most famous article on International Theory bears the title 'Why is there no International Theory?'[11] This leads students to ask:

---

11. *Diplomatic Investigations*, op. cit., ch. I.

does he believe in International Theory or does he not? How can he deny the existence of the enterprise he is engaged in? Brian Porter has recently suggested that there is no great puzzle about this: what Wight meant was that the student will not find the history of thought about International Relations in ready-made and accessible form: the pieces of the jigsaw puzzle have to be disinterred and put together.[12] This is the correct explanation of the title, and it is confirmed by the fact that in an early draft Wight used as his heading 'Why is there no *body* of International Theory?'

But there is a deeper problem in this article than the one posed by its title. Wight argues that it is no accident that International Relations has never been the subject of any great theoretical work, that there is 'a kind of disharmony between international theory and diplomatic practice, a kind of recalcitrance of international politics to being theorised about.'[13] He notes that the only acknowledged classic of International Relations — Thucydides on the *Peloponnesian War* — is a work not of theory but of history. And he goes on to say that 'the quality of international politics, the preoccupations of diplomacy, are embodied and communicated less in works of political and international theory than in historical writings.'[14]

Is Wight here proclaiming the ultimate heresy that after all, theoretical understanding of international politics is not possible, only historical understanding? Is he, so to speak, throwing in the sponge? No, he is not; this is not what he says and all of his work in this field is a denial of it — for while that work is steeped in history it is not itself history. Wight gives us the clue a little further on when he writes that the only kind of theoretical inquiry that is possible is 'the kind of rumination about human destiny to which we give the unsatisfactory name philosophy of history.'[15]

Theoretical inquiry into International Relations is therefore philosophical in character. It does not lead to cumulative knowledge after the manner of natural science. Confronted by a controversy, like the great debate which Wight explores among the three traditions, we may identify the assumptions that are made in each camp, probe them, juxtapose them, relate them to circumstances, but we cannot expect to settle the controversy except provisionally, on the basis of assumptions of our own that are themselves open to debate. All of this must follow once we grant Wight's initial assumption that theoretical inquiry into International Relations is necessarily about moral or prescriptive questions.

---

12. See Brian Porter's unpublished paper, 'Martin Wight's "International Theory": Some Reflections'. (This has since been published as 'Patterns of Thought and Practice: Martin Wight's "International Theory"' in M. Donelan (ed.), *Reason of States* (London, 1978), pp. 64–74.)
13. *Diplomatic Investigations*, op. cit., p. 33.
14. ibid., p. 32.
15. ibid., p. 33.

I believe myself, however, that an inquiry that is philosophical can be more public, more rational, more disciplined than Wight was willing to allow. In his work we may note a preference for vagueness over precision, for poetic imagery over prosaic statement, for subjective judgment over explicit formulation of a line of argument. I do not think, for example, that 'rumination' is an adequate word to describe the activity of theoretical analysis. Wight speaks of the 'fruitful imprecision' of Grotius's language, but it appears to me that this imprecision is in no way fruitful.[16] It is true, as Wight says, that the stuff of international theory is constantly bursting the bounds of the language in which we try to handle it, but this appears to me a reason for trying to find a language that is appropriate. There is a tendency to believe that those who are profound, as Martin Wight undoubtedly was, are thereby licensed to be obscure. This is the point at which I begin to part company with Martin Wight and to wonder whether there was not, after all, some value in the demand of the behaviourists that International Theory be put on a proper methodological footing.

I have tried in this lecture not to lose sight of those aspects of Wight's work with which it is possible to quarrel. Let me mention some more of them. The term Wight used to describe the enterprise he was engaged in — International Theory — is not a good one; as Professor Manning pointed out long ago it is the Relations that are International not the Theory; the enterprise is better described as Theory of International Relations.

Wight's contribution is vulnerable to the charge of being unduly Eurocentric. It is the glory of his work that it sprang from a mastery of Western culture, ancient and medieval no less than modern. But although he took some account of Islam and of Gandhi and played with the idea that there was a Chinese equivalent of the debate among the three traditions — in the conflict of Confucianism, Taoism and the School of Law — he had no deep understanding of non-Western civilizations. He saw modern international society as the product of Western culture and felt, I think, a basic doubt as to how far the non-Western majority of states today have really been incorporated within it. I should not myself leap to the conclusion that in this he was wrong, but he does sometimes display insensitivity about non-Western peoples and their aspirations today, as in his contemptuous dismissal of Kautilya or his comparison between the Afro-Asian powers and the revisionist powers of the 1930s.

Wight's immense learning sometimes does more to encumber than to enrich his arguments: his intellectual architecture is not so much classical as baroque. His learning is entirely authentic: Wight was not a cultural showman or pedant, and had a great gift of apt quotation. But in some of his writings the branches of the tree are so weighed down with historical foliage that it is difficult to find the trunk.

---

16. ibid., p. 102.

I have often felt uneasy about the extent to which Wight's view of International Relations derives from his religious beliefs. These beliefs are not obtrusive in his writings about secular matters, which apparently employ only the ordinary canons of empirical knowledge of the world. And yet one is conscious of the extent to which his view of the subject is affected by beliefs not derived in this way.

What can one learn from Martin Wight's example? He was a person of unique gifts and no one else is likely to contribute to the subject in quite the way that he did. But three aspects of his work in this field are worthy of note by others.

The first is his view that theoretical inquiry into International Relations should be focused upon the moral and normative presuppositions that underlie it. In the 1950s and 1960s there was a tendency in the Western world to leave these presuppositions out of account: to inquire into the international system without inquiring into its moral and cultural basis, to discuss policy choices — as in strategic studies or development economics — in terms of techniques rather than in terms of ends. More recently, values or ends have made a comeback, but chiefly in the form of the shouting of slogans, the fashion of so-called political commitment, which means that values are asserted and at the same time held to be beyond examination. Wight stood, it appears to me, not simply for having value premises but for inquiring into them.

The second is his attempt to associate theoretical inquiry with historical inquiry. The professional diplomatic historians, on the whole, have not been interested in large questions of theory. The theorists of International Relations have lacked the capacity or the inclination to do the historical work. Or they have approached it in the belief that it consists of 'data', to be fed into the computer, and without any real grasp of historical inquiry itself. Wight is one of the few to have bridged this gap with distinction.

The third and most important is Wight's very deep commitment to intellectual values and to the highest academic standards. Especially, perhaps, in a field such as International Relations there is a temptation to study what is ephemeral rather than of enduring importance, to be knowing rather than to say only what one truly knows, to claim results prematurely rather than to persist in the long haul. The most impressive thing about Martin Wight was his intellectual and moral integrity and *gravitas*. His writings are marked by paucity, but at least we cannot say of them, as he said of theoretical writings about International Relations before him, that they are marked also by intellectual and moral poverty.

Foreword

It may seem odd to publish posthumously, and in the much-changed world of the 1990s, a book about international relations which is based on a course of lectures given in the 1950s. However, there is no need for any apology. This remarkable study will still endure when other more topical works have been forgotten. It explores traditions of thought about international relations – traditions which influence practitioners, citizens and scholars alike – in a lively and also deeply reflective way.

Martin Wight (1913–72) was perhaps the most profound thinker on international relations of his generation of British academics. However, his work in this field was not widely known in his lifetime, principally because he published little of it: mainly the pamphlet on *Power Politics* (1946), and his various contributions to the volume of *Survey of International Affairs* on *The World in March 1939* (1952) – both appearing under the auspices of the Royal Institute of International Affairs in London. There was also the major book he co-edited with Herbert Butterfield, *Diplomatic Investigations* (1966). The perfectionist in him seems to have resisted publication when, as is always the case, there was still room for further improvement. Thus his lectures were one of his principal means – perhaps *the* principal means – by which he conveyed his unique understanding of international relations.

Hedley Bull (1932–85) described in his Martin Wight Memorial Lecture in 1976 how deeply he had been influenced by Wight's LSE lectures in the late 1950s. The text of Bull's lecture on 'Martin Wight and the Theory of International Relations' is re-published in this volume, with only very minor editorial alterations. It provides a clearer exposition of Wight's ideas, and a more direct expression of personal indebtedness, than I ever could – never having had the privilege of sitting at Martin Wight's feet. Bull's account of the effect which Wight's lectures had on him explains what had previously been a mystery to me: how Bull's first work, *The Control of the Arms Race* (1961), emerged so fully armed from the waves, with such a sure understanding of the philosophy and history of international relations.

In order of publication, though not of the date of the original text on which it is based, this is the third major posthumous work by

Martin Wight. The first was *Systems of States* (1977), edited by Hedley Bull, a collection of papers that Wight wrote in the last eight years of his life for the British Committee on the Theory of International Politics. The second was *Power Politics* (1978), edited by Hedley Bull and Carsten Holbraad, which was based on the 1946 pamphlet as revised and expanded by Wight in the last twenty years of his life. The present book, being based on lectures, and ranging even more widely than its predecessors, was bound to take longer to prepare for publication, and further delay was imposed by Hedley Bull's death in 1985. In her preface, Gabriele Wight describes the long process by which she and Brian Porter, with crucial help from Barbara Wight and others, transformed the shorthand of the lecture notes into the present book.

Although Wight's approach here is entirely consistent with his earlier published works, *International Theory: The Three Traditions* is no mere re-working of themes already covered. Nowhere else can one find so systematic and persuasive an exposition of the idea that virtually all thought about international relations, over centuries and even millenia, draws on three traditions: the Rationalist, the Realist, and the Revolutionist – or, to put a human face on abstract theory, the Grotian, the Machiavellian, and the Kantian.

It is not difficult to raise objections to the idea of forcing all the rich complexity of thought about international relations into three pigeon-holes: for example, Kant himself was more of a political Realist than his labelling as a 'Revolutionist' would imply. However, as the book progresses, it becomes increasingly apparent that the three traditions should be seen, not as pigeon-holes or labels, but rather as strands, or primary colours, which are intermixed in endless different ways by different practitioners and writers. As Wight himself puts it in the last chapter:

Classification becomes valuable, in humane studies, only at the point where it breaks down. The greatest political writers in international theory almost all straddle the frontiers dividing two of the traditions, and most of these writers transcend their own systems.

There may be other hazards in Wight's emphasis on the three traditions. There is at least an implication in it that international relations are consigned forever to be an interplay between these traditions, and that nothing fundamental changes very much. While such a view is a healthy antidote to ideas about the exceptionalism of the present, too little room is left for evolutionary, or even teleological, views of international relations. One may agree with Wight that most such views have been far too simple, and have been confounded in this century: yet as Wight himself notes, albeit briefly, there has been progess, not least in the emergence of a universal international society.

In looking at the three traditions, Wight surpasses even his own past distinguished record for seeking out apt and pithy expressions of points of view on international relations. The book is practically a dictionary of international quotations, with Aristotle rubbing shoulders with Tito, *De Jure Belli ac Pacis* with the *Daily Mail*. Wight's genius for making old writings seem fresh is nowhere better displayed than in this book. At the same time he illuminates, in a systematic and penetrating way, age-old problems of international relations: the nature and methods of diplomacy; the causes of imperialism; the tension between the 'civilized' and the 'barbarians'; the special character, and limits, of pacifism.

This book tells us much, not only about these problems, but also about Martin Wight himself. His discussion of pacifism at the end of Chapter 5, where he perceptively observes that pacifists have much in common with realists, is especially interesting when one recalls that Wight himself had been a pacifist in the late 1930s and early 1940s, gradually moving over to the broader and more mature vision of which this book is impressive evidence. Likewise there is a great deal in this book, especially in Chapter 4, which bridges the two fields in which Wight worked professionally: international relations on the one hand, and colonial administrations on the other. He shows a strong radical streak in his sympathy with the Gladstonian view: 'It is liberty alone that makes men fit for liberty.'

How relevant is this work to today's conditions? Perhaps it does not matter too much. Wight's concern to lead his listeners and readers away from the parochialism of the present is needed just as much today as it was in the 1950s. When he referred, as he often did, to contemporary issues, it was more to use them as illustrations of enduring themes than to make a definite judgement or prognosis about them. Some of the finest passages in this book are about the frailty of judgements on international issues. He shows in Chapter 6 how the same policy, even the same acts, may quite reasonably be judged a success by one generation, and a failure by the next; and how the legalism of US policy regarding the Baltic States in 1942–3 turned out, in a longer perspective, to be far-sighted realism – a view which, in 1991, could be put even more emphatically. Interestingly, he claims no superiority for the detached academic observer, and suggests persuasively in Chapter 7 that involvement can often lead to objectivity, detachment to bias.

Some of Wight's statements do undeniably read oddly today. In Chapter 4 he seems, momentarily, to take the possibility of global conquest by a single power seriously. In Chapter 6 he is too critical of George Kennan's 1951 view of the attributes one might look for in a future Russian foreign policy: these amounted to the abandonment of internal totalitarianism and external domination. Wight calls Kennan's view 'completely unrealist' and 'remote from attainability': but forty years later, Gorbachev has shown that Kennan's projected Soviet attributes were far from being absurd.

Yet such anachronisms are few and far between. In general one is impressed by the salience of this study in a much-changed world. In 1991, the statements of political leaders and scholars can still be interpreted usefully according to the classification set out by Wight in this book. The problems of national self-determination, intervention, restraint on war, alliances and international organization are still very much as Wight describes them here.

A more serious criticism of the work might be that it is incomplete. Although full of fascinating material, beautifully woven together, there are places where the text has more the character of a stimulating lecture than a definitive publication. Several chapters end in mid-air, without the kind of conclusion one might expect from so rigorous a mind as Wight's. No doubt this explains why Wight hesitated to publish, but the reader is likely to forgive this fault. Sometimes work in progress can convey more sense of a mind at work, grappling with a hard problem, than can a definitive finished product, with all the rough edges carefully sanded down.

For teachers of international relations, there has long been a need for a book which explores the history of ideas about the subject; which bridges the wholly artificial divide between history and international relations; which also bridges the artificial divide between political theory and international theory; and which shows how statesmen, as well as writers, shape and are shaped by the evolution of ideas. *International Theory: The Three Traditions* does all these things, and it does them with a skill which no writer other than Martin Wight could have matched.

Adam Roberts
Balliol College, Oxford
2 August 1991

Introduction

By 'international theory' is meant something corresponding to political theory. Political theory is a recognizable subject; it is one half of 'politics', the other being 'institutions' or 'government'. Politics is a realm of human experience continuously studied in one form or another since Plato heard Socrates arguing about justice in the market-place, and himself immediately began lecturing to Aristotle. To study politics means, primarily, entering this tradition, joining in the conversation, speculating about the state, authority, the justification and limits of power, the sources of law and political obligation, and the nature of freedom and rights. International theory is the corresponding tradition of enquiry about relations between states, the problems of obligations that arise in the absence as distinct from the presence of government, the nature of the community of which states are members, and the principles of foreign policy. In other words international theory is the political philosophy of international relations.

Now the difficulties begin: it is easy to recognize political theory, but not so easy to recognize international theory, and one might suspect that historically there was no such thing. There is no obvious tradition of enquiry, or body of theory and speculation, about relations between states, and about the problems of obligation that arise in the absence of government. So the attempt to answer the question, 'What is international theory?' only poses a second one, 'Where is international theory?' But before we try to answer this, we might ask ourselves, 'Why, if it exists, is it so hard to discover?' The answer to this question is a historical one of considerable interest. International theory can be discerned existing dimly, obscured and moreover partitioned, partly on the fringe or margin of ordinary political philosophy and partly in the province of international law. This is owing to a historical accident, due ultimately to the cultural cleavage in Western society that occurred in the sixteenth century.

One cannot talk properly about international relations before the advent of the sovereign state. This, the state which acknowledges no political superior, largely came about in Western Europe in the time of Machiavelli, at the beginning of the sixteenth century, the threshold of 'modern history'. The process of its evolution had, however, begun two centuries earlier and for the states of the Holy Roman Empire would not be completed for another century and a half. The world of feudal relationships, of a Universal Church with political and taxing power, and of an Empire with at least universal claims, was a different world from that of international relations. Now, in the sixteenth century, from Machiavelli on, the important and exciting social need was seen as the development of the sovereign state itself, the need to build up a strong central authority which would give internal order in place of feudal licence. The development of the sovereign state implied also the development of the modern states-system or modern international relations (diplomacy, war, international law, international institutions, etc.), but this was treated as a by-product or corollary of the sovereign state itself. The crystallization of the state was what excited the best minds at that time, and they gave political philosophy that concentration on the state which it has never since lost. Hence the discussion of the nature of sovereignty, of the limits of sovereign power, of popular sovereignty and contract theory, which constitute the familiar highroad of political theory. This tendency was reinforced by the historical coincidence of the Renaissance, and the rediscovery of the wisdom of antiquity.

Although Graeco-Roman civilization had international relations, and there is some important classical writing about it, especially in Thucydides' work, the bulk of classical political writing is concerned with the Polis, with politics in the accepted sense. This fact, whether due to the accidental survival of certain texts rather than others, or to an inherent bias in Graeco-Roman thought, reinforced the state-centred tradition and established its continuity into modern times. Whereas Aristotle had been known in the twelfth and thirteenth centuries, the two most important discoveries of the Renaissance were Plato, the greatest of theorists of the Polis, and Tacitus, the most penetrating analyst of absolutism and of the internal workings of empire. Tacitus, indeed, by the paradox of all the classics, gives a parallel classic account of Lenin, Stalin and Khrushchev, and the hazards of succession, in his treatment of the Julio-Claudian emperors.

The Catholic universities of Europe, with a traditional attachment to ideas of a supranational authority, continued to canvass theoretical questions concerning the relationships between states, while the Humanists and Protestants were busy with the political theory of the state. Catholic writers, particularly the Spanish neo-scholastics, made a very important addition to medieval doctrine on these matters; indeed their writings, seen in retrospect with the preoccupations of the twentieth century, seem perhaps more worthwhile than most of the rest of the political theory of the sixteenth century. But neither side was disposed to recognize the achievements of the other, and when a century later the leading Protestant nation, in the person of Grotius, turned to international law, it appeared that the development of that subject was lagging a hundred years behind that of the political theory of the state.

A notable example of this time-lag concerns the doctrine of sovereignty. It began as a theory to justify the king being master in his new modern kingdom, absolute internally. Only subsequently was it turned outwards to become the justification of equality of such sovereigns in the international community, a theory of state-sovereignty or of sovereign states.

The divisive effects upon European thought of the Renaissance and Reformation also produced a partitionment of international theory between international law (as Tocqueville said, 'the public law of Europe') and the work of philosophers. International law had its origin in the vague field where theology, ethics and law all meet and seem indistinguishable, and in its second chapter of development it had to borrow its tools and concepts largely from political philosophy. Jean Bodin in his *De Republica* (1576), is usually credited with the invention of the theory of sovereignty, the theory that every state must have a central authority which was the source of laws but not bound by them. But this doctrine of the equality of states became part of the stock-in-trade of international law only much later. Even in Grotius, there is more about sovereignty as a principle of internal organization than as the mark of membership of international society, and more about the extinction of sovereignty by dynasties dying out or through dynastic marriage than by cession or conquest.

Conversely there were political philosophers whose genius or circumstances made them more concerned with the relations between states than with the theory of the state, but whose temper was uncongenial to the theologico-ethical origins of international law, and who were thus ignored from its point of view, and never came within its purview. The best example is Machiavelli. In 1576 the Jesuits burnt Machiavelli in effigy at Ingolstadt, and secured the placing of his works on the Index. In 1950 an English Jesuit brought out a fine edition of Machiavelli's greatest work, the *Discourses*, which was the fruit of years of labour.[1] This may be seen as evidence of a *rapprochement* between the two severed paths of international theory, showing belated recognition that Machiavelli and the Spanish neo-scholastics were really fellow-workers in the vineyard of international relations. Alas, Dr Walker, his commentary bursting with sixteenth-century animus against Machiavelli, is still concerned to make his readers think of him primarily as Old Nick, and so the publication cannot be readily seen as inaugurating a permanent reconciliation.

This unhappy partition of the domain of international theory, between philosophically minded international lawyers and internationally minded political philosophers, which lasted four hundred years down to the boom in international studies this century, does not mean that there is not a considerable body of writings about international theory for him who seeks it. It is not the absence of literature which is the difficulty, to return to the question raised earlier, but its

---

1. Leslie J. Walker, *The Discourses of Niccoló Machiavelli* (London: Routledge & Kegan Paul, 1950), 2 vols.

scatteredness. It is a body of writings of varied merit: some of it, like the *Grand Design* of Henry IV's minister, Sully, and the lucubrations of the Abbé de St. Pierre, is traditionally dismissed by political philosophers proper as belonging to the curiosities of political literature, although it is not clear whether this adverse judgement is really delivered on the merits of the works concerned or springs from a prejudice against political writings which do not deal with the traditional subject-matter of the state. On the other hand, it is noticeable that some of the greatest political philosophers have been fascinated by the problems of international relations and have tried their hand at writing about them.

Kant's essay on *Perpetual Peace* was perhaps the ripest fruit of his philosophy. This is only the most illustrious example. The busy Bentham wrote about international relations, and so did Rousseau. The philosopher Hume, who produced essays on nearly everything, wrote a classic study on the balance of power. Burke spent the last years of his life obsessed with an international problem — the impact on the international system of a revolutionary state. Tocqueville, as early as 1852, related enquiries about the society of nations to other political studies, and many other political writers have scattered chapters, or provide valuable bearings, upon international theory.

The remainder of these scattered sources is to be found in the statements and policies of politicians. Here the distinction between theory and practice is not a hard-and-fast one. Machiavelli was a retired Secretary of State of the Republic of Florence; Bismarck spent his retirement writing his *Reflections and Reminiscences* which is unreliable history but perhaps the greatest book on statecraft of the nineteenth century — only Churchill, possibly, can compare with him in the twentieth. Lenin's theoretical writings were all blows struck in the day-to-day political struggle, and so were Burke's and Hamilton's. Some of the greatest statesmen have not written books or even contributed to journalism, yet their personalities reveal their political thought. The ideas which Gladstone or Lincoln, Woodrow Wilson or Lord Salisbury, represented in politics can be gathered from their speeches; and similarly one turns mainly to Nehru's for the theory of Asian neutralism and to Vyshinsky's and Khrushchev's in considering international Communism. One can even learn something about politics from listening to statesmen at press conferences or eavesdropping upon them when they are talking informally.

The development of the states-system did not become a matter of prime interest, nor its control one of prime urgency, until our own time. The generations who fought both World Wars were left to cope with the by-product of this concentration on the state. Latterly the West has grown tired of the state and sceptical about it; it is sick of sovereignty and wants to modify it. Interest today has shifted to foreign policy, to international institutions and international control, even a world state, because the states-system is now manifestly in the same sort of anarchical obsolescence as the feudal kingdoms were when Machiavelli was born. This of course is why there is the feeling that international relations is a quite new subject academically, which sprang from the head of Andrew Carnegie when he set up his Endowment for International Peace (1910), or of President Wilson when he thought up the League, or of David Davies and the Cassel Trustees when they founded chairs in Aberystwyth (1919) and London (1923) respectively. This is partly an illusion: obviously the First World War put international relations on the academic map in a way it had not been before, but there had been before then an awareness of international relations, of the states-system, as a subject of study.

This course of lectures is in the first place an experiment in classification, in typology, and in the second an exploration of continuity and recurrence, a study in the uniformity of political thought; and its leading premiss is that political ideas do not change much, and the range of ideas is limited. As D'Entrèves observed: 'Men have kept repeating the old slogans over and over again. The novelty is very often only a question of accent.'[2] And in his presidential address at the annual public session of the Académie des Sciences Morales et Politiques, in Paris on 3 April 1852, Tocqueville said:

It is unbelievable how many systems of morals and politics have been successively found, forgotten, rediscovered, forgotten again, to reappear a little later, always charming and surprising the world as if they were new, and bearing witness, not to the fecundity of the human spirit, but to the ignorance of men.

It would perhaps be permissible to apply to moral and political studies what Mme de Sévigné said so agreeably about love — that it is *un grand recommenceur* . . . They offer only a small number of truths which are not of great antiquity, and few errors which would not appear broken-down and decrepit, did we but know the date of their origin.[3]

One can compare T.S. Eliot, in *East Coker*:

And what there is to conquer
By strength and submission, has already been discovered
Once or twice, or several times, by men whom one cannot hope
To emulate — but there is no competition —
There is only the fight to recover what has been lost
And found and lost again and again: and now, under conditions
That seem unpropitious. But perhaps neither gain nor loss.
For us, there is only the trying. The rest is not our business.[4]

2. A.P. D'Entrèves, *Natural Law* (London: Hutchinson, 1951), p. 11.
3. Alexis de Tocqueville, *Oeuvres completes d'Alexis de Tocqueville* (Paris: Michel Lévy Frères, 1866), vol. IX, p. 125.
4. T.S. Eliot, 'East Coker', *Collected Poems 1909–1962* (London: Faber & Faber, 1963), p. 203.

One of the main purposes of university education is to escape from the *Zeitgeist*, from the mean, narrow, provincial spirit which is constantly assuring us that we are at the peak of human achievement, that we stand on the edge of unprecedented prosperity or an unparalleled catastrophe; that the next summit conference is going to be the most fateful in history or that the leader of the day is either the greatest, or the most disastrous, of all time. It is a liberation of the spirit to acquire perspective, to recognize that every generation is confronted by problems of the utmost subjective urgency, but that an objective grading is probably impossible; to learn that the same moral predicaments and the same ideas have been explored before. One need read very little in political theory to become aware of recurrences and repetitions. Thus, if one turns to E.H. Carr's *The Twenty Years' Crisis* after Hobbes' *Leviathan*, one cannot fail to note that the basic arguments are the same. To read about the Wars of Religion, and the theories of the Huguenots, Calvinists, and Jesuits, is at once to be struck by the parallel with modern totalitarianism, especially Communism. It is therefore possible, as Tocqueville said,

by studying the most illustrious writers who have engaged in moral and political studies throughout the centuries, to rediscover what are the principal ideas in these fields which have been in circulation among the human race — to reduce them to quite a small number of systems — and so to compare them with one another and to pass judgement on them.[5]

This is what I am going to try to do.

---

5. Alexis de Tocqueville, *Oeuvres complets*, pp. 125—6.

1: The three traditions of international theory

If one surveys the most illustrious writers who have treated of international theory since Machiavelli, and the principal ideas in this field which have been in circulation, it is strikingly plain that they fall into three groups, and the ideas into three traditions. Let them be called Rationalists, Realists, and Revolutionists: these names do not sacrifice accuracy in any degree to the charms of alliteration.

These three traditions of political thought can be in some sense related to the three interrelated political conditions which comprise the subject-matter of what is called international relations.

(a) *International anarchy*: a multiplicity of independent sovereign states acknowledging no political superior, whose relationships are ultimately regulated by warfare.
(b) *Diplomacy and commerce*: continuous and organized intercourse between these sovereign states in the pacific intervals: international and institutionalized intercourse.
(c) *The concept of a society of states, or family of nations*: although there is no political superior, nevertheless recognition that the multiplicity of sovereign states forms a moral and cultural whole, which imposes certain moral and psychological and possibly even legal (according to some theories of law) obligations — even if not political ones. As Burke observed: 'The writers on public law have often called this *aggregate* of nations a commonwealth.'[1]

The three traditions of international theory can be roughly distinguished by reference to these three interdependent conditions of international relations. The Realists are those who emphasize and concentrate upon the element of international anarchy, the Rationalists those who emphasize and concentrate on the element of international intercourse, and the Revolutionists are those who emphasize

---

1. Edmund Burke, 'Letters on a Regicide Peace', *The Works of The Right Hon. Edmund Burke* (London: Samuel Holdsworth, 1842), vol. II, p. 299.

and concentrate upon the element of the society of states, or international society. This is only a rough and initial distinction, and the three traditions must be defined and discriminated between more fully.

Revolutionists

The Revolutionists can be defined more precisely as those who believe so passionately in the moral unity of the society of states or international society, that they identify themselves with it, and therefore they both claim to speak in the name of this unity, and experience an overriding obligation to give effect to it, as the first aim of their international policies. For them, the whole of international society transcends its parts; they are cosmopolitan rather than 'internationalist', and their international theory and policy has 'a missionary character' (Dawson).

There are three outstanding examples of these international Revolutionists: the religious Revolutionists of the sixteenth and seventeenth centuries; the French Revolutionists, especially the Jacobins; and the totalitarian Revolutionists of the twentieth century.

The religious Revolutionists of the sixteenth to seventeenth century were both Protestant and Catholic. The Protestants asserted that the existing expression of the society of states was corrupt and perverted, and that it both needed reform, and was indeed through the inherent workings of history — or as they would have said, through God's providence — on the point of undergoing a reform and purge which would bring a new society of states into being. The Catholics asserted that the existing international society of Christendom, Europe, was being subverted by rebellion and heresy, and needed to be restored. The Protestant Revolutionism found its classic expression in the Calvinists, especially the French Huguenots; the Catholic in the Jesuits (this was a counter-Revolutionism, that of the Counter-Reformation, but it is nonetheless Revolutionism for our purpose). It is well known how the political philosophy of the Calvinists and the Jesuits developed along similar lines, and how each approximated to the other, with theories of power based on popular consent, of the right of resistance against royal governments, and of tyrannicide.

> A Scot and Jesuit, hand in hand,
> First taught the world to say
> That subjects ought to have command,
> And monarchs to obey

This squib produced during the English Civil War refers specifically to George Buchanan, *De Jure Regni apud Scotus* (1579), and Mariana, *De Rege et Regis Institutione* (1599).[2]

---

2. R.H. Murray, *Political Consequences of the Reformation* (London: Ernest Benn, 1926), p. 122.

There is a similar approximation in their international theory in their views on the rights or duties both of intervening in other states, and of liberating the adherents of one's own faction who are under the rule of the other faction, as well as in their doctrine about the nature of international society. The principal example on the Calvinist side is *Vindiciae contra Tyrannos* (1579), and on the Catholic side, Cardinal Bellarmine with his theory of indirect power, justifying Papal intervention (Hobbes crossed swords with him in the last book of *Leviathan*),[3] and Botero, a Piedmontese pupil of the Jesuits, in *Della Ragion di Stato* (1589).[4]

An analogous relationship of interdependence between the totalitarian Revolutionists of left and right can be seen in the twentieth century, an interdependence along with dialectical hostility, and a mutual assimilation of their international theory the extent of which will be discussed later.

There are perhaps two reasons for considering the Revolutionists before the other two traditions. The three interdependent conditions on international relations were enumerated earlier in the reverse order from that in which they came historically into being. In the historical development which led to the state of affairs which is the subject-matter of international relations, first, there was an effective society of states, the *Respublica Christiana* with a degree of constitutional unity, ecclesiastical and political, which fluctuated from time to time, but which for about five hundred years (AD 700–1200) was out of any comparison greater than the constitutional unity of the society of states since then. (In many respects the ancestor of modern Revolutionism was the medieval Catholic Church.) Secondly, there was continuous and organized intercourse between the various members of the *Respublica Christiana*. Only lastly and latest did the bonds between them become so slight that they accepted warfare as ultimately regulative of their relationship, and repudiated any allegiance to a political superior. The historical precedence of the Revolutionist society of states is one reason for considering Revolutionism first; a second reason is that it is in a special way representative of Western civilization. It exemplifies its moral dynamism and energy.

What distinguishes Western culture from the other world civilizations is its *missionary character* — its transmission from one people to another in a continuous series of spiritual movements.[5]

Western civilization has been the great ferment of change in the world, because the changing of the world became an integral part of its cultural ideal.[6]

---

3. Luigi Sturzo, *The Church and State* (London: Geoffrey Bles, 1939), p. 251.
4. ibid., p. 269.
5. C. Dawson, *Religion and the Rise of Western Culture* (London: Sheed & Ward, 1950), p. 12.
6. ibid., p. 10 (see also *Understanding Europe* (London: Sheed & Ward, 1952), p. 16).

Before we leave the Revolutionists, a possible contrast between them and the other two traditions, Realist and Rationalist, must be noted. It might be asked whether the Revolutionists form a continuous tradition of philosophical speculation, whether there is anything resembling a school of thought, an acknowledged continuity, from Calvin through Rousseau to Hitler and Stalin? It can be argued that the three examples of international Revolutionism, the Wars of Religion, the French Revolutionists, and the twentieth-century totalitarian Revolutionists, were unconnected explosions of religious fanaticism, separate convulsions related only by being symptoms of a common disease.

But there is some degree of conscious affiliation and acknowledged continuity between the totalitarians of the twentieth century and the French Revolutionists. Marxism respects Babeuf as the first Socialist, in a different way it respects Robespierre and the Jacobins as the representatives of the bourgeois revolution which was a necessary forerunner of the proletarian revolution, and the Jacobins of course were the offspring of Rousseau. Fascism not dissimilarly recognized the French Revolutionists, but rather more rudely, by taking over a great deal of their ideas and techniques (as the Communists do too), but at the same time claiming to abrogate the French Revolution, to end the period which the French Revolution had begun and which had worked out its ideas to their conclusions. (This was a favourite theme with Mussolini, the least illiterate of the Fascist leaders.) The French Convention began a new chronological era from 1792. The Italian Fascists followed suit by inaugurating the Fascist era, a new reckoning of dates from the March on Rome, and by doing so they at the same time imitated and dismissed the French Revolution. Talmon's book, *The Origins of Totalitarian Democracy*,[7] traces totalitarian democracy back to its Rousseauite source and clarifies a line of intellectual descent which had been neglected. But can the line of descent be traced further?

Only a slight acquaintance with history suggests that all the techniques of tyranny which have characterized the twentieth century find their prototypes not in what the disciples of Rousseau did in the 1790s, but in what the Catholic Church and its several Protestant Titos did, or tried to do, with their more restricted governmental equipment, in the sixteenth century, and what the Catholic Church had already done in its heyday in the Middle Ages. There is a family resemblance among Western tyrannies, but is there an affiliation of ideas?

Rousseau, as everybody knows, was a citizen of Geneva, and his statue sits on a little island there in the middle of the Rhone, where it flows out of the Western end of the lake. He was proud of his

---

7. J.L. Talmon, *The Origins of Totalitarian Democracy* (London: Secker & Warburg, 1955).

citizenship of that city-state, 'citoyen de Genève', more particularly because 'citizen' meant 'aristocrat', and not what the French Revolution made it mean. (Citizens and burghers were the two privileged orders of Geneva.)[8] He was brought up in the ideas and doctrines of the supreme figure in Genevese history, the theocratic dictator, Calvin (although he later 'converted' to Catholicism); he read the *Institutes*.[9]

Geneva indeed might be taken as the symbolical city of international Revolutionists: it is the city of Calvin, Rousseau, and the League of Nations (and some of the League's theorists may be considered Revolutionists). But this connection is external and symbolic; a real affiliation of ideas can be found on two levels, the political, and the philosophical or theological.

Although Calvin propounded doctrines which tended towards popular sovereignty, he himself did not propound that doctrine: his doctrine was the sovereignty of God. He was, strictly, a theocrat. The authority of kings and magistrates came from above, from God, not from below, from the people. Nevertheless by exalting the sovereignty of God he correspondingly minimized the differences of rank between men. In the eyes of God, all men are equal; and if a king or magistrate commands something immoral or irreligious, the natural duty of obedience is transformed into the special duty of disobedience. The last paragraph of the *Institutes* makes this point:

But in that obedience which we hold to be due to the commands of rulers, we must always make the exception, nay, must be particularly careful, that it is not incompatible with obedience to Him to Whose will the wishes of all kings should be subject, to Whose decrees their commands must yield, to Whose majesty their sceptres must bow. And indeed, how preposterous were it, in pleasing men, to incur the offence of Him for Whose sake you obey men! The Lord, therefore, is King of Kings. When He opens His sacred mouth, He alone is to be heard, instead of all and above all. We are subject to the men who rule over us, but subject only in the Lord. If they command anything against Him, let us not pay the least regard to it, nor be moved by all the dignity which they possess as magistrates — a dignity to which no injury is done when it is subordinated to the special and truly supreme power of God.[10]

And he concludes by quoting St Peter's words, 'We ought to obey God rather than men' (Acts V. 29).

This was the source of the Calvinist doctrine of the duty of resistance to tyrants and the right of deposing kings. It is only a short step from the position that the king has authority from God, and the people may judge that he has forfeited this authority, to the position that the king has authority from the people. On this principle, the

---

8. Jacques Maritain, *Three Reformers* (London: Sheed & Ward, 1941), pp. 231, 140.
9. R.H. Murray, *Political Consequences of the Reformation*, p. 111.
10. *Institutes* (1845 edn), quoted in R.H. Murray, ibid., pp. 109–10.

Scots in 1567 deposed Mary Queen of Scots and the Dutch in 1581 deposed Philip of Spain. The practice was consolidated in theory by the German Calvinist, Johannes Althusius (1557–1638), who was the first great exponent of the doctrine of the political contract in its modern form.[11] And from Althusius there is a straight road to Rousseau. There is also a deeper comparison between Rousseau and Calvin. Both of them postulated a transcendental source of authority behind the political machinery of social contracts, elective kings, and popular government. What God is for Calvin, the general will (the immanent social God) is for Rousseau, and this enables their political systems to escape through the meshes of humdrum majority rule or representative government.

It has been said that democracy is the rule of those who claim to speak 'in the name of the people'. In Rousseauite democracy, it is of those who embody the general will. Likewise theocracy in practice is the rule of those who claim to speak 'in the name of God'. And the dictatorship of the proletariat is the dictatorship of those who claim to speak 'in the name of the proletariat'. These assertions of exclusive representativeness are a constant feature of Revolutionist doctrine.

On a philosophical or theological level Rousseau was perhaps closer to Luther than Calvin. Both represent anti-intellectualist religious thought, or mysticism, and a predominance of sentiment and feeling over intellect. They reveal, too, a swollen consciousness of self, and religious egocentrism, leading to complete subjectivism. Rousseau subverted natural morality as Luther subverted supernatural morality and the doctrine of grace.[12]

Nevertheless, the Revolutionist ancestry of ideas and continuity of thought is ambiguous or uncertain. The Revolutionist tradition is less a stream than a series of waves. Here continuity is least important; there is rather a series of disconnected illustrations of the same politico-philosophical truths, as the entries in a psychiatrist's records are casually disconnected illustrations of a few common principles. It is characteristic of Revolutionism, not only in international theory, to deny its past, to try to start from scratch, to jump out of history and begin again. And when (as is usually the case) it is compelled to come to terms with its own past, it effects it by arbitrary selection and a doctrine of repudiation and supersession. Rousseau acknowledges the Reformation, but on the conscious level makes it out of date; Marxists acknowledge the Jacobins, but on a conscious level make them out of date. The family history of Revolutionism is parricidal: 'Yes: that is my father, and I have killed him, as was necessary.' This, Freud would have us believe, is the truth of all family relationships.

---

11. Johannes Althusius, *Politica medodice digesta* (publ. 1603).
12. Jacques Maritain, *Three Reformers* (London: Sheed & Ward, 1941), pp. 150, 143, 34–6 and 95.

Rationalists

The Rationalists are those who concentrate on, and believe in the value of, the element of international intercourse in a condition predominantly of international anarchy. They believe that man, although manifestly a sinful and bloodthirsty creature, is also rational. The word 'Rationalist' has suffered a considerable debasement in the passage of time. At one end of the scale. Aquinas is a Rationalist when compared to Augustine, because Augustine asserted the primacy of faith over reason, while St. Thomas asserted that faith and reason were two specifically different kinds of assent, and religion and science two distinct species of knowledge, and therefore the objects of science cannot be the objects of faith.

Rationalism is the theory that reason is a source of knowledge in itself, superior to and independent of sense perceptions. It is opposed to sensationalism. At the beginning of modern philosophy in the seventeenth century, 'Rationalism' came to have an epistemological significance, to describe a particular answer to the question, 'How do we obtain knowledge?' It described the view that reason itself, unaided by observation, can provide us with philosophical knowledge which is true knowledge. This can be arrived at by deduction from a priori concepts or necessary ideas. Rationalism tended therefore to a spiritual or aspirational conception of the universe, the world of sense experience being in some sense illusory. Descartes, Spinoza and Leibniz all propounded this theory. The Rationalists were answered by the empiricists, such as Locke, Berkeley and Hume, who answered the question 'How do we obtain knowledge?' by saying, 'through observation and sense-experience'.[13] Two centuries later, Rationalism had acquired what is now its popular sense, which is much closer to the empiricism than the Rationalism of the seventeenth century. It is the sense illustrated by the Mills, father and son: belief in accordance with the evidence, and understanding of one's real interest. It is in this sense that the 'Rationalist Press Association' is so called. Rationalism is the explanation according to reason of what appears supernatural.[14] The final debasement is the use of 'rationalization', meaning to make up plausible reasons to explain (to oneself and others) behaviour whose real motives are different or unconscious. This is not the same as making reasonable, or bringing within the empire of reason, but is disguising the predominance of unreason.

I would justify the word 'Rationalist' by taking a text from one who, in epistemological theory, was an empiricist, Locke: 'Men living together according to reason without a common superior on earth, with authority to judge between them, is properly the state of

---

13. C.E.M. Joad, *Guide to Philosophy* (London: Victor Gollancz Ltd., 1937), pp. 108–12.
14. See Hugh Trevor-Roper vs. Toynbee, *The Times*, 28 May 1954, letter.

Nature.'[15] Locke's premise is that men are reasonable, and that they live together according to reason even when they have no common government, as in the condition of international relations.

The Rationalists hold the tradition of natural law, and one might equally well call them 'naturalists' if this word were not appropriated to a school of writers on international law. The older international law writers were divided into naturalists, positivists, and Grotians. Naturalists maintain that the only law of nations is in the law of nature, that is, in first principles, and that custom and treaties make no true law; positivists maintain the reverse, that the only law of nations is what is found in custom and treaty, and the law of nature is non-legal or non-existent. The Grotians combine the two, saying both are essential to the law of nations. Naturalists do not equate with Rationalists, as I use the term. The greatest naturalist was Pufendorf, a disciple of Hobbes, who understood natural law in the new Hobbesian sense of anarchic liberty, not as a principle of social cohesion, and he truly was a Realist. Grotians are Rationalists (with deviations); but both positivists and naturalists tend to be Realists.

To call this tradition Rationalist is to associate it with the element of reason contained in the conception of natural law. The belief in natural law is a belief in a cosmic, moral constitution, appropriate to all created things including mankind; a system of eternal and immutable principles radiating from a source that transcends earthly power (either God or nature). But it is also a belief that men and women have some inherent correspondence with this law, some inherent response to it, because of their possessing a rational faculty. Reason means the capacity to know this natural law and the obligations it imposes; this law (of justice) is 'written in his heart'. Men and women in essence are rational creatures, not merely sentient beings. Reason is a reflection of the divine light in us: '*Ratio est radius divini luminis.*' This is the justification for using the word Rationalist in this special sense in connection with international theory.

The Rationalist tradition is the broad middle road of European thinking. On one side of it the ground slopes upwards towards the crags and precipices of revolutionism, whether Christian or secular; on the other side it slopes downwards towards the marshes and swamps of realism. The origin of Rationalism is with the Greeks and especially the Stoics; its upkeep was later taken over by the Catholic Church, but its great merit has been that it has never been exclusive to Catholics. In the Middle Ages Jewish and Arab thinkers travelled this road, and in modern times, Protestants, humanists and Rationalists in the modern 'Rationalist Press Association' sense. It is potentially universal to mankind. It is a road on which I suppose all of us, in certain moods, feel we really belong and it is the road with the most conscious

---

15. John Locke, *Of Civil Government* (London: Dent & Sons, 1924), book II, p. 126.

acknowledgement of continuity. On it can be seen the stout figure of Thomas Aquinas, whom Acton called 'the first Whig'; also Vitoria, O.P. (1480–1546), and Suarez, S.J. (1548–1617), the Neo-Scholastics who make the bridge between the medieval tradition of natural law and modern international thought. Hugo Grotius is there, with his offspring and descendants among Grotian writers on international law, together with Hooker, Althusius and John Locke, and the Founding Fathers of the American Republic, at least Washington, Madison and Hamilton, to say nothing of Jefferson.

It is a *broad* middle road, but just at this point it seems to become rather uncertainly wide; its edges are difficult to discern and the road itself seems sometimes disconcertingly narrow. Hamilton, for instance, seems to be on the road, but look again and he is to be found well away from it, on the turf over towards the marshes. Burke is apparently marching sturdily along the road, but his movements are erratic. Kant one would like to think is on it, but he shows a disquieting tendency to dart away, to the other side from Hamilton, towards the crags and precipices. A little later there looms up a pocket of fog, called Hegel, which makes it difficult for some time to know where the road is and who is on it. Later Mill and Cobden are there, and also Mazzini, but is he on the road or not? Its general further direction is clear, although it looks as if it has narrowed to a cart track. Tocqueville and Abraham Lincoln are on it, and the sound of Mr Gladstone's oratory comes from round the next bend. Beyond that is a glimpse of the pince-nez and silk top-hat of President Wilson, who seems to be on or near the road, and the road *appears* to lead straight up to and end at the Palais des Nations at Geneva. The ambiguity of international Rationalism in the nineteenth century is something that will be returned to and analysed later; the above describes the general tradition of international thought here called Rationalist, and perhaps illustrates also how the three traditions are not clear-cut pigeon-holes, but can overlap.

Realists

The initial pointer towards the Realists was that they are those who emphasize in international relations the element of anarchy, of power-politics, and of warfare. Everyone is a Realist nowadays, and the term in this sense needs no argument. However it is worth noting that the word Realist has suffered a more grave debasement than the word Rationalist. Originally, as the dominant school of medieval philosophy, Realism was concerned with the doctrine that universals, that is, general ideas or abstract concepts, have an objective existence, as against nominalism, which asserts that universals are mere names. Then came the Cartesian revolution, asserting the doctrine that matter as an object of perception has real existence, as against idealism, which asserts that the object of external conception consists of ideas.

Today, in contemporary political theory, it is the doctrine that conflict is inherent in relations between states. 'For the political Realist, rivalry and some form of strife among nation-states is the rule and not a mere accident of backwardness in the past.'[16] To use the word Realism implies an affirmation about what is real, what is reality. For the medieval scholastic, this lay in universals, general concepts similar to Plato's Ideas, of which all particulars are reflections. For eighteenth-century man, reality is matter, as for Dr Johnson when Bishop Berkeley's idealism was mentioned and he angrily kicked a big stone, saying 'I refute him thus'. For twentieth-century man, Realism means a frank acceptance of the disagreeable aspects of life. Realism, therefore, is violence, sin, suffering and conflict, as when Kennan spoke of 'the real things that were happening' or as a great Realist said earlier, it is the acknowledgement that 'the life of man' is 'solitary, poor, nasty, brutish and short'. This might seem a misrepresentation of modern Realism, and perhaps it is, but not of one distinguished Realist, E.H. Carr: 'Politics are made up of two elements — utopia and reality — belonging to two different planes which can never meet. Every political situation contains mutually incompatible elements of utopia and reality, or morality and power.'[17] The implications of his language are that morality is utopia; a place which *is not*, whereas reality is power. Carr does not keep the balance, the fruitful tension, between morality and power which can be found for instance in Niebuhr's *Moral Man and Immoral Society*. (Realism in this sense — the frank acceptance of the disagreeable side of life — is a word always bordering on, but never quite becoming synonymous with cynicism, and it is frequent in current colloquial usage: 'so-and-so is very upset: his wife has just run off with X' — 'Oh well, he'll have to be realistic' is an exchange you would not be surprised or even shocked to hear at any cocktail party. It is interesting that a word of philosophical origin, debased into current coinage, has passed into the vocabulary of international theory but *not* of political philosophy. This is perhaps evidence that international theory does have its own proper language and concepts, and it would be valuable to trace back the use of the word in international theory and diplomatic discussion. E.H. Carr seems to have been one of the first to use it in a theoretical way in *The Twenty Years' Crisis* but there must be antecedents.)

The Realist tradition in international theory is as familiar, virtually as self-conscious and as continuous as the Rationalist. At the beginning stands the astonishing figure of Machiavelli, the first man (since the Greeks) to look at politics without ethical presuppositions. He was in a real sense the inventor of Realism. He made a conscious break away

---

16. K.W. Thompson, 'The Study of International Politics a Survey of Trends and Developments', in *The Review of Politics*, vol. xiv (Indiana: University of Notre Dame, 1952), p. 446.

17. E.H. Carr, *The Twenty Years' Crisis* (London: Macmillan & Co., 1939) pp. 118–19.

from the theologico-ethical Rationalism dominant in the Middle Ages, and equally from the latent Revolutionism (or its antecedents) which ran back to the origins of Christianity. Bacon, himself a Machiavellian, wrote, 'we are much beholden to Machiavelli and others, that write what men do, and not what they ought to do.'[18] Hobbes stands as the only peer of Machiavelli, but others who form part of the Realist tradition are Bodin, Spinoza and Hume; in the eighteenth century, the classic age of applied Realism, *raison d'état* dominated the reigns of Frederick and Catherine; and Bismarck and Treitschke continued the tradition.

E.H. Carr has made the most comprehensive restatement, other than a Marxist or Fascist one, of the Hobbesian view of politics in recent times, and of the doctrine that it is from politics, the conflict for power, that both morality and law derive their authority. The parallel between Carr and Hobbes is close, and amusing. The last of the four parts of Hobbes' *Leviathan*, which few people read, is 'The kingdom of darkness'. It is an attack on the Roman Catholic Church which is partly theological, and tongue in cheek, but mainly political, because the Church claimed universal suzerainty still over sovereign states, which Hobbes called the 'kingdom of fairies'.[19] His attack is a mixture of irony and historical penetration. The place taken in Hobbes by the Roman Church is taken in Carr by the League of Nations, which is (on a Realist analysis) no other than the ghost of the deceased Pax Britannica, sitting crowned on the grave thereof and the principal old wives who bemuse the British public with their fables about the Kingdom of the Fairies, and its seductive enchantments, are President Wilson, Lord Cecil, Professor Toynbee, Sir Alfred Zimmern, and, at least in his pre-war championship of the League, Mr Churchill. Apart from Carr, recent figures in the Realist tradition are Morgenthau perhaps, certainly Burnham, Kennan and Butterfield.[20]

The Realist tradition on international theory has a distinguishing mark in its reliance on the inductive method. It concentrates on the actual, what is, rather than the ideal, or what ought to be; on facts rather than obligations. It appeals to the inductive method rather than to a priori reasoning. Machiavelli himself said this explicitly:

It being my intention to write a thing which shall be useful to him who apprehends it, it appears to me more appropriate to follow up the real truth of a matter than the imagination of it; for many have pictured republics and principalities which in fact have never been known or seen, because how one lives is so far distant from how one ought to live, that he who neglects what is done for what ought to be done, sooner effects his ruin than his preservation.[21]

---

18. Joseph Devey, *Works of Lord Bacon* (London: Henry G. Bohn, 1864), book VII, ch. ii, p. 281.
19. Thomas Hobbes, *Leviathan* (Oxford: Blackwell, 1946), part iv, p. 457.
20. See H. Butterfield and M. Wight, eds, *Diplomatic Investigations* (London: Allen & Unwin Ltd. 1966), p. 121.
21. Machiavelli, tr. W.K. Marriot, *The Prince* (London: J.M. Dent, 1928), ch. xv, p. 121.

This is echoed by E.H. Carr in his definition of Realism: 'The impact of thinking upon wishing which, in the development of a science, follows the breakdown, of its first visionary projects, and marks the end of its specifically utopian period, is commonly called realism.'[22] Carr's reference to the 'development of a science' is a pointer to the philosophical basis of all Realism: it is based on one or another 'scientific' theory. One can detect three such 'scientific' presuppositions which successively or simultaneously have determined the Realist tradition; they are the mechanistic, the biological, and the psychological.

With the mechanistic theory, the symbol of international politics is provided by a balance or pair of scales. It was developed in the course of the fifteenth century and was one of the most characteristic conceptions of the Renaissance. In painting and sculpture and most strikingly in architecture it was expressed in the principle of symmetry, and the search for what was believed to be the 'classical equilibrium' and found its supreme expression in Raphael. In music, in the fifteenth century, counterpoint became the principle of harmony, and counterpoint was the placing of one melody against another, each with its individual life. In science, the first field of modern physics to be explored was statics, which was concerned with bodies at rest or with forces in equilibrium. In medicine, Renaissance theory found the principle of health in the balance of the four humours; their balance produced the 'harmonic man'. (It is interesting to compare Jung's four types.) Astrology, which attained its greatest elaboration as an intellectual system in the Renaissance, was as prevalent a pseudo-science as much psychology is today; and like psychology offered interpretations and predictions of public affairs as well as personal life, and sometimes attained, by circuitous and arbitrary reasoning, conclusions already indicated by common sense, also like psychology. And in astrology great importance was attached to the symbol of *Libra*, the scales, which is the seventh constellation of the Zodiac. These pseudo-sciences, systems of imagery which seem to come half-way between religious belief and true science, colour all our thinking. (Their methods are so arbitrary by standards usually accepted as scientific that they are often repudiated by cognate scientists — psychology by medicine and ethics, alchemy by chemistry, and astrology by astronomy.) It is possible that astrology was the field from which the symbol of the balance filtered and seeped into other realms of thought. Alchemy, astrology and psychology, three pseudo-sciences of modern Western history, all contain half-lights and hints of truth, to which, no less than to human credulity, they owe their long vitality.

During the fifteenth century this mechanistic symbol of the scales, this concept of equilibrium, was introduced from the realms of

---

22. E.H. Carr, *The Twenty Years' Crisis*, p. 14.

speculative thought, art and science, into practical affairs. Double-entry book-keeping was invented in commercial Venice; instead of entering items in a ledger one below another, as a simple listing, they were entered on opposite pages, under credit and debit, income and expenditure, hence the phrase 'balancing the books'. The theory of equilibrium was introduced into politics also; the theory of balance of power was first formulated at the end of the fifteenth century and there are famous early expressions of it in Rucellai and Guicciardini, post 1494. (The mercantilist 'balance of trade', however, came into use in the seventeenth century.) The theory of the balance of power underlay all Machiavelli's pictures of international politics. Before 1494, when Lorenzo di Medici died, Italy had been 'in a way balanced'.[23] But the French invasion had upset the balance. This was, for Machiavelli, a realistic historical analysis, description not prescription, and this is characteristic of the Realist conception of the balance of power. The conception of a balance of power has become fundamental to all international theory, and it is impossible to discuss world politics without employing it, but it is important to note that although it was first formulated by the Realists in a descriptive and analytical sense, between the late sixteenth and early eighteenth centuries a displacement occurred in the principle of equilibrium, from the Realists to the Rationalists, from description to prescription, from analysis to policy, and from pure to applied international theory, so that the principle has been used since then in a double and ambiguous sense.

Machiavelli did not advocate a policy of the balance of power to remedy the ills from which Italy was suffering; he simply saw that there had been a balance between the Italian powers before 1494 which the French invasion had destroyed. The character of his prescriptions, of the policies he advocated, will be discussed later along with the general nature of Realist prescriptions and the Realist theory of foreign policy.

The highest expression of the mechanistic view of international relations is found in *War and Peace*. There are those haunting passages in which Tolstoy sees the drama of the Napoleonic Wars in terms of dynamics: hordes of men, moved by some fatality as mysterious as that which governs the migration of lemmings, pour eastwards to Moscow. This is the grand army of Napoleon. There the pendulum is at the extremity of its arc, and it swings back. Hordes of men pour westwards over the same path, and the Cossacks stable their horses in Paris.[24] This conception of international relations was so deeply and passionately held by Tolstoy that he ended the world's greatest novel with that extraordinary, sociological, section, in which he expounds

23. Machiavelli, *The Prince*, ch. xx, p. 169 (see also ch. xi, p. 92).
24. Leo Tolstoy, tr. C. Garnett (London: Penguin Books Ltd., no date), pp. 776–7, 968, 1066.

his philosophy of history and theory of international relations.
Tolstoy's fatalist Realism produced a Revolutionist response.

The second 'scientific' theory or model underlying Realist international philosophy is biological, and its source is, of course, Darwin.
But he was an unwitting source, for that gentle and retiring invalid
would have been astonished to know that he was, in an oblique way,
perhaps the most influential international theorist of the nineteenth
century.

It was in 1859 that he published *The Origin of Species*, and there
expounded the hypothesis of natural selection in biological evolution,
ratifying 'the expression often used by Mr Herbert Spencer of the
survival of the fittest', as 'more accurate'.[25] So great are the benefits
of universal education, cheap literature and rapid communication of
ideas, that within less than two generations a young man could pick
up this same hypothesis of the survival of the fittest, in Vienna, as he
loafed and ate cream cakes and read the newspapers in the cafés, or
engaged in violent political arguments in the night shelters. It was a
hypothesis wrenched from its context and degraded into the cliché,
'the struggle for existence', and applied now not to the individuals of
a biological species but to nations and races. Hitler found in it a
justification for the resistance of the Germans to the demand for equal
rights from the multitudinous subject peoples of the Habsburg Empire.
The biological theory of international realism was eagerly seized upon
by his brutal and inelastic mind, and he gave it its classic expression
(because with a crude theory the classic expression is the crudest) in
Mein Kampf.

The third scientific theory underlying international Realism is
psychological. This has become widespread in the twentieth century
as psychology has widened its scope from being a science of feeling
to a science of thought. The profoundest of Realists, Hobbes, based his
Realism on a psychological theory, which furnishes the first eight
chapters of *Leviathan*. He is known as 'the founder of empirical
psychology', and he worked out a sensationalist psychology, based on
the usual empiricist assumption that all mental life has its beginnings
in sensation. 'For there is no conception in a man's mind, which hath
not at first, totally, or by parts, been begotten upon the organs of
sense. The rest are derived from that original.'[26] He was interested in
the psychology of the individual mind less for its own sake than as a
logical foundation for his secularist, 'naturalist', doctrine of ethics and
politics. It is not fully worked out and contains internal contradictions.

The same relation between a comprehensive psychological theory
that claims to be derived from a science of behaviour and international
Realism is apparent with the development of psychology in the

25. Julian Huxley, *Living Thoughts of Darwin* (London: Cassel & Co. 1939), p. 81.
26. Thomas Hobbes, *Leviathan*, ch. i, p. 7.

twentieth century. For example Sigmund Freud's letter to Einstein of 1932: 'Here is then (in the destructive instinct) the biological justification for all those vile pernicious propensities which we are now combating. We can but own that they are more akin to nature than this our stand against them, which, in fact, remains to be accounted for.'[27]

Psychological theories might not seem prima facie to need to lead to Realism. But they do in fact, and the reason is not difficult to find. The more comprehensive an explanation of human behaviour a psychological theory claims to give, the more it tends towards determinism, and the more, therefore, it is implicitly derogatory to the claims of ethics. Underneath almost all modern psychology (unless perhaps Jungian) lies a behaviourist assumption about human nature which discards ethical values. For example, in 1951 the United Nations condemned Communist China as an aggressor, and there was pressure for a resolution to 'brand China' by American public opinion and the government; the psychological Realist is apt to describe this in terms such as 'Acting out of the American aggression-impulse'. Descriptions in such language are implicitly derogatory to moral and legal considerations, and justify the intemperate and exhilarating onslaught on psychology by R.G. Collingwood: 'as the pseudo-science of thought which claims to usurp the field of logic and ethics in all their various branches, including political science, aesthetics, economics, and whatever other criteriological sciences there may be, and finally of metaphysics.'[28] This consideration of the 'scientific' theories or philosophies underlying international Realism suggests that the characteristic kind of statement which Realists make about international relations is *sociological*. The affirmations of Realists are empirical generalizations arrived at inductively, they are statements of social laws. They do make ethical statements too, but their characteristic statement is sociological. For example: Machiavelli's 'armed prophets [Moses, Hitler] conquer; unarmed prophets [Savonarola, Trotsky] are destroyed'[29] and Carr's 'international order . . . will always be the slogan of those who feel strong enough to impose it on others'.[30] Perhaps here one can detect the essential difference between Realism, Rationalism and Revolutionism. The characteristic statement of a Rationalist about international relations is a descriptive statement arrived at deductively.

The political or international Realist is answering the question 'What is?' by a description and classification of experience, and brushes aside

27. Sigmund Freud, *Civilization, War and Death* (London: Hogarth Press, 1939), p. 93.
28. R.G. Collingwood, *An Essay on Metaphysics: Philosophical Essays* (Oxford: Clarendon Press, 1940), vol. ii, see also part ii, chs. 9–13.
29. Machiavelli, *The Prince*, p. 48.
30. E.H. Carr, *The Twenty Years' Crisis*, p. 110.

the other kinds of question: 'What is the essence of the matter?', and 'What ought to be?', the metaphysical and the ethical questions.

The Rationalist writes about international relations in terms of the metaphysical question; he is concerned with the essential nature of affairs. The most famous of all descriptions of the state is a statement of this kind, Aristotle said: 'While it comes into existence for the sake of life, it exists for the good life,'[31] and Suarez's description of international relations is similarly ontological:

The human race, though divided into no matter how many different peoples and nations has for all that a certain unity, a unity not merely physical, but also in a sense political and moral bound up by charity and compassion; wherefore though every republic or monarchy seems to be autonomous and self-sufficing, yet none of them is, but each of them needs the support and brotherhood of others, both in a material and a moral sense. (Therefore they also need some common law organizing their conduct in this kind of society).[32]

One might also cite those magniloquent and archaic homilies which the Holy See repeatedly addresses to an unheeding world.[33] There are similar Rationalist examples from Grotius to Gladstone, including Field-Marshal Smuts in the preamble to the United Nations Charter: 'We the peoples of the United Nations, determined . . . to reaffirm faith in fundamental human rights, in the dignity and worth of the human person, in the equal rights of men and women and of nations large and small.'[33a] Realists tend to make sociological, and Rationalists ontological, statements about international relations; the corresponding characteristic of the Revolutionist is to make statements of an ethical or prescriptive nature, to answer the third of the philosopher's questions. At the heart of international Revolutionism lies a prescriptive assertion, an ought, expressed as an imperative. It may take the form either of an exhortation to believers, the faithful, to hasten the international revolution which will renovate and unify the society of states, or of a threat to those who obstruct and resist the revolution. The sixteenth-century Huguenot treatise, *Vindiciae contra Tyrannos*, provides a good example of this:

All accord in this, that there is only one Church, whereof Jesus Christ is the head, the members whereof are so united and conjoined together, that if the least of them be offended or wronged, they all participate in the harm and sorrow . . .

31. Aristotle, tr. H. Rackham, *Politics* (London: W. Heineman Ltd., 1932), 1252b, p. 9.
32. Francisco Suarez, *'De Legibus ac de Deo Legislatore'*, quoted by John Eppstein in *The Catholic Tradition of the Law of Nations* (London: Burns Oates, 1935), p. 265. See also ibid., p. 272.
33. As in the Encyclicals *Mortalium Animos* (1928) and *Quadragesimo Anno* (1931) of Pius XI and *Summi Pontificatus* (1939) of Pius XII, emphasizing the brotherhood of peoples. For a fuller list of Encyclicals, with extracts, from 1878 to 1940, see *War, Conscience and the Rule of Christ* compiled by Mark FitzRoy (High Wycombe, Pax Society, 1940).
33a. *Charter of the United Nations* (New York: The UN Office of Public Information, 1963), p. 1.

He who has any sense of religion in his heart, ought no more to doubt whether he be obliged to aid the afflicted members of the church, than he would be assisting to himself in the like distress ...

As this church is one, so is she recommended and given in charge to all Christian princes in general, and to every one of them in particular ... So that if a prince who has undertaken the care of a portion of the church, as that of Germany and England, and, notwithstanding, neglect and forsake another part that is oppressed, and which he might succour, he doubtless abandons the church [the church being one] which he is bound to preserve and defend.[34]

Ergo, it is his duty to conduct ideological interventions abroad. This is the reasoning of international Revolutionists whether they are speaking of the church, the human race, or the working class. Their tone is exhortatory, imperative, prescriptive: 'workers of the world, unite.' Stalin's oath at Lenin's funeral was: 'We vow to you, Comrade Lenin, that we will not spare our lives to strengthen and extend the union of the toilers of the whole world — the Communist International!'[35] Perhaps the simplest instances of Revolutionist exhortation are afforded by the choruses of two familiar songs:

> To arms you sons of France!
> To arms your ranks advance
> March on, march on,
> Serfdom is past,
> Set free the world at last![36]

* * *

> Then comrades come rally!
> And the last fight let us face:
> The International
> Unites the human race![37]

These unsophisticated choruses could be said to have been more potent statements of international theory than the lucubrations of many philosophers.

To say that the characteristic Rationalist statement is ontological does not say it excludes the ethical sphere, and the concept of duty: it obviously *includes* it. But the characteristic Revolutionist statement, imperative in nature, does exclude the conceptions of ontology and teleology, or at least it does not formulate them even if it can be construed as implying them. Even Marxism can be construed as a theory of natural right.[38] Both the Rationalist and the Revolutionist norm is derived from a transcendental source, and the Revolutionist norm from an immanentist process.

34. Junius Brutus tr., *A Defence of Liberty against Tyrants* (London: Bell and Son Ltd., 1924), pp. 216–17.
35. *History of the Communist Party of the Soviet Union* (Moscow: Foreign Languages Publishing House, 1945), p. 269.
36. *The Left Song Book* (Victor Gollancz Ltd., 1938), p. 15.
37. ibid., p. 9.
38. See A.P. D'Entrèves, *Natural Law* (London: Hutchinson University Library, 1951), p. 113.

To conclude, international Realism tends to describe international relations in sociological terms; international Rationalism, in teleological terms; and international Revolutionism, in ethical and prescriptive terms and in the imperative mood. This is a general survey of the three traditions; the following chapters present a series of paradigms which illustrate their differences more clearly.

2: Theory of human nature

All political theory presupposes some kind of theory about human nature, some basic anthropological theory.

Realists

Realists tend to be pessimistic about human nature, or rather, if 'pessimism' suggests a regret about the badness of what is recognized to be bad, the consistent Realist has no regrets; he sees human nature as plain bad. Mankind is divided into rogues and fools, and the rogues prey on the fools. Edmund, in *King Lear*, is the classic Realist about human nature, rejecting conventional astrological interpretations of human badness as examples of human folly.[1] 'Homo homini lupus' — 'Man is a wolf among men' — said the Roman poet Plautus succinctly,[2] and Freud stated categorically: 'the tendency to aggression is an innate independent instinctual disposition in man' . . . 'the greatest obstacle to civilization [is] the constitutional tendency in men to aggressions against one another . . .'[3] Hobbes gives a detailed account of human nature:

In the nature of man, we find three principal causes of quarrel. First, competition; secondly, diffidence; thirdly, glory.
The first, maketh men invade for gain; the second, for safety; and the third, for reputation. The first use violence, to make themselves masters of other men's persons, wives, children, and cattle; the second, to defend them; the third for trifles, as a word, a smile, a different opinion, and any other sign of under-value, either direct in their person, or by reflexion in their kindred, their friends, their nation, their professions, or their name.
Hereby it is manifest, that during the time men live without a common

---

1. See *King Lear*, act I, scene ii, line 120ff.
2. See Plautus, *Asinaria*, Act II.4.88.
3. Sigmund Freud, *Civilisation, War and Death* (London: Hogarth Press, 1939), pp. 55, 77.

power to keep them all in awe, they are in that condition which is called war; and such a war, as is of every man, against every man.[4]

This is the 'Bellum omnium contra omnes'.
Machiavelli had a similar opinion of mankind:

Because this is to be asserted in general of men, that they are ungrateful, fickle, false, cowards, covetous, and as long as you succeed they are yours entirely; they will offer you their blood, property, life, and children, as is said above, when the need is far distant; but when it approaches they turn against you . . . [he later goes on] 'A wise lord ought not to keep faith . . . If men were entirely good this precept would not hold, but because they are bad, and will not keep faith with you, you too are not bound to observe it with them.[5]

And Tolstoy, in *War and Peace* writes: 'Davoust was not like Araktcheev a coward, but he was as exacting and as cruel, and as unable to express his devotion except by cruelty.' 'In the mechanism of the state organism these men are as necessary as wolves in the organism of nature.'[6]
A.J.P. Taylor wrote of Bismarck:

Though Bismarck lacked humbug, he did not lack principles. Only they were not liberal principles. They were principles founded in distrust of human nature, principles of doubt and restraint. When men dislike Bismarck for his realism, what they really dislike is reality. Take his most famous sentence: 'The great questions of our time will not be settled by resolutions and majority votes — that was the mistake of the men of 1848 and 1849 — but by blood and iron.' Who can deny that this is true as a statement of fact? What settled the question of Nazi domination of Europe — resolutions or the allied armies? What will settle the question of Korea — majority votes at Lake Success or American strength? This is a very different matter from saying that principles and beliefs are ineffective. They can be extremely effective if translated into blood and iron and not simply into resolutions and majority votes.[7]

However this Realist theory of the badness of human nature leads to a paradoxical political conclusion, the Hobbesian paradox, namely that the social contract may throw up a tyrant worse than the state of nature.[8]
Latter-day Realists tend to be less outspoken and robust in their statements about human nature than their predecessors (except for the Fascist writers who have little standing where academic consideration

---

4. Thomas Hobbes, ed. M. Oakeshott, *Leviathan* (Oxford: Basil Blackwell, 1946), ch. 13, p. 81.
5. Niccoló Machiavelli, *The Prince* (London: J.M. Dent, 1928), ch. xvii, p. 134, ch. xviii, p. 142.
6. Leo Tolstoy, tr. C. Garnett, *War and Peace* (London: Penguin Books), p. 580.
7. A.J.P. Taylor, *Rumours of Wars* (London: Hamish Hamilton, 1952), p. 44.
8. See chapter 1: The three traditions.

is concerned), and the reason may be found in the changing cultural and sociological conditioning of international theory. Whereas sixteenth- and seventeenth-century theorists wrote for an élite, princes and aristocrats, who alone understood and controlled foreign policy, modern international theorists write for the common man, and for democracy, which it has been a dogma since 1789 to regard as inherently good and perfectible. Modern theories of human badness are wrapped up in psychological guise, which makes them acceptable; modern Realists have to pretend to be, if they are not actually, infected with Revolutionism.

Revolutionists

Revolutionists tend to be optimistic and perfectionist about human nature; but like the Realists' pessimistic assumption about human nature, the Revolutionists' optimism is paradoxical. 'Man is born free, everywhere he is in chains', is the Rousseauite paradox parallel to the Hobbesian. If he was born free, how does he come to be in chains? How did the golden age of natural man decline into the *ancien régime* of the Bourbons and Habsburgs? It is because men, who manage to be exceptions to the rule that all are naturally good and free, have put him in chains.

In Marxist writings and statements one can frequently detect the same Rousseauite paradox. In one and the same sentence the world will be described (a) as inhabited by peace-loving toiling millions, the naturally good mass of the world's population — 'The Communist movement created by Lenin has grown into a powerful, invincible force' (Mikhailov); and (b) with a change in the lighting, as infested and riddled and potentially controlled, not only by secret enemies in the pay of the imperialists, but also by vestiges, even in the souls of the peace-loving masses, of bourgeois ideology, psychology and morality:

The Soviet rulers . . . genuinely think that their system is the best in the world and that it is bound to triumph. On the other hand, absurdly enough, they live in an atmosphere of ceaseless fear, expecting conspiracies and wars of intervention at any moment. In fact they are very like a gambler who believes that he has invented an infallible 'system', yet is terrified of being robbed or even assassinated on the way to the casino.[9]

It is worth noting that to use the word 'paradox' of Realism and Revolutionism is not, nor intended to be, derogatory. Every philosophy of life, in proportion to its fidelity in interpreting the

---

9. A.J.P. Taylor, *Rumours of Wars*, p. 234.

substance of human experience, must resort to and embody paradox. A philosophy of life free of paradox is either one which has not investigated its own assumptions, or is so shallow as not to be worthy of consideration.

The regenerate, the elect, the party, sometimes speak of themselves as the majority of the human race, faced with only a small rump or residue of heretics and wreckers; sometimes as a small chosen disciplined élite, setting themselves to do battle with the slothful and backsliding mass of mankind. Either way, it is the task of the regenerate to coerce the remainder of the human race into goodness; to force them to be free. If they are not good they can and must be made good.

The forces of peace were capable of exploding the imperialists' war conspiracy. The genius of Lenin and Stalin has shown to all mankind the path to a new life. 'Tomorrow, if not today, the peoples of the entire world will adopt that path. There is and can be no other path'.[10]

In Revolutionist practice, the duty of coercing the human race will often be fulfilled by the method of extermination. Persons believing that the class-war can be progressively eased up and relaxed, as the Soviet Union grows stronger: 'can have nothing to do with our party. They are traitors or fools who must be ousted like vermin.'[11] Nor is this only practice. Revolutionism is characterized by what during the French Revolution was called the theory of depopulation. It is really an extreme form of optimism to believe that by decimating the human race you can make the residue virtuous, and that such methods will not affect the results.

Rationalists

Rationalists are neither pessimistic nor optimistic about human nature, but place the paradox which lies in our experience of human nature squarely in the centre of their theory of it. Thus they describe human nature in terms of a tension, and have to define it by a paradox. Grotius said: 'God has . . . forbidden submission to those reckless impulses which, contrary to our own and others' good, prevent us observing the rules of reason and Nature'[12] and A.J.P. Taylor expressed it thus:

---

10. L.I. Mikhailov, quoting a directive from Stalin on intensifying the class war, 21 January 1953; (*Manchester Guardian*, 22 January 1953).
11. ibid., L.I. Mikhailov.
12. Hugo Grotius, tr. W.S.M. Knight, *The Law of War and Peace, Selections from De Jure Belli ac Pacis 1625* (London: Peace Book Co., 1939), para. 13, p. 32.

There is a third way between Utopianism and despair. That is to take the world as it is and to improve it; to have faith without a creed, hope without illusions, love without God. The Western world is committed to the proposition that rational man will in the end prove stronger and more successful than irrational man.[13]

Both in its Christian and in its secular form, the Rationalist tradition appeals to reason. It affirms that besides being a sinful, pugnacious and irrational animal, man is also rational, and through his reason he can attain a considerable degree of success in adjusting his political and social arrangements. Society is not a picture of fools being duped by rogues, but of a largely successful field of co-operation between rational persons. The Rationalist is therefore a reformist, the practitioner of piecemeal social engineering.

A theory of human nature carries as its shadow, more or less clarified and acknowledged, a theory of history. Realists tend to see history as cyclical, the repetition of conquests, revolutions and defeats. This, incidentally, encourages the Realist tendency to treat international relations sociologically, since Realists find in history a great storehouse of examples and lessons. Revolutionists, by contrast, tend to see history as linear, moving upwards towards an apocalyptic denouement which is either just about to take place or has taken place in the present generation. It is clear that the revolutionary *élan* and dynamic in international politics is derived from a sense of partnership in the messianic fulfilment: the overthrow of Antichrist and establishment of pure religion; the destruction of tyranny and establishment of liberty, equality and fraternity; or the inevitable doom of capitalism and the world-wide triumph of the revolution. Rationalists, in their theory of history, may be expected to be cautious and agnostic. H.A.L. Fisher could be cited as an example:

Men wiser and more learned than I have discerned in history a plot, a rhythm, a predetermined pattern. These harmonies are concealed from me. I can see only one emergency following upon another . . . only one safe rule for the historian: that he should recognize in the development of human destinies the play of the contingent and the unforeseen. This is not a doctrine of cynicism and despair. The fact of progress is written large and plain on the page of history; but progress is not a law of nature. The ground gained by one generation may be lost by the next. The thoughts of men may flow into the channels which lead to disaster and barbarism.[14]

---

13. A.J.P. Taylor, *Rumours of Wars*, p. 262.
14. H.A.L. Fisher, *A History of Europe* (London: Edward Arnold, 1936), preface, p. v.

3: Theory of international society

The central question of classical political theory is, 'What is the state?', 'What is civil society?' The analogue question of international theory is, 'What is international society?'

International society is, prima facie, a political and social fact, attested to by the diplomatic system, diplomatic society, the acceptance of international law and writings of international lawyers, and also, by a certain instinct of sociability, one whose effects are widely diffused among almost all individuals, from tourist curiosity to a deep sense of kinship with all mankind.

Men have been arguing for centuries about what the state really is, what its purpose is, how it holds together and why it should hold together; there is far more scope for argument about the nature of the much more shadowy and insubstantial entity called international society. Is it really a society or only a field of sentiment? Does it create legal obligations? By the end of the sixteenth century it was already being discussed in these terms, and three broad answers have been offered, which can be identified as those of the Realists, Rationalists and Revolutionists.

Realists

The answer of the Realists is not the oldest, but it is the simplest; and in a sense it was a Realist, Machiavelli, who first discussed international relations in a way which made it possible to formulate an answer. Moreover, it was another great Realist, Hobbes, who first established the terms in which the question was to be answered. It seems to have been Hobbes who first laid down the equation: *international relations/society equals the state of nature*, and from the mid-seventeenth century this became the basic assumption of international theory. The equation may have been pre-Hobbesian; it can certainly be found in his contemporary, Spinoza, and later continental writers, such as Vattel, who appeals to *De Cive*, ch. xiv, para. 4. where Hobbes defines the law of nations as natural law applied to states (which are as moral persons). It is also explicit in *Leviathan*, part I, ch. 13.[1]

The social contract, for Hobbes, covers the individuals who have contracted together; there remains the question first, of those who have not yet made a contract, and come to live a civic life in states, e.g. the American Indians; and the second, the question of the relationship between those who have made *different* social contracts, between the separate moral, corporate persons brought into existence by these separate contracts. The answer to the first is obvious; that those who have not yet made a contract still live in a pre-contractual condition, which is the state of nature. The same answer is given to the second question. The separate moral persons, or states, brought into existence by separate social contracts are also, *inter se*, in a pre-contractual condition, which is the state of nature. So the initial question, 'What is international society?' seems to resolve itself into the question, 'What is the state of nature?', and the answers to both questions will be the same.

Hobbes' answer about the state of nature is familiar; he saw it as a war of all against all (not just of individuals, but rather of families or patriarchal governments). The state of nature is a war of everyone against everyone, and the answer to the question, 'What is international society?', is 'nothing'. There is no natural society or community of states; society is created by a social contract; the state of nature is by definition pre-contractual and non-social, so to speak of a society of nations is contradictory. This was implicitly the position of Bodin, and clearly, the more a thinker emphasizes sovereignty, and the authority, dignity and coherence of the state (as Bodin does), the more he will tend to discount a suggestion that the state is a member of a wider society of states. This is also, explicitly, the position of Spinoza, Rousseau, and of Hegel, although the latter expresses it in characteristically inspissated language: the state alone is actual and rational, international relations 'are on the largest scale a maelstrom of external contingency and the inner particularity of passions, private interests and selfish ends, abilities and virtues, vices, force and wrong. All these whirl together . . .'[2] This is equally the position of Fichte and Hitler. It is also expressed by Morgenthau, when he says: 'Above the national societies there exists no international society so integrated as to be able to define for them the concrete meaning of justice or equality, as national societies do for their individual members.'[3]

---

1. Thomas Hobbes, *Leviathan* (London: J.M. Dent, 1934), part I, ch. 13. See also J.L. Brierly, *The Basis of Obligation in International Law* (Oxford: Clarendon Press, 1958), p. 33.
2. Friedrich Hegel, tr. T.M. Knox, *Philosophy of Right* (Oxford: Clarendon Press, 1949), para. 340.
3. Hans J. Morgenthau, *In Defense of the National Interest* (New York: Alfred A. Knopf, 1951), p. 34. See also *Dilemmas of Politics* (University of Chicago Press, 1958), pp. 80–1.

The common assertion of all these writers, and many others, with varying shades of emphasis, is that really there is no such thing as international society, and the evidence for its existence does not bear examination. International law is too nebulous and too constantly violated to be understood as more than a peacetime convenience of sovereign states; the diplomatic system is a network which came into existence and continues for the purposes of aggrandisement and protection; and the sentiment of humanity invariably evaporates at the moment when, on the supposition of an international society, it is most needed: to prevent a war. In other words, there can be no world society without a world state. And in some moods, and in some circumstances, it is difficult to deny that this explains the facts of international relations.

Practising diplomats often assume, it might almost be true to say that they normally assume, that international society does not exist. Bismarck used to show impatience when the words 'Christendom' or 'Europe' were introduced into diplomatic language, (usually by the Russians and their Foreign Minister, Gorchakov). In the pre-1914 German documents there is a marginal note by Bismarck on a memorandum drafted by Gorchakov: 'Talk about Europe is off the point: it is a geographical notion [these words in French, then in English]: Who is Europe?' and once when Gorchakov in person was urging on Bismarck the view that the Eastern Question was not a German or Russian, but a European question, Bismarck gave the devastating reply: 'I have always found the word Europe on the lips of those politicians who wanted something from other Powers which they dared not demand in their own name.'[4]

In these cases, the answer to the question 'What is international society' is clearly 'nothing'. However, there is a secondary, alternative answer that Realists sometimes give, which is, that international society is nothing but the great powers; the great powers constitute what international society there is. When Napoleon met Alexander at Tilsit in 1807, the brilliant conqueror overwhelmed the emotional young Russian with flattery; between them they could settle the destiny of the world: 'What is Europe, if it is not you and I?'[5] One hundred and fifty years later, Alexander's successor, the First Secretary of the Soviet Union, said very nearly the same thing.

In July 1956, on Soviet Aviation Day, at a dinner given for the leading foreign Air Force chiefs, one of the American guests reported Khrushchev thus:

He had also rude things to say about the smaller countries of Europe, such as

---

4. A.J.P. Taylor, *Bismarck The Man and the Statesman* (London: Hamish Hamilton, 1955), p. 167.
5. C.R.M.F. Cruttwell, *British History, 1760–1822* (London: G. Bell & Sons, 1928), p. 63.

Belgium, Holland, Italy, Norway, and Russia's own satellites in Eastern Europe. He said: 'A little country doesn't count any more in the modern world. In fact, the only two countries that matter are Russia and the United States. And Russia is superior. The other countries have no real say'. The American added that by this time Khrushchev was beginning to look a little anxious, as if his tongue had been too free.[6]

An American instance of the same line of thinking can be seen at the Congress of Panama in 1826. Henry Clay, an early advocate of Pan-Americanism, spoke in the US Congress in support of US participation to create 'an American system'. But John Quincy Adams (president of the United States, 1825–9), wrote in his *Diary*, 'as for an American system, we have it — we constitute the whole of it.'[7] This American answer to the question 'What is international society?' is in accordance with the principle of monopoly of power. If the answer is to be offered, that international society is nothing but the great powers, then some social relationship and degree of co-operation between these powers is assumed. Here Bismarck has the last word: a Russian diplomat once used the word 'Christendom' to Bismarck. Bismarck said 'what do you mean by Christendom?' The diplomatist answered, 'well — several Great Powers'. Bismarck replied, 'what if they are not in agreement?'[8]

We may explore the logic of this little dialogue in the case of the United Nations. The Hobbesian state of nature leads by the inexorable steps of Hobbesian logic to the Hobbesian social contract. The equation between the state of nature and the state of war demands the drastic remedy of the unlimited contract, and the complete surrender of rights in a state of nature to a despot, who may then retrogrant such civil rights as he thinks fit. The United Nations Charter (with some qualifications) is such an unlimited contract; it is a Hobbesian contract. It is not wholly fanciful to say that the inarticulate premise on which the Charter rests is that there is no such thing as international society, or that international relations are a state of war. Indeed this is a bare literal description of fact about the condition of things when the Charter was drafted, at Dumbarton Oaks, in the autumn of 1944, and in San Francisco, in April 1945, when the Third Reich and the Japanese Empire were still raging undefeated. There *was* a state of war then; there *was* no international society, or only potentially so. Thus:

We the peoples of the United Nations determined to save succeeding

---

6. Account of a dinner given by Marshal Lhukov, Russian Defence Minister, *Daily Mail*, 10 July 1956.
7. Dexter Perkins, ed. S.F. Beamis, 'John Quincy Adams', in *American Secretaries of State and their Diplomacy*, vol. IV, p. 52.
8. W.K. Hancock, *Survey of British Commonwealth Affairs* (London: Oxford University Press, 1937), vol. I, p. 460n.

generations from the scourge of war, which twice in our lifetime has brought untold sorrow to mankind . . .[9]

we came together. And what did we do?

reduced all [our] wills . . . to one will: . . . [we] appointed one man, or assembly of men, to bear [our] person, . . . and acknowledge [ourselves] to be author of whatsoever he that so beareth [our] person shall act or cause to be acted, in those things which concern the common peace and safety . . .[10]

The Smutsian pretence in the preamble, of 'we the peoples', we human individuals being party to the contract, is dropped as the Charter trundles on to Article 24, where the sovereign states, who alone are international persons and can make an international contract, perform this solemn transaction: they 'confer on the Security Council primary responsibility for the maintenance of international peace and security, and agree that in carrying out its duties under this responsibility the Security Council acts on their behalf'. In the very next article they pledge themselves 'to accept and carry out the decisions of the Security Council in accordance with the present Charter' (Article 25); and in Article 48 they authorize the Security Council to determine what action they themselves are to take, to carry out the Security Council's decisions.[11] In fact, they set up for themselves a Hobbesian sovereign, not 'we the people', but the states, members of the United Nations. The Security Council is the Hobbesian sovereign of the United Nations.

There is a small point which further illustrates the Hobbesian character of the United Nations. The Hobbesian contract is meant to be irrevocable; you cannot contract out without injustice, as the sovereign gives rise to justice.[12] An examination of the Charter will show that there is no provision for a member to resign from the United Nations. The covenant of the League of Nations had an article,[13] permitting withdrawal, but there is no counterpart in the Charter. You can be suspended from the exercise of rights and privileges and even be expelled[14] (just as the Hobbesian sovereign can banish his subject),[15] but there is no article of the Charter permitting a member to resign. 'States would have no right of withdrawing voluntarily; the intention is that membership of the Organisation shall be

9. L.M. Goodrich and E. Hambro, *Charter of the United Nations Commentary and Documents* (Boston: World Peace Foundation, 1946), preamble, p. 338.
10. Thomas Hobbes, *Leviathan*, ch. xvii, p. 89.
11. *Charter of the United Nations*, Art. 24, 25, 28.
12. But see the discussion that follows for the exception to this rule.
13. *Commentary on the League of Nations Covenant* (London: HMSO, 1919), Cmd. 151, Art. 1(3), p. 3.
14. *Charter of the United Nations*, Art. 5, 6, pp. 340, 341.
15. Thomas Hobbes, *Leviathan*, ch. xxi, p. 117.

permanent.'[16] This led to some misgivings among the small powers at San Francisco: 'Will you walk into our parlour, said the great powers to the small'; and to the debate and then Declaration of Interpretation that it was the 'highest duty' to remain a member.[17]

The common statement of the paradox of the Hobbesian contract is that the sovereign, with a despotic concentration of authority, may be either intolerable, worse than the state of nature (but Hobbes could not admit the possibility of this in theory), or inefficient (and Hobbes could not avoid recognizing this). 'The obligation of subjects to the sovereign, is understood to last as long, and no longer, than the power lasteth, by which he is able to protect them.'[18] Of course the Hobbesian sovereign of the United Nations has been inefficient; it has been a schizophrenic paralytic. Since the Security Council requires the unanimity of the great powers for action, it has scarcely ever acted.

The Realist theory of the badness of human nature leads to a paradox, for the classic Realist solution to the problem of anarchy, of the 'warre of every man against every man', is to concentrate power in the hands of a single authority and to hope that this despot will prove a partial exception to the rule that men are bad and should be regarded with distrust. This is the Hobbesian paradox. And those who framed the Charter of the UN expressed it in modern terms:

The principle on which the Charter is based is that power must be commensurate with responsibility, and it is on the Great Powers the Charter places the main responsibility for the maintenance of international peace and security . . . Thus the successful working of the United Nations depends on the preservation of the unanimity of the Great Powers [i.e. on the Hobbesian sovereign not being irresolute or schizophrenic] . . . if this unanimity is seriously undermined no provision of the Charter is likely to be of much avail . . . It is . . . clear that no enforcement action by the Organization can be taken against a Great Power itself without a major war. If such a situation arises the United Nations will have failed in its purpose and all members will have to act as seems best in the circumstances.[19]

In other words, the social contract will be dissolved. As Hobbes sadly admits 'when . . . there is no farther protection of subjects in their loyalty, then is the Commonwealth DISSOLVED, and every man at liberty to protect himself by such courses as his own discretion shall suggest unto him.'[20]

It is perhaps difficult to find the United Nations intellectually

---

16. *Dumbarton Oaks Documents on International Organisation* (Washington, DC: Dept. of State Publication 2192, Conference Series 56, 1944), Cmd. 6571, para. 22.
17. See Summary of Rousseau's argument for a federated Europe 'to force rulers, so to speak to be just and pacific' in F.M. Stawell, *The Growth of International Thought* (London: Thornton Butterworth Ltd., 1929).
18. Thomas Hobbes, *Leviathan*, ch. xxi, p. 116.
19. *Commentary on the League of Nations Covenant*, paras. 85, 87, 88.
20. Thomas Hobbes, *Leviathan*, ch. xxix, pp. 177–8.

appetizing; but one of its few thrills is in seeing how the penetrating vision of a great political philosopher has this kind of prophetic quality. Hobbes saw so deeply into the nature of political life that now after three centuries, when the whirligig of time has brought round conditions similar to those he constructed in the logic of abstract fantasy, things happen much as he said they would.[21]

The above describes the extreme Realist position on this matter. There is also a general or conventional Realist position, which can be illustrated from the positivists of international law.

It is the basic proposition of legal positivists that international law emanates from the free will of sovereign independent states. There is no law except what is 'posited' by sovereign powers, and therefore international law is the finite, sum-total of explicit agreements between powers, treaties, and customs to which they can be supposed to have tacitly consented. International society, for legal positivists, is the sum-total of agreements between states; i.e. it is no more than what its members agree it to be. Positivists perpetuate the contractual theory of society which in ordinary political philosophy is generally discredited. They emphasize that it is *states* that are the subjects of international law, and states alone are the units of the international juridical community. For the thorough-going legal positivist, international society is a society of personified Hobbesian or Hegelian sovereigns, who can suffer no authority superior to themselves, and whose will is the only source of law. In fact, it is pretty little of a society, and positivism has some difficulty in constructing a theory of legal obligation to explain in what sense international law is binding at all, or rather, in making a purely consensus theory of obligation fit the facts of international legal life.

The idea that states alone have an international legal personality, are the subjects of international law, and the members, or units, of international society, is one emphasized by legal positivists (who are a kind of Realist). It has been the preponderant doctrine of international lawyers for the last three hundred years (in spite of a persistent subdued note of criticism about it). It has been the majority report, but there has been a minority report also. In the sixteenth and early seventeenth centuries it was not clear that only states or sovereigns could be subjects of international law and members of international society; indeed it was generally assumed that individuals were as well. To the question, who are the members of international society?, there are three possible, theoretical answers. The first is that of the positivists: only states are. The second is that only individuals are: states are institutions only, and personified states are fictions; in the last analysis, international society is a society of the whole human race.

---

21. See in this connection, not only general Realism today, but the renaissance of Hobbesian studies; Oakeshott, Strauss, Collingwood, to name but three. [Written in the 1950s – Eds.]

The third answer is that both states and individuals are capable of being members, and this last is Grotius's answer. Grotius has at least eight different phrases for international society: the common society of the human race (in two forms); human society; the great community; the great university; the great society of peoples; the mutual society of peoples; the city of the world; the society of the globe.

Depending on the texts, one can argue that Grotius saw international society either as *societas gentium, civitatum, populorum* or as *societas humani generis*. In fact he saw it as both; and although this is usually explained by the undeveloped state of international law in his day, it can equally be argued that the fruitful confusion of his terminology corresponds to the fruitful confusion of the facts of international life.

There have always been parts of international law which seem to regard the individual as the subject of rights and duties, and which permit direct enforcement by or against him, for example, the law of diplomatic privileges; of extradition; piracy; prize; foreigners when abroad, etc.[22]

Positivists treat these as exceptional or insignificant, and argue to show that they do not upset the positivist premise that states alone possess international personality; but there have always been lawyers who take these points to argue, conversely, that the positivists have mistaken the nature of international society and law.[23]

The Central American Court of Justice, instituted in 1907, had the jurisdiction to hear a claim by an individual against a state; and since 1919 it has been possible to argue that the League, the United Nations, the International Labour Organization, and the Universal Postal Union are international legal persons, and to point to the International Military Tribunal after the Second World War as the beginnings of international criminal jurisdiction over delinquent individuals. The Smutsian flourish with which the Charter begins, 'We the peoples of the United Nations', though belied by what follows, points to some fruitful confusion, as we see in Grotius.

This whole line of reasoning, which sees international law as potentially a law having for its subjects both institutions and individuals, just as municipal law does, we may call Rationalist.

Rationalists

Half a century before Hobbes another answer had been developed to the question, 'What is international society?', which for a long time

---

22. J.L. Brierly, *The Basis of Obligation in International Law*, p. 52, T.J. Lawrence, *The Principles of International Law* (Macmillan Co., 1925) sect. 42, pp. 65, 66.
23. e.g. John Westlake, T.J. Lawrence, J.L. Brierly.

had the support of more international theorists than the Realist answer. This school of thought posits that in the state of nature men are still bound by the law of nature, by which is meant the pre-Hobbesian moral law of nature (which Hobbes debunked), not the scientific, quasi-psychological law of nature Hobbes substituted for it.

Sovereignty had indeed passed to different states, by social contracts, but the original unity of the human race survived; there was a law of nations acknowledged by sovereigns, even if violated, and this was the original natural law, which was legally binding and not just a moral imperative. This school, which was developing the main tradition of medieval thought, assumed that law was the source of society, prior to society, and not vice versa; they thought of law as issuing from some transcendent source, such as God's will.

This created a problem: if there is a natural law, and if the existence of law itself creates a society, and if, on the other hand, it is the social contract which brings civil society into existence, what becomes of the absolute distinction between the state of nature and man's social condition? This is not just a verbal problem; it is related to the experience of international relations. The answer was, of course, that there is no such absolute distinction between the state of nature and the social condition. The latter is indeed inaugurated by the social contract, but this does not mean that the pre-contractual condition, the state of nature, is non-social.

Grotius settled this question on the verbal level, by propounding the doctrine of sociability. It was indeed the social contract which inaugurated the condition of society, but the state of nature was a condition of sociability, of the capacity for becoming social.[24] The law of nature commands sociable behaviour; state of nature, therefore, is a condition of sociability, if not of society. It is a condition of common intercourse, containing the germ of society, a condition of peace, but unstable, formless, insecure, and liable to collapse into war. Thus the antithesis between natural and social conditions blurred: the transition to civil society is not a breach with the moral law of nature but a development of it.

This is the argument Locke uses against Hobbes, although he does not name him. Hobbes not only said that international society equals the state of nature, he added that the state of nature equals the state of war.[25] Locke is concerned to refute this: the state of nature is not a state of war; all that the two conditions have in common is the absence of a political superior. The state of war is a state of enmity,

---

24. Some useful definitions:
      socius = ally, partner
      societas = partnership
   Pliny, *sociabilis*: disposed to become a partner
   socialitas: condition of being a partner
   Grotius, *sociabilitas*: capacity for partnership
25. John Locke, *Of Civil Government* (London: Dent & Sons, 1924), bk. II, ch. 3.

malice and mutual destruction; the state of nature is one of goodwill, mutual assistance and preservation. This view of the state of nature clearly offers a different answer to the question about international society. Given this view, international society is a true society, but institutionally deficient; lacking a common superior or judiciary. While the Realist will say that force is the dominant mode of intercourse between nations, the Rationalist argues that, on the contrary, custom is. He sees international society as a customary society, and he will not make the Realists' cynical sneers against international law, nor the Revolutionists' agitated demands upon it. He sees it as essentially a kind of customary law, with defects, but also with the tenacity of that kind of law.

It is not easy to make a satisfactory distinction between force and custom, to find the point where one ends and the other begins, nor to derive a quantitative measurement; but it might be argued cogently that at any given moment the greater part of the totality of international relationships reposes on custom rather than force. For example, the majority of the world's frontiers are grounded on custom rather than force (where custom equals the absence of an active will to change the frontier). This can be true without invalidating the Realist truth that most frontiers are disputed; it is possible that these truths, Realist and Rationalist, are complementary, not contradictory. On the Rationalist view, the role of force would then be simply to remedy the insufficiencies of custom; where the Realist says that custom gives a coating to acts of force, the Rationalist says that force steps in where custom breaks down.

The Rationalist view was formulated with precision by Francisco Suarez S.J. (1548–1617): although every state is a perfect community, yet it is none the less a member of a universal body or whole; this membership is the basis of international law.

The universal body he described as 'a political and moral quasi-society' — *societas quasi politica et moralis*; Grotius spoke of *'societas humana'* holding states to be *'membra unisus corporis'*; and Tocqueville described such a universal body too: 'the society of nations in which each separate people is, as it were, a citizen — a society always semi-barbarous, even in the most civilised epochs, whatever efforts are made to improve and regulate the relations of those who compose it.'[26]

Just as the Realist doctrine that the state of nature is a state of war leads to an unlimited contract; so the Rationalist doctrine that the state of nature is a quasi-social condition, institutionally deficient, leads to a limited contract; a contract of the Lockian type. If one can detect the sardonic smile of Hobbes between the lines of the UN Charter,

---

26. Alexis de Tocqueville, 'Discours prononcé à la séance publique annuelle de l'Académie de Sciences Morales et Politiques', 3 April 1852, *Oeuvres* (Paris: Michel Lévy Frères, 1866), vol. ix, pp. 120–1. (Author's translation.)

one can discern the bland and amicable assumptions of Locke in the Covenant of the League. It was 'founded on the assumption of mutual good faith'.[27] The men who drafted the Covenant thought of the First World War not as the total breakdown of international society, but as an exceptional and abnormal interruption of international relations. International society had been deficient in the means for the pacific settlement of disputes, and it was necessary to provide what Locke called an 'umpirage . . . for ending all the differences that may arise amongst' states. For this a limited contract was sufficient. 'The document that has emerged from these discussions is not the constitution of a super-state, but, as its title explains, a solemn agreement among sovereign states, which consent to limit their complete freedom of action on certain points for the greater good of themselves and the world at large.'[28]

Natural rights, the liberty of the state of nature, were reserved to the individual in civil society; states did not lose their sovereignty, they simply undertook to limit the exercise of their sovereignty. The paradox of the Charter is that it endorses the sovereignty of members in letter, but curtails that sovereignty in substance; e.g. the unanimity rule is abolished. The power conferred on the legislature was in the nature of a trust 'the supreme power cannot take from any man any part of his property without his own consent'.[29] The Covenant binds the organs of the League to observe the rules of law and existing treaties much more definitely and explicitly than does the UN. Locke gave a negative answer to the question whether the contract binds permanently, and the Covenant permitted withdrawal from the League. The Covenant did not establish a 'legislature' in Locke's sense, and it is not a complete Lockian contract, nor is the Charter a full Hobbesian contract. However, the difference between the Covenant and the Charter is, in essence, the difference between Locke and Hobbes.

Revolutionists

The Revolutionists' position stands on the other side of Rationalism from Realism. Unlike the other two it was not, on the whole, expressed in social-contract state-of-nature terms; for where the Realists made an absolute cleavage between the state of nature and civil society, and the Rationalists blurred this distinction into one of degree only, the Revolutionists obliterated it altogether, as being of no importance. What they were doing was to revive, or perpetuate, the minority medieval idea of a single human republic, an *imperium*

---

27. *Commentary on the League of Nations Covenant*, Cmd. 151, p. 15.
28. ibid., p. 12.
29. John Locke, *Of Civil Government*, bk. II, p. 187.

mundi (Dante), or to harden international society into a world-state, to define it and constitute it as a super-state.

Among international lawyers the most celebrated exponent of this view was Christian Wolff (professor at Halle University, 1679–1754). He propounded the idea that international society was a *civitas maxima*, a great society or super-state, of which individual states were citizens, and which could exercise authority over them. This view caused much debate in the eighteenth century. The greatest international theorist then was Vattel, the Swiss, whose book on the law of nations became a standard authority second only to Grotius, and is still cited. Vattel acknowledged a great debt to Wolff, but expressly dissociated himself from the dangerous *civitas maxima* idea:

I find the fiction of such a (great) republic neither reasonable nor well enough founded . . . I recognize no other natural society among Nations than that which nature has set up among men in general. It is essential to every civil society that each member should yield certain of his rights to the general body, and that there should be some authority capable of giving commands, prescribing laws, and compelling those who refuse to obey. Such an idea [he concludes rather priggishly] is not to be thought of as between independent Nations.[30]

Thus, before he begins his own book, Vattel quite deliberately aligns himself as a Rationalist.

The *civitas maxima* idea was not invented by Wolff; he happened to put it in a popular form. In the sixteenth century it was developed both by Catholics, for example Francesco de Vitoria O.P. (1480–1546), who spoke of a human commonwealth, including all states as members, with majority decisions binding; and by Protestants, for example Gentili (professor of civil law at Oxford, 1552–1608), an Italian protestant refugee, who advised Elizabeth's government, and held that the 'government of the world is in the power of the assembly of the majority of the world'. It was expounded, above all, by Calvin.

The essential characteristic of Revolutionist theory is that it assimilates international relations to a condition of domestic politics. The more international society is conceived of as a *civitas maxima*, the more international relations will be conceived as the domestic politics of the universal *civitas*. There are three possible ways of trying to bring about this assimilation; doctrinal uniformity, doctrinal imperialism, and cosmopolitanism.

Doctrinal uniformity

Revolutionist theory demands homogeneity among the members of

---

30. E. de Vattel, *The Law of Nations* (Institution of Washington: Carnegie, 1916), vol. iii, preface, p. 9a.

international society, i.e. states; it requires doctrinal and structural conformity, and ideological homogeneity between states. The classic statement of this kind of Revolutionism is Kant's Essay on *Perpetual Peace*. He works out an ideal, make-believe, treaty of eternal peace, of which the first definitive article is that the constitution of each state should be republican. (It is not necessary here to examine what he meant by 'republican', nor the reasoning which led him to this conclusion.) There could be no international peace until all governments were of the same ideological compulsion.

But the principle of the ideological uniformity or conformity of members of international society can be employed by ideologists of more than one kind. Kant's principle was applied by Alexander I and Metternich in the Holy Alliance, in the counter-Revolutionist sense; every member of international society must be legitimist. The Holy Alliance was to the French Revolution what fascism is to communism. The three autocrats, the rulers of Russia, Austria and Prussia, described themselves as 'fellow countrymen' — they had taken over the revolutionary concept of fraternity. In the Holy Alliance the single sovereign was God, to the French Revolutionaries the sovereign was . . . 'the rights of man'. Mazzini gave the principle a violent push in the opposite direction, so that it swung to a more extreme point than Kant: there is no valid international society until all its members are nation-states. This was the principle of self-determination which triumphed in 1919. There was a Revolutionist tinge given to the League of Nations by Wilson's initial demand that it be a league of democratic nations; a plan which was not in fact carried out. Wilson's earlier speeches and his refusal to negotiate with imperial Germany show him to be quite half-Revolutionist; the Fourteen Points, however, are not, and it can be argued that the League was not. The attempt by the United Nations to exclude Spain from international society in 1946 was an example of post-Second World War Revolutionism: ensuring the ideological homogeneity of its members in the sense of their being anti-fascist or 'peace loving'. The same principle, drawn ultimately from Mazzini and Wilson, gave its driving force to the Bandung bloc and the anti-colonial campaign. The demand was for international society to be made homogeneous; it was to be a society of self-determining nation-states; imperialism was to be liquidated; historic monstrosities like continued Dutch rule in West New Guinea, and the Portuguese Empire, could not be tolerated; South Africa, so far as possible, had to be reduced to conformity. 'Wherever, whenever and however it appears, colonialism is an evil thing and one which must be eradicated from the earth.'[31]

---

31. Sukarno, speech by President Sukarno of Indonesia at the opening of the Bandung Conference, *Asia-Africa speaks from Bandung* (Djakarta: The Ministry of Foreign Affairs, Republic of Indonesia, 1955), p. 23.

Doctrinal imperialism

The second way in which Revolutionist theory can try to actualize *civitas maxima* and assimilate international relations to domestic politics is by ideological or doctrinal imperialism; that is by a single great power trying to spread a creed and impose uniformity. There are many examples of this: Stalinism did it to Eastern Europe; the first French Republic imposed the rights of man wherever its armies could conquer; Philip of Spain believed it was his duty to suppress heresy, not only in his own vast dominions, but throughout Christendom as well: it was his duty to prevent Henry of Navarre from attaining the throne of France, and to depose the bastard Elizabeth, from the throne of England, who to the injury of being a heretic had added the insult of rejecting his offers of marriage.

The common theory underlying these attempts at ideological imperialism may be called the theory of the chosen people, or the imperial vocation. This has two sources:

(a) *The Old Testament.* This, of course, is where the phrase 'chosen people' originates. The Jews were the original chosen people in history, and the first nation to have this unique, exclusive sense of mission, claiming to be the bearers of the meaning of history. European history and civilization has been haunted by the Jews, by the thought of this inscrutable people with their cosmic providential claims; and hence comes the long story of anti-semitism and persecution of the Jews.

But a more sophisticated way of coming to terms with the Jews has been to take over their claims, to conceive of oneself as the chosen people. 'National Socialism was a perversion of the Old Testament, the self-appointment of a new chosen people, appropriating the promise without the judgement. Hitler's hatred of the Jews had its roots in this spiritual usurpation.'[32] There is a short step from this to his belief in Germany as the master race. Rauschning wrote about Hitler:

His own esoteric doctrine implies an almost metaphysical antagonism to the Jew. Israel, the historical people of the Spiritual God, cannot but be the irreconcilable enemy of the new, the German, Chosen People. One god excludes the other. At the back of Hitler's anti-semitism there is revealed an actual war of the Gods.[33]

England, in the seventeenth century, displayed a belief in herself as the land of the chosen people, when for a moment she became a dominant power in Europe under Cromwell, the English Napoleon: 'God is decreeing to begin some new and great period in his church,

32. Martin Wight, 'Germany' in *The World in March 1939*, Survey of International Affairs 1939–46 (London: Oxford University Press, 1952), p. 323.
33. Hermann Rauschning, *Hitler Speaks* (London: Thornton Butterworth Ltd., 1939), p. 232.

even to the reforming of reformation itself; and as his manner is, first to his Englishmen . . .'[34] and 'Let not England forget her precedence of teaching nations how to live'.[35] Puritan England, like Lutheran Germany, was steeped in the Old Testament. One can see a similar belief in the United States, with its 'manifest destiny' and descriptions such as 'the American; this New Man?';[36] 'a new nation, conceived in liberty, and dedicated to the proposition that all men are created equal'.[37]

(b) *Virgil*. There is a second source of this idea of imperial vocation, quite distinct from the first. Virgil's *Aeneid* has influenced European history more deeply than any book except the Bible; more deeply probably than Aristotle. In Aeneas, Virgil created the astonishing figure of a man with a mission, fate-driven, god-impelled, the supreme literary symbol of vocation, of personal destiny. When, in pursuit of his mission to re-found Troy in Italy, Aeneas lands in Italy, he is welcomed by Evander, King of Pallanteum: 'Through divers mishaps, through so many perilous chances we fare towards Latium, where the fates point out a home of rest. There 'tis granted to Troy's realm to rise again . . .'[38] 'Tis at the call of fate thou comest hither.' Aeneas answers: '*Ego poscor Olympo*' 'Tis I who am summoned of Heaven.'[39] This is the supreme expression of the imperial mission of Rome; and belief in this mission influenced Augustus and pervaded mediëval culture. The belief was channelled in the direction of international theory by Dante's *De Monarchia*. Dante's dependence on Virgil can be seen in the *Divine Comedy*, and *De Monarchia* is studded with Virgilian quotations. It is a completely satisfying piece of intellectual architecture, granted its premises. Its tight argument is that: mankind is one (idea of humanity); mankind can only fulfil itself under a single government; and Providence has designed for this role the Roman Empire. Today, if one accepts the first two points, it is easy to substitute the United States for the Roman Empire. It is Dante who lies behind various Latin versions of the imperial vocation, for example France as 'la grande nation', and Mazzini's belief in a third, 'Mazzinian' Rome. The Russian mission combines the Old Testament with the Byzantine Roman source.

---

34. John Milton, *Areopagitica* (Cambridge: University Press, 1928), p. 51.
35. John Milton, *Doctrine and Discipline of Divorce*, Pamphlet, 1643.
36. First used by John L. O'Sullivan, editor of *Democratic Review* in July–August 1845.
37. Abraham Lincoln, 'Gettysburg Address, 19 November 1863', *Speeches and Letters* (London: J.M. Dent and Sons Ltd., 1936), p. 213.
38. Virgil, tr. H.R. Fairclough, *Aeneid* (London: William Heinemann, 1947), vol. i, p. 255.
39. ibid., vol. II, pp. 93, 96–7.

Cosmopolitanism

The third way that Revolutionism attempts to actualize *civitas maxima* is by proclaiming a world society of individuals, which over-rides nations or states, diminishing or dismissing this middle link. It rejects the idea of a society of states and says that the only true international society is one of individuals. This is cosmopolitanism: *cosmopolis* equals world city equals *civitas maxima*. This is the most revolutionary of Revolutionist theories and it implies the total dissolution of international relations. For this reason it is theoretically the least important, and no major work of international theory propounds such a doctrine. However in practice it is influential.

The essence, or central theme, of what is loosely called 'idealism' in international politics, when 'idealists' are contrasted with 'Realists', can perhaps be found here, in the appeal to *cosmopolis*, the appeal from the fictitious international society of sovereign states to the true international society of human beings.

Idealists must recognize as a basic condition for the realization of the liberal and humane values the creation of a brotherhood of mankind in which all men, regardless of physiological, social, religious, or political distinctions, will have equal partnership and in which human conflicts will be settled by reason, morality, and law rather than by physical power, coercion or violence.[40]

The idealist wants the creation of a brotherhood of mankind in which international politics will be assimilated to the condition of domestic politics. This is the natural impulse of the layman when he is first brought up against the hard barriers of international life: passports, visas, frontier posts, historic hatred, nationalist press campaigns. It is the reaction of the individual who travels, or who attends some sporting, academic or scientific congress. These private, non-governmental, international organizations encourage cosmopolitanism because there people of different nationalities, with strong professional common interests, meet one another as individuals, and realize that, under the skin and behind the language barrier, all men are brothers.

It is a strand, although not a dominant one, in the movement for world federations so far as it seeks to adapt the Western tradition of constitutionalism, which is Rationalist, to international relations. It is an abiding strand in the American outlook:

It is important to bear in mind that in international affairs it *is* governments, not peoples, with whom we have to deal. Many Americans do not like this. The American mind entertains a yearning for relations from people to people, unmarred by the pernicious interference of governments.[41]

---

40. R.E. Osgood, *Ideals and Self-Interest in America's Foreign Relations* (Chicago: University of Chicago Press, 1953), pp. 6–7.
41. George F. Kennan, *Realities of American Foreign Policy* (London, Oxford University Press, 1954), p. 42.

There is frequently a difference between our attitude toward foreigners as individuals and as 'types' or representatives of states or governments we find obnoxious. For many, this is one of the great obstacles in the study of international relations: the kink in the political space between a people and its government, between humanity and diplomacy, which the cosmopolitan seeks to smooth out, by ignoring the government and diplomacy.

The desire of Revolutionists to assimilate international to domestic politics is one feature of Revolutionism; another generalization one can make about them is that they are all concerned with aspiration rather than fact. Their assertion is about what ought to be, not what is. (The deductive, doctrinaire, imperative character of Revolutionist thinking has already been noted.) The central problem of Revolutionism, the great crux, is the disharmony or gap between Revolutionist prescription and the actual state of international relations. After all, all states are *not* self-determining nations; colonialism still exists; capitalism has not yet collapsed and nor has the communist empire. International society remains intractably various and heterogeneous, and this is the Revolutionist's problem.

For him, mankind is naturally good and destined for salvation, but it is empirically divided between those who accept the Revolutionist blueprint and those who are recalcitrant (always the majority). For the Jesuits it is the faithful versus the heretics; for Calvinists, the elect, 'saints', versus the reprobate; for the Jacobins, the virtuous against the corrupt ('*les pourris*'); for Marxists, the progressives or proletariat against the reactionaries or bourgeoisie. The following excerpt illustrates the latter case: H.G. Wells in conversation with Stalin: 'The big ship is humanity, not a class. — Stalin: "You, Mr Wells, evidently start out with the assumption that all men are good. I, however, do not forget that there are many wicked men. I do not believe in the goodness of the bourgeoisie".'[42] G.A. Tokaev describes how the official bureaucracy crudely reduced everything to a struggle against 'the vestiges of capitalism in the consciousness of man'. So whatever underhand thing a man did, whether deliberately or not, it was labelled as a vestige of capitalism (Tokaev and his friends considered this a vulgar over-simplification).[43]

To ask, 'What do Revolutionists do about this central problem?' leads to another distinction between them, cutting across the threefold distinction already made. It is a distinction of practice, and of theory. In *Faith and History* Niebuhr distinguishes between hard and soft utopians. These categories can be borrowed to differentiate between hard Revolutionists, like Lenin, and soft Revolutionists, like Kant, William Jennings Bryan, Andrew Carnegie, Woodrow Wilson, Cordell

---

42. *Stalin–Wells Talks*, The Verbatim Record and a Discussion (London: The New Statesman and Nation, 1934), p. 11.
43. G.A. Tokaev, *Betrayal of an Ideal* (London: Harvill Press, 1954), Introduction.

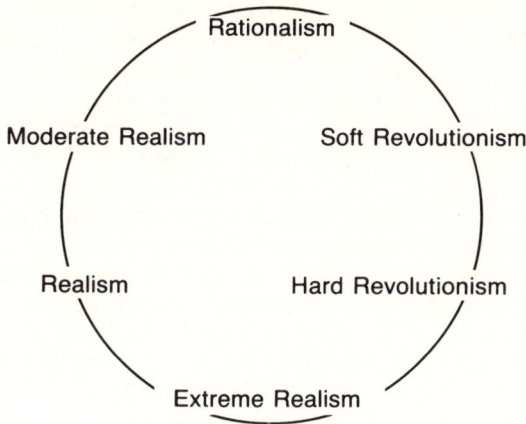

Figure 1 Proximity of the traditions

Hull, Franklin Roosevelt, Henry Wallace, the British and French neutralists, and Nehru. Hard Revolutionists believe in creating the brotherhood of mankind, or *civitas maxima*, in which international politics will be assimilated to the condition of domestic politics, by violence. Soft Revolutionists aim at this through yearning and talk; there are fewer in the United States now than in Europe. Henry Wallace was one of the last in the United States: 'War is impossible because of the H-Bomb: therefore ban the bomb, disarm, and talk.'[44] Konni Zilliacus wrote: 'Will we never learn that there is no way to end the cold war and the arms race except to negotiate with the Soviet Union, and the only basis on which we can find common ground for negotiation is the Charter of the United Nations?'[45]

The picture of the three traditions we now have can be represented diagrammatically (see Figure 1). Of the three kinds of Revolutionist theory discussed, clearly the first (doctrinal uniformity), is the least extreme. It assumes that a society of states will continue, and allows the majority, the ideologically pure, to encourage or coerce the minority, or impure, into conformity. Since sovereign states have hitherto been various in doctrine and structure, in practice this doctrine leads to subversion or intervention, or proves unsuccessful. An example of its unsuccess is the ostracism of Spain by the United Nations in 1946; ten years later Spain was admitted to the UN. In practice, the first kind of Revolutionism is unsuccessful unless it is a function of the second kind, doctrinal imperialism. An ideological empire will tend to promote uniformity among others, to create as far as it

---

44. Henry Wallace: Vice-President to Roosevelt 1941–45 when replaced by Truman; unsuccessfully ran for President, 1948.
45. Letter to *The Manchester Guardian*, airmail edition, 17 January 1957.

can a uniform society of states as a step towards dissolving this society into a cosmopolitan world-state. Napoleon and the French Republic, Hitler in 1938–41, and Stalinism in Eastern Europe all provide examples of this, and show how the three kinds of Revolutionism intertwine.

These dry theories and formulas of dusty dons and German professors about human commonwealths and *civitates maximae* can become politically explosive. The assertion that international society is a *civitas maxima*, a super-state (and 'is' here means 'is essentially', 'ought to be' or 'is destined to be'), raises at once the question of conformity and non-conformity. What is to be done about the citizens of the *civitas maxima*, i.e. states, which reject its authority in principle or counteract it in practice? One answer was given for the Revolutionist in the *Vindiciae contra Tyrannos* (1579), which deduced from the unity of human society the right of intervention to protect the oppressed. This is an early statement of the Revolutionist idea that horizontal ties are more important than, and may override, vertical ties, and in this way Revolutionism assimilates international relations to domestic politics. 'Workers of the world unite!'

The theory of international society, therefore, can be summed up in three Latin tags, answering the question, 'What is international society?'. For the Realist it is '*bellum omnium contra omnes*' (Hobbes); for the Rationalist, '*societas quasi politica et moralis*' (Suarez); and for the Revolutionist, '*civitas maxima*' (Wolff); or, in short:

1. It is not a society, rather an arena.
2. It is a society but different from the state.
3. It is a state (or ought to be).

4: *Theory of mankind: 'barbarians'*

The first question to be considered was, 'What is international society?' There is another that follows upon this, which it would be easy to overlook and lose in the earlier question, which is, 'How far does international society (supposing there be one) extend?'

If international society is not co-extensive with the human race, then what of the human beings and societies which are external to it? This is not an abstract question; it has been, and may again be, highly concrete. Every international society known to us has covered less than the whole habitable surface of the globe and has therefore been aware of other societies outside itself. The Greeks and Romans called these societies 'barbarians', with no presumption of cultural inferiority, only cultural difference (unlike the Chinese who, it is true, regard barbarians as inferior).[1] In the sixteenth century our international society was aware, on the one hand, of a highly organized and menacing society in the East, in some ways more civilized than Europe, the Ottoman Empire, and, on the other hand, of exotic new societies in the West, in new-found America, which were weaker, but in many ways not less civilized. (As for example, Dürer, who was fascinated and delighted, on a visit to Antwerp in 1520, by 'the first wonderful objects' brought back from the newly discovered Aztec culture.)[2] There was, then, a theoretical problem of how to account for these societies, and what kind of obligation might subsist between Europe and them.

Western international society came to include the greater part of the world at the second Hague Conference in 1907, when Asian and Latin American states were first generally represented at an international

---

1. A. Toynbee, *A Study of History* (London: Oxford University Press, 1934), vol. I, p. 161.
2. Heinrich Wölfflin, tr. Alistair and Heidi Grieve, *Die Kunst Albrecht Dürer's* (London: Phaidon Press Ltd., 1971), p. 243.

gathering, and this was confirmed by the League of Nations in 1920. But the problem was not extinguished. Arguably it was more reasonable in the years after 1945 to see world politics as divided into two international societies: that of Western European origin, and the new Communist one, their overlapping, as for example in the United Nations, being less important than their mutual exclusiveness, as in the non-recognition of Red China.

But there is another problem too, for there are still new societies outside international society, or rather, pockets within it. One need not speculate about explorers in the Amazon jungle finding lost civilizations, or abominable snowmen turning out to be men leading a social life in the snows; in 1954 the Australians discovered, in south-west New Guinea, fertile landlocked valleys, hitherto unknown, surrounded by mountain-ranges rising to 14,000 feet and inhabited by apparently 100,000 tribesmen. The New Guinea aviation director said it was impossible to tell from the air whether the people were pygmies or of normal size, but their villages were well designed and surrounded by great moats, and the External Territories Department of Australia found itself plunged at once in the same controversy that agitated the Spanish Government in the sixteenth century over what to do about the American Indians.[3]

It is one of the charms of international relations that more than any of the social sciences it approximates to science fiction. Already international lawyers are beginning to discuss whether international law applies to outer space, and whether there is a law of discovery and occupation. It is significant of the state of our culture that virtually all science fiction imagines a condition of natural hostility between the invented creatures of outer-space and ourselves; this makes for more gripping drama of course but it is significant.

The question of relations with barbarians was a political problem forming a bridge between international relations and colonial administrations. Non-self-governing peoples, colonial populations, were barbarians who had been absorbed into international society but not yet been digested.

Thus the 'Theory of mankind', for want of a better name, verges upon a theory of colonial administration.

Realists

It would be easy deductively to trace the Realist position about relations with barbarians; if international society does not exist, but if it is only an arena of power politics, a war of all against all, then what lies beyond this arena is obviously the same only more so. The

---

3. News reports, *The Times*, 12 and 17 June, 1954.

moderate Realist will allow that what Rationalists call international society is at least a diplomatic community, where some rudimentary social obligation operates as described in the language of positivist jurisprudence. Outside the diplomatic community there is plainly no element of social obligation whatever and here there is a war of all against all unrestrained by any tincture of morality, but only a law of self-preservation or law of the jungle.

Surprisingly, perhaps, it was Aristotle who first taught this; it was a basic tenet of Greek international theory. The Greeks had an international society, but no system of resident embassies. The Oracle of Delphi was like the papacy, and the Aetolian League and Achaean League played their part in international, or interstate, law. But society stopped short sharply at the limit of Greek-speaking communities, and beyond them was a state of war. This is explicitly stated by Aristotle, and it is worth remembering that this is an Aristotle who is usually overlooked. Aristotle is thought of as the father of the Whigs of constitutionalism, and the theory of the mixed constitution; the ancestor of Bagehot and the godfather of Gladstone and Jo Grimond. It is forgotten that Aristotle was adopted, with as much reason, by the German romantic philosophers like Hegel; this was the Aristotle of the city-state as proto-totalitarian, the total community, religious and secular: '. . . the city state is prior in nature to the household and to each of us individually. For the whole must necessarily be prior to the part.'[4] This is the Aristotle who made the state-yearning Germans conceive of themselves as the successors to the Greeks.

Aristotle is a better source of totalitarianism than Plato. Plato was a metaphysician, primarily a religious philosopher, who envisaged no concrete peoples as his 'Guardian' or 'Rulers': 'It is the main task of the *Republic* to introduce explicitly and formally the life of Theoria or Contemplation, in the teeth of the evil society.'[5] Aristotle, in contrast, was primarily a political philosopher and natural scientist. And this was the Aristotle who taught that barbarians, non-Greeks, were slaves by nature.

Among the barbarians . . . no naturally ruling element exists . . . This is why our poets have said, 'Meet it is that barbarous peoples should be governed by the Greeks', the assumption being that barbarian and slave are by nature one and the same . . . [the Greeks] are driven, in effect to admit that there are some (i.e. the barbarians) who are everywhere and inherently slaves and others (i.e. the Greeks) who are everywhere and inherently free . . . the art of war is in some sense a natural mode of acquisition. Hunting is a part of that art; and hunting ought to be practised — not only against wild animals, but also. against human beings who are intended by nature to be ruled by others

---

4. Aristotle, tr. H. Rackham, *Politics* (London: William Heinemann Ltd., 1932), p. 11.
5. A.S. Ferguson, 'The Platonic Choice of Lives', *Philosophical Quarterly*, vol. I, no. 1, October 1950.

and refuse to obey that intention — because war of this order is naturally just.[6]

At a meeting of the Aetolian League in 200 BC to discuss resistance to Rome, the Macedonian ambassador spoke thus:

Aetolians, Acarnanians, the Macedonians, men of the same speech, are united or disunited by trivial causes that arise from time to time; with aliens, with barbarians, all Greeks wage and will wage eternal war; For they are enemies by the will of nature, which is eternal, and not from reasons that change from day to day.[7]

It follows from such a premise that the problem of relations with barbarians is not a *moral* problem at all, but purely one of expediency; they were slaves by nature and so far as power extended they could be warred upon, pillaged and exploited. This was the Greek tradition. The distinguishing factor of the barbarians for Hellenic civilization was linguistic and cultural; the barbarian did not speak Greek. In Western civilization there was a new distinction, a religious one; the barbarian was non-Christian and called 'pagan' or 'heathen' instead. Instead of Hellas against the barbarians, it was Christendom against the pagans. Christian Realism, however, was no less apparent than classical Greek Realism. The Song of Roland (eleventh century) talks of: 'Paien unt tort a chrestiens unt dreit' (The pagans have sin and the Christians have right).[8]

The medieval and modern Western Realism talked of here is the philosophy of a frontier society. It is of course on the frontiers of international society that barbarians are normally encountered, and Realism about relations with barbarians is the predominant political theory of a frontier society. The sociological generalization may be hazarded, that Realism flourishes when a frontier society is confident and expanding, not when it is on the defensive and frightened. Then one is likely to find frontiersmen showing grudging respect or even admiration for barbarians, even imitating them, just as the crusading kingdoms in Spain and the Levant became assimilated to their Muslim enemy, who was vastly more civilized than they, and which became the channel for the acculturation of medieval Christendom. Nor does Realism flourish when a frontier society is triumphant and sated. Then one is likely to find barbarians herded into reserves and given tolerance and patronage, now renamed 'natives', usually. A Department of Barbarian Affairs may be set up to protect them from exploitation, to regulate the amount of liquor they can obtain, and to see that

---

6. Ernest Barker, *The Politics of Aristotle* (Oxford: The Clarendon Press, 1946), pp. 3, 16, 21.
7. *Livy*, tr. Evan T. Sage (London: William Heinemann Ltd., 1953), vol. IX, book XXXI, xxix, p. 87.
8. *The Song of Roland* (Faber & Faber 1937), v. 1015.

the brighter specimens get presented to the Queen if she comes round. It is when a frontier society is dynamic and aggressive, untroubled by doubts about its own purposes or strength, that the Realist theory of the limits of international society flourishes. Western civilization has shown a unique power of expansion and self-confidence, and has produced a unique crop of Realism. I shall mention the background of two sectors of Western frontier society, the German-Dutch and the Anglo-Saxon.

Germany in the early Middle Ages was the Eastern march or frontier of Christendom against the pagan Slavs. (The English and French words 'slave' and 'esclave' come from 'slav'; the Medieval Latin 'sclavus' means 'Slav captive'.) From the tenth to the fourteenth centuries German settlers colonized the North European plain from the Elbe to the Niemen, clearing the forests and draining the marshes[9] in a great effort that deserves comparison with the movement of the American frontier from the Ohio River to the Pacific Coast, after the signing of the Treaty of Paris in 1783, giving the Confederation independence, or of the Russian frontier from the River Ob in 1529 across the Siberian plain to the Pacific Coast. The heathen population here had to be converted, was usually reduced to serfdom or slavery, but was sometimes wiped out. Sometimes the forward movement took a new impetus in the form of a crusade, preached under the slogan of baptism or extermination, which attracted settlers. The greatest organ of this movement was the Teutonic Knights, a crusading military order founded in 1190, who conquered East Prussia and set up a state there, (like the Mormon state in Utah), which was the origin of the future Prussia, with its virtues and vices: austere military honour and arrogant militarism.[10] Lithuanian manhunts in the fifteenth century became a fashionable pastime for the nobility of the Empire, who gathered annually for the 'sport' as people now assemble at the Olympic Games;[11] this was the decadence of German colonization. Germany had ceased to be the frontier; there was instead an outer ring of Latin Christian peoples, the Poles, Bohemians and Hungarians, all interpenetrated and partly dominated by enclaves of German colonists. Germany then entered her time of weakness; the Reformation and Counter-Reformation, Thirty Years' War, and Napoleonic subjugation, followed.

German Realism about barbarians was given a new spurt by the impact of the Greek tradition in the efflorescence of German romanticism. (This Greek tradition of Realism was not influential in Machiavelli, who was captivated by the Romans and for whom the problem of barbarians had not yet appeared.) It comes into its own with the German romantics; thus Hegel writes:

---

9. H.A.L. Fisher, *A History of Europe* (London: Edward Arnold, 1938), p. 203.
10. See Eisenstein's film of 'Alexander Nevsky', 1938.
11. Henri Pirenne, *A History of Europe* (London: George Allen & Unwin, 1939), p. 476.

A nation does not begin by being a state. The transition from a family, a horde, a clan, a multitude, etc. to political conditions is the realization of the Idea in the form of that nation . . .

It is the absolute right of the Idea to step into existence in clear-cut laws and objective institutions, beginning with marriage and agriculture, whether this right be actualized in the form of divine legislation and favour, or in the form of force and wrong . . . The same consideration justifies civilised nations in regarding and treating as barbarians those who lag behind them in institutions which are the essential monuments of the state. Thus a pastoral people may treat hunters as barbarians, and both of these are barbarians from the point of view of agriculturalists, etc. The civilised nation is conscious that the rights of barbarians are unequal to its own and treats their autonomy only as a formality.[12]

Mommsen likewise speaks of 'the law, that a people which has grown into a state absorbs its neighbours who are in political infancy, and a civilised people absorbs its neighbours who are in intellectual infancy . . . this law . . . is as universally valid and as much a law of nature as the law of gravity.' By virtue of it, Rome 'was entitled to reduce to subjugation' the decadent Greeks, and was entitled 'to dispossess the peoples of lower grades of culture in the West' such as the Celts, Germans, Libyans etc.; 'just as England with equal right has in Asia reduced to subjection a civilization of rival standing but politically impotent, and in America and Australia has marked and ennobled, and still continues to mark and ennoble, extensive barbarian countries with the impress of its nationality.'[13] By this point the absence of any moral obligation to barbarians has become a right of conquest and dispossession, and that civilized states will behave in this way had become a universally valid law of nature.

German Realism about barbarians reached its culminating expression in National Socialism.

Therefore we National Socialists have purposely drawn a line through the line of conduct followed by pre-War Germany in foreign policy . . . We finally put a stop to the colonial and trade policy of pre-War times and pass over to the territorial policy of the future.

But when we speak of new territory in Europe today we must principally think of Russia and the border states subject to her . . .

Today there are 80 million Germans in Europe. And our foreign policy will be recognised as rightly conducted only when, after barely a hundred years, there will be 250 million Germans living on this Continent, not packed together as coolies in the factories of another Continent but as tillers of the soil and workers whose labour will be a mutual assurance for their existence.[14]

---

12. Friedrich Hegel, tr. with notes by T.M. Knox, *Philosophy of Right* (Oxford: Clarendon Press, 1949), pp. 218, 219.
13. Theodor Mommsen, tr. W.P. Dickson, *The History of Rome* (London: J M Dent & Sons, 1930), vol. IV, p. 196.
14. Adolf Hitler, tr. James Murphy, *Mein Kampf* (London: Hurst & Blackett Ltd., 1939), pp. 553, 549, cf. 128.

What will happen to the existing inhabitants of this territory was left unsaid; it was the Nuremberg Trials which revealed what it was. This famous quotation from *Mein Kampf* illustrates the importance of reading the published works of dictators as a guide to their future policy; and National Socialism illustrates the constant relevance of history. Here, in the first half of the twelfth century, is a manifesto by bishops and princes of Saxony appealing for settlers:

The Slavs are an abominable people, but their land is very rich in flesh, honey, grain, birds, and abounding in all product of fertility of the earth when cultivated so that none can be compared with it . . . Wherefore, O Saxons, Franks, Lotharingians, men of Flanders most famous, here you can both save your souls and if it please you acquire the best of land to live in.[15]

At the Nuremberg Parteitag in September 1936 Hitler declared in a celebrated indiscretion which provoked a rejoinder from Stalin and a clumsy disavowal by the Germans: 'If we had at our disposal the incalculable wealth and stores of raw material of the Ural Mountains and the unending fertile plains of the Ukraine to be exploited under National Socialist leadership, then we would produce, and our German people would swim in plenty.'[16] The motive of the salvation of individual souls has dropped out, to be replaced by the preservation of the German race.

The Anglo-Saxon tradition of Realism in relation to barbarians is more familiar than the German one which has just been traced. It involves not the Slav frontier, but the Celtic and Red Indian, and it has such monuments, between 1550 and 1900, as the plantation of Ireland and Cromwell's massacres; the transatlantic Slave Trade (ended 1806); the colonization of North America and the Indian wars (the last Indian war was the Sioux war of 1890); and the colonization of Australia and extermination of the Aborigines, especially in Tasmania. One might also add the Indian Mutiny, the Anglo-Chinese wars, and the Boxer Rebellion.

Among the elements of a Realist theory of relations with barbarians one can distinguish four doctrines, one positive and the other three negative. The positive doctrine is that *civilization has the absolute right to expand itself*. The Realist has a verbal difficulty with the theory of international society because he does not really believe there is such a thing and can only use the phrase in inverted commas; but when he deals with the theory of barbarians he can speak of civilization even if he thinks of civilization as a war of all against all, of haves against have-nots, at least it is the opposite of barbarism. This is the

---

15. Rudolf Kötzschke, *Quellen zur Geschichte der Ostdeutschen Kolonisation im Zwölften bis vierzehnten Jahrhundert* (Leipzig: Teubner, 1912), p. 10, freely translated in H.A.L. Fisher, *A History of Europe*, p. 203.
16. N.H. Baynes, 'Speech to the Labour Front at the Nuremberg Parteitag', *Hitler: Speeches* vol. I, p. 929 in *Survey of International Affairs 1936* (London: Oxford University Press, 1936), pp. 381–2 and note.

traditional language of international lawyers, when they say that international law is the law governing the relations of 'civilized' states. The definition of civilization here is presupposed, it is something historical. That civilization has the right to expand, to impose itself, is clearly stated in Mommsen [quoted above] and, for example, by John Quincy Adams in 1802 speaking to the Sons of the Pilgrims Society[17] and by others:

It is the mission of civilised nations to carry the banner of civilisation into barbarous and heathen lands. This boon has hitherto followed in the train of conquest and subjection, and has been forced upon nations, not from any motives of benevolence but from the natural superiority of civilisation over barbarism which must triumph when they are brought into constant and immediate contact.[18]

The thoroughgoing Realist will extend this principle of expansion from a civilization to the individual powers within a civilization. This is the premise of nineteenth-century European imperialism; and it is the premise underlying the forcing of European trade on China and Japan, two seclusionist empires, in the Anglo-Chinese War of 1839–42 and the Anglo-Franco-Chinese War of 1856–60; and on Japan, by Commodore Perry in 1853–4, by the British bombardment of Kagoshima in 1863, and by the four-power naval demonstration in Osaka Bay in 1865, involving the British, French, Dutch and Americans. Here are the instructions to Commodore Perry, 5 November 1852:

When vessels are wrecked or driven ashore on the island their crews are subjected to the most cruel treatment. Two instances of this have recently occurred . . .
Every nation has undoubtedly the right to determine for itself the extent to which it will hold intercourse with other nations. The same law of nations, however, which protects a nation in the exercise of this right imposes upon her certain duties which she cannot justly disregard. Among these duties none is more imperative than that which requires her to succour and relieve those persons who are cast by the perils of the oceans upon her shores . . .
If a nation not only habitually and systematically disregards it, but treats such unfortunate persons as if they were the most atrocious criminals, such nations may justly be considered as the most common enemy of mankind . . .
It can hardly be doubted that if Japan were situated as near the continent of Europe or America as it is to that of Asia, its government would long since have been either treated as barbarians, or been compelled to respect those usages of civilised states of which it receives the protection . . .[19]

---

17. See W.C. Macleod, *The American Indian Frontier* (London: Dawson of Pall Mall, 1928), p. 463n.
18. Brodie Cruikshank, *18 Years on the Gold Coast of Africa*, Reprint of 1853 (London: Cassell, 1966), p. 7.
19. Ruhl J. Bartlett, sel. and ed. *The Record of American Diplomacy* (New York: Alfred Knopf, 1947), p. 268–9.

The deeper American motive was not to compel the humane treatment of shipwrecked sailors but 'to establish commercial intercourse with a country whose large population and reputed wealth hold out great temptations to mercantile enterprise.'[20] Accordingly the objects sought by the United States Government were: a permanent arrangement for the protection of wrecked seamen or vessels driven to shelter; the provision for United States vessels to refuel and refit; and the permission to enter one or more ports for the purposes of commerce.

The first of the negative strands in this Anglo-Saxon Realist theory is that *barbarians have no rights*; or, put another way, they are outside the law, whether the natural law or *jus gentium*. It was discussed in these terms in the sixteenth century, especially in Spain. There were those who were sufficiently Rationalist to assume that international society was governed by law, whether natural or *jus gentium*, but they argued that there was no law outside international society to guarantee the rights to barbarians. Consequently barbarians had rights neither of occupancy, nor of being conquered, nor of making treaties. That barbarians have no rights of occupancy is the basis of all English colonization, the fundamental assertion distinguishing English Protestant tradition from the Catholic tradition about barbarians. John Wyclif's doctrine of dominion founded on grace[21] stated that all authority belongs to God, and God delegates it to all who are capable of reflecting his rational nature, who are obedient to his will and in a state of grace. This was both egalitarian and radical because his authority was delegated to all, not just to St. Peter's successors, but also exclusive, because it was delegated to those in a state of grace, that is, not to infidels and idolators. Heathens, pagans and barbarians had no valid dominion. Wyclif did not draw this conclusion, and it was condemned by the Council of Trent, but it shaped or reflected all English political thought and jurisprudence subsequently.

Early English colonization charters, in the sixteenth and seventeenth centuries, gave individuals or companies the authority to settle and colonize 'land not occupied by any Christian prince';[22] in other words, land occupied by barbarians was unoccupied land. This was the philosophical premise on which the American colonies and consequently the United States itself were erected. It may be true that the North American Indians were thinly scattered and 'primitively' organized, but the theory was decisive, because 'occupation' in law meant something that most barbarians were incapable of doing. In Spanish America things were a little more complicated. Montezuma

---

20. ibid., Instructions, *ab init*.
21. Ernest Nys, *Les Origines du droit international* (Paris: Alfred Castaigne, 1894), pp. 147–9.
22. ibid., p. 368.

thought Cortés was the god Quetzalcoatl and he swore fealty to the Emperor Charles V, whose representative Cortés was; he swore away his country's independence.[23] The subsequent revolt of the Mexicans was then a revolt against lawful authority. In Peru, Pizarro wanted to repeat Cortés' method: he kidnapped Atahualpa, the Inca, and then, fearing revolt, put him to death. The transfer of authority was less clearly made, and was disgraced by murder and massacre, but it was arguable that there was a right of conquest.

The doctrine that barbarians have no rights of occupancy passed into international law:

Tracts swarmed over by savage tribes have again and again been appropriated, and even the attainment by the original inhabitants of some slight degree of civilization and political coherence has not sufficed to bar the acquisition of their territory by occupancy. All territory not in the possession of states who are members of the family of nations and subjects of International Law must be considered as technically *res-nullius* and therefore open to occupation. The rights of the natives are moral, not legal. International morality, not International Law, demands that they be treated with consideration.[24]

The doctrine that rights of barbarians are moral, not legal, is a Realist one, because even if such rights are allowed to be legal they will probably be violated, and if they are only moral they will have little effect. English jurisprudence ascribed no rights to barbarians not even the right of being conquered, for the right of conquest implies a pre-existing right of the conquered to rule themselves, which is transferred to the conquerors. Nor even did it ascribe to barbarians a right to defend themselves. William Dampier (1652–1715) a pirate, later captain in the Royal Navy and pilot of the vessel which rescued Alexander Selkirk, wrote in *Voyage round the World*, 1697, of the natives of Papua as: 'A fierce and intractable race of savages who, when fired upon, did not scruple to retaliate.'

Barbarians have no rights of making treaties because they are not subjects of international law; but the imperialist expansion in the nineteenth century took place largely by means of treaties. Numerous African chiefs or Asian sultans made treaties with Queen Victoria, as Indian tribes in North America made treaties with the United States Government in Washington.[25] These treaties were always liable to cause embarrassment, not only because they were contracted with savages who had no rights, but also because they were contracted by

---

23. Maurice Collis, *Cortés and Montezuma* (London: Faber & Faber, 1954), pp. 147–8.
24. T.J. Lawrence, *The Principles of International Law* (London: Macmillan & Co Ltd., 1925), p. 148.
25. For example: Treaty of Waitangi 1840, Bond of 1844 between Fanti Chiefs and Crown appealed to by Cahana nationalists, Agreement with Sultan of Maldive Islands, 1887, Agreement with Sultan of Zanzibar, 1890, Uganda Agreement 1900, Agreements with Malay Sultans, esp. agreement of 1909 setting up Federated Malay Studies, Lobengula's treaty, 1888 in Matabeleland.

persons, whether officials or private explorers, who had no proper authority. The governor of the New Zealand Company, J. Somes, wrote to Lord Stanley, Secretary of State for War and the Colonies, in 1843:

We have always had very serious doubts whether the Treaty of Waitangi, made with naked savages by a consul invested with no plenipotentiary powers, without ratification by the Crown, could be treated by lawyers as anything but a praiseworthy device for amusing and pacifying savages for the moment.[26]

One can compare Hegel again: 'The civilised nation is conscious that the rights of barbarians are unequal to its own and treats their autonomy only as a formality.'[27] The basic law of the British constitution is Realist, and therefore the criticism followed that such treaties with barbarians as mentioned above were not treaties in international law, since native rulers did not enjoy sovereignty in international law, nor had they any validity in the constitutional law of the British Empire. If they imposed obligations, these were of a moral, not a legal order, and if they were disregarded by the Crown there was no redress.[28] They were sometimes regarded as obsolete and no longer binding, but were often scrupulously observed.

The treaties made with Indian princes (the treaties of the protectorate) were not valid in international law, both because they surrendered control of foreign policy and relations, and because they were not contracted by subjects of international law. A general character of the treaties of protectorates was that they could not be repudiated by the protected party; they were 'unequal treaties', not only in respect of power but also in respect of legal status. Indian 'native states' had internal sovereignty and their relations with the Empire were defined by treaty, but these treaties were subject to the reservation that they might be disregarded when the supreme interests of the Empire were involved, or even when the interests of the native states themselves were gravely affected. They amounted to little more than statements of the limitations which the imperial government placed on its own actions. In 1891, by notification in the official *Gazette*, the Government of India declared that the principles of international law had no bearing on the relations between the Queen-Empress and the states under her suzerainty. (Yet the rulers of the native states were not ordinary British subjects, nor even British protected persons.)[29]

---

26. See letters by J. Somes, Appendix to the 'Report on the New Zealand Committee', *British Parliamentary Papers*, vol. XIII, 1844.
27. See above, p. 54.
28. Martin Wight, *British Colonial Constitutions 1947* (Oxford: Clarendon Press, 1952), pp. 8–9.
29. Professor Alan M. James warned that the above passage should be understood in political rather than legal terms. His observations on protected states can be found in Alan M. James, *Sovereign Statehood* (London: Allen & Unwin, 1986), pp. 99–104 (Eds). See also W.E. Hall, *A Treatise on International Law* (Oxford: Clarendon Press, 1924), p. 28n.

Compare the Indian tribes of North America: originally each colony
dealt as it pleased with its neighbour Indians, on Realist principles, but
in the Seven Years' War the Crown took over Indian affairs because
the Indians held the balance of power between the English and the
French, or were allied with the French. The Crown treated the Indian
tribes as independent nations under British protection (their lands
were their own), but also refused to allow Indians full title to their
lands, claiming sovereignty up to the Mississippi. There was an inconsistency in practice and in theory; the political independence of the
Indians was recognized, but the Crown claimed an option on the
purchase of Indian lands, and neither individual British subjects nor
foreign powers were allowed to buy them.[30] The United States
inherited the rights and the policy of the Crown, and the Constitution
of the United States reserved to the federal government, as against the
states, the right to make treaties and regulate trade with the
Indians.[31] The individual states resented this. Georgia quarrelled with
the Cherokees in the 1820s, and in 1827 the legislature refused to
recognize the Cherokee government, and declared the Cherokee lands
to be the public domain of the state.[32] The Supreme Court
invalidated the Georgia statute in *Cherokee Nation* v. *Georgia, and
Worcester* v. *Georgia* (1832). President Jackson said of the Chief
Justice: 'John Marshall has made his decision, now let him enforce
it.'[33] The Indians and the missionaries got verdicts against Georgia,
but the state effectively nullified the legal victory, thus anticipating the
struggle between the states and the Supreme Court over desegrega-
tion.[34]

The United States policy towards the Indians, and the status of the
Indians, was full of anomalies and contradictions. The Indian tribes
were regarded as foreign nations, and their land was 'the Indian country', yet these nations and lands were within the bounds of the United
States.[35] There were schemes in the eighteenth and early nineteenth
centuries for admitting the Indian tribes in due course into the Union,
allowing them to send 'a deputy of their choice' to Congress — as
later the Filipinos, Hawaians and Puerto Ricans did[36] — but this idea
died away. In 1834 the Intercourse Act extended the jurisdiction of
the United States to the Indian country allowing it to punish crimes
involving a non-Indian; in the 1871 Revised Statutes, treaty-making
with the Indian tribes was ended, and from then on no Indian tribe

---

30. W.C. Macleod, *The American Indian Frontier*, pp. 402–4.
31. ibid., pp. 442, 553.
32. ibid., pp. 464–5.
33. H.W. Faulkner, *A Short History of the American People* (London: George Allen &
    Unwin Ltd., 1938), p. 193.
34. D.W. Brogan, *The American Political System* (London: Hamish Hamilton, 1945),
    p. 29.
35. W.C. Macleod, *The American Indian Frontier*, p. 533.
36. ibid., pp. 445, 535.

was to be recognized as an independent nation with whom a treaty was possible, although in *Lone Wolf* v. *Hitchcock* it was held that Congress had no power to abrogate a treaty between the United States and an Indian tribe. The Indians were thenceforth to be 'wards' of the United States to be dealt with by congressional enactment.[37] In an Act of 1885, the United States assumed general criminal jurisdiction in Indian reservations; in 1887, the General Allotment Act led to the division of tribal lands among individuals. After twenty-five years Indians could become citizens if esteemed worthy by the authorities and they could then sell out their land (compare Communist policy of giving land to peasants). In 1924, Congress enacted that all Indians become citizens; two-thirds of Indians already were under partial enactment.[38]

The doctrine that barbarians have no rights was reimported by Hitler from the frontiers to the centre of international society, and vividly expressed when in March 1939 he erected Bohemia into a protectorate. Britain and other powers had invented these categories for handling barbarian nations; Hitler too would have his colonial empire in the very middle of Europe, reducing many 'famous and ancient states of Europe' to rightlessness, since they were Slav barbarians. The deepest reason why the West was shocked by Hitler was his introducing colonial methods of power politics, their own colonial methods, into international relations. Non-European nations could not share European horror at Hitler's methods, even his massacre of the Jews: the Second World War was for them a European civil war and its methods they had seen before.

Another strand of this Realist theory is that *barbarians may be exploited*. This lies behind the mercantilist theory of the colonies: 'Colonies differ from provinces of the Kingdom as the means differ from the end', Louis XV instructed the governor of Martinique in 1765. 'Colonies are made by the metropolis and for the metropolis' ('La colonie, disait Diderot, n'existe que par et pour la metropole').[39] The lust for gold in the conquistadores underlay their atrocities. The epigraph for all this is in *Gulliver's Travels*:

For instance, a crew of pirates are driven by a storm they know not whither, at length a boy discovers land from the topmast, they go on shore to rob and plunder, they see an harmless people, are entertained with kindness, they give the country a new name, they take formal possession of it for their King, they set up a rotten plank or a stone for a memorial, they murder two or three dozen of the natives, bring away a couple more by force for a sample, return home, and get their pardon. Here commences a new dominion acquired with a title by *divine right*. Ships are sent with the first opportunity, the natives driven out or destroyed, their princes tortured to discover their gold, a free

---

37. ibid., pp. 535–6.
38. ibid. chap. 'The Liquidation of the Indian Problem in the United States', pp. 533ff.
39. *Encyclopédie politique de la France et du monde*, (Editions de L'Union Française, 1951), vol. III, p. 36.

licence given to all acts of inhumanity and lust, the earth reeking with the blood of its inhabitants: and this execrable crew of butchers employed in so pious an expedition, is a *modern colony* sent to convert and civilize an idolatrous and barbarous people.[40]

That *barbarians are not human* followed easily from the doctrine that they have no rights; indeed it was its premise. They are incapable of rights because incapable of reason; '*insensati vel amentes*', argued Jean Ginés de Sepulveda, against François de Vitoria who took up the Indians' cause against the exploits of Pizarro. It was the great controversy in the wake of the Mexican conquest.[41] This indeed has often been the first reaction to people of markedly different culture from ourselves, that they are sinister or crazy; and to the sixteenth-century Spaniard it seemed still more so if they were from the Aztec civilization. Beeson, an early emigrant to Oregon in the 1850s, writes of the covered-wagon epoch:

The majority of the first emigration to Oregon were from Missouri; and among them it was customary to speak of the Indian man as a buck; of the woman as a squaw; until, at length in the general acceptance of these terms, they ceased to recognize the rights of humanity in those to whom they were so applied. By a very natural and easy transition, from being spoken of as brutes, they came to be thought of as game to be shot, or as vermin to be destroyed. This shows the force of association, [Beeson adds] and the wrong of speaking in derogatory terms of those we regard as our inferiors.[42]

Three policies are likely to follow on from the idea that certain types are sub-human: if tractable and muscular, they will be enslaved; if intractable and useless, exterminated; and if there are too many to be exterminated and they are difficult to organize they will be segregated. The most obvious example of enslavement is of course the transatlantic slave trade, when ten million were uprooted.

Among the varied examples of extermination one might contrast German and Spanish cruelty: the Teutonic Knights in Lithuania, and the Spanish in the Carib Indies; with English callousness in treating the Aborigines in Tasmania. The Germans probably exterminated more intensively, and the Anglo-Saxons more extensively than other peoples. The American-Indian frontier provides a horrific example. That 'the only good Indian is a dead Indian'[43] was generally accepted

---

40. Jonathan Swift, *Gulliver's Travels* (London: Oxford University Press, 1938), pt. IV, pp. 351–2.
41. 'Reste l'argument principal: les Indiens sont privés de raison, *insensati vel amentes*: les creatures non raisonables ne peuvent avoir des droits, par consequent ni proprieté ni souveraineté,' François de Vitoria, *Les Fondateurs du droit international* (Paris: V. Giard & E. Brière, 1904), p. 18.
42. W.C. Macleod, *The American Indian Frontier*, p. 485.
43. Attrib. to Philip Sheridan (1831–88) at Fort Cobb, *Dictionary of Quotations* (London: Oxford University Press, 1953), p. 499.

by the settlers, and there was a monotonous massacring of non-combatants, and burning of villages with women and children. The Puritan colonists saw themselves as new Israelites settling in a new Canaan: 'It was a fearful sight to see them frying in the fire, and the streams of blood quenching the same, and horrible was the stink and stench thereof. But the victory seemed a sweet sacrifice and they gave praise thereof to God.'[44]

Of the burning of Pequot village near the Mystic River Connecticut in 1637 Bradford's *History of Plymouth Plantation* records: 'When Mather [Richard Mather, Puritan Minister settled in Massachusetts, 1596–1669] heard of the massacre, he entered his pulpit and 'gave praise to God, thanking him that on this day we have sent six hundred heathen souls to hell.'[45] In 1641 the Dutch offered the first scalp-bounty; the last scalp-bounty was in Indiana in 1814.[46] The West coast tribes in California were destroyed between 1850 and 1870. The diary of a settler recalls for April 1871:

The next day the whites trail the Indians with dogs, corner them in a cave, and kill about thirty . . . In the cave with the meat were some Indian children. Kingsley could not bear to kill children with his 56 calibre rifle. 'It tore them up so bad'. So he did it with his 38 calibre Smith and Wesson revolver.[47]

Witness Israeli tendencies to extermination: 'On the night of 9–10 April 1948 a commando detachment systematically massacred all 254 inhabitants, men, women and children, of the Arab village of Deir Y'assin.'[48]

A report from *The Manchester Guardian*, 30 October 1958, illustrates the same tendency, in this case in South Africa:

Pretoria, October 29. A white South African, Hendrik Claassens (41), charged with assaulting speakers at a rally addressed by an African chief, said in court here today: 'If it was in my power I would have annihilated the whole lot of them.' He added that he went to a meeting of the Pretoria Political Study Group on August 22 'with the express purpose of breaking it up'.
Claassens was alleged to have led a group of about thirty men in storming the platform while Chief Albert Luthuli, president of the African National Congress was speaking. He said he hit the chairman of the meeting in self-defence. He was shocked that an African should address white people. 'I would have hit white liberals and given them a thrashing', he added . . . Reuter.

---

44. W. Bradford, *History of Plymouth Plantation* in W.C. Macleod, *The American Indian Frontier*, p. 216.
45. ibid., p. 216.
46. ibid., pp. 223, 488.
47. ibid., p. 487.
48. M. Rodinson, *Israel and the Arabs* (London: Penguin Special, 1968), p. 39.

The third policy, segregation, can be illustrated by the existence of ghettos for Jews, reservations for (surviving) American Indians, or by the caste system in India, which suited perfectly the Protestant Realism of the British in India:

For good or ill, the English Protestant rulers of India have distinguished themselves from all other contemporary Western rulers over non-Western peoples by the rigidity with which they have held aloof from their subjects. They took to the Hindu institution of caste as readily as if they had not found it established in India when they came but had invented it for their own convenience.[49]

There are two observations which may be made about these examples: first, why dig up so much ancient dirt about the British and Americans? These are 'old unhappy far-off things and battles long ago'. But it is good to remember, if we pride ourselves on our democratic greatness, the unpleasant foundations it rests on. If we do not, our enemies or our victims' descendants are only too willing to remind us. A second observation might be that there is little proper *theory* here. It is a description of a state of mind rather than a system of belief, a matter of social psychology rather than political theory: but this is to describe its quality, not belittle it. Realism about barbarians is a basic political attitude, a bedrock political fact, which circumstances every now and then bring us down to (for example, the Mau Mau); and it can be described in simple axioms like 'the only good Indian is a dead Indian', and does not need, or lend itself to, more sophisticated elaboration. When more sophisticated formulation occurs, we are compelled to wonder if this is still *Realism*. The illustrations of Realism about barbarians have come from the Puritans and the Nazis, and these were both referred to in preceding pages to illustrate Revolutionism (Puritans being Calvinists). This points to an inherent ambiguity, perhaps, or an inherent tendency of Revolutionism to turn into Realism. Nazi theory was undoubtedly Realist about barbarians, it defined civilization as German-European and attributed thereto the absolute right of aggressive expansion. The Nazis denied rights to all non-Europeans as barbarians and, like their Wilhelmine predecessors, would have graded them in degrees of sub-humanity, and enslaved, segregated and exterminated them. On the other hand, Nazism was Revolutionist in character, both in its chosen people doctrine (a very acute case), and in its doctrine of world revolution and renovation. Here lies the essential difference between Nazism and other kinds of Revolutionism; the world renovation aimed at by other Revolutionists, such as the Jacobins or Communists, is something in principle inclusive, which all men can share. Conversion to the true creed is possible. Nazism combined the Revolutionist dynamic with exclusiveness. World renovation was to be on biological principles; it would be

---

49. Arnold Toynbee, *A Study of History*, vol. I, p. 213.

imposed by the Germans on other peoples, who would be arranged in biological hierarchy. Conversion was impossible, despite 'honorary Aryans' and alliances of expediency with Italy and Japan (Japan was a more notable breach with racial theory). Your status was determined by heredity and blood.

So Nazi racialism is on the border-line between Revolutionism and Realism. It is untrue to say that it had nothing to offer the world (is it not still alive?); it offered the supposedly biologically better, the opportunity of putting the supposedly biologically worse in their proper place. This was the cement of the New Order in Europe, and it was a terrifyingly attractive offer; why else did Italy accept racial laws? The ruling groups in Eastern Europe were given the opportunity to deal with their own Jews. It offered (or offers) the opportunity to all nations to adopt Realist principles for dealing with their own 'barbarians', be they Jews, Blacks, Irish, Cypriots, or whoever.

As Burke once said:

It is but too true, that the love, and even the very idea, of genuine liberty is extremely rare. It is but too true, that there are many, whose whole scheme of freedom is made up of pride, perverseness, and insolence. They feel themselves in a state of thraldom, they imagine that their souls are cooped and cabined in, unless they have some man, or some body of men, dependent on their mercy.

The desire of having some one below them descends to those who are the very lowest of all . . . This disposition is the true source of the passion, which many men, in very humble life, have taken to the American war. *Our* subjects in America; *our* colonies; *our* dependants.[50]

Or we may cite a more recent example in the British reaction to Suez: 'having a smack at the Gyppos'.

The other existing representative of Realism towards barbarians is Afrikaaner policy in South Africa — the policy of apartheid. The roots of this may be Dutch or German; the Dutch were Realist in their policy towards the Red Indians, and the Dutch in Manhattan offered the first scalp-bounties; Afrikaaner nationalism is seclusionist; there is a desire to escape from international society (comparable to that of Japan or China), and it is thus not Revolutionist like the Nazi idea of world-renovation was. There is, perhaps, a residual introverted Revolutionism in the claimed Old Testament basis for apartheid, but it is escapist, not world-renewing. Towards 'barbarians' apartheid is distinctly Realist, wavering between segregation (pure apartheid) and enslavement (practical apartheid), extermination being impossible.

Let the last word about Realism towards 'barbarians' be said by Hobbes, in a passage where he pushes his inexorable political logic to the length of foreseeing the dilemmas of the twentieth century. He

---

50. Edmund Burke, *The Works of the Right Hon. Edmund Burke* (London: Samuel Holdsworth, 1842), vol. I, p. 270.

points out that one corollary of a welfare state is direction of labour, as well as full employment:

Whereas many men, by accident inevitable, become unable to maintain themselves by their labour; they ought not to be left to the charity of private persons; but to be provided for . . . by the Lawes of the Commonwealth . . . But for such as have strong bodies, the case is otherwise: they are to be forced to work; and to avoid the excuse of not finding employment, there ought to be such Lawes, as may encourage all manner of Arts; as Navigation, Agriculture, Fishing, and all manner of Manufacture that requires labour.

But he continues:

The multitude of poor, and yet strong people still increasing, they are to be transplanted into Countries not sufficiently inhabited: where nevertheless, they are not to exterminate those they find there; but constrain them to inhabit closer together, and not range a great deal of ground, to snatch what they find; but to court each little plot with art and labour, to give them their sustenance in due season.
And when all the world is overcharged with Inhabitants, then the last remedy of all is Warre; which provideth for every man, by Victory, or Death.[51]

It is the Realist who sees that the problem of relations with 'barbarians' is the remorseless outward expansion of civilized society into the surrounding vacuum, which leads in due course to world overpopulation, and finds that the last remedy for this is war.

Rationalists

China

Chinese political theory provides a good bridge from the Realists to the Rationalists; again there is, apparently, a triad of philosophical traditions. The Rationalist philosophy is provided by Confucianism, which is amorphous, adaptable and various. It is perhaps comparable with Hinduism or even Christianity, but at its core one finds an individual, and an attitude of mind. The individual is the shrewd wise sage, conveying his wisdom in pithy sometimes enigmatic sayings. He is the archetype of Chinese educators, who became the most learned scholar of his day, and ended as a minister, diplomat, and finally elder statesman. (Goethe, perhaps, provides the closest Western comparison.) The attitude of mind, or philosophical disposition, is partly a moral one, providing an ethical philosophy: 'The true greatness and originality of Confucius consists in his having given this

---

51. Thomas Hobbes, *Leviathan* (Oxford: Blackwell, 1946), ch. 30, p. 185.

ritual order an ethical content.'[1] It is morality based on the reciprocity principle; a moral self-culture involving 'the superior man'. It is also a political attitude, concerned about the principles of government, interested in 'benevolent government' and government by moral example; and also it is conservative and traditionalist, concerned with the rediscovery of ancient standards of discipline and obedience. It has a broad resemblance to Western Rationalism.

The Revolutionist strand is Taoism. Tao means way, the way of life, or truth; it is the 'nature' of the Stoics, both a doctrine and a moral principle. It represents the cosmic pattern, the unchanging unity behind all phenomena.[2] This is the fundamental Chinese conception. Confucianism is one variation on it, and the pursuit of Tao was Confucius' own great endeavour. But 'Taoism' became appropriated to a separate and special variation, associated with the dubious name of Lao Tzu, Confucius' earlier contemporary. The attitude of mind or philosophical disposition of Taoism might be sketched thus: religion is emphasized more than morality and it involved mysticism and yoga. Mo Tzu and his school *c.* 300 BC believed in a personal supreme being. Also, individual, rather than socio-political morality is emphasized. Morality is personal and altruistic rather than social and utilitarian, with doctrines of universal love, compassion and responsibility for others (Mencius 372–289 BC).[3] A third strand of the Taoist attitude of mind is quietism; there is a distrust of politics and government which is almost anarchism: government itself is seen as the cause of evil and crime. Taoism is as amorphous and pervasive as Confucianism, but it is the subordinate of these two attitudes in Chinese civilization.

The Realist strand in Chinese philosophy comes from Fa Chia and the school of law. Law should replace morality, and there must be reliance on the law, with a system of punishments and rewards. There is a rejection of tradition and of supernatural religion; and there are no private standards of ethics. The only right is what rulers want, what is good for the state; this is of course totalitarian. Government must be based on 'the actual facts of the world as it now exists'.[4]

The Chinese theory of barbarians seems to have been mainly Realist, with occasional flickers towards Rationalism. Confucianism may represent the general Rationalist posture, yet it is very much a Sinocentric philosophy, a system calculated for the Middle Kingdom, which does not claim to offer a way of life for mankind as a whole. The Confucian

---

1. C. Dawson, *Progress and Religion* (London: Sheed & Ward, 1931), p. 122.
2. Arthur Waley, *The Way and its Power* (London: George Allen & Unwin, 1936), pp. 50–1.
3. Arthur Waley, *Three Ways of Thought in Ancient China* (London: George Allen & Unwin, 1939), pp. 115ff., 163ff.
4. Han Fei Tzu, quoted by Arthur Waley, *Three Ways of Thought in Ancient China*, p. 199.

attitude to barbarians seems to be that in so far as they civilize, or sinocize, themselves, they qualify themselves for virtue, otherwise they remain in outer darkness. As for Realism, Chinese Realism about barbarians is characteristically defensive and passive. China, the Middle Kingdom, was a stable international society with a remote and seldom recognized penumbra of barbarians.

It had its phases of imperialism and expansion, but never a fit of world-conquering fanaticism, like the Greeks under Alexander, the Arabs under the first four Caliphs, the Mongols under Genghis Khan or the West since 1500. It was a serene, balanced, gyroscopic society. Its classical self-description is Chien Lung's answer to Lord Macartney 1793.

You, O King, live beyond the confines of many seas; nevertheless, impelled by your humble desire to partake of the benefits of our civilization, you have despatched a mission respectfully bearing your memorial . . . I have perused your memorial: the earnest terms in which it is couched reveal a respectful humility on your part, which is highly praiseworthy.

In consideration of the fact that your Ambassador and his deputy have come a long way with your memorial and tribute, I have shown them high favour and have allowed them to be introduced into my presence. To manifest my indulgence, I have entertained them at a banquet and made them numerous gifts . . .

As to your entreaty to send one of your nationals to be accredited to my Celestial Court and to be in control of your country's trade with China, this request is contrary to all usage of my Dynasty and cannot possibly be entertained . . . If you assert that your reverence for Our Celestial Dynasty fills you with a desire to acquire our civilization, our ceremonies and code of laws differ so completely from your own that, even if your Envoy were able to acquire the rudiments of our civilization, you could not possibly transplant our manners and customs to your alien soil. Therefore, however adept the Envoy might become, nothing would be gained thereby.

Swaying the wide world, I have but one aim in view, namely, to maintain a perfect governance and to fulfil the duties of the State. Strange and costly objects do not interest me. If I have commanded that the tribute offerings sent by you, O King, are to be accepted, this was solely in consideration for the spirit which prompted you to despatch them from afar. Our Dynasty's majestic virtue has penetrated into every country under Heaven, and kings of all nations have offered their costly tribute by land and sea. As your Ambassador can see for himself, we possess all things. I set no value on objects strange or ingenious, and have no use for your country's manufactures.[5]

When the South Sea barbarians pushed their way in they were seen as foreign devils — one communication begins: 'To his excellency the Great English Devil, Consul X' — with strange ways: 'He was quite a friendly mandarin, taking a practical view of national dress, who

---

5. Quoted from A.F. Whyte, *China and Foreign Powers* (London: Milford, 1927), appendix, p. 41, in Arnold Toynbee, *A Study of History* (London: Oxford University Press, 1935), vol. I, p. 161.

said in conversation: "I can't think why you foreigners wear your clothes so tight; it must be very difficult to catch the fleas." [6]

Through the nineteenth century there was a balance of respect-in-hatred; then in 1900 at the time of the Boxer Rebellion the Empress Dowager's order came to 'Exterminate the Foreigners!' Mao Tse-tung was seven then (he was born in 1893). All of this is relevant to Mao's regime: he expelled or imprisoned foreigners, and eradicated missions, schools and businesses. In his attitude towards barbarians one can argue that Mao showed traditional defensive Realism, as Pannikar says, rather than unprecedented Marxism.

Europe

Rationalism in Europe begins with the great debate in Spain in the second quarter of the sixteenth century about the Indians, which was the origin of modern international law. Sepulveda, the chaplain of Charles V and tutor of Philip II, wrote the first reasoned treatise of Realism about barbarians, justifying the subjugation of primitive peoples by those more civilized. Las Casas, a Dominican and great humanitarian, made fourteen journeys to America collecting information, and he pleaded with Charles V and the Pope for just and humane treatment of the Indians. In 1550 there was a public dispute between Sepulveda and Las Casas at Valladolid before a committee of theologians and jurists, on the question of whether it was permitted to make war on American Indians to subject them to Spanish rule and Christianity. It seems that Las Casas won. This 'great debate', in the long run, transformed the Spanish Empire:

In theory and in practice, in policy and in law, the rapacity and crusading zeal of the *conquistadores* quickly gave way to a sane, conscientious and prudent imperialism which could face its critics boldly and with confidence. Partly for that reason, the conquest proved remarkably enduring.[7]

Charles V, as he traipsed around his vast empire like a Habsburg Dulles, coping with the Lutheran revolt and with papal neutralism; facing Turkish power from Vienna to the Balearics, and the unrelenting hostility of France; with Cortés in his train, a bore and an embarrassment like so many retired generals; repeatedly came back to study and listen about this question in Spain.

This 'great debate' also laid the foundations for modern international law. It was not the development of the diplomatic system in Europe, nor war in Europe, nor the disintegration of Christendom and

---

6. H.A. Giles, *The Civilization of China* (London: Thornton Butterworth Ltd., 1929), pp. 214, 217.
7. J.H. Parry, *New Cambridge Modern History* (Cambridge: University Press, 1958), vol. II, p. 589.

the need for its reunion that provided the occasion for international law; it was this problem of the barbarians. The first great treatises on international law were by Vitoria, O.P. (1480–1546), professor of theology at Salamanca. His 'Relectiones de Indis' were lectures of 1532, investigating the legality and morality of Spanish rule in the Indies, and explicitly condemning much of the Conquest. Vitoria's doctrine was that there is a world-wide legal community; this was novel, for in medieval thought the international legal community was confined to the Respublica Christiana. But Vitoria wrote that all peoples of the world form a '*societas naturalis*'. Therefore barbarians are within the law and enjoy its protection; they have full ownership and true dominion over their territories. It follows that the Spaniards have no right to use violence to deprive them of their country, to compel them to embrace Christianity, or to punish their odious crimes at home.[8]

Conversely, civilized peoples when among barbarians are under the law, and enjoy rights too. The Spaniards in America were no mere intruders from the fact of having crossed the Atlantic. There is a natural society and fellowship between the Spaniards and the Indians, and the Spaniards have the right to travel freely, to enter and to settle. 'It would not be permitted to France to forbid Spaniards to travel or even to live in France, or vice versa, provided that they did not break the law. Barbarians cannot have *more* rights than this.'[9] This condemns the hermit kingdoms, for example China, Japan, the USSR, or White Australia. Immigration is a natural right; '*jus communicationis*'. Vitoria could not yet see, what was not recognized until the twentieth century, that when a vigorous society comes into contact with a weaker, the weaker often withers up. Here was another field where *laissez-faire* meant the right of the stronger, and such rights had to be curtailed if the weak were to be protected. This was recognized by anthropologists, but it is difficult to see a direct influence on colonial policy; the protection of barbarian societies has normally involved segregation in reserves, that is, pushing the barbarians into a corner and leaving the greater part of the land free for the settlers. There have been examples of putting settlers in reserves, for example the White Highlands of Kenya, but such reserves have usually expanded, and it is fair to say that there is no example of a barbarian reserve increasing its size. The British policy in Palestine, under the Mandate, of limiting Jewish immigration was conceived as a protection for the Arab society but proved impossible to maintain. Perhaps the best example of the successful protection of a numerically weaker society at the expense of a universal right of

8. See G.H.J. van der Molen, *Alberico Gentile* (Amsterdam: H.J. Paris, 1937), p. 108, and *Les Fondateurs du droit international* (Paris: V. Giard & E. Brière, 1904), pp. 7–8.
9. *Les Fondateurs du droit international*, p. 8.

settlement is White Australia policy, where a mere ten million Australians have preserved themselves against their more numerous non-white neighbours to the north. Another right of the Spaniards when among barbarians, according to Vitoria, is the right to trade, *jus commerçii*; and also, the right to trade in ideas, to preach the Gospel to the Indians; the right of propaganda. Indians do not have any duty to be converted, but they do have a duty to give missionaries the freedom to preach.[10]

Vitoria asserted that barbarians are within the law, and seems to mean by this, *jus gentium*, giving the phrase at first its usual signification as 'law of nations'. *'Gentes'* means people of the world of mankind; *'jus gentium'* is the practice of mankind, or ordinary custom, and it must be understood as signifying much more what is now called private international law, rather than public law, a law mutually binding individuals who are foreigners.[11] Public international law was *'jus fetiale'*. In the Roman Republic, civil rights and civil law were confined to the citizens of Rome; it was unclear what law the courts could administer for the many foreigners, Italians from other cities, and merchants and traders, who thronged to Rome to do business, to marry, or to settle. Roman magistrates apparently created a body of rules, less technical than Roman law, based on fair dealing, common sense, and the highest common factor of the customs prevailing among foreigners in Rome; 'in fact commercial law'.[12] This came to be known as *'jus gentium'* and was entirely created by the courts, not through enactment. One could compare the British officials in India who, in building up the legal system, used a foundation of Muslim and Hindu custom modified by their own sense of the fair and just, plus the occasional bold application of English law if it could be remembered.[13]

By the end of the Roman Republic, when Rome had become a world-state, *'jus gentium'* had lost much of its distinctness, and was 'a reforming influence rather than a branch of law'.[14]

This was due perhaps to the notion that it was systematized common sense, but this brought *'jus gentium'* very near to natural law. There were obvious divergences: slavery was an institution of, and justified by, *'jus gentium'*, although it conflicted with natural law; but the practical aspects of *'jus gentium'* were ousted by its 'philosophical' sense. If it was 'common sense' law, it was a *common* sense

10. ibid., p. 9.
11. But see James Bryce, *Studies in History and Jurisprudence* (Oxford: Clarendon Press, 1901), vol. II, p. 572, n. 2.
12. F. de Zulueta, 'The Development of Law under the Republic', *Cambridge Ancient History* (Cambridge University Press, 1951), vol. IX, ch. XXI, p. 867.
13. James Bryce, *Studies in History and Jurisprudence*, vol. I, pp. 97–101, vol. II, p. 573.
14. W.W. Buckland, 'Classical Roman Law', *Cambridge Ancient History*, vol. XI, p. 808.

law, a body of rules of presumed universality, appealing immediately by their inherent reasonableness. It was appealing to natural reason — and this is similar to natural law.[15] In classical Roman law in the second century AD these Siamese twins had attained a juxtaposition that they kept ever after. Natural law was the ethical standard of conduct, the ideal of good legislation attainable by natural reason; *'jus gentium'* was world law,[16] the essence of the usages of mankind distilled by natural reason. These two concepts of natural law and *'jus gentium'*, and the relationship between them, were further developed and elaborated by, among others, Aquinas, Vitoria, Gentili and Grotius. Early international lawyers often failed to distinguish between the two, although there was perhaps the germ of a notion that natural law applied to barbarian relations, while *'jus gentium'* was for Christendom.[17]. Eventually the notion of *'jus gentium'* disappeared between natural law and the developing positive law.[18]

The idea of a world-wide legal community was a fundamental Rationalist idea in relation to barbarians. Gentili said *societas gentium* comprises all nations of the world, including those not yet discovered;[19] and Hooker maintained that: 'we covet (if it might be) to have a kind of society and fellowship even with all mankind. Which thing Socrates intending to signify, professed himself a citizen, not of this or that commonwealth, but of the world.'[20]

Grotius, too, saw a society of mankind, bound by a general law of mankind. But it proved impossible to persist in this generous view; Christendom or Europe was the cultural unit and historical reality which defined the effective international society. The word 'Christendom' was used in international treaties till Vernius in 1598, and in projects of international organisation into the seventeenth century, for example, in Sully's Grand Design.[21] Indeed the ecumenical legal theorists themselves allowed this. Vitoria asserted a general law of mankind binding Christians and barbarians, but within Christendom there was still a special international regime with its special organ in the Papacy, which in certain circumstances could exercise temporal power over princes, intervening in wars or providing arbitration.[22] This of course was the medieval conception. Grotius also saw special

---

15. See ibid., p. 810, and James Bryce, *Studies in History and Jurisprudence*, vol. II, p. 583.
16. See F. de Zulueta, *Cambridge Ancient History*, vol. IX, p. 866.
17. See van der Molen, *Alberico Gentili*, p. 115.
18. Otto Gierke, tr. Ernest Barker, *Natural Law and the Theory of Society 1500–1800* (Cambridge: University Press, 1934), vol. I, p. 38.
19. See van der Molen, *Alberico Gentili*, p. 115.
20. *The Works of Richard Hooker* (Oxford: Clarendon Press, 1863), vol. I, bk. i, p. 250.
21. See Denys Hay, *Europe The Emergence of an Idea* (Edinburgh: University Press, 1957), pp. 114-5.
22. Walter Schiffer, *The Legal Community of Mankind* (New York: Columbia University Press, 1954), p. 31.

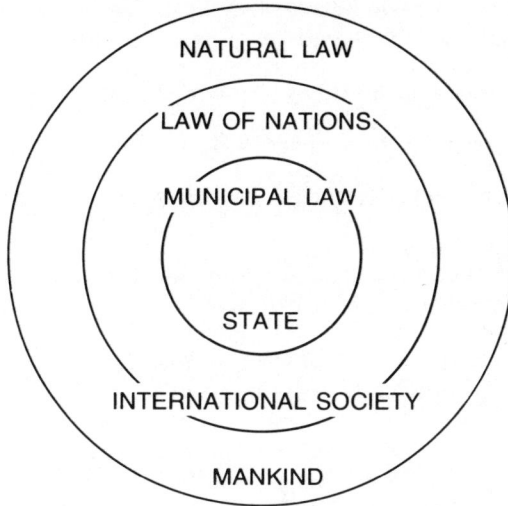

Figure 2 Three stages of society and law

bonds uniting Christendom. Christendom was an inner circle of kingdoms and republics with the duty (and tradition) of confederating against Moslem attacks and making contributions of men or money according to their strength.[23] Grotius wrote in *De Jure Belli ac Pacis* that poisoning weapons and waters 'is contrary to the law of nations, not indeed of all nations but of European nations and of such others as attain to the higher standard of Europe'.[24] A picture began to emerge of three concentric circles; the inner circle was the state, with its municipal law, or '*jus civile*'; the second circle was international society, subject to a volitional, positive law of nations; and the third, outer circle, surrounding the other two, was mankind, subject to natural law (see Figure 2). This natural law was confused with the '*jus gentium*' of the second circle by Vitoria; but became more distinct as international society turned to positive law, until, with the growth of positivist realism, it became the sphere of no law or morality.

Dr Johnson, a Christian Tory, might be taken as an example of one with a Rationalist attitude towards barbarians. He believed in both the primacy of Europe, and in natural law. When Boswell said he would like to travel in a country totally different from what he was used to, for example Turkey, he said: 'Yes Sir; there are two objects of curiosity, — the Christian world, and the Mahometan world. All the

23. C. van Vollenhoven, *The Framework of Grotius' Book De Jure Belli ac Pacis (1625)* (Amsterdam: Noord-Hollandsche Uitgeversmaatschappi, 1932), pp. 8, 87.
24. Hugo Grotius, tr. F.W. Kelsey, *On the Law of War and Peace* (Oxford: Clarendon Press, 1925), bk. III, ch. IV, p. 653.

rest may be considered as barbarous.'[25] On the island of Col, Johnson learned that their landlady had never visited the mainland:

Johnson: That is rather being behind-hand with life. I would at least go and see Glenelg.
Boswell: You yourself, sir, have never seen, till now, anything but your native island.
Johnson: But sir, by seeing London, I have seen as much of life as the world can shew.
Boswell: You have not seen Pekin.
Johnson: What is Pekin? ten thousand Londoners would drive all the people of Pekin: they would drive them like deer.[26]

Dr Johnson also had a hatred of slavery and the slave trade: 'Upon one occasion, when in company with some very grave man at Oxford, his toast was, "Here's to the next insurrection of the negroes in the West Indies." '[27] This was a reason if not the main reason, for his hatred of Americans. He hated them partly for their Whig and rebellious principles, but he hated equally the West Indian settlers who did not rebel. 'How is it that we hear the loudest *yelps* for liberty among the drivers of negroes?'[28] When Boswell said he might send Johnson a letter from Salamanca, Johnson replied: 'I love the University of Salamanca; for when the Spaniards were in doubt as to the lawfulness of their conquering America, the University of Salamanca gave it as their opinion that it was not lawful.'[29] This view was reflected in his attitude towards the Irish:

He had great compassion for the miseries and distresses of the Irish nation, particularly the Papists; and severely reprobated the barbarous debilitating policy of the British government, which, he said, was the most detestable mode of persecution. To a gentleman, who hinted such policy might be necessary to support the authority of the English government, he replied by saying, 'Let the authority of the English government perish, rather than be iniquity . . .'[30]

The model of the three concentric circles showing three stages of society and law, described above, is reflected in Kant's three 'Definitive Articles for Eternal Peace'. The first article, or central circle, is a republican constitution in every state; the second article, the next circle, is a law of nations founded on a federation of free states, and the third article, the outermost circle, is a cosmopolitan

25. James Boswell, *Life of Samuel Johnson* (London: Oxford University Press, 1946), vol. II, p. 480.
26. James Boswell, *The Journal of a Tour to the Hebrides with Samuel Johnson* (London: Dent, 1958), p. 74.
27. James Boswell, *Life of Samuel Johnson*, vol. II, pp. 153-4.
28. ibid., vol. II, p. 154.
29. ibid., vol. I, p. 303.
30. ibid., vol. I, pp. 415-6.

or world law limited to conditions of universal hospitality. Hospitality 'means the right of a foreigner not to be treated with hostility when he arrives upon the soil of another'.[31] This is comparable to Vitoria's right to travel, or *'jus communicationes'*.

Kant supports his third definitive article by discussing relations with barbarians, especially China and Japan, and this suggests that his circles are geographically concentric; but probably he is proposing an additional kind of international law to bind individuals and reinforce international law proper, a right of friendly intercourse.[32] Just as the original distinction between kinds of law as one of dignity or logical priority was replaced by that of geographical remoteness, so this was now replaced in its turn by a distinction in the range of subjects of international law, or its 'depth'.

It was not Kant who filled in the third circle of the Rationalist theory of barbarians but a contemporary of his, Burke, and what Burke filled in there was the word 'trusteeship'. Here he is on the charter of the East India Company:

All political power which is set over men, and . . . all privilege claimed or exercised in exclusion of them, being wholly artificial, and for so much a decoration from the natural quality of mankind at large, ought to be some way or other exercised ultimately for their benefit.

If this is true with regard to every species of political dominion, and every description of commercial privilege, none of which can be original, self-derived rights, or grants for the mere benefit of the holders, then such rights, or privileges, or whatever else you choose to call them, are all in the strictest sense a *trust*; and it is of the very essence of every trust to be rendered *accountable*; and even totally to *cease*, when it substantially varies from the purposes for which alone it could have a lawful existence.[33]

Now this idea of trusteeship is not in Vitoria and the Spanish Rationalist theory of barbarians, though it may have been implicit there, but it is the central Whig principle, as expounded by Locke:

the legislative [power] being only a fiduciary power to act for certain ends, there remains still in the people a supreme power to remove or alter the legislative, when they find the legislative act contrary to the *trust* reposed in them. For all power given with trust for the attaining an end being limited by that end, whenever that end is manifestly neglected or opposed, the *trust* must necessarily be forfeited, and the power devolve into the hands of those that gave it, who may place it anew where they shall think best for their safety and security.[34]

---

31. Carl J. Friedrich, ed., *The Philosophy of Kant* (New York: Modern Library, 1949), p. 446.
32. See Walter Schiffer, *The Legal Community of Mankind*, p. 112, Hegel, *Rechtslehre*, para. 62, and W. Hastie, tr., *The Philosophy of Law* (Edinburgh: T. & T. Clark, 1887), pp. 226–7.
33. Edmund Burke, 'Speech on Mr Fox's East India Bill, 1783', *The Works of the Right Hon. Edmund Burke* (London: Samuel Holdsworth, 1842), vol. I, p. 276.
34. John Locke, *Of Civil Government* (London: Dent, no date), ch. xiii, para. 149, p. 192.

But what a transformation the idea of trusteeship undergoes from Locke to Burke! For Locke it is a doctrine justifying a community in getting rid of a ruler whom members of the community had contracted to set over their affairs; for Burke, it is a doctrine justifying a community in thrusting its rule upon barbarians who had never asked for it. For Locke, it means the right of rebellion; for Burke, it means the right of empire. This is one of the best examples of how theories, with the passage of time, turn into their opposites. Burke was aware of this himself; in this same speech on Fox's East India Bill he goes on to a splendid philippic against the last twenty years' plunder and violence by the East India Company (perhaps much exaggerated). He tells his audience that there is not a single prince or potentate they have come in contact with whom they have not sold: the Rohillas for example were sold to the Nabob of Oude who thirsted for their rich country but could not conquer them himself, so for £400,000 he had the loan of an English brigade and colonel who defeated the brave Rohillas without provocation and their country was then burned and ravaged.[35]

Also, he claims there is not a single treaty the Company has made, which it has not broken, and there is not a single Indian state or power allied to the Company, or which has trusted in it, which is not ruined. He concludes: 'All these circumstances are not, I confess, very favourable to the idea of our attempting to govern India at all. But there we are: there we are placed by the Sovereign Disposer; and we must do the best we can in our situation. The situation of man is the preceptor of his duty.'[36]

This is a point at which Rationalism comes near to Realism: in the acquisition and growth of power there comes a time when it is no longer any use agonizing over the misdeeds by which that power was established, one can only go ahead and exercise the power responsibly. To abdicate the power becomes morally impossible because it would leave an anarchy causing worse evils than those now past and repented. This was what Burke meant by saying: 'we must do the best we can in our situation. The situation of man is the preceptor of his duty.' The motives and methods by which empires are acquired are fortunately not the same as those by which they are administered. The Rationalist Realist will even make a mild counter-attack, and say with Brogan that 'there is something unnatural in imperialism, in the rule of peoples by strangers' but 'that the fundamental pathological condition is usually in the situation of the ruled'.[37]

Thus it could be said, the disintegration of the Mogul Empire was

35. John Morley, *Edmund Burke* (London: Macmillan 1867), pp. 204–5, and V.A. Smith, *The Oxford History of India* (Oxford: Clarendon Press, 1919), pp. 517–8.
36. Edmund Burke, *The Works of Edmund Burke*, vol. I, p. 283.
37. See D.W. Brogan, *The English People* (London: Hamish Hamilton, 1944), ch. VI, pp. 141ff.

India's fault, not the East India Company's. Arguably, it was the internal condition of India and Indonesia that made Western rule possible; the Western adventurers did not originally have technical superiority, this came with the empire. They filled a vacuum.[38]

This Rationalist argument that we must do the best we can in our situation is of course capable, like every other, of perversion. After all, 'our situation', in international politics, is defined by ourselves and it is easy to define it so as to suit our appetites and wishes. Thus almost the same pious form of words can be used, the same principles formulated, not only to justify not abdicating an administration or government that has lasted a couple of generations, on the grounds that the political order would disappear and anarchy would result with a vast increase of suffering (Burke's argument); but also to justify extending a government by annexing a new province. The appeal to situational logic is capable of dangerous flexibility. The United States began the Spanish–American War in 1898 to free Cuba, and ended by annexing the Philippines. McKinley justified this by exactly Burke's argument and language; he wrote to the commissioners negotiating the peace settlement:

The march of events rules and overrules human action. We cannot be unmindful that without any design on our part the war has brought us new responsibilities and duties which we must meet and discharge as becomes a great nation on whose growth and career from the beginning the Rules of Nations has plainly written the high command and pledge of civilisation.'[39]

This differs from Burke, in fact, because he appeals to justification-by-necessity. Anyway, from Burke's enunciation of the doctrine of trusteeship, and still more from the impeachment of Warren Hastings, the British Empire was reformed. Macaulay answered Burke's strictures on the Government of India in 1833,[40] and from then the Rationalist's theory of barbarians was fully developed, as a counterpart to the triumphant expansion of Western civilization.

It is a principle of Rationalist theory that barbarians have rights under natural or moral law. Gladstone wrote, during the Midlothian Campaign, after the second Afghan war:

Never suffer appeals to national pride to blind you to the dictates of justice . . . The errors of former times are recorded for our instruction, that we may avoid their repetition . . . Remember the rights of the savage, as we call him. Remember that the happiness of his humble home, remember that the sanctity of life in the hill villages of Afghanistan, among the winter snows, is as inviolable in the eye of Almighty God as can be your own.[41]

---

38. See V.A. Smith, *The Oxford History of India*, pp. 465, 558.
39. Reinhold Niebuhr, *Moral Man and Immoral Society* (New York: Charles Scribner & Sons, 1949), p. 101.
40. T.B. Macaulay, *Selected Speeches* (London: Oxford University Press, 1935), p. 136.
41. W.E. Gladstone at Dalkeith, 26 November 1879, quoted by Philip Magnus, *Gladstone* (London: John Murray, 1954), p. 262.

Also, treaties with barbarians are valid and must be observed. This principle got into British colonial law; in the Royal instructions of 1937 to the governor of the Aden Protectorate, it says: 'In the exercise of the powers conferred on him the Governor shall respect existing native laws and customs except so far as the same may be opposed to justice or morality and shall in all things observe the Treaties concluded with the Chief of the Protectorate.'[42] And in the Royal instructions in 1946 to the governor of Nigeria:

Nothing in any ordinance contained shall take away or affect any rights secured to any natives in the Protectorate by any treaties or agreements made on behalf or with the sanction of her late Majesty Queen Victoria, her heirs and successors, and all such treaties and agreements shall be and remain operative and in force, and all pledges and undertakings therein contained shall remain mutually binding on all parties to the same.[43]

A further principle of the Rationalist theory of barbarians is that international society has a 'dual mandate' (this is the name of Lord Lugard's book of 1922). Colonial powers are seen as trustees both for the advancement of the subject races, and for the development of their material resources for the benefit of mankind.

The mandate system, under article 22 of the League of Nations, seemed to be the culmination of the trusteeship doctrine. This now applied in due legal form to the whole residue of the world (the shrinking third concentric circle), which could not yet achieve statehood and membership of the League of Nations.

To those colonies and territories which as a consequence of the late war have ceased to be under the sovereignty of the States which formerly governed them and which are inhabited by peoples not yet able to stand by themselves under the strenuous conditions of the modern world, there should be applied the principle that the well-being and development of such peoples form a sacred trust of civilisation and that securities for the performance of this should be embodied in this Covenant.[44]

There was a certain amount of humbug about this, a dual humbug; Britain wanted to annex the German colonies and also the Ottoman Empire from Egypt to Baghdad; this was disedifying in itself, and led to disagreements between the Allies. Consequently the mandate system was invented and it was formulated in terms not of the advantages to the mandatory, but of the protection of the peoples not able to stand by themselves. Lugard was honest:

---

42. Martin Wight, *British Colonial Constitutions 1947* (Oxford: Clarendon Press, 1952), p. 168.
43. ibid., p. 231.
44. F.P. Walters, 'Article 22.1', *A History of the League of Nations* (London: Oxford University Press, 1952), vol. I, p. 56.

Let it be admitted at the outset that European brains, capital, and energy have not been, and never will be, expended in developing the resources of Africa from motives of pure philanthropy; that Europe is in Africa for the mutual benefit of her own industrial classes, and of the native races in their progress to a higher plane; that the benefit can be made reciprocal, and that it is the aim and desire of civilised administration to fulfil this dual mandate.[45]

Here we have the Rationalist version of the Realist principle that civilization has a right to expand, a right in so far as it can be made of mutual benefit.

If one asks, 'What rights do barbarians have?', the answer is, not full rights, not equal rights, but appropriate rights. What corresponds to a trustee is a *ward*, and there is the crux of the Rationalist doctrine: for a ward is in a state of legal tutelage; he has rights but cannot, in his own person, claim those rights or influence their formulation and scope, or claim that they are insufficient. In domestic society, society itself protects them on his behalf; international society is less well able to do so. The Permanent Mandates Commission under the League, and the Trusteeship Organisation under the United Nations were two experiments in making trustees accountable to international society. Probably the Permanent Mandates Commission was more successful; its members were experts, not political appointees. This issue of giving effect to a ward's rights becomes acute at the point where the ward wants to cease to be a ward, and to assume the rights of independent adulthood. Here the Rationalist tradition bifurcates into a conservative and a liberal wing.

The conservative Rationalist advocates the principle that the trustee has exclusive definition of his ward's rights; this is paternalism. British paternalism is complicated because in theory it was the paternalism of a democratic parliament. The ultimate guardian of the rights of the barbarian wards of Britain was not the Colonial Office but the British citizen, or British elector. He proved himself sensitive to issues of colonial rights where he understood them, and did not, for example, surrender the tutelage of the High Commission Territories to South Africa (Botswana/Bechuanaland, Swaziland and Lesotho/Basutoland). But it was notorious that nothing emptied the House of Commons so quickly as a colonial debate, and in practical terms paternalism culminated in the proposition: 'I shall decide when it is time for you to be independent' (that is, to join international society), where 'I' meant the Colonial Office.

Here is a report from a press conference given by Sir Andrew Cohen, the governor of Uganda, one of the most liberal of British colonial governors, in 1954:

---

45. F.D. Lugard, *Dual Mandate in British Tropical Africa* (Edinburgh and London: Blackwood & Sons, 1922), p. 617.

Sir Andrew's conclusion was that the logical extension of the argument put to him that the will of the people should prevail was to give them self-government now. The crux, he said, though many people disliked it, as he was inclined himself [to dislike it], was that either the British Government or the Baganda were responsible for the country and must have the power to take the final decision. This should not be exercised unreasonably — Sir Andrew said that on various matters he had given way — but when it came to the question of the ultimate structure of the country the last word had to rest with the Government and ultimately with Parliament. It was not a question of what was popular but of what was right.[46]

It is a good example of what we mean by paternalism: Father knows best; it is for your own good; you don't know what is good for you; and it hurts me more than it hurts you.[47] In Rationalist politics in general, the distinction between what is popular and what is right is purely academic, because the convention is established that what is popular is acted upon, however much it may seem, in the detached view of the moralist, that what is popular is crazy, misinformed, and pregnant with disaster. But in the Rationalist theory of relations with barbarians what is popular does not, by virtue of its popularity, command authority, so that colonial peoples sometimes had the despairing feeling that the more they progressed economically and culturally, the more independence receded. 'It is a melancholy and depressing reflection for them to perceive that their prospects of self-government, or even joinder in government seem to be in inverse ratio to their progress under tutelage in European civilisation.'[48]

This paternalist principle was constantly under fire at the United Nations, where anti-colonial powers of the Afro-Asian bloc tried to revise the Charter (or violate it) by taking away from the colonial powers the decision as to when a non-self-governing territory became ripe for independence. In response Henry Hopkinson, the British Minister of State for Colonial Affairs, said, in 1952 in the United Nations that

the word 'colonialism', in its objectives and purposes, is indistinguishable from the United Nations schemes and other programmes for the economic and social development of backward countries, except in one important respect. This is that the United Kingdom, and the United Kingdom alone, have the responsibility for guiding our territories towards political self-government. This responsibility and duty, from which we cannot divest ourselves, applies equally to colonies and protectorates.[49]

---

46. Probably after addressing a Commonwealth Parliamentary Association meeting, 22 February 1954.
47. Martin Wight, *The Gold Coast Legislative Council* (London: Faber & Faber Ltd., 1946), pp. 82–4.
48. 'Petition to the Crown of the Gold Coast Aborigines', *Rights Protection Society* (London: 1934), p. 19.
49. Henry Hopkinson, *Fourth Committee of the UN General Assembly, VII Session 1952* (New York: Headquarters, Summary Records of Meetings, October–19 December 1952), 1421, p. 6.

Paternalism becomes the philosophy of the last ditch. Macaulay was a paternalist about India:

The destinies of our Indian empire are covered with thick darkness . . . It may be that the public mind of India may expand under our system till it has outgrown that system; that by good government we may educate our subjects into a capacity for better government; that, having become instructed in European knowledge, they may, in some future age, demand European institutions. Whether such a day will ever come I know not. But never will I attempt to avert or retard it. Whenever it comes, it will be the proudest day in English history.[50]

The time-span then was beyond any measurement, and remained so, for every colonial empire, until the Second World War; it was Hitler and Tojo who broke the mould of colonial paternalism, yet it was already acknowledged in theory that the function of the Rationalist tutelage of barbarians was to work for its own extinction, to make itself unnecessary; this was the liberal side of the Rationalist theory. It was seen by Lugard himself, that the very discontent of colonial peoples was a measure of their progress; and by his greatest disciple, Margery Perham, 'that there comes a time when the most liberal rulers can no longer help a dependent people'.[51] This led to a principle, already enunciated with simplicity by Gladstone: 'It is liberty alone that makes men fit for liberty.' This principle had its effect on British colonialism and its chief show-piece was Ceylon (now Sri Lanka), which Taya Zinkin described as late as 1956 as 'the best advertisement for colonialism', and the governor general described as 'the best Colony ever' and 'the safest bet in Asia'.[52] There were two special commissions on constitutional reform in Ceylon, in 1928 and 1945, each engendering new constitutions. The first concluded: 'We feel that there is considerable justification for the argument that only by exercising the vote can the political intelligence to use it be developed';[53] and the second:

We think it better to devise a Constitution somewhat in advance of the stage already reached rather than behind it, trusting in the power of education and the lessons of experience to promote further development. The enlargement of liberty is always attended by risk, but it is well to bear in mind a wise observation attributed to Aristotle. 'The only way of learning to play the flute is to play the flute'.[54]

---

50. T.B. Macaulay, 'Speech on the Government of India', Selected Speeches, 1833, p. 155.
51. Margery Perham, *Native Administration in Nigeria* (London: Oxford University Press, 1937), p. 363.
52. *The Manchester Guardian*, 2 April 1956, p. 5.
53. Donoughmore Report, 1928, VII, Cmd. 3131.
54. Soulbury Report, 1945/6, Cmd. 6677.

The second commission had read the report of the first, and put its principle with more wit and learning.

That 'it is liberty alone that makes men fit for liberty' is a good principle, but it raises the question: 'How do you know when men possess liberty?' The paternalist answer is, that men have liberty when the paternalist thinks they have such liberty as is good for them. This was the position of King Charles I, which he stated in his speech from the scaffold in Whitehall:

For the people, I desire their liberty and freedom as much as anybody whomsoever; but I must tell you that their liberty and freedom consists in having government, in those laws by which their life and goods may be most their own. It is not their having a share in government; that is nothing pertaining to them . . .[55]

The liberal answer to this paternalist position was stated by Burke (in whom, if you read him discursively, you can find everything):

If there be one fact in the world perfectly clear, it is this: 'That the disposition of the people of America is wholly averse to any other than a free government'; and this is indication enough to any honest statesman, how he ought to adapt whatever power he finds in his hands to their case.

If any ask me, what a free government is, I answer, that, for any practical purpose, it is what the people think so; and that they, and not I, are the natural, lawful, and competent judges of this matter.[56]

It is the same principle that lurked behind the debate about Cyprus in the 1950s. This quotation can be seen as a counterpart to that of Hobbes on world overpopulation and war as 'the last remedy of all', which ended the exposition of the Realist position, above. The natural law theory underlies Burke's position: 'they, and not I, are the natural, lawful, and competent judges of this matter.' (By municipal law the Americans were rebels, but under natural law, to which the Declaration of Independence appealed, they were not.) There is a paradox in the Rationalist theory, in that the liberal thread of itself is not strong enough to triumph over paternalism.

Revolutionists

If one sums up the Realist theory of barbarians as: barbarians have no rights (exploitation), and the Rationalist theory as: barbarians have

---

55. Quoted in O. Firth, *Cromwell* (New York and London: G.P. Putnam's Sons, 1900), p. 228.
56. Edmund Burke, 'Letter to the Sheriffs of Bristol, 1777', *The Works of Edmund Burke*, vol. I, p. 217.

appropriate rights (trusteeship), then the equivalent Revolutionist theory would be: barbarians have equal rights, (assimilation). However, this is not simple: to whom do barbarians have equal rights, and does this mean *full* rights (the rights of man), and a right not to be assimilated, if they so wish? Whatever the answers, Revolutionists and Rationalists agree about the principle of the brotherhood of man, and the Revolutionists assert it with an emphasis suggesting that they deny not only the Rationalist's cautious qualifications about it, but any qualifications at all. The concept of the brotherhood of mankind goes back to the ideas of one particular man: to the most attractive of the Balkan princes, King Alexander III of Macedon (popularly known as Alexander the Great) — the greatest Albanian who ever lived. Alexander was educated by Aristotle, tutor at the court of Macedon, who instructed him (presumably) that the city-state was the highest political form attainable by man, that all non-Greek speakers were barbarians, and that barbarians were slaves by nature. Aristotle, after his seven years in Macedon, founded the Lyceum, with Alexander's patronage. He outlived Alexander, dying in 322 BC, and so he saw all of his pupil's career. He told Alexander to behave to Greeks as leader, to barbarians as master; to treat Greeks as friends and relatives, barbarians as animals or plants.[1] All this Alexander swept away.

Alexander replaced the city-state by world empire, and the distinction between Greek and barbarian by the ideal of *Homonoia* or *Concordia*, meaning 'union of hearts' or 'being of one mind together'.[2] Certain incidents in his life reflect this. After a visit to Ammonium (Siwah) in the Libyan desert he is reported to have said: 'God is the common father of all men but he makes the best ones peculiarly his own.'[3] This is the first known statement that all men are brothers, at least in the West. He conquered as far as the Punjab, where his Macedonian veterans refused to go further; then he returned to Babylonia to organize his empire. He pursued a policy of racial fusion; he was the Great King of Asia as well as king of Macedon. He wore Persian dress, married a Persian princess, promoted intermarriage by his officers and enrolled 'natives' in his Macedonian military formations. This last led to a Macedonian mutiny at Opis (near the present Baghdad), where the whole army demanded to go home.[4] Alexander dismissed the whole army from his service, shut himself up for two days, and then summoned the Persian leaders and began to form a Persian army whose regiments bore the old Macedonian names. This broke down the Macedonians; they came weeping to his tent and reconciliation followed. At a banquet given for nine thousand, Greeks,

---

1. Eratosthenes, in W.W. Tarn, *Alexander the Great* (Cambridge: University Press, 1948), vol. II, p. 439.
2. ibid., p. 400.
3. Plutarch, ibid., p. 435.
4. ibid., vol. I, p. 115.

Persians and all races shared a huge silver drinking-bowl as a loving-cup. His prayer on that occasion was, that he 'prayed for the other good things, and for *Homonoia*, and for partnership in the realm between Macedonians and Persians'.[5] According to Eratosthenes, 'he believed that he had a mission from God to harmonise men generally and to be the reconciler of the world, bringing men from everywhere into a unity and mixing their lives and customs, their marriages and social ways, as in a loving-cup.'[6]

At a British Academy Lecture given in 1933, Sir William Tarn, Alexander's biographer, identified three facets of Alexander's idea. First, all men are brothers; he was the first man in the West to apply this to all mankind without the distinction between Greek and barbarian. He believed it was his own divine mission to be the harmonizer and reconciler of the world, to bring all men to live as brothers in *Homonoia*, with a unity of heart and mind, and he also wanted all the peoples in his empire to be partners, not subjects: this he never lived to achieve.[7]

After Alexander, the stoic philosopher Zeno (335–263 BC) ultimately envisaged the universe as one great city of gods and men, without distinction of race; so did Marcus Aurelius: 'For me as Antoninus my city and fatherland is Rome, but as man the world.' 'Man is the citizen of the supreme city in which other cities are as it were houses.' 'In what other universal constitution can the whole race of men have a share?'[8] Alexander's ideas were reflected, later, by Christianity. In Christ 'there is neither Greek nor Jew, circumcision nor uncircumcision, Barbarian, Scythian, bond nor free: but Christ is all and in all.'[9] This became the pattern of Revolutionist fraternalism: whether it was 'In Christ', 'In the principles of the Rights of Man' or 'In Marxism–Leninism'; there are no distinctions between humanity. Perhaps the most complete fulfilment of this idea is found in Islam. It is certainly present in Catholic universalism, which proclaims the universal jurisdiction of the Pope, as Vicar of Christ, with authority which extends not only over Christians, but over Jews and infidels.[10] Christendom or Western civilization was the only civilization, except for Islam, to formulate these universalist claims and then attempt to give them political expression. This is the root of most Western imperialism. Dante's *De Monarchia* marks the high point of universalist imperialism. In the first book he considers the 'ultimate end of

5. ibid., vol. II, p. 444.
6. ibid., pp. 439–40.
7. ibid., pp. 400, 447–8.
8. Marcus Aurelius, 'Meditations', quoted in *The Cambridge Ancient History* (Cambridge: University Press, 1936), vol. XI, p. 367.
9. St. Paul's 'Letter to the Colossians', III, 11, King James version.
10. R.W. Carlyle, *A History of Medieval and Political Theory in the West* (Edinburgh and London: Blackwood & Sons Ltd., 1950), vol. V, p. 323.

human society as a whole'.[11] The specific capacity of men, differentiating them from all other creatures, is their intellectual potentiality. This potentiality cannot be translated into action by single individuals; intellectual fulfilment requires social conditions and the cooperation of mankind as a whole: 'The task proper to mankind considered as a whole is to fulfil the total capacity of the possible intellect all the time, primarily by speculation and secondarily . . . by action.'[12] Universal peace is a necessary condition for this. This is, says Gilson, 'the first known expression of the modern idea of humanity,'[13] that is, of mankind not only as a brotherhood but as a community having a common purpose and common task. Dante argued from this premise of *universalis civilitas humani generis* to a universal empire or world-state, which alone could give the peace necessary for the fulfilment of human purpose. This was both modernized and transposed into the Rationalist's key when Vitoria claimed that the human race composed a *legal* community (the beginning of international law), but jettisoned the imperialism, that is, there should be no world-state.

There are two sets of circumstances in which the Revolutionist doctrine about relations with barbarians can manifest itself; when the initiative comes from barbarians themselves, and when the initiative comes from Revolutionists inside international society. The prototype of a barbarian initiative is offered by the Black Rebellion in Haiti, French Santo Domingo, during the French Revolution.[14] In 1789 Haiti had perhaps 14,000 whites, 4,000 free mulattos and 172,000 black slaves. The French Revolution in Paris touched off successive revolts in Haiti of whites, mulattos and blacks. The rich planters supported the Revolution, like their brethren in the United States, but excluded the mulattos from civil rights. The mulattos rebelled, and were crushed by the whites with great cruelty; the blacks revolted (at first in the name of the *ancien régime*!) and the surviving mulattos joined them. All this happened with only the remotest control from Paris. The revolutionary Assemblies legislated for the colonies ignorantly and blindly, and behind events. On 28 March 1792, the legislative Assembly extended full political rights to all free blacks, and on 4 February 1794 the Convention abolished slavery by acclamation throughout the French empire (this was forty years before British abolition of slavery in 1833), even though the rights, granted in conditions of insurrection and civil war, were never more than theoretical. By contrast Sierra Leone was founded in 1787 for the 'black poor', with

---

11. Dante Alighieri, ed. Donald Nicholl, *Monarchy* (London: Weidenfeld & Nicholson, 1954), p. 5.
12. ibid., p. 8.
13. Etienne Gilson, *Dante the Philosopher* (London: Sheed & Ward, 1952), p. 179.
14. Salvador de Madariaga, *The Fall of the Spanish American Empire* (London: Hollis & Carter, 1947), pp. 317ff.

the full civil rights of Englishmen.[15] In Haiti there was chaos, war, and intervention by the Spanish and English, but at the same time the gradual consolidation of black power took place under a black soldier of genius, Toussaint L'Ouverture. The French recognized him as the chief military authority in 1794, and later he declared a Black Republic, and became 'the first independent sovereign in the New World outside the republic of the United States'.[16] He has no little historical importance. The success of the black rebellion was watched by the New World, and became a precedent for revolution and independence throughout Latin America ten years later; and it disenchanted Napoleon with the West Indies and made him sell Louisiana to Jefferson. Haiti is the oldest black state, and the black revolution in Haiti was the historical precursor of Latin American enfranchisement and admission to international society in the Hague Conference of 1907, and subsequently of Asian–African enfranchisement and admission to international society, mainly since 1945, achieved on the whole with less violence.

All these movements have the political philosophy of the outsider or barbarian, which has since been called anticolonialism, and this philosophy comprises four strands. The first strand is an assertion of an absolute right to freedom. The Rationalist tradition we saw divided into a paternalist, and a radical or liberal, interpretation of the trusteeship principle. The Revolutionist tradition emphatically endorses the radical stand, as exemplified in Gladstone's, 'It is liberty alone that makes men fit for liberty'. It was again asserted by India in the United Nations: 'India would never concede that people were not ready for self-government';[17] '. . . India, speaking for all those countries in Asia which had so often been told that they are not ripe for independence . . . wished to state that at the moment all peoples, whatever stage of development they had reached, had the right to govern themselves.'[18]

The second strand is egalitarianism; although the new nations were legally free, colonialism had left vast economic inequalities between their poverty and the colonial powers' wealth. The root of non-alignment policy was a desire to press on with solving internal problems and achieve economic growth; but it had its emotional expression too. When Christopher Shawcross QC was banned from re-entering Ghana in 1957, the *Daily Sketch* wrote that 'Nkrumah still has to show us that Ghana is a worthy member of the British Commonwealth'. The Ghana *Evening News* retorted:

---

15. Martin Wight, *The Development of the Legislative Council 1606–1945* (London: Faber & Faber, 1945), p. 43.
16. Salvador de Madariaga, *The Fall of the Spanish American Empire*, p. 321.
17. V.K. Krishna Menon defending the timetable in the report on Tanganyika to the Trusteeship Council of the UN, published January 1955.
18. Mrs Lakshmi Menon in 1950 at the UN General Assembly 5th Session, *Yearbook of the UN*, 1950.

Our independence is sacred to us. We sacrificed a lot for it and we mean to defend it by every legitimate means at our disposal. We refuse to accept the proposition that we are inferior to Great Britain or any other nation. We are men of equal stature. The same respect we give to Britain should be accorded to us. Ghana is no more a footstool of Britain.[19]

A third strand in this anti-colonialist philosophy can perhaps be described as an absence of fraternity. There is a resentment, and a proletarian pose in many anti-colonial statements, a kind of outsider consciousness. This is the most frequently marked aspect of Bandung philosophy, and deserves a little analysis. It was generally accepted that Asia wanted to imitate and equal the West, and at the same time repudiate its ways, as Russia and Japan had done in their day; and this desire for equality easily became self-pity at having to demand it, and resentment against those from whom it had to be asked. Racial discrimination continues to produce the deepest sensitivity. Old phrases like 'the white man's burden', '*mission civilisatrice*', and 'the yellow peril', are almost forgotten in the West, but remain fresh in Asian–African minds. Freedom from contempt is the first freedom wanted.

This led to what might almost be seen as inverted racialism: 'As I survey this Hall and the distinguished guests gathered here, my heart is filled with emotion. This is the first intercontinental conference of coloured people in the history of mankind.' This was President Sukarno at the opening speech at Bandung.[20] (One might compare the emphasis on 'the African personality' at the All-African People's Conference in Accra, in December 1958.) The *Middle East Journal* reported in 1955 that: 'Most Indians actually believe that the US dropped the atom-bomb on the Japanese rather than the Germans because she wanted to spare white Europeans but did not care about killing Asians. This also, they believe, is why the US tests the H-bomb only in the Pacific.'[21] A Makerere student said in Uganda in 1955: 'Africans are not concerned about whether Kenyatta was guilty or not. The issue has become one of black against white.'[22]

There is also a posture of moral and legal condemnation: 'We are not here today to decide whether or not a wrong has been done. We are met here as those who are convinced that a wrong has been done,' said a delegate at the Arab–Asian Conference on Indonesia in Delhi in January 1949.[23] And at the Bandung Conference Sukarno

---

19. As reported in the *Manchester Guardian*, 20 September 1957.
20. Achmed Sukarno, *Asia–Africa speaks from Bandung* (Djakarta: The Ministry of Foreign Affairs, Republic of Indonesia, 1955), p. 19.
21. 'India and the Cold War', *Middle East Journal*, vol. IX (1955), no. 3, p. 263.
22. George W. Shepherd, Jr., *Christianity and Crisis*, 6 February 1956, p. 5.
23. For a summary report see: Keesing's *Contemporary Archives* (London, Keesing's Publications Ltd., 1948–50), vol. VII, p. 9733.

proclaimed: 'Wherever, whenever and however it appears, colonialism is an evil thing, and one which must be eradicated from the earth.'[24] The West is blamed, not only for having exploited Asia and Africa, but for Asia and Africa having been so weak that they could be dominated by the West. It seemed that Asia and Africa, dissatisfied with their own backwardness, projected this dissatisfaction outwards as a grievance against the West. The logical extreme of this view came in two remarks made at the All-African People's Conference in December 1958: 'The Europeans in Africa are not here to be rulers and master of the Africans. They are here to be ruled and mastered by the Africans'[25] and: 'We do not want to get rid of our chains, we want them to chain up colonialists.'[26]

Along with this there was often an assumption of moral superiority:

In these urgent and vital tasks, where the wisdom of the West has failed, is it possible that the nations of Asia and Africa can hope to succeed? I think it is. Have the nations of this region in fact anything to offer? I think they have. Has the time come to offer it? I think it has. I say, then, in all seriousness and in all humility, that the peoples of this region have it in their power to apply to the problems of the present day world, and for the first time in their history, that traditional respect for the spiritual values of life and for the dignity of the human personality, which is the distinguishing feature of all their religions.[27]

This was Sir John Kotelawala, then Prime Minister of Ceylon, at Bandung, the best phrase-maker there, with an interesting appropriation of the claims formerly made for itself by the Christian West. Along with a certain self-pity — 'For many generations our people were the voiceless ones in the world, disregarded and living in poverty and humiliation' — there was an assumption of superiority:

In a world driven to the verge of madness by the omnipresent spectres of fear and violence and hatred, from which it is unable to escape, it is our historic privilege and our solemn duty to offer the hope, however belated and remote, of a way out . . . We have, I venture to believe, something which the great and mighty lack. That something is the strength of our weakness.[28]

There was a feeling of revolutionary exaltation and emotionalism verging on anti-reason: 'It is better to be carried away by emotions than bogged down by legal sophistications.'[29]

24. A. Sukarno, *Asia–Africa speaks from Bandung*, p. 23.
25. Nstu Mokhele of Basutoland.
26. Bhoke Munanka of Tanganyika.
27. Sir John Kotelawala, *Asia–Africa speaks from Bandung*, p. 52.
28. ibid., pp. 20, 53.
29. Ashmed S. Bokhari, Pakistan Delegate in the UN General Assembly, as reported in the *Christian Science Monitor* (Boston, Mass.), 20 November 1952.

In the same month, the Saudi Arabian delegate in the Social, Cultural and Humanitarian Committee of the General Assembly, denounced the *New York Times* for making propaganda against the right of self-determination. He could not consider objectively an editorial which ·had said: 'that national sovereignty, described as a "magic phrase" instead of settling certain problems . . . most often created new and even more serious ones.'[30] Sukarno again, at the opening of the Bandung Conference, provides an example of this emotionalism: 'In your deliberations, don't be guided by these fears [H-bomb, world tensions, etc.], but be guided by hopes and determination, be guided by ideals, and yes, be guided by dreams.'[31]

Revisionism and interventionism, which form the fourth strand of anti-colonialism, follow from the libertarian premise; as Nehru told the UN General Assembly in 1948: 'We in Asia, who have ourselves suffered all the evils of colonialism and of imperial domination, have committed ourselves inevitably to the freedom of every other colonial country.'[32] Thus there was Egyptian intervention in Algeria; and Radio Cairo broadcast in Swahili, giving the Mau Mau as a model of liberation movements. The Guatemalan delegate announced, with an interesting transposition of paternalism: 'South Africa must find its own way out, but we must help it. We must help it with a paternal assistance.'[33] Intervention is divided by a thin line both from liberation and aggression; the most striking example of an aggressive utterance, because it was a striking lapse by Nehru, is his speech to the Upper House in Delhi in September 1955: 'his government was not prepared to tolerate the presence of the Portuguese in Goa, even if the Goans wanted them.'[34]

It is interesting to note that all these attitudes and policies were found in the Axis Powers between the wars; a demand for equality of rights, and a grievance against the injustices of Versailles. It was Mussolini who invented the proletarian conception, the 'have-not' states, in an international setting. There was great resentment of Western patronage, as expressed by Hitler: 'It would be a good thing if in Great Britain people would gradually drop certain airs which they have inherited from the Versailles epoch. We cannot tolerate any longer the tutelage of governesses';[35] and: 'The Western Democracies are dominated by the desire to rule the world and will not regard

---

30. 449th Meeting of the Third Committee, 'Social Humanitarian and Cultural Questions' (19 November 1952), p. 192.
31. A. Sukarno, *Asia–Africa speaks from Bandung*, p. 22.
32. Jawaharlal Nehru, UN General Assembly, Paris, Palais de Chaillot, *Official Records, 3.1948*, 1, Plenary Meetings, 3 November 1948.
33. Guatemalan delegate, UN General Assembly, 2 November 1955, reported in the *Johannesburg Star*, 3 November 1955.
34. Nehru reported in *The Manchester Guardian*, 7 September 1955, p. 12.
35. Adolf Hitler, 'Speech at Saarbruecken, 9 October 1938', N.H. Baynes, ed., *The Speeches of Adolf Hitler* (London: Oxford University Press, 1942), vol. II, p. 1536.

Germany and Italy as in their class. This psychological element of contempt is perhaps the worst thing about the whole business.'[36] Germany and Italy were the barbarians, or under-privileged, of the European community.

This particular psychology of resentment in the have-not powers is new to the twentieth century. It is interesting that attitudes first found in the have-nots who were the weaker powers of European society, and whose claim to a 'place in the sun' (as the Kaiser put it) was a claim for equal opportunity to exploit barbarians, were then reproduced by the barbarians themselves on their having gate-crashed international society. But Germany and Italy were not the earliest have-nots. In the sixteenth-century Spain and Portugal were the powerful nations, and England, Holland and France were the have-nots. But the English of the first Elizabethan age did not have this self-pity, resentment, and proletarian pose. They had instead self-confidence, an assurance that free Protestants were better than Inquisition-ridden Spaniards. When Sir Francis Drake singed the king of Spain's beard by burning the Spanish fleet in Cadiz harbour, when he sailed round Cape Horn and came up the Pacific coast of South America to deliver a resounding kick in the unsuspecting pants of the Spanish empire, there was a sporting spirit about it (after all, 'he was an Englishman'), a certain gaiety in taking on the world champion. Why the resentment creeps in in the twentieth century is unclear. It could be due to mass-civilization, or perhaps to international proletarianism.[37]

The more usual circumstance in which the Revolutionist doctrine of relations with barbarians has been developed is when the initiative comes from Revolutionists within international society. At its simplest, Revolutionists stir up barbarians to support a revolution, or rather to undermine the old order. On a small scale it happened in the French Revolution. The black revolution in Haiti began by local initiative; then the revolt of slaves spread to other West Indian islands, where Britain was predominant, and to Jamaica itself. Once the war between France and Europe was ablaze, the French saw the advantage of these allies, and French agents stirred them up. But once the military expansionism of the French Revolution was over, it developed, in peace, a new policy and doctrine towards barbarians, one of assimilation. To say 'in peace' is relative here: the abandonment of the universal mission of Jacobinism meant peace with other European powers, but there was continued selective military expansion against barbarians. The conquest of Algeria in the 1830s was not a European war, and nor was the conquest of Indo-China in the 1860s and 1880s. The establishment of the greatest of all European territorial empires in Africa was

---

36. Hitler to Ciano, 13 August 1939, *Nazi Conspiracy and Aggression* (Washington, DC: US Government Printing Office, 1946), vol. VIII, p. 527.
37. Or perhaps, race theory in the case of the Germans. (Eds.)

done in co-operation with other European powers in the scramble for Africa; the French have assimilated no colonial people without prior establishment of political power. But this was nineteenth-century expansion, when France was one partner, not the leader in the general expansion of international society. Assimilation is the conventional antithesis of British colonial policy. Trusteeship derives from Burke and assimilation from the Rights of Man; it is the extension of the Rights of Man to all whom France has ruled. In practice this has meant turning them into Frenchmen; the French are sublimely incapable of distinguishing between the universal Rights of Man and French culture, or nationalism. The equation of France with civilization is deep-rooted, and of course older than the French Revolution. France was the leader, the flower of medieval Christendom and the eldest daughter of the Church. The Arabic, Turkish and Persian word for Europeans as a whole is 'Franks' and Western Europe is 'Feringhistan' (because the French took the lead in the Crusades). The chief commercial street in Smyrna (Izmir in Turkey) before the fire of 1922 was 'la Rue Franque'; and the Turkish for syphilis is 'Frank Zahmeti';[38] and, of course, French was the formal language of international society.

The conventional antithesis between assimilation and trusteeship was never complete in practice, but the astonishing thing to the outsider's eye was France's success in turning her colonial subjects into Frenchmen. The Indo-Chinese, the Senegalese, and blacks from Martinique were polished examples of French culture. Even Haiti remained 'French' culturally and spiritually, like the French Caribbean and New Orleans until the election of François Duvalier 'Papa Doc' in 1957. This spiritual impulse, building a cultural communion, is what kept the French Union alive despite all its tribulations, and it may well go deeper and have more lasting effects than the British Commonwealth. But from the Revolutionist assertion that barbarians have equal rights there follows the question whether they have a right *not* to be assimilated. Theoretically, no: when Guinea alone voted for independence and against remaining in the French Union in 1958, the reaction of de Gaulle and France was different from Britain's tolerant acceptance when Ireland or Burma seceded from the Commonwealth. With these countries, except for political formalities, British links remained much as they had been, but Guinea underwent a deeply felt emotional excommunication and disinheritance.

The pattern of the French Revolution was repeated by Bolshevism. Apparently already in 1918 or 1919 Trotsky coined the famous phrase that the road to London and Paris lay through Calcutta and Peking, which meant the reorientation of Soviet foreign policy away from the hope of European revolution; and one of the first achievements of Soviet foreign policy was the Congress of Eastern Peoples at Baku in

---

38. Arnold Toynbee, *A Study of History* (London: Oxford University Press, 1939), vol. I, p. 33n.

1920, for stirring up the colonial masses: 'We are ready to help any revolutionary struggle against the English Government . . . Our task is to help the East to liberate itself from English imperialism.'[39] Stalin wrote in *Pravda* in November 1918:

Indeed the great international importance of the October Revolution consists mainly in that this revolution has widened the scope of the national question, transforming it from a partial question of struggling against national oppression into a general question of liberating the oppressed nations, colonies and semi-colonies from imperialism . . .
. . . has thereby erected a bridge between the socialist West and the enslaved East, by setting up a new front of revolutions extending from the proletarians of the West on through the Russian Revolution to the oppressed nations of the East *against* world imperialism.
This . . . explains the indescribable enthusiasm now displayed by the toiling and exploited masses of the East and West with regard to the Russian proletariat. This largely explains the brutal fury with which the imperialist robbers of the whole world have hurled themselves against Soviet Russia.[40]

Lenin accepted this reorientation at the end of his life; he wrote on 2 March 1923:

In the last analysis, the outcome of the struggle will be determined by the fact that Russia, India, China, etc., constitute an overwhelming majority of the population of the globe. And it is precisely this majority of the population that, during the past few years, has been drawn into the struggle for this emancipation with extraordinary rapidity, so that in this respect there cannot be the slightest shadow of doubt what the final outcome of the world struggle will be. In this sense, the final victory of Socialism is fully and absolutely assured.[41]

He had his second stroke on 9 March, which forced him to abandon all work and retire to Gorki's country house for the rest of his life.

This might be called the quantitative principle in politics. Perhaps in the final analysis in the struggle between the West and the Communist bloc is the opposition between the belief that in the long run politics are decided by quality, and the belief that they are decided by quantity — is there a Gresham's law in politics? Quantitative politics are a feature of revolutionary situations; there is always a sense of an irresistible mass or mobs. At the trial of Lilburne, in 1653, there were 6000 spectators and leaflets were passed round with the refrain: 'And

39. G. Zinoviev, opening speech, quoted by E.H. Carr, *The Bolshevik Revolution* (London: Macmillan & Co., 1953), vol. III, p. 261.
40. Joseph Stalin, *The October Revolution and the National Question*; *A Handbook of Marxism* (London: Victor Gollancz, 1935), pp. 820–1.
41. V.I. Lenin, 'Better Fewer, but Better', *Selected Works* (Moscow and Leningrad: Co-operative Publishing Society of Foreign Workers in the USSR, 1936), vol. IX, p. 400.

what, shall then honest John Lilbourn die? Three score thousand will know the reason why';[42] and at the trial of the seven Bishops in 1688, including Sir Jonathan Trelawny, the bishop of Bristol, crowds of Cornishmen sang

> And have they fixed the where and when?
> And shall Trelawny die?
> Here's twenty thousand Cornish men
> Will know the reason why![43]

But before the twentieth century the quantitative principle only appeared occasionally; with industrialized mass-society, it may become decisive. Lenin himself announced its basic form in another famous saying: 'Politics begin where the masses are, not where there are thousands, but millions, that is where serious politics begin.'[44] Applied to relations with barbarians, or world politics, the principle may be formulated in two propositions, inseparable from each other: first, the Revolution will triumph because the vast majority of the human race are behind it; secondly, the vast majority of the human race are behind the Revolution because it is the fulfilment of history. Which is emphasized more depends on your reading of Communism.

The quantitative principle, incidentally, was developed by Vyshinsky into a defence of Soviet policy in the United Nations, and especially the veto, in its early days. In a General Assembly debate on the international control of atomic energy in Paris in 1948, he said:

The majority resolution totally neglected the view of the minority and forgot the immense number of peoples which was represented by the Soviet-led minority. 'They forgot that a majority here is a minority in the world and a minority here is a majority in the world. The majority disregards the opinions of the peoples of the world, therefore it is necessary for us to formulate our views so that the outside world shall hear the voice of truth.'[45]

This was the great justification of the use of the veto by Russia at the time when the veto was paralysing the Security Council and bringing Russia herself into disrepute. Vyshinsky said:

The veto was a very powerful political weapon. No one who held such a

---

42. G.M. Trevelyan, *England under the Stuarts* (London: Methuen & Co. Ltd., 1930), p. 294.
43. 'Song of the Western Men' by the Revd. R.S. Hawker (1803–1875). 'The last three lines existed since the imprisonment of the seven Bishops by James II in 1688.' *Oxford Dictionary of Quotations* (London: Oxford University Press, 1982), p. 243.4.
44. V.I. Lenin, 'Report on War and Peace, to the 7th Party Congress, 1918', *Selected Works*, vol. VII, p. 295.
45. UN General Assembly 156th Plenary Meetings, 4 November 1948 (Official Records), p. 408, as quoted by the Special Correspondent, *The Manchester Guardian*, 5 November 1948.

weapon would be foolish enough to let it go in the midst of a political struggle; those who were in the minority admitted that frankly and based
themselves on the Charter, while those in the majority gave generous-
sounding assurances of their willingness to dispense with the veto, but were
in fact not at all disposed to do so and would not do so if they were in a
minority.[46]

This was the party line in the Korean War, when the United Nations
imposed sanctions on an aggressor: the *Daily Worker* diplomatic
correspondent on 9 October 1950 argued that those who voted
against the resolution on Korea, or abstained, had far larger populations than those who voted for it. The five opposing countries,
including the Soviet Union, totalled 238 million; the eight abstaining,
including India and Indonesia, 435 million; and China, which would
have voted against if represented, had a population of 475 million.
This added up to 1148 million. The 'American voting machine',
consisting of forty-seven countries, totalled 649 million. 'But these
figures . . . do not tell the whole story. For the Governments of many
of the countries in the American bloc do not represent the wishes of
their population.'[47]

This kind of argument was used by Asians and Africans themselves:
in 1950 in the General assembly the Indian resolution to seat
Communist China was defeated by 33 votes against, 16 in favour, and
10 abstentions, and critics claimed it was 'overwhelmingly' defeated.
Sir Benegal Rau challenged this by population-counting. The population of the states which voted for the resolution was 809 million, of
the states against, 412 million, and of the abstainers, 117 million. Two
years later, also in the General Assembly, Mrs Pandit said:

The question of apartheid was raised by States with a population of 600
million people, and they took the stand that the Union Government by its
policies was repudiating the dictates of the collective conscience of mankind
as contained in the Charter, in direct opposition to the trend of world
opinion.[48]

What is 'democracy' in an international organization? 'World public
opinion' becomes a much less vague and ineffectual deity if it can be
decked out with rough statistics. Sukarno used the majority-of-
mankind argument at Bandung:

What can we do? We can do much! We can inject the voice of reason into
world affairs. We can mobilise all the spiritual, all the moral, all the political
strength of Asia and Africa on the side of peace. We, the peoples of Asia and

---

46. A. Vyshinsky, 24 November 1948, Ad Hoc Political Committee, Summary Records
    of Meetings, 1948, Paris, Palais de Chaillot.
47. *Daily Worker*, 9 October 1950.
48. Mrs V.L. Pandit, as reported in *The Times* on 13 November 1952.

Africa, 1,400 million strong, far more than half the human population of the world, we can mobilise what I have called the moral voice of nations in favour of peace. We can demonstrate to the minority of the world, which lives on the other continents, that we, the majority, are for peace, not for war.[49]

In 1952 V.K Krishna Menon argued the under-representation of Asia in the United Nations and its bodies; but in 1956, when the Asian–African bloc became the largest in the General Assembly, it could be said this was the turning point, and from then on the majority inside did correspond to the majority outside, although still through the representation of states not of human beings. The quantitative principle is, then, a principle of Revolutionists in drawing barbarians into international society.

Another feature which both Bolshevism and Jacobinism displayed is the assimilation of the barbarian peoples colonized. A comparison of French and Soviet colonial policies would show variations on the theme of assimilation. Here, just one contrast may be noted: France has turned her barbarian subjects or associates into Frenchmen, but Russia has not similarly sought to turn hers into Russians, only into Communists. Soviet colonial policy aimed at cultural national self-determination. The official aim of the Soviet Union and the Communist Party was to preserve the cultural variety of the national life of its peoples within the framework of a socialist economy. The principle theoretical contribution to Marxist doctrine of both Stalin and Tito (Lenin's chief successors before Mao) concerned the cultural independence of national groups within the Communist federation. Perhaps in practice Soviet colonial policy is a policy of Russification, as was the Tsarist policy, probably there is even a colour-bar between Russian party officials and technicians and the 'natives' in Central Asia; but in theory, there is no identification between Communist doctrine and Russian national culture. The Soviet Union is the first and only country in the world whose name has no territorial or national connotation. The USSR is the only power which could conquer the world and absorb all other political units without having to revise its official appellation. One can contrast here China: the Chinese, the sons of Han, preponderate more in the celestial Chinese empire (whose frontiers are roughly those of the People's Republic) than the Russians do in the Russian empire (whose frontiers are roughly those of the USSR); there are fewer national minorities in China than Russia, it is a more homogeneous empire. Chinese self-assurance is as serene as that of the French; the equation 'China means civilization' is older and deeper than 'France means civilization'. Chinese colonial policy, as noted earlier, aims simply to turn barbarians into sons of Han, to effect

---

49. A. Sukarno, *Asia-Africa speaks from Bandung*, p. 24.

true assimilation. There is no comparable Russian self-assurance, rather, Russia has an inferiority complex *vis-à-vis* the West; the Russians, unlike the Chinese or the French, can remember having been themselves barbarians and outsiders. Russian messianism is alternately explosive and shrinking, pushing out to lead the world and then contracting into itself in Dostoievskian alternation. It is yet to be seen which will prove the stronger and more durable attitude in the struggle for mastery of the Communist world, and perhaps eventually of the globe.

If the question is raised in relation to Marxism, whether barbarians have the right *not* to be assimilated, the answer lies on a familiar stretch of road of Leninist doctrine, involving a controversy about whether national self-determination includes the right of secession. According to Lenin, bourgeois imperialists had hypocritically waged the First World War under the banner of 'national self-determination', Britain for Belgium, Germany for Poland;[50] and the Soviet Government had recognized the self-determination of Finland, the Baltic States, Poland, Georgia, Armenia and Azerbaijan, but these seceded borderlands inevitably fell into slavery to international imperialism; their secession was counter-revolutionary. By 1923 there had been an agrarian revolution in three Caucasian republics, whose so-called national governments had to appeal to the imperialists of Western Europe, the British and the French, against their own workers and peasants, and were then chased out. In 1940 the same thing happened in the Baltic States, which were being penetrated by German imperialists. If one takes what Stalin wrote between 1918 and 1923 about the counter-Revolutionism of the demand for secession 'under contemporary international conditions',[51] this principle can be formulated: that so long as there is a single bourgeois imperialist state left in the world, that state will by definition be in a condition of hostility to the Socialist world; that no secession from, or refusal of assimilation to, the Socialist camp can therefore be neutral, it must have the character of a movement towards the imperialist camp; that therefore any secession from the Socialist camp is counter-revolutionary; and that self-determination is therefore admissible only in one direction, that is, in the direction in which history itself is moving, in the direction of Socialism as defined by the masters of the Socialist camp.

This characteristic of Revolutionist thinking is familiar; it can be called, for want of a better phrase, the one-way rule. The Revolutionist has a familiarity with the process of destiny, the cosmic mechanism, which permits him to say to his critics in every important issue, 'heads I win, tails you lose'. 'All the principles we might agree upon are admissible if their application leads in my direction,

---

50. V.I. Lenin, 'Socialism and War, 1915', *A Handbook of Marxism*, pp. 686–7.
51. *Pravda*, 10 October 1920.

inadmissible if their application leads in yours.' This is the monopoly of the ace of trumps. It can be looked at in more depth. At the beginning of this section it was suggested that the pattern of Revolutionist doctrine towards barbarians is found in St. Paul's teaching, that in Christ, 'there is neither Greek nor Jew', in Lenin, in relation to the rights of man, in the Socialist Revolution, there is neither civilized nor barbarian. But what happens, in terms of this doctrine, if for good or bad reasons you are not 'in Christ'? The original answer perhaps is that those who are in Christ will continue to love you just the same; but the political and historical answer has been different. Already by AD250, Cyprian the bishop of Carthage, martyred under Valerian in AD258, had formulated the famous principle on which the Church was to act when, after Constantine's conversion, it became politically predominant: *'Nemini salus . . . nisi in Ecclesia'* — outside the Church there is no salvation.[52]

Perhaps one way of stating the essence of international Revolutionism is to say that it aims to transform international society into a church, which is a different form of organization from states, societies of states, or even world states. It is impossible to describe international Revolutionism without using the language of ecclesiastical politics. This observation can be carried right back and applied to Dante.[53] Dante clamours for a universal monarch, a supreme shepherd of the human race, through whose authority men will be governed for their own good instead of being exploited for particular ends which are not their own. This is his own ideal, his own passion; it is not scholastic, Thomas Aquinas never mentions an emperor in all his writings.

By a curious paradox, Dante was able to raise up a universal monarch vis-a-vis to the universal Pope . . . If the *genus humanum* ('human race') of Dante is really the first known expression of the modern idea of Humanity, we may say that the conception of Humanity first presented itself to the European consciousness merely as a secularized imitation of the religious notion of a Church.[54]

Dante's ideal was 'the incarnation of a moral end as well as of a legal principle'.[55]

Revolutionists go out, with missionary fervour, to convert barbarians and bring them into the fold; but it is difficult to avoid the implication in ecclesiastical politics, that barbarians are brought in as

---

52. Th. C. Cyprianus: Epistle iv, ch. 4, in Arnold Toynbee, *A Study of History*, vol. VIII, p. 111n.
53. The two best books on Dante's politics are Etienne Gilson, *Dante the Philosopher*, and A.P. D'Entrèves, *Dante as a Political Thinker* (Oxford: Clarendon Press, 1952), Gilson makes this point and D'Entrèves develops it.
54. E. Gilson, *Dante the Philosopher*, p. 179.
55. A.P. D'Entrèves, *Dante as a Political Thinker*, p. 50.

reinforcements against somebody else. This appears in St. Paul's account of his mission to the Gentiles and its relation to the Jews:

Now I ask myself, 'Was this fall of theirs (Israel) an utter disaster?' It was not! For through their failure the benefit of salvation has passed to the Gentiles, with the result that Israel is made to see and feel what it has missed. And if its failure has meant such a priceless benefit for the world at large, think what tremendous advantages its fulfilling of God's plan could mean![56]

Camus develops this concept in *The Rebel* (*L'Homme révolté*), one of the existentialist works of political philosophy, and the best modern analysis of Revolutionism. Its profound but simple pages analyse and criticize Marxism in its own terms: the dialectical miracle, the transformation of quantity into quality, comes about actually with the decision to call the total servitude of individuals in a totalitarian regime, 'the freedom of man', in the collective sense.[57] The dialectical transition from the government of people to the administration of objects is actually brought about in Russian slave camps by confusing people with objects.[58] Camus argues that Communism aims at the ancient dream of the universal city, the Stoic cosmopolis, the city of mankind: 'By the logic of history and doctrine, the Universal City, which was to have been realised by the spontaneous insurrection of the oppressed, has been little by little replaced by the empire, imposed by means of power.' And he adds finally, 'beyond the confines of the empire there is no salvation'.[59]

---

56. St. Paul, tr. J.B. Phillips, 'Letter to the Romans xi, v. 11–12', *Letters to Young Churches* (London: Fontana Books, Collins, 1957), p. 42.
57. A. Camus, *The Rebel* (*L'Homme Révolté*) (London: Hamish Hamilton, 1953), p. 203.
58. ibid., p. 208.
59. ibid., pp. 204, 208.

5: *Theory of national power*

The doctrine of human nature provides the foundations for all political theory; the basement of the building is the general doctrine about the nature and purpose of political power. The theory of national power asks what the basic method of international action is; 'How do we act?'

Rationalists

The fundamental problem of politics is the justification of power. Power represents a problem; it is frightening, and needs to be harnessed and directed. Rationalists distrust not men (as the Realists do), but certain conditions of which power is the most important, which arise with the aggregation of men in political society. Power is not self-justifying; it must be justified by reference to some source outside or beyond itself, and thus be transformed into 'authority'.

When Rationalists assert that man, the individual, is logically and morally prior to the state, that political institutions are made for man and not man for political institutions, they are denying the finality of human institutions; saying that there are inherent limits to the exercise of authority and declaring that the ultimate meaning is found in some category other than politics. Aristotle would say, it is to be found in virtue; others in self-fulfilment according to some transcendent ideal of goodness and justice, whose sanction is found in the human conscience. Politics unrelated to this ultimate category are invalid politics. As Grotius says in the *Prolegomena*, power divorced from justice can no longer command assent, and Tawney has commented in *The Western Political Tradition*:

The conception of Natural Law is not now in fashion; but the truth once expressed by it — the truth that there is a political morality which is in the nature of things, since it has its source in the character of man as a rational being — it not one to be discarded.

And again: totalitarianism failed in the past in the West because of

the conviction of the existence of a higher law than any represented by the powers in this world. That denial of the finality of human institutions is both for practice and for theory a key position. It makes it not a paradox to assert that the most significant characteristic of the western political tradition — its peril, but also its glory and salvation — consists in a quality which, from Socrates to the least of those who have resisted dictators, has drawn its nourishment from sources so profound as to cause the word 'political' to be an inadequate expression of the obligations felt to be imposed by it.[1]

This view, of course, supposes moral realism, realism in the classical or philosophical, not the modern or political sense. That is, the doctrine that goodness, oughtness and value, the moral norms, are grounded in nature, independently of human interest and opinion; that they are existential categories corresponding with the data of moral experience. Moral realism in politics means the doctrine of natural law, and 'natural law' is a phrase so soiled by verbal battles and seeming to confine the subject within the confines of legal justice theory, that it would be an advantage to speak of moral realism instead.[2]

Natural law has been described as 'the law behind the law', the moral law behind the legal law. There have been innumerable attempts to discredit and debunk it, but as Gierke (its greatest historian) wrote: 'If it is denied entry into the body of positive law, it flutters around the room like a ghost and threatens to turn into a vampire which sucks the blood from the body of law.'[3] In the philosophical, juristic debate it may seem that defenders of natural law have the upper hand, but there are two practical difficulties or inadequacies about natural law, both that it seems too vague and imprecise, and that it seems too lofty and difficult. 'The unconverted philosophical reader is likely to complain of the chief doctrines here expounded, not so much that they are false, as that they have not a sufficiently definite sense to be informative or enlightening. How exactly does one distinguish between "natural" and "unnatural" behaviour?'[4] The vagueness of natural law is illustrated by these descriptions in John Wild, *Plato's Modern Enemies*:

Cooperative activity which fulfils the nature of man is good. That which frustrates or obstructs such activity is unjust and evil. Thus, [quoting Grotius]

---

1. R.H. Tawney, 'The Burge Memorial Lecture', *The Western Political Tradition* (London: SCM Press, 1949), pp. 12, 15–16.
2. C.J. Wild, *Plato's Modern Enemies and the Theory of Natural Law* (Chicago: University of Chicago Press, 1953), p. 111.
3. O. von Gierke, *Natural Law and the Theory of Society*, vol. I, p. 226 quoted by A.P. D'Entrèves, *Natural Law* (London: Hutchinson, 1951), p. 113.
4. C.H. Whiteley review of 'The Return to Reason', ed. J. Wild, *Philosophy* vol. xxix, no. 111, October 1954, p. 362.

'to take from another for the sake of one's own convenience is against nature
. . . because if this were ordinarily done the common life of men would be
impossible'[5] . . . The Universal declaration of Human Rights . . . is based
upon the natural-law philosophy . . . of Plato. That which furthers the realization of the nature of man is liberating; that which thwarts and impedes that
nature is tyrannical.[6]

Natural law can give us respectable philosophical grounds for believing that promises, or treaties, ought to be honoured, or that wars
should not be waged with unnecessary cruelty to civilians; but there
would probably be acceptance of these ethical generalities anyway,
without an analysis of their philosophical foundations, and they do
not help very much in settling international problems. In practice,
'natural justice' means the ethical prejudices of the person who
administers it. Natural law does have a practical value when it
reasserts itself surprisingly, for example, as the ethical basis of the
Nuremberg Tribunal. There it permitted the condemnation of men
who had not violated positive law, rejecting the defence of superior
orders as an inadequate justification for obeying unjust orders; but this
was an exceptional circumstance.

The sanction of natural law is ultimately the human conscience. It
comes down to the archetypal figures of Antigone in literature, and
Socrates in history:

Men of Athens, I respect and love you; but I shall obey God rather than you,
and while I live and am able to continue, I shall never give up philosophy or
stop exhorting you and pointing out the truth.[7]

This expression of individual conscientious defiance of unjust power
is very difficult and very rare, rarer than one thinks. There is glib talk
about the unquenchable spirit of freedom in man, exemplified by,
perhaps, the Hungarian revolt of 1956, but a mass uprising is very
different, and requires a different order of moral courage, from a
lonely individual defiance. Thomas More, a Renaissance Socrates, is a
clear example; but St. Joan was an enemy commander and prisoner of
war for her captors; Gandhi was the leader of a mass movement, an
ambiguous politician–saint, and anyway did not suffer the ultimate
penalty; and people like Sacco and Vanzetti, and Ethel Rosenberg, are
dubious examples because they had political rather than moral
motives. Masaryk's suicide in 1948 was a notable gesture of fidelity to
conscience, but perhaps the best modern examples are the Germans of
the resistance: the Germans, so hopeless at political opposition,
produced individual heroes like Dietrich Bonhoeffer and Rupert Mayer
S.J. (but not the July 20th plotters, who resorted to violence).

---

5. C.J. Wild, *Plato's Modern Enemies*, quoting Grotius, p. 120.
6. ibid., p. 36.
7. Plato, tr. H.N. Fowler, *Apologies of Socrates* (London: Heineman, 1943), p. 109.

The public example of Socratic martyrdom, the lonely conscientious defiance of unjust power, has become far more difficult today with the widespread development of torture, brain washing and totalitarian penal seclusion. Furthermore one can doubt the moral status of Socrates in much twentieth-century opinion. Julien Benda puts it paradoxically:

The intellectual who nowadays condemns the realism of the State of which he is a citizen, does real harm to that State. Whence it follows that the State, in the name of those practical interests which it exists to preserve, has the right and perhaps the duty to crush him. So this seems to be the correct order of things: the intellectual, true to his essence, denounces the realism of States, whereupon the States, true to their essence, make him drink hemlock.[8]

The doctrine of natural law, or moral Realism in politics, with its sanction in the human conscience, means that the ultimate reality of politics and the guarantee of political health, lies not in democracy, votes, self-determination, economic aid, etc, and all those idols of the market place, but in the lonely individual, passing judgement on the false justice and lawless power of his judges and torturers. This is not the indecent exception in politics, as one likes to think, but the repeated source of political renewal, the ultimate ground of political health; and this of course is a very hard doctrine, so hard as to be out of relation to what is normally meant by politics.

The two objections to natural law, that it is 'too vague' and 'too difficult', can be answered by challenging the way the objections are formulated: too vague, too hard, for what? The wording implies that natural law is too vague and too hard to be useful; but it does not claim utility, but truth. It is a basic ethical category, founded on ontological principles; it makes a statement about reality, about the moral cosmos. It is not a political nostrum, like world federalism, or banning the bomb. If it seems vague, it is only because it offers general principles whose details must be filled in by the infinite variety of concrete political experience. 'There is a universally valid hierarchy of ends, but there are no universally valid rules of action.'[9]

Natural law will not tell us whether to recognize Red China, to pool atomic knowledge, or to join or withdraw from the Common Market. If it seems a vague and difficult doctrine, it is only because the human condition in politics has not been recognized.

Realists

Realists emphasize a different aspect of the central problem of politics.

---

8. Julien Benda, *La Trahison des clercs* (Paris: Bernard Grassét, 1928), p. 265.
9. Leo Strauss, *Natural Right and History* (Chicago: University of Chicago Press, 1953), p. 162.

They, too, have a respectable ancestry (more respectable even than Machiavelli). Aristotle said: 'Man is by nature a political animal . . . the city state is prior in nature to the household and to each of us individually. For the whole must necessarily be prior to the part.'[10] This doctrine, as appropriated by the Rationalists — 'that the rudiments of sociability and social organisation are never absent from any group of human beings living together'[11] — was revived and made influential in the seventeenth century by Grotius. Man only fulfils himself in a political community; this was the theory of the Greek city-state, and it haunted Renaissance theory. It was the ultimate source of Hegel's vision of the total community — 'the true city in which man is one with the gods, where the finite and infinite are united in the totality of a living community.'[12]

But modern Realism advanced a new doctrine which was implicit in Machiavelli. He conceived of politics as the practical art of obtaining and preserving state power as an end in itself; political power in itself was the natural and sufficient end of government. For Rationalists, the art of government and the business of politics is a means to an end — the security and comparative freedom of the rational man. For Machiavelli, the individual is the raw material of government, from which the ruler manufactures state power. This is implicit in Machiavelli, Bodin and Bacon, indeed in the whole development of the modern sovereign state in defiance of supra-national religious loyalties. Realism asserts the finality of politics: of all human institutions the political category contains the ultimate meaning; politics is for politics' sake. It is implicitly also in Hobbes' argument for (a) an empirical sensational psychology; (b) the doctrine that philosophy treats only of causal processes: therefore no philosophy is possible of anything eternal or transcendent; and (c) the State — 'that great Leviathan, — or rather (to speak more reverently) that *Mortall God*, to which we owe under the *immortall God*, our peace and defence'.[13]

But the doctrine is implicit chiefly in Hobbes' doctrine that morality and law derive their authority from power, not vice versa. 'Before the names of Just, and Unjust can have place, there must be some coercive Power.'[14] Power is not subordinate to justice, it is anterior to it; furthermore, 'religion is not philosophy but law'.[15] It is our duty to accept the theology promulgated by the state, not because it is true, but because it is official. Our duty to God cannot conflict with our duty to the sovereign, for we only know our duty to God from the

---

10. Aristotle, tr. H. Rackham, *Politics* (London: Heineman, 1932), 1253a, pp. 9, 11.
11. A.E. Taylor, *Thomas Hobbes* (London: Archibald Constable & Co., 1908), pp. 72–3.
12. C. Dawson, *Understanding Europe* (New York: Sheed & Ward, 1952), p. 195.
13. A.E. Taylor quoting *Leviathan*, ch. XVII, in *Thomas Hobbes*, pp. 31, 117.
14. Thomas Hobbes, *Leviathan* (London: Dent, no date), ch. XV, p. 74.
15. A.E. Taylor, *Thomas Hobbes*, p. 32.

Scriptures, and both their canonical character and their true interpretation are authorized by the sovereign, who is the final court of
appeal.

The essence of the Realist doctrine of political obligation is that
politics is the source of morality and law, that power is therefore self-
justifying, and the category of politics contains the ultimate meaning.
Thus E.H. Carr: 'Any international moral order must rest on some
hegemony of power'; and 'Behind all law there is [the] necessary
political background. The ultimate authority of law derives from
politics.'[16] Morgenthau wrote that 'There is a profound and neglected
truth hidden in Hobbes' extreme dictum that the state creates morality
as well as law and that there is neither morality nor law outside the
state.'[17] He holds that within the state, moral values acquire a
concrete meaning; but if one asks a thoroughgoing Realist, 'What is
the purpose of the state?', he would answer that it is an organization
primarily for maintaining power, and this answer would preclude, or
intend to, any further question about 'What is the power for?' The
state is an organization for survival in an international anarchy, and its
policy is determined by the pressure of conflict in the international
anarchy. It is an organization for which guns mean more than butter,
security more than liberty, and foreign policy more than domestic.
(For Rationalists, the reverse holds true: domestic policy is prior to
foreign policy; and the latter serves the ends of the former. The
Foreign Office is the watch-dog at the gate of a well-conducted household.) The doctrine of the primacy of foreign policy is a characteristically Realist doctrine. *'Das Primat der Aussenpolitik'* was coined by
Ranke, who wrote a classic on the foreign policy of every European
great power. A.J.P. Taylor wrote:

One of the great blunders of modern political thinking is to invent an abstract
entity called the State. Many States can be organizations for welfare or internal
order, or whatever else suits the theorist. But some half-dozen States, called
the Great Powers, are organizations primarily for power — that is, for fighting
wars or for preventing them. Hence all analogies between the Habsburg
Monarchy and, say, Switzerland break down. The Habsburg Monarchy was a
Great Power or it was nothing. If it could have survived in war against other
Great Powers it would not have undergone national disintegration.[18]

The doctrine of the state as an organization of power, with its
corollary of the doctrine of the primacy of foreign policy, can lead to
a power-political theory of history, which presents history as the
conflict and sequence of powers, not of classes, and is at least as valid

---

16. E.H. Carr, *Twenty Years' Crisis 1919–1939* (London: Macmillan & Co., 1939), pp.
    213, 231.
17. Hans J. Morgenthau, *In Defence of the National Interest* (New York: Alfred Knopf,
    1951), p. 34.
18. A.J.P. Taylor, *Rumours of Wars* (London: Hamish Hamilton, 1952), p. 71.

as an economic interpretation. This is the theory of Treitschke, Spengler and Toynbee. As Spengler said: 'domestic politics exist simply in order that foreign politics may be possible.'[19]

Revolutionists

Revolutionists, unlike Realists, do not find power self-justifying. For them, the justification of power does not reside in the fact of power but in something beyond itself. Carr has remarked that: 'consistent realism excludes four things which appear to be essential ingredients of all effective political thinking: a finite goal, an emotional appeal, a right of moral judgement and a ground for action.'[20]

These four requirements are provided by Revolutionism. (Indeed, the finite goal is an infinite one for religious Revolutionists; and the ground for action is a duty, or political imperative.) They all converge and result in a rejection of the existing organization and distribution of power. But the criterion whereby the existing system of power is judged wanting is not, as with the Rationalists, derived from outside the political category. Whereas the Rationalist denies the ultimacy of politics and finality of human institutions, the Revolutionist condemns the existing system of power by a standard external to that system of power but drawn from within the political category. He resembles the Realist in finding the ultimate meaning within the realm of politics; indeed he divinizes the political category: it is politics which prescribe human goals, the right of moral judgement and duty of action. This is clearly true of secular Revolutionism, both hard and soft, of Jacobins, Marxists and democratic utopians. It is probably also true to some extent of the early religious Revolutionists. The religious quarrel of the sixteenth century was basically concerned with the nature of the Church, to which the debate on other doctrines was subordinate, but the controversy was ecclesiological rather than theological, and ecclesiology is the most purely political department of religion.

There is a pattern of relationship between the three traditions which will reappear in other paradigms. It is tempting to say, as a broad statement of this relationship, that Revolutionists resemble Rationalists in their principles and Realists in their practice, but it is clear that this is too simple, and can go only a little way without serious qualification. It is precisely because Revolutionists do not really resemble Rationalists in their principles that they can approximate to Realists in their practice; and precisely because they do not resemble Realists in their principles, they can appeal to, or dupe, Rationalists in spite of their practice. The distinctions between them must be pushed back to

---

19. Oswald Spengler, tr. C.F. Atkinson, *The Decline of the West* (London: George Allen & Unwin Ltd., no date), vol. II, p. 398.
20. E.H. Carr, *Twenty Years' Crisis*, p. 113.

their doctrines of man and their theories of history. To recapitulate, these distinctions can be summed up in three celebrated dicta:

Realism expressed by Bacon and quoted before : 'Thank God for Machiavelli and his kind of writer, who tell us not what men ought to do but what they in fact do.'[21] What they in fact do is more important, more real, than what they ought to do, which is mere speculation. Men exist and are graspable in their acts, not their ideals; in the results of their actions, not their motives. There are certain recurrences or uniformities in men's acts which can be revealed by study.

Rationalism comes back with the answer, through the mouth of Acton: 'The great task is to discover, not what governments prescribe, but what they ought to prescribe, for no prescription is valid against the conscience of mankind.'[22] Ideals and moral law are more important, more real, than the flux of the phenomenal world. History in the long run is not, as Gibbon said 'the register of the crimes, follies and misfortunes of mankind', but the story of the human conscience.

Revolutionism cuts across this debate of the hypocritical versus the sentimental bourgeoisie, with the ringing voice of Marx: 'The Philosophers have only *interpreted* the world in various ways; the point however is to *change* it'[23] (inscribed on his grave in Highgate cemetery, London). Do not talk about duty, conscience and other idealist abstractions: say simply that the business of men is to assist the immanent purpose of history towards its revolutionary fulfilment, towards the radical reconstitution of international society; to assist it, or to be crushed: 'To exchange the weapons of criticism for the criticism of weapons.' Stalin said:

The Bolsheviks were not mere pacifists who sighed for peace, as the majority of the Left Social Democrats did. The Bolsheviks advocated an active revolutionary struggle of peace, to the point of overthrowing the rule of the bellicose imperialist bourgeoisie.[24]

If Revolutionists resemble Rationalists in believing that the justification of power does not reside in the fact of power, they may perhaps resemble Realists in their use of power. Here we may note *en passant* the dialectical interdependence of Revolutionists and Realists which we shall consider more fully later.

---

21. *Works of Lord Bacon* (London: Henry G. Bohn, 1864), bk. VII, ch. ii, p. 281, quoted above in 'The Three Traditions', p. 17.
22. J.E.E. Dahlberg-Acton, *The History of Freedom* (London: Macmillan & Co. Ltd., 1922), p. 24.
23. Karl Marx, 'Thesis on Feuerbach 1845 no. XI', *A Handbook of Marxism* (London: Gollancz, 1935), p. 231.
24. Joseph Stalin, *History of the Communist Party of the Soviet Union* (Moscow: Bolsheviks Foreign Languages Publishing House, 1945), p. 167.

On the level of the paradigm being discussed at present, the distinction between the three theories might be illustrated by giving precision to three overlapping words: power; authority, and force.
Power is the Realists' concept. It is the capacity of existing political organizations to secure compliance; of states to impose their will, both internally and externally.
Authority is the Rationalists' concept. It is power that is justified by consonance with moral principles; the capacity of states to secure assent and co-operation, freely given, internally and externally.
Force is the Revolutionists' concept. It is the capacity to overthrow power, to destroy existing political organizations in the name of Revolutionist doctrine; the capacity to demolish in order to carry out the necessary reconstruction.

'Force' is a keyword in Leninist thought and always has the connotation of something liberating; of a violence which breaks the calls of custom, the mould of history. It destroys established power and bogus authority, and liberates new social elements and impulses. 'Force is the midwife of society . . .';[25] force is the labour-pains of history, history groaning and travailing with its progeny. Force is 'the instrument by the aid of which social movement forces its way through and shatters the dead, fossilized, political forms.'[26]

Great questions in the life of nations are settled only by force. The reactionary classes are usually themselves the first to resort to violence, to civil war; they are the first to 'place the bayonet on the agenda', as Russian autocracy does . . .[27] [and]
'. . . great historical questions can be solved only by violence.'[28]

If one looks at the Revolutionist doctrine with regard to foreign policy, the contrast between the Revolutionists and the Rationalists, and the assimilation between them and the Realists, can be seen. It is characteristic of international Revolutionism that it cannot rest satisfied with the rule of the saints in a single country. This can be achieved, as in Geneva under Calvin; France under the Convention; Russia under Lenin, but this is regarded essentially not as a final, but as an initial, achievement. It is not possible, in Revolutionist doctrine, for the revolutionary state to settle down to the pursuit of the good life, and for its foreign policy to become ancillary merely to its domestic policy, protecting the revolution already achieved. This acquiescence in the rule of the saints in a single country may be forced upon it as a tactical necessity, but it is not compatible permanently with the Revolutionist creed. Lenin's doctrine that the uneven

---

25. Karl Marx, *A Handbook of Marxism*, p. 391.
26. Friedrich Engels, 'Anti-Dühring', *A Handbook of Marxism*, p. 278.
27. V.I. Lenin, 'Two Tactics of Social Democracy 1905', *Selected Works* (Moscow: Co-operative Publishing Society, 1933), vol. III, pp. 126–7.
28. ibid., p. 312.

development of capitalism made the simultaneous victory of socialism in all countries impossible, so that socialism would triumph first in one or two countries, did not mean the abandonment of the duty to promote world revolution.

The Revolutionist, if asked whether he attaches more importance to foreign or domestic policy will probably say that it is a stupid question: the two are indissolubly linked; they are the obverse and reverse of the same coin. What matters is the *kind* of state it is. He believes in first, the primacy of doctrine, and secondly in the domestic embodiment of that doctrine, which determines external policy. If you have the right kind of state you will have the right kind of policy. 'The foreign policy of a given state is a function of its inner system of class-relations, and not vice versa',[29] and 'the nation-State will act towards other nation-States as it acts towards its own citizens.'[30] Hitler states that 'every important success in the field of foreign politics must call forth a favourable reaction at home'.[31] Thus one can see the horizontal stratification of Revolutionism again: a belief that 'democratic' or 'communist' states are peaceable while capitalist or autocratic states are inherently warlike.

Inverted Revolutionism

There is another political position to be considered before leaving the theory of national power and obligation. It is a position which has taken the Rationalist distrust of power to the point of repudiation. It denies that politics can be made an instrument of justice; admits of no grounds for political obligation; and denies the political category altogether. In the political theory of the state, such a philosophical position is called anarchism, and it is not relevant here; in international theory, such a position is usually called pacifism, and it is an important, fascinating, and academically neglected part of the subject. But pacifism is a broad and rather woolly term in which it is necessary to make distinctions; the dominant kind of pacifism today may be described as inverted Revolutionism, and it is as different from soft as from hard Revolutionism. It is 'inverted' because it repudiates the use of power altogether; it is 'Revolutionist' because it sees this repudiation as a principle of universal validity, and energetically promotes its acceptance. It has a missionary character.

The inverted Revolutionism has two main sources: one is Hindu philosophy and the example of Gandhi; the other is Anglo-Saxon

29. Palme Dutt, *World Politics, 1918–1936* (London: V. Gollancz Ltd., 1936), p. 181.
30. Harold Laski, *Grammar of Politics* (London: George Allen & Unwin Ltd., 1941), p. 238.
31. Adolf Hitler, tr. James Murphy, *Mein Kampf* (London: Hurst & Blackett Ltd., 1935), p. 495.

Christianity and the example of the Quakers. However its most articulate theorist was a Russian, Tolstoy. He himself drew on the Christian tradition, and indeed inverted Revolutionism is a revival, or survival, of primitive Christian Revolutionism. The early Christian Church had a strongly marked non-political or anti-political strand of thought. Political power was regarded with passivity, acquiescence, or sometimes emphatic denunciation. It was also Revolutionist: it had a militant missionary character. St Paul's letters are as full of military metaphors as Marxist writings; the Christian life was seen in terms of warfare and struggle. The Early Church underwent two more or less simultaneous developments:

(a) The early tendency for the military character of Christian life to be translated out of the metaphorical and spiritual sphere into the literal and material sphere. There were early sects whose missionary zeal outran their charity, and who struggled to spread the Gospel, or wrestled with its enemies, with fists, clubs and swords. Spiritual Revolutionism turned into political Revolutionism.

(b) When Christianity became the established official religion of the Roman Empire in the fourth century, other latent elements in its original thought were developed, which enabled it to accommodate itself to the acceptance and exercise of power, and its political philosophy became primarily Rationalist in character, largely through the agency of St. Augustine. Here, Revolutionism turned into Rationalism.

Through the Middle Ages, these two elements in the political character of Christianity co-existed and had achieved a kind of stable equilibrium. The official political philosophy of the Catholic Church was Rationalist, or Aristotelian; but marginally, and in practice, the Church exhibited Revolutionism of the political kind, both in its policy towards the infidels outside Christendom with the Crusades; and in its policy towards heretics, with the Albigensian Crusade and the Inquisition. There are also irregular and sporadic evidences of primitive, spiritual Revolutionism in different sects: primitive, pacifist, and anarchist; heretical and, as with the Franciscans, orthodox.

In the sixteenth century the equilibrium broke down. Political Revolutionism burst out volcanically, with destructive floods of lava. (It is worth noting that all Revolutionism is of a Christian pattern, whether Rousseauite or Marxist: the patent is Christian, and perhaps the responsibility too. The ancient world has no tradition of political thought comparable to Revolutionism.) Spiritual Revolutionism, the earliest and most primitive stratum of all, also erupted: the Anabaptists, Quakers and pacifists — all Inverted Revolutionists.

But if the spiritual tradition of Inverted Revolutionism is predominantly Christian, its intellectual root is a Realist analysis of politics. The early Quakers — for whom men were like 'raging lions' etc. — are good examples of this,[32] as also is Tolstoy. Inverted Revolutionism in its classic form is fed by a pessimistic estimate of human nature, not an optimistic one. This bleak view of mankind may explain why pacifists, if they descend from being above the battle to entering the fray, tend to adopt a Realist stance. The same unblinkered view of human nature, together with other aspects of Realism, is likewise to be found in the Arthasastra of Kautilya (fourth century BC);[33] in Hindu political thinking there is no Rationalist tradition.

We could formulate the distinction between the three doctrines in terms already suggested: Rationalism equals politics for the sake of the good life; Realism equals politics for politics' sake; Revolutionism equals politics for the sake of the doctrine.

---

32. See G.W. Knowles, ed., *Some Quaker Peace Documents 1654-1920* (London: Grotius Society, 1921).
33. See Kautilya, tr. Dr A. Shamasastry, *Arthasastra* (Mysore: Weslyan Mission Press, 1929).

6: Theory of national interest

National power and national interest are correlative: one concerns capability, the other right. They are the obverse and reverse of the same coin. The question of international society is the modern expression of what used to be called the question of the state of nature; and the question of national interests is the modern formulation of that which used to be discussed as the question of natural liberties. These are liberties in the state of nature, or natural rights. Liberties lead to rights, which imply duties, which in turn lead to the modern concept of interest and the legal concept of sovereignty. All these threads are interwoven in this paradigm (and talk of 'rights' introduces an ethical connotation which leads to the theory of international obligation (chapter IX). The 'interest' illustrates the difference between individual and state morality. In the Granville versus Beaconsfield debate on 17 January 1878, Disraeli told the House of Lords: 'When we talk of "British Interest" we mean material British interests — interests of that character which are sources of the wealth or securities for the strength of the country.'[1]

This definition provides a provisional identification of Rationalist and Realist views, but Realists tend to extend all interests into vital ones, blurring the distinction. It is impossible to define 'national interest' without taking a stand on the issue of the compatibility of one nation's interests with another's (and also the problem of the internal compatibility of a nation's interests, as had to be done over Munich and Suez).

Realists

The Realist doctrine is perhaps the simplest to pin down. If there is no international society, if powers are in a state of nature *vis-à-vis* one

---

1. *Hansard's Parliamentary Debates*, vol. CCXXXVII, col. 34.

another, in a war of all against all, then international relations is a condition of the conflict of interests.

The Realist premise therefore is that whatever national interest is, it is likely to be in conflict with other national interests; and thus the basic national interest is to maintain freedom of action: 'Princes ought as far as possible to escape from the condition of being at the discretion of another Power' (Machiavelli).[2] One can state this more broadly in the words of another Italian statesman. On 16 October 1914 Salandra, the Italian prime minister, took over the Foreign Office; asked what Italian policy about the Great War was, he replied '*sacro egoismo par l'Italia*', and subsequently indeed Italy displayed independence of action. Salandra's words are famous for their naked Realism, but Viviani had said much the same when he answered the German ultimatum in August 1914: 'France will consult her own interests.'[3] The same position was more genially and less repellently expressed by Sumner Welles, former Under Secretary of State and Roosevelt's personal envoy: 'It is axiomatic that the foreign policy of the United States, like that of any other nation, should be based upon enlightened selfishness. It should be determined from the standpoint of what is of the most advantage to the long-range interest of its people.'[4]

To assert that a country's fundamental interest is to preserve its freedom of action, to assert that it will 'consult its own interests', implies another assertion: that a power has the exclusive right to decide what its interests are. Freedom of action implies freedom of decision; and freedom to decide what one's interests are implies freedom to decide what one's duties are. In the older language of international theory, the freedom to decide what one's duties are is one of the natural liberties of nations, one of the basic liberties of the state of nature. This was formulated in the eighteenth century, when the doctrine of natural law was transformed into that of natural rights. The *norma agendi*, the objective rule of action, became a *facultas agendi*, a subjective right to act. 'Wolff . . . declares quite flatly that the (subjective meaning) is the only proper meaning of *ius naturae* and that "whenever we speak of natural law (*ius naturae*), we never intend the law of nature, but rather the right which belongs to man on the strength of that law, that is naturally."'[5] Vattel wrote:

Since Nations are free and independent of one another as men are by nature, it follows that it is for each Nation to decide what its conscience demands of it, what it can or can not do . . . and therefore it is for each Nation to

---

2. Machiavelli, *The Prince* (London: J.M. Dent & Sons, 1928), ch. XXI, p. 181.
3. C.R.M.F. Cruttwell, *A History of the Great War* (Oxford: Clarendon Press, 1934), p. 133.
4. Sumner Welles, *The Time for Decision* (London: Hamish Hamilton, 1944), p. 307.
5. A.P. D'Entrèves quotes 'Ius naturae Methodo Scientifica Pertractatum', 1741, tom. I, Prol., para 3 in *Natural Law* (London: Hutchinson, 1951), p. 60.

consider and determine what duties it can fulfil towards others without failing in its duty towards itself. Hence in all cases in which it belongs to a Nation to judge of the extent of its duty, no other Nation may force it to act one way or another.[6]

This is the passage which Vollenhoven, the great champion of Grotius, uses to indict Vattel for having betrayed Grotius and seceded to the camp of Realism.[7] No power can, or may, define another power's interests or duty; it has neither the capacity nor the right to do so. Like much that the Realists assert this seems to have a measure of empirical validation. In practice states are unaccustomed to accept definitions of their interests and duties proffered by other states. 'I did not become the King's First Minister in order to preside over the liquidation of the British Empire,'[8] noted Churchill when Roosevelt suggested a certain course of interest and duty for Britain. *Mutatis mutandis* this position has been adopted by many leaders of states since, as when in 1957 Ben Gurion was advised to withdraw from the Gaza strip and the Gulf of Aqabah, and the Soviet Union repeatedly since the war was urged to loosen its grip on Eastern Europe. The premise underlying the principle that no power can or may define another's interests or duty is that none can be a disinterested judge of another's interests. This follows from the assumption of a conflict of interests in the state of nature. Each power is driven by its own self interests and is therefore limited by these, and can only judge the interests of another power through the spectacles of its own. It can no more make a disinterested recommendation about the interests of another power than a businessman can make a disinterested recommendation about the interests of a rival firm; the advice is tainted at source. The humane Realist, when he reflects on this, can express it in terms of an epistemological scepticism, as does Kennan in his most celebrated dictum: [we should] 'have the modesty to admit that our own national interest is all that we are really capable of knowing and understanding.'[9]

There is a note of regret about this: it would be nice to understand the national interests of other powers but we are just unable to do so. It is as much as we can do (he almost seems to say) to know what our own interest is, let alone focus on other people's. This is diplomatic solipsism.

---

6. E. de Vattel, translation of the edition of 1758, *The Classics of International Law* (Washington, DC: Carnegie Institution of Washington, 1916), vol. III, pp. 6, 7.
7. C. van Vollenhoven, 'Three Stages', *The Evolution of The Law of Nations* (The Hague: Martinus Vijhoff, 1919), p. 28.
8. Winston S. Churchill, 'Mansion House Speech, 10th November, 1942', *The End of the Beginning* (London: Cassel & Company Ltd., 1943), p. 215.
9. George F. Kennan, *American Diplomacy* (Chicago: University of Chicago Press, 1955), p. 100.

The doctrine of the freedom of action, decision, and definition of interests, is the particular inference to be drawn from the premise of a basic conflict of interests; it is the inference when considering each power individually. However, not only freedom, but power is needed to pursue interests, and there is a general inference to be made, when considering the totality of power-relationships. (Realists repudiate the existence of 'international society' so some alternative phrase such as 'totality of power-relationships' must be substituted.) The inference is that one power's security is another power's insecurity. There is no general welfare or security which in theory might be expanded and distributed so that every power could enjoy its just share; there is only individual welfare and security, and what one power enjoys another is deprived of. Security, for the Realist, is a function of power; power is a relational concept. The 'power of the United States', or of Israel, means their power to deal with 'any possible aggressor', that diplomatic euphemism with a precise application. Security, equally, is a relational concept: security against whom? Every arms-race proves, if proof were needed, that an increased sense of security on the part of one power means an increased sense of insecurity on the part of another. Consequently there can be no such thing as a general security treaty. Talk of world security, or regional security, is just hot air; the question is: 'Security for whom, against whom?' Politicians talk of 'security' in Europe or the Middle East, with NATO and other pacts, as if it were general security; but of course it means security for their side against the other, and increased insecurity on the other. The general object of national interest and policy is national security. This is not abstract and general, like peace (peace cannot be the object of policy), but concrete and self-regarding: 'In Defense of the National Interest.'

Revolutionists

If the Realist doctrine of national interest starts from the premise of a conflict of interests, and asserts the autonomy of the national interest, then Revolutionist doctrine clearly starts from the opposite premise, of an international community and solidarity of interest. This is an assertion that the interest of the *civitas maxima*, the society of states and fraternity of mankind, is both definable and attainable. It overrides any supposed parochial national interest, because it includes all true national interests, as the greater includes the less. This is one of the points at which international theory comes closest to the theory of history, for the Revolutionist doctrine of a permanent international solidarity of interest implies that this convergence of interests is going to be brought into being by the immanent movement of history. It is like Adam Smith's 'invisible hand', which leads the self-seeking industrialist 'to promote an end which was no part of his intentions'. (It is worth noting that the doctrine of *laissez-faire*, which was the guiding philosophy of Britain during her Victorian predominance, was as authentically Revolutionist a doctrine as Jacobinism for Revolutionary France. Its supreme theoretical exponent was Cobden.) Or again, it is Burke's 'divine tactic', or Hegel's 'cunning of the idea', or Marx's dialectic. This general conception of the immanent weaving together of particular interests into a general good is often called the 'harmony of interests' and it was attacked under this name by Carr.[10] This is a misnomer, and if it is not too late, 'harmony of interests' should be rescued to describe the contrasted Rationalist doctrine. In strict musical metaphor, the Revolutionist doctrine should be unison of interests; it is a progressive convergence, an immanent solidarity of interests. It is expressed in Kant's *Perpetual Peace*, where the philosophy of history comes through very strongly to carry the international theory over difficult patches. For example, naively, at the end of Appendix 1 on the discrepancy between morals and politics:

The process of creation by which such a brood of corrupt beings [as men] has been put upon earth, can . . . be justified by no theory of Providence, if we assume that it never will be better, nor can be better, with the human race . . . We shall inevitably be driven to a position of despair . . . if we do not admit that the pure principles of right and justice have objective reality and can be realized in fact.[11]

In other words, the facts are so horrible that one must make a wild leap of faith and believe that progress is going to transform them. Kant almost leaps into inverted Revolutionism, pure pacifism. The idea of the immanent solidarity of interests is expressed at the beginning of the First Supplement, entitled 'The Guarantee of Perpetual Peace'. The guarantee is nature herself: 'The mechanical course of nature visibly exhibits a design to bring forth concord out of the discord of men, even against their will'[12] and a little later:

What does nature do about the end which man's reason presents to him as a duty; what does she do for the furtherance of his moral purpose in life? . . . When I say of nature that she wills a certain thing to be done I do not mean that she imposes upon us a duty to do it, for only the Practical Reason as essentially free from constraint, can do this; but I mean that she does it herself whether we be willing or not. '*Fata volentem ducunt, nolentem trahunt*'. [The fates lead the willing and drag the unwilling (Proverbial)].[13]

This is the presupposition in terms of a theory of history.

On the diplomatic plane, a belief in the immanent solidarity of international interests was interestingly expressed by Attlee in November

---

10. See E.H. Carr, *The Twenty Years' Crisis* (London: Macmillan Co. Ltd., 1939).
11. W. Hastie, *Kant's Principles of Politics* (Edinburgh: T. Clark, 1891), p. 136.
12. ibid., p. 105.
13. ibid., pp. 110, 111.

1946, at a White House dinner for him and Mackenzie King. It is probably one of his last foreign policy statements in which a socialist ideology can be detected:

What we are out for today is to try and devise a world policy of the common man . . . What we need most of all is a universal foreign policy directed not to any immediate aim of any particular country but one that is conceived in the interest of all the people of the world. That does not mean we do not take into account our particular differences, but it seems to me today our over-riding interests of world civilisation come first.[14]

The idea reappears often enough; it is here expressed with clarity and naivety. World civilization has overriding interests, therefore we need a universal foreign policy conceived in the interest of all the people of the world, a world policy of the common man. But it is not clear whether this 'universal foreign policy' is to be that of all foreign offices, pursuing in unison the overriding interests of world civiliza-tion in preference to their several national interests; or whether, perhaps, the people of the world are to strike out into this universal foreign policy by short-circuiting the foreign offices. These are crucial questions to which soft Revolutionism can never give a satisfactory answer, so it tends in practice to fall back on the compromises and make-shifts inherent in Rationalism. Clear and authoritative answers, however, are given by hard Revolutionists, because they are prepared to recognize the empirical gulf between the ideal assertion of an inter-national community of interests, and the actuality of the multilateral repudiation of this community. The rule of the people is the rule of the spokesmen of the people; the international community of interest is the interest of the spokesmen of the international community. Hard Revolutionism asserts the doctrine of the real will embodied in some particular state. 'It is our duty to think of the interests of the Soviet people, the interests of the Union of Soviet Socialist Republics — all the more because we are firmly convinced that the interests of the USSR coincide with the fundamental interests of the peoples of other countries',[15] and ' "The solid peaceful policy" of the Soviet Union answers the interests of the American people and the broad masses of all other people, — except those "who are stuffing their pockets with armaments dividends" '.[16]

So the Revolutionists assert an international community of interest which in practice comes to mean that the Revolutionist state defines and expresses the real interest and will of the international community. Thus it follows that one power *can* define the interests

---

14. Reported in *The Manchester Guardian*, 12 November 1946.
15. V. Mikhailovich Molotov's speech to the Supreme Soviet, 31 August 1939, 'Four speeches by V. Molotov', *Soviet Peace Policy* (Lawrence & Wishart, 1941), p. 14.
16. A. Andreyevich Gromyko to the Political Committee of the UN General Assembly, 26 March 1953 as reported in *The Manchester Guardian*, 27 March 1953.

of others. In diplomatic practice, of course, it is improper for one power to define another's interests. Stronger powers do of course bully and influence weaker ones, but this is normally done without violating the decent appearances of natural liberty, and without formulating propositions about the 'real' interest of the weaker party. The exceptions are usually so glaring that they almost always draw attention to, and condemn, themselves, because no pretence of disinterestedness is possible.

It would not be fair to say that an attempt to tell another power what its interests are is always an index of Revolutionism. On 10 February 1957 a Washington dispatch in the *New York Times* reported that the United States government was 'angry and frustrated' over the Israeli refusal to withdraw from the Gaza strip and Gulf of Aqabah. It listed the reasons for this anger and frustration, the first of which was: 'The government believes Israel's defiance of the United Nations . . . will inevitably damage her own longterm self interest.' This touching concern for the interests of Israel probably sprang not from Revolutionist philosophy (unless one wants to emphasize the undeniably counter-Revolutionist features of Dulles's diplomacy), but from mere diplomatic embarrassment, which appears in the last of the reasons listed: 'By facing a showdown with the United Nations, Israel has put the United States in the awkward position of having to choose sides between the two.'

Nevertheless, Revolutionist states do tend to tell other states their business, and pose as their protectors. To do so was a prominent feature of Nazi diplomacy. On 6 April 1941, the day Germany invaded Yugoslavia and Greece, Ribbentrop held a press conference of the foreign press in Berlin. He said that all that had been demanded of Yugoslavia was her loyal co-operation with the Axis in bringing about a new order in Europe: 'It was Germany's only aim to secure a position for Yugoslavia in this new European order, in accordance with Yugoslavia's best interests.'[17] On the same day a German note was sent to Greece saying that the Greek government would have best served the interests of the Greek people by remaining neutral (overlooking that Greece was drawn into the war through having been attacked by Mussolini). With Hitler, this capacity to decide what were the interests of other states was developed to the point where it became a weakness. On 23 August 1939 he held a staff meeting in the Berghof, when he sought to persuade his generals and admirals, with all the force of his earnest rhetoric, that if there was a German–Polish conflict, England would not intervene because in such circumstances England 'had no need to wage war and consequently would not wage war'. Grand-Admiral Erich Raeder described at Nuremberg how he walked away from this meeting with his Chief of Staff of Naval Operations feeling depressed, and they agreed:

17. *New York Times*, 7 April 1941.

that England had never as yet kept itself from a war because — seen objectively — it had no need to wage it (in that case it would indeed have waged few wars), but on the contrary England entered upon a war precisely if it believed it necessary to wage war in its own interest.[18]

This mistake of Hitler's, a mistake which had historic consequences, is an extreme example of the unrealism of Revolutionism, and can be erected as a trophy at the limit of the enquiry in this direction.

One last aspect of the solidarity of international interest deserves to be mentioned. The international community of interest is the interest of the spokesman of the international community, and can only be defined by him. It is for the teacher to say what is in the interest of the school as a whole, not any of the delinquent pupils who are ripe for expulsion. It is a familiar phenomenon that all categories of Revolutionist thought are particular and exclusive, not universal or general. They are private to the point of being privileged, since they are exclusive to the Revolutionist movement and may not be used by anybody else. Before Revolutionism establishes a new class-system in society, it erects a caste-system in philosophy. Revolutionists are exempt from the general moral rule that men must be judged by the immediate consequences of their actions as well as by their purposes. They are incapable of the predicates 'imperialist' or 'aggressor' even when there is identity of action; and they are incapable, *ex officio*, of being the objects of the anti-colonial campaign. They have the exclusive right to define the international community of interests. This was amusingly illustrated in July 1946, in the early twilight of the Cold War, when Bevin tried to appeal to a waning sense of solidarity. He said: 'I think the Soviet government, as well as the United States government, really recognizes the tremendous importance which the preservation of [Britain's] position in the Middle East has for the maintenance of peace throughout the world.' *Izvestia* reacted against this attempt to steal Communist language and pedantically replied: 'it should be pointed out that this statement on the Soviet attitude to [British] policy does not in any way correspond to the facts and is merely an ill-founded attempt to hide behind the back of the Soviet Union.'[19]

A special corollary of the Revolutionist doctrine of national interest relates to foreign policy in representative democracies. The normal assumption in any settled state (and this means, not so much a mature and experienced power as one not guided by the caprice of a tyrant like Mussolini or Franco) is that of a continuity of foreign policy. It is common to Realists and Rationalists. A state's vital interests are

---

18. *Nazi Conspiracy and Aggression* (Washington, DC: US Government Printing Office, 1946), vol. VIII, p. 701.
19. BBC Monitoring Report, 3 and 4 July 1946, quoting *Izvestia*, 4 July 1946, quoted in *The Times*, 5 July 1946.

determined by long-term, immutable conditions: geographical, economic, demographic, power-political; and the policy for handling these conditions tends to become traditional, although flexible. There is a recognizable general continuity in the foreign policy of America, Russia, or Britain which shows a general consensus between one regime and another about the national interest of each power respectively. When the German ambassador complained to the British Foreign Secretary in 1886 that the foreign policy of one government was overturned by the next, Rosebery replied that this was true, but that a successful foreign policy would not be. The condition of continuity was success. This expresses the normal assumption of Realists and Rationalists. It is not when a change or modification of foreign policy is made on a particular issue, but when the principle of the continuity of foreign policy itself is challenged, that one detects Revolutionism. In the Republican campaign of 1952 there was a suggestion that the foreign policy of the Democratic administration had been so negligent of the true interests of the United States and the Free World that a totally new foreign policy was required, pure and untainted, which would paradoxically not only be more effective in handling the Communist menace, but also would put an end to the existing war against it. This is an example of the Revolutionism which consists in counter-Revolutionism. This issue has haunted British foreign policy for as long as there has been a Labour opposition in parliament. It became explicit during the 1945 election when the principle of the continuity of foreign policy was repeatedly attacked by Laski, the Party chairman. 'I don't believe in taking foreign policy out of politics. [I don't believe in keeping it] pure and clear, in a kind of Tory vacuum where Labour people may gaze upon it, but where we are told to keep our hands off.'[20] 'We do not propose to accept the Tory doctrine of the continuity of foreign policy, because we have no interest in the continuity of Conservative policy.'[21] 'We Socialists are only committed to decisions which result in coherence with Socialism.'[22]

Socialism took precedence over traditionally conceived national interest. In practice Attlee and Bevin proved as effective exponents of traditional national interest as their predecessors, but the search for a specifically socialist foreign policy still occupies left-wing members of the Labour party, as against the concern for how Labour can intelligently pursue the agreed national interest.

---

20. Harold Laski, Speech at Newark, 16 June 1945, reported in *Reynolds News*, 17 June 1945.
21. 'What Mr Laski said', Churchill's letter to Attlee, 2 July 1945, reported in *The Times*, 3 July 1945.
22. ibid.

Rationalists

In our mapping of the territory occupied by the Realists, the dividing line with the Rationalists has already been approached. When Sumner Welles said it was axiomatic that foreign policy should be based on enlightened selfishness he posed the question: What is 'enlightened' selfishness? (see above p. 112) There are at least three possible answers. The first is intelligent self-interest; enlightenment is far-sightedness, and understanding the complexities of the situation. Enlightened self-interest is that which calculates all obstacles and contingencies in the path to fulfilment. A second answer is a selfishness which, negatively, seeks not to violate or affront the self-interest of others. It is a self-interest so intelligent and penetrating that it recognizes that one of the chief obstacles on the path to fulfilment is the reactions of other persons or states, and therefore seeks to avoid stirring up trouble. A third answer is a selfishness which gives positive consideration to the interests of other persons or states, and consents to modify and limit itself out of respect for these other interests, because it recognizes their right to exist. One might doubt whether a self-interest modified to this extent is really 'self-interest' at all; it would be compounded as much of enlightenment as of self-interest. Such an understanding of 'enlightened selfishness' is well within the territory of Rationalism. Because a phrase like enlightened self-interest is capable of progressive shades of meaning those using the phrase may pass insensibly from one meaning to another, even without realizing the implications of what they are saying.

The journey from Realism to Rationalism can be seen by a critical consideration of George Kennan. He made the realistic and sceptical assertion that one is really only capable of knowing one's own national interest (see above p. 113). However in *Realities of American Foreign Policy* he says: 'I do not wish ever to see the conduct of this nation in . . . its foreign relations animated by anything else than decency, generosity, moderation and consideration for others.'[23] The contradiction is evident. Generosity, moderation and consideration for others presupposes that you can estimate the interests of those towards whom you are being generous, moderate and considerate. This is much more characteristic of Kennan's position than the first famous sentence, taken out of context. Kennan stands out in the public life of the West as a foreign policy publicist who was most scrupulous and respectful in considering the interests of Russia. He tried to see each situation through Soviet eyes, condemning and discarding elements of doctrinal imperialism, and isolating and emphasizing a core of Soviet national interest which he urged the United States to respect. For example, he urged recognition of Russia's interests in Eastern Europe (1957 Senate

---

23. George F. Kennan, *Realities of American Foreign Policy* (London: Geoffrey Cumberlege, Oxford University Press, 1954), p. 61.

Committee) and the importance of not facing her with a challenge to those interests which would make it impossible for her to climb down. The statement quoted earlier, that 'we should have the modesty to admit that our own national interest is all that we are really capable of knowing and understanding', might be paraphrased, in the general context of Kennan's thought, as: we must not be arrogant and importunate about telling other powers what their interests are, although we have a distinct conception of the general interest within which their interests can be accommodated to our own. This would be an acceptable maxim of personal relations as well as of international, and this again is the heart of Rationalist country.

Similar critical consideration can be applied to Morgenthau. In *In Defense of the National Interest* he says: 'All the successful statesmen of modern times from Richelieu to Churchill have made the national interest the ultimate standard of their policies, and none of the great moralists in international affairs has attained his goals.'[24] But is this true? It begs the question, particularly, of what the criterion of success is in politics. Morgenthau, it seems, means that the successful statesman is the statesman who follows the national interest. But the criterion of political success is very elusive, and Morgenthau is unhistorical and unphilosophical in talking as if success is something obvious and agreed. He is unhistorical, because this, precisely, is one of the great themes of historians' debate, as they unceasingly remasticate the cud of historical reputation, reassessing achievement and reversing judgements in the light of new perspectives; he is unphilosophical, because in this endless debate different people and generations strike different balances between the criterion of technical success, mere expertise, and the moral criterion. This latter itself is twofold, involving the judgement of loftiness of motive, and the judgement of the ultimate contribution to human good.

When Bismarck died, in 1898, he was adulated by Germany and the world as one of the great men of history: creator of a united Germany, master diplomat, who achieved dazzling technical success. A generation later, with his united Germany ruined and defeated, his reputation slumped: he was seen as the man who destroyed constitutionalism in Prussia, the principal exponent of *Realpolitik*, of the international arrogance and bullying which had brought Germany to ruin, and a great misleader and deceiver. By contrast President Wilson, when he died, was a failure, a futile obstinate theorist. A generation later, when destiny had pummelled America out of isolationism and into the leadership of a new League of Nations, his reputation reascended, and his moral grandeur of vision was seen as a kind of success in history, eclipsing his technical incompetence in handling Senate or United States opinion.

---

24. Hans J. Morgenthau, *In Defense of the National Interest* (New York: Alfred A. Knopf, 1951), p. 34.

One should not be completely sceptical: a historiographical consensus does emerge about politicians or statesmen who seem to solve the problem of their times and whose solution has some survival value. Richelieu, Morgenthau's first example, is a good instance. He aimed to strengthen the French monarchy over the Huguenots at home and give France ascendancy over the Habsburgs abroad, and his work lasted a hundred and fifty years. Modern historians have argued that his domestic policy was one of the ultimate causes of the French Revolution; and that his foreign policy was the main cause of the demoralization of international politics, and the extinction of the last traces of the old European commonwealth and the triumph of naked *Realpolitik*. But even if his success was a morally dubious success, it is still probably as definite a success as one can find.

What about Churchill? True, he brought Britain through the Second World War on the winning side, but that was not his sole aim. On the level of technical politics, he had at least two others. He wished to restore the balance of power in Europe, and in this he failed. The balance was as badly deranged by Russian power after the war as it had been by German power before it. This is normally blamed on Roosevelt and Yalta, but it is as much Churchill's fault as anybody else's. The Soviet–British alliance treaty of 1942 assumed British recognition of all Stalin's gains under the Nazi-Soviet Pact of 1939; it originally contained a clause recognizing Soviet absorption of the Baltic States, and Churchill urged this on Roosevelt, who refused to consent. American legalism at that juncture was far-sighted realism. In 1943 Russia broke off diplomatic relations with the Polish government-in-exile. Churchill urged the Poles to appease Russia by voluntarily ceding Polish territory east of the Curzon line, but the Poles refused. At Tehran, on British initiative, the Big Three decided that the Curzon line should be the future Polish frontier, and Britain and the United States extracted no quid pro quo from Russia in the shape of firm guarantees for the independence of what remained of Poland. 'If the Americans in the end went faster and farther than the British in appeasing Russia, they could fairly argue that it was the British who first taught them to sin.'[25]

A second of Churchill's aims was to preserve the British Empire. 'I have not become the King's First Minister in order to preside over the liquidation of the British Empire' (quoted above p. 113). He had opposed the India Act of 1935 which granted responsible government to India. But in 1945 Churchill was dismissed from office and in the next few years the British Empire was largely liquidated. In 1956 Churchill's political heir, Eden, undertook the Suez adventure which probably marks the end of Great Britain as a great power. All this was the opposite of what Churchill wanted and stood for: so was he a success? Like Clemenceau, he seems one of those great figures who

---

25. G.F. Hudson, *Questions of East and West* (London: Odham Press Ltd., 1953), p. 13.

sometimes appear at the end of a period to sum up the past rather than to shape the future. Most people would agree that he was a great man, and there is a personal and moral grandeur about him, but this is a different proposition from saying he was a success.

(It is interesting to note some distinctions in language and concept between the three traditions: for the Realist, the highest commendation of a statesman is to say he was successful; for the Rationalist, it is to say he was 'great'; for the Revolutionist the highest commendation is to be 'right', and the content of 'rightness' is determined by Revolutionist doctrine. In Marxism what is required is to be 'correct', scientifically; for the soft Revolutionist or Dulles-type Counter-Revolutionist, it is to be 'morally right'.)

Morgenthau claims that Churchill made the national interest the 'ultimate standard' of his policy. There is a difficulty here with the extravagance of Morgenthau's language. If the 'ultimate standard' means that, in the last analysis, Churchill did what he thought best for the national interest, it is true; but there are very few statesmen for whom it is not true, so the statement is uninformative and undifferentiating. If the implication is that the national interest was the normal standard of Churchill's policy, a characteristic of his statecraft, then it is not true. It would be true of Richelieu, but one must not fail to perceive the difference in quality between Richelieu and Churchill. The mark of Churchill's idea of national interest is that he saw it as part of a wider whole, 'the liberties of Europe'. The difference between Chamberlain and Churchill, for example, is that between an exclusive and an inclusive conception of national interest. For Chamberlain, Czechoslovakia was 'a far-away people of whom we know nothing'; for Churchill, she is one of the 'famous and ancient states of Europe' whose interests coincided with our own. As a supporter of the League, of collective security, and the balance of power, Churchill saw Britain's national interest in the wider context of European interests, and this runs though all his speeches. It is more characteristic, and more important, than the desperate appeasement of Stalin that has been noted. After the war, the peoples of Europe did not hail and revere him as their liberator, showering him with honours, and the freedom of their capital cities, because they thought he had served British national interests faithfully, but because they saw him as having served their interests too, those of 'Europe', or 'civilization'.

There is another question to be asked about Morgenthau's statement: is it true that 'none of the great moralists in international affairs has attained his goals'? The great moralists are not enumerated or exemplified: Wilson and F.D. Roosevelt are probably among them, and the question of Wilson's success or failure has already been discussed. Both Attlee and Gladstone, also, would probably be considered 'moralists'. Attlee will go down in history as the man who gave independence to India, Pakistan, Burma and Ceylon. To maintain an empire in South Asia was probably far beyond Britain's strength after 1945 and therefore abdication was in her national interest; but this was not Attlee's motive, although no doubt it reconciled his military and official advisers. Attlee acted on principle, as an old Fabian socialist. Does he fall under the condemnation of the moralist?

Gladstone, possibly the greatest moralist in English political history, supported self-determination for the Italians from Austrian rule and the Balkan peoples from Turkish oppression. This sentimental leaning, shared by most of the British governing class, did not involve Britain in any sacrifice, only a little judicious diplomatic and naval support. But in his seventies Gladstone came to the moral conviction that what was sauce for the goose was sauce for the gander, and if freedom was good for the oppressed nations of southern Europe then it was good also for the oppressed nations of the British Isles. He devoted the last thirteen years of his life (which included his last two premierships) to the cause of Irish Home Rule, and most of his contemporaries thought this was clearly against the national interest. He split his party, and he did not in his lifetime convert the British people, but twenty-four years after his death Ireland gained her national independence. Was he a success or a failure — in the sense of a moralist who failed to attain his goals? He himself, if he had seen the sequel, would almost certainly have denied that he had failed. Gladstone enlarged the boundaries of British political morality and he was the only foreign statesman whose name was remembered and revered by the people of Italy, the Balkan states and Ireland, down until the totalitarian revolutions of the 1930s obliterated earlier memories.

There are clearly some political acts and policies which are difficult to fit into an exclusive national self-interest pattern. The abolition of the slave trade, and such surrenders of territory as Castlereagh's return to the French of their captured colonies in 1814, are examples, but the motive can usually be seen as an enhancement of the national standing or prestige: 'I am sure our reputation on the continent as a feature of strength, power, and confidence, is of more real moment to us than an acquisition [thus] made.'[26] Castlereagh's undoubted pursuit of the national interest was qualitatively different from Richelieu's or from Canning's return to isolationism; he strove for union of interests among the great powers, for 'habitual confidential and free intercourse between the Ministers of the Great Powers *as a body*'.[27] He wrote to Liverpool from the conference at Aix-la-Chapelle October 1818:

It is satisfactory to observe how little embarrassment and how much solid good grow out of these reunions, which sound so terrible at a distance. It really appears to me to be a new discovery in the European Government, at once extinguishing the cobwebs with which diplomacy obscures the horizon;

---

26. C.K. Webster, *The Foreign Policy of Castlereagh* (London: G. Bell & Sons Ltd., 1931), vol. I, 1812–15, p. 273.
27. ibid., vol. II, 1815–22, p. 56.

bringing the whole hearing of the system into its true light and giving to the counsels of the Great Powers the efficiency and almost the simplicity of a single state.[28]

And to the Cabinet he wrote: 'the Great Powers feel that they have not only a common interest but a common duty [to Europe].'[29]

These examples show that it is false schematizing and untrue to political experience to divide statesmen into Realists, who follow the national interest and are successes, and moralists, who do not follow it and who are failures. There is an infinite series of gradations, and it might be true to say that the majority of statesmen whom posterity remembers and finds worth arguing about lie between the extremes. They represent self-interest with varying degrees of enlightenment, and pursue national interest with varying degrees of consideration for the interests of other powers. Morgenthau admits of this possibility of the accommodation of national interests. In *In Defense of the National Interest* he says:

The task of ascertaining what one's own nation needs and wants in order to be secure, and what the other nation needs and wants in order to be secure, and whether there is inescapable conflict or the possibility of accommodation between these needs and wants — this task is an intellectual one, the highest of those constructive tasks which the Hamiltons, the Pitts, the Cannings, the Disraelis, and the Churchills face and solve, and whose existence is ignored by the amateurs.[30]

This position, regarding the adjustment of national interest as an intellectual task, can be taken to illuminate the second stage of enlightened self-interest suggested earlier (p. 120): a self-interest intelligent enough to recognize that reactions of other states are among the complexities of the situation within which national self-interest must be pursued. In *Politics among Nations* Morgenthau uses different language: if we see all nations, including our own, as pursuing their respective interests, we are safeguarded from moral self-righteousness and can do justice to all.

We are able to judge other nations as we judge our own and . . . we are then capable of pursuing policies that respect the interest of other nations, while protecting and promoting those of our own. Moderation in policy cannot fail to reflect the moderation of moral judgement.[31]

Here he talks of not only 'ascertaining' the other nation's interests but 'respect' for them; not only an intellectual but a moral task.

---

28. ibid., vol. II, p. 153.
29. ibid., vol. II, p. 160.
30. Hans J. Morgenthau, *In Defense of the National Interest*, p. 149.
31. Hans J. Morgenthau, *Politics among Nations* (New York: Alfred A. Knopf, 1954), p. 10.

Morgenthau, like Kennan, has one foot planted in Rationalist territory.

The Rationalist doctrine of national interest, then, assumes a tension of interests between states which sometimes but not normally rises into a conflict of interests, but it asserts a wide possibility of mutually adjusting these interests. The great aim of statecraft, of foreign policy, is to pursue and safeguard the national interest within the setting of a respect for the interests of others, or of international society as a whole. Thus for the Rationalist, the interesting and important thing about Castlereagh, Churchill, Roosevelt or Dulles, is not whether the ultimate standard of their policy was the national interest, but how and with what discrimination they struck the balance between national interest and wider interests. We find the Rationalist position formulated well in Washington's Farewell Address:

It will be worthy of a free enlightened, and at no distant period a great nation to give to mankind the magnanimous and too novel example of a people always guided by an exalted justice and benevolence.

If we remain one people, under an efficient government, the period is not far off . . . when we may choose peace or war, as our interest, guided by justice, shall counsel.[32]

While the Realist will tend to extend the principle of vital interests (which means precisely those interests which cannot be adjusted or accommodated but will be fought over) until all national interests become vital, so the Rationalist will seek to contract the operation of this principle, and minimize the number of particular interests that are designated as vital.

It is the true art of policy that each Nation should so interpret its own vital interests that they will not be inconsistent with or antagonistic to the interests of other nations. Each nation must aim at connecting its own security, not with the conquest and subordination of others, but with their equal independence and security.[33]

Churchill, in the House of Commons on 27 February 1945 said:

I have high hopes that when the war is over good arrangements can be made for securing the peace and progress of the Arab world and generally the Middle East, and then Great Britain and the United States, which is taking an increasing interest in these regions, will be able to play a valuable part in proving that well-known maxim of the old Free Trader, 'All legitimate interests are in harmony'.[34]

---

32. Ruhl J. Bartlett, ed., *The Record of American Diplomacy* (New York: Alfred A. Knopf, 1947) pp. 86, 88.
33. J. Headlam-Morley, *Studies in Diplomatic History* (London: Methuen and Co. Ltd., 1930), p. 166.
34. *Hansard's Parliamentary Debates*, vol. 408, col. 1289.

This quotation is interesting because in its reference to the Middle East it suggests the limits of the truth of the Rationalist doctrine, and this is exactly the Realists' critique. Rationalists are led to assume the accommodatability of interests wishfully, and assertions about a harmony of interests are always statements of aspiration, not of fact.

Here, fortified by Churchillian language, one would like to rescue the phrase 'harmony of interests'. It ought *not* to mean the Revolutionists' progressive convergence or immanent solidarity of interests, if the metaphor is respected. Harmony, after all, is a combination of sounds of different pitch, not a reduction of all sounds to the same pitch. Harmony is the product of a musical act, not of historical evolution; it is conformity to harmonic laws, and there are always discords, dissonances and cacophonies which cannot be brought under those laws. This is much closer to the Rationalist conception of the relation between national interests. It is not a conflict of interests, nor an immanent solidarity of interests, but a partially resoluble tension of interests, open to reconciliation. This is nearer the true meaning of harmony. Perhaps the phrase 'harmony of interests' cannot be recovered for this usage, and it does not matter so long as one recognizes that there are two distinct positions, and knows which it is that is designated thus.

A great part of international politics has been conducted under the aspect of a largely resoluble tension of interests. When there is a Revolutionist power on the scene, of course, tensions of interest become unresoluble because such a power creates a holy war with any powers which do not accept its definition of their interests. (But the politics of NATO, for instance, were conducted on the assumption of a resoluble tension of national interests until the alliance was virtually wrecked, if only temporarily, by Eden and Dulles which seemed indeed to prove the Realist case, that all national interests are ultimately in conflict). A much longer-lasting example of the politics of Rationalism was the Concert of Europe, with its sequel, or epilogue, in the League of the 1920s. The Concert was based on the tacit understanding between great powers that there were certain standards of moderation or good faith which governed their relations with one another and with weaker powers. This understanding was fractured by the First World War, and then shattered by Mussolini, the Japanese attack on Manchuria, and the Nazi Revolution. The official protocol of the Belgian Conference of 1831 contains this sentence: 'Each nation has its individual rights; but Europe has also her rights; it is social order that has given them to her.'[35] This is an interesting proposition because it is an official diplomatic statement, and because it sums up neatly the tripartite conception of social order (something Marxists can

---

35. H.L. Bulwer, ed., *The Life of Henry John Temple Viscount Palmerston* (London: Richard Bentley, 1871), vol. II, appendix, p. 391.

analyse), embodied in an international society, in which the rights of the international society and of sovereign states are balanced. Among English statesmen, Gladstone had the most highly developed theory of the Concert. He habitually thought in terms of European interests rather than parochial British interests: he did not fail to recognize the latter, but believed that true British interest could not be incompatible with European interests. Yet Gladstone was not a Revolutionist; he did not believe that the true interests of Europe were identical with Britain's, and he was not out to reconstruct international society in accordance with a doctrine. He met and judged each claim for international justice as it arose. He described the Concert of Europe in realistic terms as a tradition of co-operation which neutralized the selfish aims of each great power. 'Common action is fatal to selfish aims . . . When two Great Powers enter into an alliance for a common object, they not only assist one another, but each acts as a check upon the other.'[36] This idea has been applied to the League and the United Nations by their more intelligent interpreters.

In Rationalist theory, therefore, there is a resoluble tension of interests between powers, a balance between the interests of international society as a whole and individual powers. The criteria of statecraft are skill, judgement, and moral insight in estimating other powers' interests and those of international society as a whole. There is a middle path between the Realist doctrine of the absolute autonomy and subjectivity of national interest, and the Revolutionist doctrine of the dogmatic objectivity of national interest, defined by doctrinal authority. In the Rationalist conception, while it may be impertinent to define another power's interests and duties, it is possible to make broad statements of a common international interest, which includes particular interests, especially through the constitutional machinery and organizations of international society. 'The task of a diplomatic agent is to reconcile the interests of his own nation with those of others.'[37]

Extreme examples would be the great quasi-legislative acts of international society: those peace settlements which are not only territorial, but also legislate in more general matters. In June 1815 the Final Act of the Congress of Vienna included the suppression of the slave trade, and of the Barbary pirates; settled the rank of diplomatic representatives; guaranteed the civil rights of Jews in Germany; and neutralized Switzerland. The neutralization of Belgium was agreed upon by the Powers in 1839. The Treaty of Paris of 1856 set up an international commission to regulate traffic on the Danube, the

---

36. W.E. Gladstone's Speech at West Calder, 27 November 1879, *Selected Speeches on Foreign Policy 1738–1914* (London: Worlds Classics, Humphrey Milford, Oxford University Press, 1914), p. 372.
37. E. Satow, *A Guide to Diplomatic Practice* (London: Longman Green & Co., 1922), vol. I, p. VI.

Congress also defined limitations of warfare and rights of neutrals in war. In 1919 the Treaty of Versailles allowed for minority treaties, and introduced the mandates system and the International Labour Organization, as well as a system for the pacific settlement of disputes. All international agreements creating new states are examples too; from declaring Greece an independent state in 1830, through the Berlin Act of 1878 which created Serbia and Romania, down to the recognition of Israel by the United Nations in 1947. The Hague Conferences with their prolific conventions for the regulation of warfare form part of the Rationalist tradition too. The large school of Rationalist writers before 1939 formed the orthodoxy of international theory, and interpreted and extolled these legislative achievements as developing constitutionalism, and fulfilling the Grotian tradition. There were none of first eminence, no Grotiuses, Burkes or Hegels, but many respected names: Alfred Zimmern, Norman Angell, Leonard Woolf, Gilbert Murray, de Madariaga, and Oppenheim. They were subject to a devastating Realist counter-attack by the writers of the age of Hitler, E.H. Carr and others, for describing a utopian, not real world, where all these 'legislative' achievements were unconcerned with vital interests. But Grotius, after all, was not describing the Thirty Years' War, but factors in human nature and politics suppressed or latent at that time, which it was desirable to emphasize as bulwarks or breakwaters against the total dissolution of civilized living and the complete triumph of barbarism. Conceptions of constitutionalism applied to international relations are usually Rationalist, in the tradition of Aristotle and Grotius, who saw the whole of international relations as subject to the rule of law.

This Rationalist theory has various corollaries. First, it denies the Realist principle that the security of one power is in inverse ratio to that of others, that security itself is a relational concept. Whereas the Realist identifies security with power and makes security a function of power, the Rationalist separates power from security. It is true that if one says that the power of a state has increased, by the invention of a new weapon for example, one might equally say that the power of all other states has decreased: the one proposition contains the other. But power, says the Rationalist, is not identical with security. Security consists in other factors besides national power: the strength and reliability of allies, and the absence of conflicting interests, for example. In theory, maximum security would be attained by minimizing all national power; if all armed forces were abolished, leaving only police forces, the security of every power would be enhanced. Security, like prosperity, is an objective towards which all powers can, conceivably, move simultaneously. It is the argument set out in W.T.R. Fox, *The Super-Powers*.[38]

---

38. W.T.R. Fox, *The Super-Powers* (New York: Harcourt, Brace & Co., 1944).

A second corollary of the Rationalist theory is an attitude rather than a principle: it is a presumption in favour of small powers. The Realist makes a presumption in favour of great powers: that is, either an intellectual acceptance (perhaps reluctant) of their primacy in international politics; or a moral and emotional approval of this primacy, as for example the rather jejune doctrine fashionable in the early days of the United Nations that power goes with responsibility. It is the Realists who advocate spheres of influence in which great powers will govern their smaller neighbours, from the Nazi theory of *Grossraumordnung* which they said they had contributed to international law; to Morgenthau's advocacy of dividing the world into spheres of influence between the United States and Russia.[39] And it is the Realists who rejoice over the passing of small powers: 'The day of small nations has long passed away, the day of Empires has come' (Joseph Chamberlain, 1904). 'The small country can survive only by seeking permanent association with a great power.'[40] Realists argue that small powers have limited interests, and a petty, parochial vision. They lack the broad world-picture of great powers and are mainly devoted to intrigue, squabbling and horse-trading.

But the Rationalist makes the contrary presumption: he fears and suspects power, so he fears and suspects great powers more than small powers. He doubts whether great powers can be transformed into great responsibles, and believes that small powers have been truer spokesmen of civilized values than great ones. Small powers were the authors of whatever success the League of Nations enjoyed; the great powers sabotaged it. The Rationalist may be embarrassed by extending his thesis to the United Nations, where predominant groups of small powers are themselves less animated by Rationalist principles than they were in the League, but from the late 1950s many Rationalist arguments about small powers were to be found — how they were law-abiding, ready to make sacrifices, dependable, peace-loving and so on — in the columns of the *New York Times* and in respect of the UN peace-keeping force. The theme was that *small* powers, not great powers, are the responsible ones.

This presumption in favour of small powers is a late development of Rationalist constitutionalism, a result of the enfranchisement of small powers in the twentieth century, of the Hague conferences, and the League. It is unclear whether it can be traced back to early Rationalism. It is not connected with the legal doctrine of equality of states; this fiction is due to the naturalists of the eighteenth century, who were in effect, although not in form, a Realist school. They emphasized that there is no international law except the law of nature

---

39. Hans J. Morgenthau, *In Defense of the National Interest*, pp. 150ff.
40. E.H. Carr, *Conditions of Peace* (London: Macmillan & Co Ltd., 1942), p. 55.

(of the Hobbesian kind), in which all states had perfect liberty.[41] However it is worth noting that in the Melian Dialogue[42] it is the great power, Athens, which talks of self-interest (Realism), and the small power, Melos, which talks of the general interest (Rationalism). In Thucydides the particular event is the vehicle of a general truth: small powers are normally the chief spokesmen of general principles, of moral law and natural law, because they have no other defence.

If the Rationalists' belief in a resoluble tension of interests in international society makes them advocates and theorists of international constitutionalism and organization, are they not, in their own pragmatic, undramatic way, seeking the assimilation of international to domestic politics; the establishment of the *civitas maxima*, albeit constitutional, which we have seen as the mark of Revolutionism? Broadly, of course, the answer is yes. But there is a line of distinction one can trace between the two traditions. It is, a priori, a distinction perhaps between the theory of unitary government and the theory of federal government. Rationalists are federalists, or rather confederalists. (A theory of confederation, if one were to be written, would be less than the original thirteen American states would have been satisfied with, but more than members of the international society at large have ever been content with.)

Unlike Revolutionists, Rationalists have an international doctrine of states' rights. At the beginning of the chapter it was suggested that the theory of national interest was comprised of the theory of the natural liberties of states, of national duty, of sovereignty (politically, not legally) and of domestic jurisdiction. If the coin of national interest is turned over to its other side one can formulate a theory of international right, a sub-paradigm of the theory of national interest.

A theory of international right would formulate a balance between the rights of separate nations and the rights of international society as a whole. This would be almost the same thing as a theory of intervention; intervention is a phenomenon of international politics where international right clashes with national interest, and where international politics intersect with domestic. This is the central theme of Burke's polemics against the French revolutionary state. Intervention is the characteristic mode whereby Revolutionism works towards its *civitas maxima*. The constitutional co-operation between states, in Concerts, Leagues, UNs, is the corresponding mode whereby the Rationalist works, not towards the *civitas maxima*, but towards mitigating international anarchy.

These two opposing positions with regard to a theory of international right can be formulated in more detail.

---

41. See G. Butler & S. Maccoby, *The Development of International Law* (London: Longmans, Green & Co., 1928), pp. 248–53.
42. Thucydides (London: J.M. Dent & Sons Ltd., 1936), verses 84–117, pp. 393–401.

International right: Rationalism

This is Burke's position. Right is conferred by prescription and acceptance. To paraphrase Kent's *Commentaries on American Law*:[43]

(a) Every state has the right to regulate its own affairs freely, without
intervention.
(b) No state has the right to establish government on principles of
hostility to other governments, and intervention is permissible
against such a state.
(c) Every state has the duty of accommodating its national interests,
so far as possible, to those of other states.

This last point has already been examined: it is true within the
limitations of the second point. Accommodation of interests is
impossible without some degree of good faith. Burke said, referring to
the 'ill faith and treachery' of the French revolutionary government:
'The very idea of a negotiation for peace, whatever the inward
sentiments of the party may be, implies some confidence in their faith,
some degree of belief in the professions which are made concerning
it.'[44]
This is the whole theme of international politics from 1789 down
to 1830, when the force of French Revolutionism and the Holy
Alliance counter-Revolutionism was beginning to abate. Throughout
this period British policy walked the Rationalist tightrope. Through
Burke, it strongly opposed the violent interventionism and
imperialism of the French Revolution.

This power, by the very condition of its existence, by its very essential
constitution, is in a state of hostility with us, and with all civilized people.
With a fixed design they have outlawed themselves, and to their power
outlawed all other nations.
They made a schism with the whole universe, and that schism extended to
almost everything great and small.[45]

Through Castlereagh, when the pendulum had swung back, British
policy diplomatically opposed the discreeter intervention of the Holy
Alliance.
It is also a theme, although not the whole theme, of international
politics since 1945, and nowhere is the Rationalist position better
stated than by Kennan in *America and the Russian Future*:

43. Chancellor James Kent (1763–1847), 4th ed, *Commentaries on American Law*
(New York 1840), 4 vols.; see also J.T. Abdy, ed., *Kent's Commentaries on International Law* (Cambridge: Deighton Bell & Co., 1877).
44. Edmund Burke, *Writings and Speeches* (London: The Worlds Classics, Henry
Frowde, Oxford University Press, 1907), ch. VI, p. 119.
45. ibid., ch. VI., pp. 146, 147, 158.

What attributes are we, as responsible members of the world community, entitled to look for in the personality of a foreign state, and of Russia in particular?

1. We may look . . . for a Russian government which . . . would not take the ideological position that its own purposes cannot finally prosper unless all systems of government not under its control are subverted and eventually destroyed.

2. [We are entitled to expect the Russian government will stop short of internal totalitarianism, because] excess of internal authority leads inevitably to unsocial and aggressive conduct as a government among governments, and is a matter of concern to the international community.

3. [We may hope it will refrain from oppressing other peoples capable of national freedom. If Russia] is prepared to do these things, then Americans will not need to concern themselves more deeply with her nature and purposes; the basic needs of a more stable world order will then have been met, and the area in which a foreign people can usefully have thoughts and suggestions will have been filled.[46]

This is superbly Rationalist, as one can see by considering how completely unrealist it is, and how remote from attainability. Compared with this, Burke, who deplored the recognition of a Revolutionary power and argued for a long, relentless, unsparing war against it, seems to pass from Rationalism to counter-Revolutionism.

International right: Revolutionism

Right is conferred, not by prescription and acceptance, but by doctrine. (a) Every people has the right, or duty, of conforming its own affairs to the doctrinal norm; that is, no established state possesses right: all may be overturned when challenged from within by their peoples, or by politically active spokesmen of their peoples. (b) No heretical state has the right to prevent the establishment of the doctrinal norm in other states. (c) Any state embodying the doctrinal norm has the duty of hostility to other states; no accommodation of interests is possible. (In the first and last of these points it is unclear whether to use 'right' or 'duty'. This illustrates the immaturity of international theory compared with ordinary political or moral theory. The theory of ethics has, from generations of discussion, refined and clarified its concepts so that it is a solecism to confuse the terms 'right', 'duty' and 'good'. Right and duty are not necessarily correlative. But in international theory this ploughing of the linguistic and conceptual soil remains to be done.)[47]

Embodied in each of these theories is a doctrine of non-

---

46. George F. Kennan, *America and the Russian Future* (Chicago: University of Chicago Press, 1951), pp. 128, 130, 134.
47. See E.F. Carritt, *The Theory of Morals* (London: Humphrey Milford, Oxford University Press, 1928), pp. 100–1.

intervention. The Rationalist doctrine is simple and two-dimensional; the Revolutionist one complex and three-dimensional. For Rationalism, non-intervention is the norm, because by the first principle of the theory of international right, every state has the right to regulate its own affairs freely, without intervention. It admits of exceptions: if a state adopts a form of government based on principles of hostility to other nations, intervention is permissible in the interests of the international community. 'The only safe principle is that of the Law of Nations — That no state has a right to endanger its neighbours by its internal Proceedings, and that if it does, provided they exercise a sound discretion, Their right of Interference is clear.'[48] This marks Castlereagh's closest approximation to the Holy Alliance and is the extreme statement of Rationalist doctrine. It has seldom been acted on: not against Nazi Germany, for example.

The Revolutionist doctrine of non-intervention differs from the Rationalist in two ways, both as regards ends and as regards means, in what it presumes and in what it prescribes. Rationalism makes a presumption in favour of existing international society, as Burke does; Revolutionism makes a presumption against it. International order has to be straightened out before it is morally validated; hence the right or duty of every people to conform their own affairs to the doctrinal norm, and the moral prohibition against any state intervening to prevent this. The Rationalist theory of non-intervention, as applied to the old order, is immoral, because it bolsters an immoral international order. This was the theme elaborated by Mazzini, and is probably his principal contribution to international theory:

It was to be observed of this principle of Non-interference, that the very terms in which it is put forth, necessarily presuppose something, take something for granted. When it is said that the true principle of the mutual relations of nations is the principle of 'Non-Intervention', a state of things is presupposed in which all the due conditions of Nationality have been attended to. It is between certain things called *Nations* that the principle of Non-Intervention is to hold; the principle of Non-Intervention is not to take effect except on the supposition that the parties concerned are distinct Nations.[49]

Mazzini was indignant with England, which by adhering to the non-intervention principle was supporting Austrian rule in Italy and Hungary, and Russian rule in Poland; and intervening *against* these nations struggling to be free. (The position was complicated by the Holy Alliance, the counter-Revolutionist enemy, which was busy intervening up and down Europe to suppress these nationalist

---

48. Viscount Castlereagh, 'Memorandum of 19 October 1818', in H. Temperley and L.M. Penson, *Foundations of British Foreign Policy* (Cambridge: Cambridge University Press, 1938), p. 44.
49. 'Non-Intervention 1851', *Life and Writings of Joseph Mazzini* (London: Smith Elder, 1870), vol. VI, p. 301.

movements, and thereby violating the second principle of the Revolutionist theory of international right.) Mazzini again: 'The same theory which proclaims Non-interference as the first law of international politics, must include, as a secondary law, the right of interference to make good all prior infractions of the law of Non-interference.'[50]

These prior infractions of the law of non-interference are in effect identical with the injustices in the international order which need straightening out at any time: that is, that the Austrians are ruling in Italy and the Russians in Poland, or the Portuguese in Goa, the French in Algeria and the British in Cyprus. The principles of Afro-Asian anti-colonialism are identical with those of Mazzini, and the indignation he felt for the slothfully non-intervening English is the same as that which Nehru felt over Goa, and the Arabs over Algeria, against the Americans.

Rationalist doctrine is confined to the realm of diplomacy, to relations between state and state, and thus it is two-dimensional. Revolutionist doctrine embraces a third dimension, which from a diplomatic standpoint is underground: relations between peoples. Rationalists believe in non-intervention because, on the whole, they do not want to intervene; Revolutionists believe in it because they do not want to be intervened against. They withdraw all right of intervention from the diplomatic level, in relations between states (the level on which they usually have neither the desire nor capacity to intervene), and concentrate the right of intervention on the underground cosmopolitan level of relations between peoples, where their intervening is usually conducted. Thus Chou En-lai declared in June 1954 on his way back from the Geneva Conference: 'Revolution cannot be exported [a standard Marxist bromide], and at the same time outside interference with the expressed will of the people should not be permitted.'[51]

There is an exact analogy between the Revolutionist use of the doctrine of non-intervention in international politics, and his use of the doctrine of civil liberties in the domestic politics of non-Revolutionist countries. In each case a Rationalist principle is appealed to for non-Rationalist, rather anti-Rationalist, purposes; and Rationalists are made the prisoners of their own principles. Macaulay explains in a famous passage:

The doctrine which, from the very first origin of religious dissensions, has been held by all bigots of all sects, when condensed into a few words, and stripped of all rhetorical disguise, is simply this: I am in the right, and you are in the wrong. When you are the stronger, you ought to tolerate me; for it is your duty to tolerate truth. But when I am the stronger, I shall persecute you; for it is my duty to persecute error.[52]

---

50. ibid., vol. VI, p. 305.
51. Quoted by Coral Bell, *Survey of International Affairs 1954* (London: Oxford University Press, 1957), section II, p. 86.
52. T.B. Macaulay, 'Essay on Mackintosh's History of the Revolution', *Critical and Historical Essays* (London and Glasgow: Collins, 1965), p. 189.

This can be adapted to say that the Revolutionist theory of international right, stripped of all its rhetorical disguise, is simply: that when you are in the ascendancy in international society you ought not to intervene against us, because it is your duty to respect the rights of states to regulate their own affairs freely; but when we are in the ascendancy we shall intervene against you, because it is our duty to encourage every people to conform their affairs to the doctrinal norm.

The theory of international right is primarily an issue between Revolutionists and Rationalists. A corresponding Realist theory can be constructed, without much difficulty, from Machiavelli, Carr and Morgenthau, to provide a setting for Talleyrand's dictum: 'Non-intervention is a political and metaphysical term meaning the same thing as intervention.'[53]

---

53. Quoted by Thomas Raikes, *A Portion of the Journal from 1831–1847* (London: Longman, 1856), vol. I, p. 106.

7: *Theory of diplomacy: foreign policy*

The theory of diplomacy signifies diplomacy in the widest sense of the term; it means not just intercourse between governments through their resident missions, but all international intercourse, its purposes and objects, in time of peace. If the theory of international society, which the three traditions see in different ways, is conceived as the statics of international relations, then the theory of diplomacy, and perhaps the theory of war also, may be seen as its dynamics.

Contractual theory

The idea of the social contract provided, in the seventeenth and eighteenth centuries, an explanation for the origins of society, and the requisite myth of political obligation; however it was never directly applied to international relations. But why should there not be a social contract between the societies themselves brought into existence by the several contracts? This had not happened; but why was it not recommended, or seen as desirable? This question presented itself to contract theorists, who comprised international lawyers as much as political philosophers, and in a sense they keep on coming back to it. A number of political thinkers contributed to the argument.

Machiavelli was a pre-contractual thinker; but the founders of international law, who established an anti-Machiavellian position, the Spanish neo-Scholastics who preceded Grotius, spoke of a society of nations or of mankind, and by so doing posed the question whether it was a society needing a contract. Vitoria (1480–1546) speaks of a *societas naturalis* of nations,[1] and in a dim way prefigures contract theory: the original state of nature saw common ownership; then the nations formed themselves and appropriated territories but as it were simultaneously and by mutual agreement, each nation reserving its

---

1. *Les Fondateurs du Droit International* (Paris: V. Giard & E. Brière, 1904), pp. 7–8.

natural rights to persist in international relations henceforward, such as the right of commerce. Suarez (1548–1617) speaks of mankind, however much divided into states, having a kind of political and moral unity. Even though each state is a perfect community, an organic whole, which is coherent and has everything it needs within itself, and no external superior, nevertheless it is a limb of the human race needing mutual aid, society and communication. Even if economic self-sufficiency were possible, free trade would be better for mankind as a whole.

Here there are already three notions: that an aggregate of nations is an international society; that a dim kind of social contract may bind them; but that states, however, are perfect communities. Grotius (1583–1645) like Suarez postulates an international society: the 'common society of the human race'; 'the great community' or 'great university'. In *De Iure Praedae* (The Law of Prize and Booty), he speaks of 'the city of the world, the society of the earth *'illa mundi civitas, societas orbis'*.[2] But he expressly says he does not believe in a super-state. He is the first writer after Dante to consider practically the possibility of a world-state (earlier writers had dismissed the claims of the Roman Empire as obsolete), but he warns against Dante's arguments that a world state would be advantageous for the human race: 'The advantages are in fact offset by the disadvantages. For as a ship may attain to such a size that it cannot be steered, so also the number of inhabitants and the distance between places may be so great as not to tolerate a single government.'[3]

Then comes Hobbes (1588–1679) and overturns it all at a blow. He 'discovered', or teaches, that international relations is no more than the state of nature, that is the Hobbesian state of nature, the pre-contractual conditions of a war of all against all, 'and the life of man solitary, poore, nasty, brutish and short'.[4] In the thirteenth chapter of *Leviathan*, having described the state of nature, he says it may be thought that such a condition never existed, but urges the reader to look at the savage people in North America, and the perpetual condition of sovereign states given their mutual fear, insecurity, and competition in armaments (p. 65). Later he says that the law of nations, which concerns the offices of one sovereign to another, is identical with the law of nature (both terms used differently from Grotius): 'And every sovereign hath the same right, in procuring the safety of his people, that any particular man can have, in procuring the safety of his own body.'[5] This identification of the state of nature

---

2. C. van Vollenhoven, *The Framework of Grotius' Book De Jure Belli ac Pacis* (1625) (Amsterdam: Uitgave van de N.V. Noord-Hollandsche Uitgeversmaatschappij, 1932), p. 11.
3. Hugo Grotius, tr. F.W. Kelsey, *De Jure Belli ac Pacis* (London: Wildy & Son Ltd., 1964), bk. II, ch. XIII, para. XIII, p. 552.
4. Thomas Hobbes, *Leviathan* (London: J.M. Dent & Sons Ltd.), ch. 13, p. 65.
5. ibid., p. 189.

with inter-state relations is also made in Hobbes' *De Cive*, and became a commonplace of international law through Pufendorf (1632–94).

Nature of international society

The Machiavellian is nominalist about international society: there is no 'international society', only a war of all against all. There is a states-system, a diplomatic system, which is an arena of power politics, and 'international society' which, as a legal fiction, is perhaps useful so long as you do not begin believing in it. What sort of a society could it be that comprised the Cold War? — and the Arab–Israeli situation? The latter may be compared to a primitive vendetta-ridden state of affairs as in Sicily, but in such a case already 'society' has a different meaning from its usual one, and international society differs as much again. 'The two most prominent character-istics of the international society are the fewness of its members and their heterogeneity,' wrote Brierly.[6] There are eighty-one members of the United Nations [in 1958/9; double the number in 1989/90 — Eds], probably the smallest aggregate to which the word 'society' has ever been applied; and the heterogeneity or inequality of its members is shown by the fiction of equality (except in the Security Council) between China and Belgium, the United States and Guatemala, or the Soviet Union and Mongolia. From these two characteristics, fewness and inequality, follow certain conclusions, which clear-sighted inter-national lawyers have drawn. Law proceeds by making general rules, seeing individuals as types of legal situations, and striking an average of society to which it applies. The smaller the numerical membership of a society, and the more various its members, the more difficult is it to make rules not unjust to extreme cases: this is one reason for the weakness of international law. As a *reductio ad absurdum*, imagine a society of four members: an ogre twenty feet high, flesh-eating, preferably human; an Englishman six feet high, speaking no Japanese; a Japanese samurai, a military noble, speaking no English; and a Central African pygmy, early palaeolithic; and all on an island the size of Malta. This is a parable of what is called international society.

As well as with the founders of international law, for the Machia-vellian too, international society is a society of perfect societies, because the state is the final term of political organization. This is not Hegelianism, but a matter of fact. The state is the body that affords the protection and organizes the welfare of its members. The majority of states today may well be tyrannical or corrupt, but would not the inhabitants of every state be worse off if that state dissolved

---

6. J.L. Brierly, *The Outlook for International Law* (Oxford: Clarendon Press, 1945), p. 40.

altogether?[7] Nobody is prepared to transfer the state's functions to an international body, neither its defence nor its welfare functions; even rebels (for example in Hungary in 1956) want a different state, not a loss of sovereignty, and show themselves just as jealous of statehood once in power.

For the Kantian, all this is abstract and unreal. The trouble arises from overlooking that all societies are comprised of men. These states, with their supposed finality, are only aggregates of human beings, and international society is only these same aggregates under a different aspect. None of them can be understood unless one first understands 'the laws of the human heart' (Rousseau). The state today is no more final than the city-state or a feudal principality; the Soviet Union is no more final than the Principality of Kiev or the Grand Duchy of Moscow; the United States no more so than the Seven Nations of the Iroquois; the United Kingdom no more so than the kingdom of Wessex. Moreover, the Machiavellian analysis is as usual not penetrating enough. To make a cogent case against the existence of international society one should point out that this supposed society has always been fuzzy at the edges, and of indistinct membership (and it might be argued that it is difficult to believe in the existence of a society whose membership you cannot clearly define). There has always been a margin of uncertainty about the family of nations, or society of states; look at Turkey and Russia in the seventeenth and eighteenth centuries, or China, Persia, Siam, and Japan in the nineteenth century. Only in this century has clarity appeared, and it is seen that international society is coterminous with all mankind: with this definition all the difficulties disappear.

Here the Grotian might intervene. He would agree with what has been said: of course societies are composed of individuals and of course international society equals mankind as a whole; but still, the discussion is specifically about the international problems of today, and what the Machiavellian says about international society is descriptively true. However what he says does not disprove international society to exist, but simply describes it. It *is* a society of other societies characterized by fewness and inequality, but this does not mean it is no society. There are several kinds of argument to show that international society is indeed a society; one of the most important is the existence of international institutions. It is clear that where there is *law*, there is a society; similarly where there are *institutions*, there is a society. 'Institutions' here does not mean determinate organizations housed in determinate buildings, such as the League of Nations in the Palais des Nations, or the United Nations in the East River building; but rather what historians and sociologists mean: 'Recognized and established usages governing the relations between individuals or

---

7. The more recent histories of the Lebanon and Uganda have shown the tragic effects of the virtual disappearance of the state. [Eds].

groups';[8] for example, 'property', or 'marriage'. An institution in this sense is 'an enduring, complex, integrated, organized behaviour pattern through which social control is exerted and by means of which the fundamental social desires or needs are met'.[9]

The Grotian would distinguish various institutions of international society which have been apparent since about 1500. Diplomacy itself is an institution for negotiations; alliances are an institution for effecting a common interest, for giving protection or exerting pressure; and the balance of power is an institution for maintaining the independence of members of international society. A guarantee is a unilateral offer of support or defence; and whereas an alliance is an arrangement of mutual obligation, a guarantee is a one-sided undertaking by a mediator, a pledge to uphold a particular settlement; for example Britain's guarantee of Belgian neutrality in 1839 or the tripartite guarantee of Israel's frontiers in 1950. Arbitration is an institution for the settlement of minor differences; and war is an institution for the final settlement of differences. These basic international institutions are combined in various degrees in the political structures such as the United Nations and the League of Nations, which are 'institutions' in the narrower sense; but they are recognized and established usages which have been traceable since the time of Machiavelli.

To this, the Machiavellian would answer that he is interested to see the traces of Realism in the Grotian's remarks; what he says about alliances, the balance of power and war needs separate discussion (and will be subjected to destructive analysis). Meanwhile he would comment thus on the legalism of the other categories: it is true that guarantees and arbitration play a part in diplomatic verbiage, but they are quite unreal. Nothing is ever done by reason of them that would not have been done without them; thus Britain went to war in 1914 in self-interest, not for Belgium; the Munich guarantee to Czechoslovakia in 1938 was to no effect, and nor was the tripartite guarantee to Israel in 1950. It is only by courtesy that they can be called 'established usages' of international life; everybody can remember examples of guarantees and arbitration precisely because they are so few and so exceptional. And only by courtesy can they be said to 'exercise social control' over states.

For the Machiavellian, by postulating institutions of this kind the Grotian begs the question. He argues that the institutions are evidence for international society, but they are *not* institutions in any acceptable sense, and the Machiavellian never believed in international society. He would abandon the notion of 'institutions' and talk rather of 'laws'. There are ways of behaviour in international relations, behaviour patterns, that have the character of political 'laws' (in a

8. Morris Ginsberg, *Sociology* (London: Thornton Butterworth Ltd., 1934), p. 42.
9. H.P. Fairchild, ed., *Dictionary of Sociology* (Iowa: Littlefield, Adams & Co., 1955), p. 157.

descriptive, not a normative sense), and these are a more satisfactory starting point for understanding the relations between states. They are descriptive laws concerning relationships.

The relation of victors and vanquished is the basic law, or 'institution', of international life. It underlies everything else: the relation between defensive powers and potential aggressors, or the status quo and revisionism, are only versions of it. This relationship was the great determining fact that underlay the history of the League of Nations. But, indeed, it has been recognized by every diplomatist and every statesman; thus Saburov wrote to Jomini on 12 May 1880:

To arrive at an era of lasting peace there must be victors and vanquished. That is the law of the world. In 1815 France was the great vanquished one. A European Concert was set up; but what was its character? It was a Concert of satisfied victors, which could last just so long as was necessary for the vanquished to recover and work for revenge. It lasted forty years.

Today (1880) the situation is not so very dissimilar. The vanquished is the same; there is a European Concert, but in the given situation, is it possible to find in it the stamp of sincerity? I do not think so. Under the appearance of general agreement is concealed the lack of real alliances.[10]

This is a penetrating passage because it brings out not only the basic relationship of victors and vanquished, but scarcely less the basic law that the common interest among victors disappears once victory has been achieved.

The second basic relationship is the pattern (rather than the balance) of power. There is a system of odds-and-evens (Namier) or a chequerboard system. It is a law of international politics that common frontiers are disputed frontiers, neighbours are enemies; your 'natural ally' is the power behind your neighbour. Hence there is a 'sandwich system of alliances' and, conversely, encirclement.[11] One can see the universal truth of this in the enmities and alliances that have existed between Portugal and Spain; Spain, France and Germany; France, England and Scotland; France, Germany and Russia; Egypt, Israel and Syria; or Afghanistan, Pakistan and India.[12] When the Afghan premier visited Delhi in January 1951, Rajagopalachari, the Indian Minister of Home Affairs said: 'It is no secret that our foreign policy holds Indo-Afghan friendship to be essential; and when we two are bound in friendship we will squeeze anyone in between in the same embrace of affection — a pincer movement for peace, so to speak.' Of course, this law must be interpreted intelligently, and there are cases when, for

10. J.Y. Simpson, *The Saburov Memoirs or Bismarck and Russia* (Cambridge: University Press, 1929), p. 137.
11. See L.B. Namier, *Conflict Studies in Contemporary History* (London: Macmillan & Co., 1942), p. 14.
12. Since the author wrote, the Indo-Soviet versus Sino-Pakistani linkages have provided an excellent example of the 'chequer-board' phenomenon [Eds].

obvious reasons, neighbours have been more inclined to friendship than enmity: the United States and Canada since 1815; Prussia and Russia in the era of Bismarck; Russia and China when faced with the greater threat of Japan. A corollary of this is that some states prefer to turn to a remoter ally, for example Turkey's friendship, through much of its modern history, first with Britain, and latterly with the United States.

At this point the Kantian can mediate, because he sees both laws and institutions in international politics. He regrets the Machiavellian's preoccupation with sterile, unpurposive conflict, and his insistence on postulating states as hard monolithic units. The Machiavellian is entirely concerned with horizontal relations of state against state; not with the class-structure of states and the class-structure of international society itself. Consider the first law, the relation of victor and vanquished: the principle is not at fault, but its application misses the real point. Who are the abiding victors and vanquished? It was remarked earlier how international society is fuzzy at the edges; ever since 1492 there has been a two-decker structure: the acknowledged (self-proclaimed) family of nations on the upper floor, which has exploited, levied tribute on, and submerged three-quarters of mankind on the bottom floor. What financed the Spanish conquests in the sixteenth century? — the Indies; and the English in the eighteenth century? — India and the slave trade. What financed the great powers of the Concert before 1914? — the colonial partition of the world. Here, the non-European and colonial peoples have been the perpetual vanquished, the international proletariat. The Machiavellian victor–vanquished relationships are like quarrels among elegant society in the drawing-room, oblivious of the misery below the stairs. What really does it matter in history if now France, now Germany is vanquished?

The Machiavellian argued that the victor–vanquished relationship underlay the period of the League of Nations, but let us see where it applies in the period of the United Nations. In the post-war era it is the victor–vanquished relation in this deep, social sense that has for the first time become the dominant theme of international relations, and thus has become ripe to be resolved. Now, for the first time, international society has become formally coterminous with the human race, and the hereditary vanquished have been emancipated. Here is a much deeper level of analysis than the Machiavellian attempts, and one that embodies an interpretation of international politics, because it shows in which direction international politics are going.

The second law, the pattern of power, is open to the same criticism: it is true as far as it goes. But the proper application of this principle is not in terms of arbitrary, sterile, geographical juxtapositions, but in terms of dynamic social movements and classes. Your natural ally is not the power on the other flank of your neighbour, but your neighbour's dissatisfied subjects. Palmerstonian Britain's natural affinities in the nineteenth century were with the liberal movements in Europe; America's natural affinities today are with the enslaved peoples of Eastern Europe; and Russia's today are with the remaining peoples in colonial bondage. It is this pattern of power in depth that gives meaning to international politics.

As to international institutions, the Kantian does not see much value in what the Grotian has said. He dislikes the implicit denigration of the United Nations by defining 'institution' so as to exclude it (after all, to most people the UN is the international institution *par excellence*); and he is astonished that the Grotian offers such hoary fallacies and obsolete delusions as the balance of power, and war (*war!*), as international institutions. As examples of international institutions (a 'behaviour pattern exerting social control') he would suggest two which he thinks far more important. First, the commercial spirit, 'which cannot exist with a state of war, and which sooner or later masters each nation'.[13] This is the same as Cobden's 'Free trade' ('free trade, peace, goodwill among Nations' is the Cobden club motto). It is a quaint shorthand for the whole process of social change, industrialization, and growing material interdependence which both the Grotian and Machiavellian neglect. The second institution is world public opinion, the most powerful of all in the long run. It brought about national self-determination from 1815, and has compelled colonial powers to dismantle their empires; it is the animating principle of the United Nations. It is shorthand, perhaps, for the whole process of intellectual change, education, and the growing spiritual and moral interdependence of mankind. Kant wrote: 'Enlightenment is a great good which must ever draw mankind away from the egoistic expansive tendencies of its rulers . . . it must by and by reach the throne, and have influence (even) upon the principles of government';[14] and: 'The maxims of philosophers . . . shall be consulted' [for they are enlightened public opinion].[15]

Principles of basic statecraft

(The term diplomacy shall be kept for the harder, more precise usage of negotiation between states.) It is important to remember that actual policies are products of situations, of the framework of necessity, as much as — even more than — principles or theories; yet differences of theoretical inclination can be discerned. One can attribute two basic principles to the Machiavellian and two counter-principles to the Grotian. The Machiavellian assumes the desirability of political self-sufficiency ('Go it alone'), and he adopts the principle of divide and rule. The Grotian assumes the desirability of co-operation, and adopts

---

13. Emmanuel Kant, *Perpetual Peace* (London: Peace Book Co., 1939), p. 41.
14. Carl J. Friedrich, ed., 'Idea for a Universal History with Cosmopolitan Intent', *The Philosophy of Kant* (New York: The Modern Library, 1949), p. 28.
15. ibid., p. 455.

the principle of concert. For the Machiavellian, the fundamentals of international life are fairly clear. There are well over one hundred power units called states co-existing and colliding on the surface of this planet without any political superior. They are in a constant state of mutual insecurity, their first concern is, and has to be, self-preservation, and they seek this, so far as they can, by self-sufficiency in defence, in weapons. Political self-sufficiency is not always attainable, but is ultimately desirable. There is a reality of conflicting interests in international affairs, and international relations are a struggle for power with certain recognised gambits; all relationships are relationships of power. Therefore the highest political good is to be independent, be a successful lone wolf, and go it alone. 'It is necessary to consider . . . whether a prince has such power that, in case of need, he can support himself with his own resources, or whether he has always need of the assistance of others.'[16] 'Princes ought to avoid as much as possible being at the discretion of any one.'[17]

Thus Canning wrote in 1823 to the British ambassador in St. Petersburg, when Castlereagh's congress system had finally broken down: '. . . and so things are getting back to a wholesome state again. Every nation for itself, and God for us all. Only bid your Emperor be quiet, for the time for Areopagus, and the like of that, is gone by.'[18] ('Each for himself and God for us all, as the elephant said when he danced among the chickens.)'[19] Bismarck in his Memoirs records that the Empress Maria of Russia remarked to a German diplomat, '*Votre amitié est trop platonique*', and observes: 'It is true that the friendship of . . . one Great Power for the others always remains Platonic to a certain extent; for no Great Power can place itself exclusively at the service of another.'[20]

This is not simply because dependence on, or service to, another power restrains one from 'going it alone' in the sense of pursuing one's own private interests; it is also because dependence on, or service to, another power involves one in that power's enmities, and limits the freedom to be friendly to other powers. Bismarck goes on: 'a Great Power will always have to keep in view not only existing, but future, relations to others, and must, as far as possible, avoid lasting fundamental hostility with any of them.' This basic desire not to be at the discretion of another, to be able to go it alone, is obviously present as a force tending to the break-up of military blocs and to the extension of the nuclear club.

---

16. Niccoló Machiavelli, *The Prince* (London: Dent & Sons Ltd., 1928), ch. X, p. 85.
17. ibid., ch. XXI, p. 181.
18. A.G. Stapleton, *George Canning and his Times* (London: John. W. Parker & Sons, 1859), p. 370.
19. G.L. Prestige quoting Henry Scott Holland in *The Life of Charles Gore* (London: W. Heinemann, 1935), p. 93.
20. Otto von Bismarck, tr. A.J. Butler, *Reflections and Reminiscences* (London: Smith, Elder & Co., 1898), vol. II, p. 235.

The Grotian would argue that this emphasis on strategic and military considerations gives a distorted, lop-sided view of international relations. Sometimes it leads to obvious error. It is plainly not true that powers normally seek self-sufficiency in defence and in isolation. They seek security in co-operation and defensive alliances, because in international society at any given time there are always more law-abiding powers, who want to see peace maintained, than aggressive powers, who want to upset things. This is the chief political common interest underlying international society, holding together the family of nations and tempering the anarchy you see. International co-operation is something experienced all the time, through economic commercial interdependence, cultural links, and the acceptance of humanitarian duties such as providing for famine-stricken regions now as in earlier times (Vattel). The Grotian will always tend to see a methodological failing in the Machiavellian, a selective viewpoint of pre-selected evidence or aspects and a narrowness of vision. Which is the more important and logically prior fact: that there are strains in NATO? or that there is a sufficient common purpose and co-operativeness among the Atlantic powers for NATO to have come into existence in the first place? It is worth noting the greatness and breadth of Bismarck who feared dependence on other powers not because it restrained one's sovereign right to be unfriendly to the world as circumstances required, but because it hampered one's sovereign need to be friendly to the world, to pursue the community of interests, as circumstances required.

Subordinate to this general contrast of positions there is another illustrative one. The Machiavellian, asserting self-sufficiency, maintains the principle that the outsider cannot judge; the Grotian, asserting interdependence, maintains the principle that society is an interested party, and has a valid judgement. That the outsider cannot judge is the familiar position of the Realist politician. To take two extreme examples: the Nazis insisted in the early 1930s that the outside world could not judge the Jewish problem in Germany; other peoples may have had more civilized Jews, and assimilated them, but the Germans had lived with their Jews through defeat and inflation and their Jews were a special problem. The South Africans today — the European and pink ones — insist that the outside world cannot judge what it is like for a small European community to live in the midst of a sea of vastly more numerous Africans. What do you know about it? It is outside your experience; who are you to judge?

Thus the Machiavellian's position is not only that involvement gives you an exclusive right to settle the matter as you see fit, without interference, but also that involvement gives you the exclusive insight into the nature of the dispute. Involvement entails knowledge, and this means objectivity, while detachment entails ignorance and this means bias. Thus during the conflict and complications surrounding Japan and the Manchurian question (1931–2), the Japanese consistently argued that outsiders lacked an understanding of the acute causes and nature of Sino-Japanese tension, and therefore were in a position neither to pass moral judgement on Japan's actions nor to declare the manner in which the controversy should be settled. The Japanese reply to the League Council (23 February 1932) was that if she had not 'unreservedly put herself in the hands' of the League, it was because 'she believes that she is naturally and necessarily in a far better position to appreciate the facts than any distant Power can possibly be'.[21] Similarly, the French were antagonized by the indignation and disapproval in the world press over Algeria. Those who had received letters from their sons serving in Algeria naturally supposed that *they* had an understanding of the reality whereas foreigners did not. The outside world does not know what it is talking about; outsiders cannot judge; the man on the spot knows best.

By contrast, for the Grotian, the outsider does have a valid judgement. This is a doctrine of general concern: no disputes or issues can be regarded as private, because in all of them society itself is an interested party, and consequently neutrals and outsiders have a right to judge. Moreover, such a position has not only this moral side, but also an epistemological one; it makes an assumption about political knowledge. It involves a negative premiss: that involvement entails not knowledge and insight, but a deformation of judgement. Neither men nor states are good judges in their own causes, and men trained by a special experience have their vision limited by the special character of that experience. There is a Grotian tradition of suspicion of experts. Thus Lord Cecil said: 'Lawyers were obstructing international arbitration in the same measure as naval experts were hampering international disarmament',[22] and, 'I am not so much afraid of the Common people. It is the experts who give me qualms'.[23] Lord Salisbury wrote to Lord Lytton, in 1877:

No lesson seems to me to be so deeply inculcated by the experience of life as that you should never trust experts. If you believe the doctors, nothing is wholesome; if you believe the theologians, nothing is innocent; if you believe the soldiers, nothing is safe. They all require to have their strong wine diluted by a very large admixture of insipid common sense;[24]

and Palmerston: 'When I wish to be misinformed about a country I ask the man who has lived there thirty years.'[25] Too great familiarity can hinder just observation, and not only does involvement lead to distorted knowledge, but non-involvement is almost a necessary

21. *League of Nations Official Journal*, Jan.–June 1932 (London: G. Allen & Unwin Ltd.), p. 385.
22. *The Times*, 12 May 1929.
23. *News Chronicle*, 10 April 1946.
24. Lady Gwendolen Cecil, *Life of Robert, Marquis of Salisbury* (London: Hodder & Stoughton, 1921), vol. II, p. 153.
25. Quoted by A.P. Thornton, *The Imperial Idea and its Enemies* (London: Macmillan & Co. Ltd., 1959), p. 41.

ingredient of clear knowledge. To judge correctly, one must remain an outsider, though a well-informed one.

The principle of divide-and-rule is fundamental to Machiavellian statecraft. The phrase becomes current in the sixteenth century; it is the '*diviser pour régner*' of Catherine de Medici; and much used throughout the nineteenth century. The principle was first formulated by Philip de Commynes of Louis XI (1461–83). 'King Louis our master understood breaking and dividing of leagues better than any prince that I ever knew' . . . 'he was a perfect master in that science.'[26] He was given advice by Francesco Sforza, duke of Milan (1450–1466), which he valued as much as military assistance: to break up the confederacy of his enemies by any terms whatsoever, to break up their forces, but to keep his own forces intact.[27]

Divide-and-rule is a principle with two applications: it applies with regard to subordinates or subjects, in colonial policy or towards satellites; this is its original sense. Secondly it applies with regard to equals as a policy in international relations, in foreign policy. As regards subordinates or subjects, in colonial policy, the Machiavellian would say that it is manifestly a method followed in fact by most imperial powers. Traditional Chinese policy is expressed in the proverb, 'use barbarians to check barbarians'; and the Byzantine Empire had the same policy, of inciting or subsidizing foreign tribes to attack one another: 'First, I seek to explain what are the nations that can aid or injure the Romans . . . which of them can be fought and conquered; how this is to be done in each case, and what other nation should be used for the purpose.'[28] 'It was a basic rule in Byzantine foreign politics to induce some other nation to oppose the enemy, and so to cut down the expenses and risks of a war.'[29]

The same rule was followed by the British in India. During the Mutiny all larger native (protected) states remained loyal, either because they were more backward and there was less popular discontent, or because they had a shrewder understanding of the reserves of British strength. After the Mutiny, the former British policy of annexing native states, and the belief that direct administration within British India was superior to that of any native states, disappeared, and they became built into the structure of the Raj.[30] Checker-boarding all India, they became like a network of friendly fortresses in debatable territory, 'loyal' obstacles to another rebellion sweeping India. Again

26. Philip de Commynes, tr. A.R. Scoble, *French Memoirs* (London: Henry G. Bohn, 1855), vol. I, p. 89.
27. ibid., p. 52.
28. Ernest Barker, *Social and Political Thought in Byzantium* (Oxford: Clarendon Press, 1957), p. 102.
29. Steven Runciman, *Byzantine Civilisation* (London: Edward Arnold & Co., 1936), p. 158.
30. V.A. Smith, *The Oxford History of India* (Oxford: Clarendon Press, 1919), pp. 721–2, 739.

the British played off the 'loyal' Mohammedan minority against the disaffected Hindu majority. Was either policy conscious and deliberate or was it pursued in absence of mind? In 1909 the Indian Councils Act (the Morley-Minto reforms) first introduced communal representation into the legislative council, that is, representation for special interests and minorities. Lady Minto in her journal artlessly records a letter from an official: '. . . a very, very big thing has happened today. A work of statesmanship that will affect India and Indian history for many a long year. It is nothing less than the pulling back of 62 millions of people from joining the ranks of the seditious opposition.'[31] Ultimately this policy led to the creation of Pakistan; but it is probably to be attributed not to any Machiavellian policy but to circumstances. Indirect rule in colonial policy postponed colonial unity; it slowed up the process of political sophistication. In the Middle East, too, Britain played off the Jews against the Arabs; and the desert nationalism of Hussein's sons in Jordan and Iraq against the middle-class urban nationalism of the cities in Palestine and Iraq (just as she played off the native states in India, which were easier to deal with, against Congress).

The Latin Americans accuse the United States of a similar policy in Latin America. Bolivar summoned the first inter-American congress at Panama in 1826 to create a common policy in foreign affairs. This was boycotted by the United States, which declared 'we are the American system'. There is a Latin American belief that the United States has played off Brazil against Argentina, dictators against democracies, and reactionaries against liberals; though to a detached eye American policy might seem aimed more to keep the European powers out of Latin America (the Monroe Doctrine), and thereafter to wield supremacy by the unscrupulous methods she condemned in other powers. For Soviet Russia there is the problem of national self-determination in central and southern Asia, and whether the peoples there form a single potential nationality because they speak Turkic languages. The Russians have long disliked the pan-Turk and pan-Turanian movement. When Enver Pasha led a revolt against the Bolshevik rule in central Asia in the early 1920s, the Soviet government had to make a practical administrative decision, and it decided on a multi-national rather than a pan-Turk solution. In 1947 Dimitrov (the Bulgarian) was the prime mover of projects for a South Slav union, especially between Bulgaria and Yugoslavia. In January 1948, *Pravda* damned federations and customs unions; what these countries needed, it said, was the maintenance of independence through a strengthening of internal democratic forces.[32] Tito accused Stalin of

31. Mary, Countess of Minto, *India, Minto and Morley 1905–10* (London: Macmillan & Co. Ltd., 1934), pp. 47–8.
32. Peter Calvocoressi, *Survey of International Affairs 1947–1948* (London: Oxford University Press, 1952), p. 175.

'divide-and-rule' and attributed his own expulsion from the Cominform to the growing tendency to unity of south-east Europe. The principle could also be seen in French policy in Syria and Lebanon. The invention of the Lebanon as a Christian Arab state, with a different past from Syria in general, meant that Christian Arabs, who had been the pioneers of Arab nationalism, were now diverted and equipped with a minority consciousness and fears of being swamped by Arab unity.

The principle of divide-and-rule is often attributed to Machiavelli but this is only partially true. In the Discourses he says: 'To attack a divided city in the hope that its divisions will facilitate the conquest of it is bad policy.'[33] He argues that disunity in a republic is due to idleness and peace, but unity is the result of war and fear, therefore it is foolish to hope that your enemies will be paralysed by their divisions in war-time (as Hitler seems to have hoped Britain and the United States would be); the much more likely effect of war is to arouse to a united effort. One gets the better of divided cities not by attack, but 'by the artifices men use in time of peace'.

The way to set about this is to win the confidence of the city which is disunited; and to act as arbitrator between the parties so long as they do not come to blows, and if they do come to blows begin fighting to give tardy support to the weaker party, both with a view to keeping them at it and wearing them out; and, again, because stronger measures would make it clear that you were out to subjugate them yourself.[34]

This is the economical and discreet employment of divide-and-rule to gain ascendancy, in limited circumstances. As to the use of this policy to maintain ascendancy, he condemns it: 'Those who hold that to retain possession of cities one must needs keep them divided . . . are mistaken.'[35] He then describes how unity may be restored and stresses the futility of trying to keep subject cities divided. To do so will lower the standard of political life in the subject city and probably retroactively corrupt political life in your own republic, as when, in our own times, the policy of promoting a European settlement in Africa led to the situation where the Conservatives thought themselves patrons of the settlers, and Labour, patrons of the Africans; or when the Irish question, in 1912–14, led to Ulster nearly wrecking British politics.[36]

Moreover, when war comes, the enemy will have a fifth column in a divided city, in the faction which hates you most. This was

33. Niccoló Machiavelli, *The Discourses of Niccoló Machiavelli* (London: Routledge Kegan Paul, 1950), bk. II, ch. 25, p. 435.
34. ibid., p. 436.
35. ibid., bk. III, ch. 27, p. 540.
36. Keith Hancock, *Survey of British Commonwealth Affairs* (London: Oxford University Press, 1937), vol. I, pp. 466–7.

emphasized in the *Prince*:

This may have been well enough in those times when Italy was in a way balanced, but I do not believe that it can be accepted as a precept for today, because I do not believe that factions can ever be of use; rather, it is certain that when the enemy comes upon you in divided cities you are quickly lost, because the weakest party will always assist the outside forces and the other will not be able to resist.[37]

Here we have a good illustration of how far Machiavelli was from cheap Machiavellianism, and how his recommendations are more penetrating, and one jump ahead, of his self-appointed disciples. Machiavelli had seen the states-system of small states in Italy overwhelmed by the larger, more backward kingdoms outside, as Europe has been by the United States and Russia. The ultimate test he applied to all policies was, how will it stand up in the supreme crisis, when the state is threatened with total conquest? His conclusion in this case, in a word, was that divide-and-rule as a maxim in colonial policy, with subject peoples, is self-defeating and dangerous, because it invited your enemy to adopt divide-and-rule against you in foreign policy.

The Grotian counter-principle is that of concert; but first of all the Grotian provides a critique of divide-and-rule. It is a characteristic crudity of Machiavellian thinking to judge actions by their results, and, more particularly, to infer intentions from results. If a political pattern is apparent which can be described as one power ruling by dividing, playing off groups or powers against one another, then the Machiavellian assumes at once that the power had such a purpose. But this need not be so, and it must not be assumed to be so without adequate evidence. If Louis XI told Commynes that it was his master-principle to break up hostile coalitions, then that is true of Louis XI (though in fact there is nothing in Commynes to prove it was not his own interpretation). If there is documentary historical evidence that the India Office or the Governor-General in India formulated a policy of playing off the Muslims against the Hindus (or the Colonial Office the Jews against the Arabs), then British policy in India (or the Middle East) must be interpreted in this light; but if such evidence is lacking, there is no need to accept this interpretation, and perhaps there is a duty not to, in proportion as other interpretations are available. It became part of the Soviet charges against the West after 1945 that the Western Powers had wanted Germany and Russia to exhaust themselves in the war on the Eastern Front, leaving the Western powers as *tertius gaudens*. This is essentially a historical question: if there is documentary evidence that Roosevelt or Churchill had this intention the charge is proved; if the proof is lacking, then Molotov was wrong, and the evidence of minor figures talking thus is irrelevant. Of course a policy of divide-

---

37. Niccoló Machiavelli, *The Prince*, p. 169 (cf. Discourses, vol. III, ch. 27, p. 542).

and-rule is possible, but note that it has a pejorative flavour. On the whole it is a polemical formula, a charge, which describes your rivals' policies rather than your own: there is a consensus of reprobation and disapproval about it. Aristotle describes divide-and-rule in the *Politics* as the policy of the tyrant: 'Still another line of policy is to sow mutual distrust and to foster discord between friend and friend; between people and notables; between one section of the rich and another.'[38] He also describes it as a mistake in the policy of demagogues and oligarchs to divide the state into two.[39]

A policy of divide-and-rule is not a necessary inference from the existence of political divisions. For example, political divisions might be due to considerations of administrative convenience or efficiency; there are many good administrative arguments for smaller units of government, just as there are for larger. The decision of the Soviet government to treat central Asia as a region of several sub-nationalities rather than one large pan-Turkic nationality may have been primarily due to the practical requirements of handling a large agrarian or nomadic population scattered over a vast area. Again, political divisions might be due to considerations of natural right: the right of minorities to develop their independent existence without being swamped and dissolved in alien majorities. (It has been noted already that the Grotian believes political variety, or multiformity, to be a good *in se*.) 'The combination of different nations in one state is as necessary a condition of civilised life as the combination of men in society.'[40]

The linguistic fragmentation of India since independence provides a large part of the explanation for the appearance of divide-and-rule in British colonial policy there. British (and Dutch) colonial administrations in Asia and Africa made great use of anthropologists; thus they came to understand the minorities (for example the Nagas on the Indo-Burmese frontier) and on the whole left them alone. Colonial nationalists saw this as a policy of divide-and-rule; having acquired independence, they ignored the anthropologists and tried to assimilate the minorities to their new nation-state. For example, the British had patronized the Karens in Burma, and for the first time the Karens felt free to move to the plains and the delta. Christian missionaries had been successful among them, and had recruited extensively for the British military force in Burma; many remained loyal in the Second World War, serving with the British and Americans, and suffering reprisals from the pro-Japanese among the Burmese. With independence, the Karens demanded an autonomous state and revolted in

38. Aristotle, tr. E. Barker, *The Politics of Aristotle* (Oxford: Clarendon Press, 1946), p. 245.
39. ibid., p. 233.
40. John E. Dalberg-Acton, 'Nationality', *The History of Freedom and other Essays* (London: Macmillan & Co. Ltd., 1922), p. 290.

1948; it was the worst rebellion the Union government suffered. British sympathy with the 'loyal' Karens was expressed unofficially, but the British government and ambassador helped the Burmese Union government by reporting on private adventurers and supplying it with arms.[41]

For the Grotian, the true principle of statecraft should be unite and influence, as the example of the Karens and Burmese shows. It is not a portmanteau principle like divide-and-rule pretends to be; it is limited in its application by the natural rights of the groups one seeks to unite. Another example is the foundation of the League of Arab States by the British Foreign Office in 1943, during the war. It believed that it would be easier to deal with a united satisfied state than with a multitude of frustrated small ones, convinced their unity was obstructed. The Machiavellian interpretation is that Britain aimed to strengthen the Arab moderates, who believed in co-operation with Britain, against the zealots and radicals; and to remove the Palestine question from the political arena.

The principle of unite-and-influence rests on two assumptions: that goodwill can evoke friendship and reciprocal goodwill; and that common interests can be found and from these co-operation will flow. This is the principle of concert, in nineteenth-century language. There is a tradition running through British foreign policy of the nineteenth century of trying to work with the power whose independent action was most feared; this was done by Canning, Palmerston, and Gladstone, and the power was usually Russia. Canning in 1826 sent Wellington to St. Petersburg over the Greek question; independent Russian action against Turkey was feared, and the Russian partnership invoked. The Duke's instructions were to achieve a 'confidential concert between Russia and England'[42] to prevent or postpone war. Palmerston followed this policy in the Mehemet Ali crisis of 1839–40, believing it was better not to leave to Russia alone the task of defending Constantinople: '. . . it seemed to me that there was no wise medium between confidence and distrust: and that if we tie up Russia by treaty we may trust her, and trusting her, we had better mix no evidence of suspicion with our confidence.'[43]

Gladstone referred to these precedents in the Balkan crisis of the 1870s. The best way of watching Russia or Austria is to become competitors with them for the affections of the Christian nations in south-east Europe. When two great powers enter into an alliance for a common object, they not only assist one another, but act as a check upon one another (speech in St. James's Hall, London, December

---

41. See Hugh Tinker, *The Union Of Burma* (London: Oxford University Press, 1957).
42. R.W. Seton-Watson, 'Wellington Despatches, 10 February 1826', *Britain in Europe 1789–1914* (Cambridge: University Press, 1937), p. 109.
43. H.L. Bulwer, 'Letter of H.L. Bulwer, 24 September 1839', *The Life of Henry John Temple, Viscount Palmerston* (London: Richard Bentley, 1871), vol. II, p. 301.

1876).[44] In a further speech in 1879, on the theory of the concert of Europe, Gladstone said that: 'by keeping all [powers] in union together you neutralize and fetter and bind up the selfish aims of each . . . common action means common objects; you cannot unite powers except for objects connected with the common good of them all.'[45] Here the two assumptions of unite-and-influence (goodwill can evoke goodwill; common interests can be found) are joined by a third: common action neutralizes antagonisms and selfish aims, and establishes a system of mutual checks.[46] This is the most elaborate theoretical formulation of the principle of concert in the nineteenth century, and it is the foundation of the doctrine of collective security. One can see its vitality today in the idea that the West should compete with Russia for the affections of the uncommitted world.

Hitherto we have followed a two-sided dialogue between the Machiavellian and the Grotian. The Kantian principles of basic state-craft are somewhat different. Instead of assuming the desirability of political self-sufficiency, like the Machiavellian, or of political interdependence, like the Grotian, the Kantian assumes the desirability of abolishing foreign politics altogether; and instead of the principle of divide-and-rule, or that of concert, he adopts isolationism. The Kantian, as we have seen, would abolish foreign policy; he is fundamentally a disbeliever in international society, and a believer rather in mankind. The organization of international society into states is for him tedious, trivial and transitory; it is bound to pass away, and all foreign policies and the diplomatic system itself are so many obsolescent obstructions to the free working of the 'commercial spirit' (growing material interdependence) and of world public opinion (growing moral interdependence). It is natural therefore that the primary instinct of the Kantian is to sweep away the whole of the traditional diplomatic system, to step out of it, as out of rags, and clothe himself in beliefs and ideology alone.

Trotsky was made the first Soviet Commissar for Foreign Relations because he was the right man 'to confront Europe' on behalf of the Revolution; but he described his programme thus: 'I will issue a few revolutionary proclamations to the peoples of the world and then shut up shop.'[47] Similar ideas were expressed in the French Revolution. When the Republican war party, the Brissotins and Girondins,

44. *The Times*, 9 December 1876.
45. E.R. Jones, ed. 'Right Principles of Foreign Policy' (West Calder Midlothian, 27 November 1879), *Selected Speeches on British Foreign Policy 1738–1914* (London: Oxford University Press, 1924), p. 372.
46. Lady Gwendolen Cecil, *The Life of Robert, Marquis of Salisbury*, vol. II, pp. 331–2.
47. L.D. Trotski's Autobiography 'Moya Zhizn' (Berlin, 1930), vol. II, p. 64. Quoted by E.H. Carr, *The Bolshevik Revolution 1917–1923* (London: Macmillan & Co. Ltd., 1953), vol. III, p. 16.

overthrew the Royalist peace party, the Feuillants, in March 1792, their foreign minister was Dumouriez.[48] He expounded his policy in a memorandum written the year before and read it at the Jacobin Club. Of all the departments of state, he said, the Foreign Ministry is the least complicated and involves the least mystery. French foreign relations should be based on the Declaration of the Rights of Man. A great, free righteous people was the natural ally of every people in Europe; it should not have separate alliances binding it to the fate, interests, or passions of this and that people. Within fifty years at most all Europe would be republican and a new diplomacy, open and above-board, would dissipate the mysteries and intrigues of the old.[49]

Mazzini's standpoint in the Risorgimento against Cavour was exactly the same. Cavour was a master-diplomatist, a great practical Machiavellian, whose aim was to aggrandize Piedmont by utilizing Italian national sentiment. He wanted simply to make Italy independent of Austrian control, and as late as 1856 he dismissed the idea of Italian unity as sheer nonsense. Italian unification as it was actually achieved in 1859–60 was a triumph of opportunism, of an empirical muddling through; the only firm framework of his policy was his alliance with Napoleon III (even if it proved not so firm later), towards whom he was as Syngman Rhee or Chiang Kai-shek to the United States in the 1950s. Passionately opposed to him was Mazzini, the Gandhi of the nineteenth century, and saint of nationalism. For him pure passionate idealism was enough; he had an honest faith in a mission or a principle, in the myth of 'Italy', or 'Young Italy', and believed that its practical expression was popular insurrection. If one could purify the hearts of the people, and teach them of their sacred national cause, then they would spontaneously arise, and their oppressors, the Austrian and the Italian, would flee, and the nation be free. He was disgusted with Cavour's 'Machiavellianism' and diplomatic calculus; he believed diplomacy was always useless and generally harmful. In September 1860 he believed the French alliance might fail at any moment; and a nice calculation of what was possible or expedient was simply a paralysing influence against action: 'Diplomacy signifies the treaties of 1815 . . . Nice and Savoy snatched away from Italy . . . Diplomacy means a wavering indecision before the idea of unity . . . and negotiations with the Bourbons at Naples . . . Diplomacy means leaving Garibaldi to fight his battles alone.'[50] The struggle between Mazzini and Cavour is fascinating. It provides the fullest

48. Dumouriez was later the victor of Valmy, and conqueror of Belgium, although he failed to conquer Holland; he became a traitor to the Revolution and lived in exile in England from 1800 to 1822 and died aged 83. He is buried at Henley.
49. J.M. Thompson, *Leaders of the French Revolution* (Oxford: Basil Blackwell, 1932), p. 256.
50. From *L'Unita Italiana* (Florence), 1 September 1860, quoted in D. Mack Smith, *Cavour and Garibaldi 1860* (Cambridge: University Press, 1954), p. 247.

theoretical debate in the history of international politics between the school of diplomacy (Machiavelli–Cavour), and the school of anti-diplomacy (Kant-Mazzini), each side having its outstanding protagonist. It also shows the most striking practical successes of anti-diplomacy, in Garibaldi's conquest of Sicily and Naples.

The same puritanical aversion from diplomacy is the ideological basis of American isolationism. This isolationism is not simply due to being in the position of a self-sufficient great power, geographically remote and inviolable, and exploiting a virgin continent; it springs also from the conception of the United States as a new society, the exemplar of mankind, with a permanent revolution.

A free, enlightened, and . . . great nation [giving] mankind the magnanimous and too novel example of a people always guided by an exalted justice and benevolence . . . [That is why] the great rule of conduct for us in regard to foreign nations is, in extending our commercial relations to have with them as little *political* connection as possible . . . Why, by interweaving our destiny with that of any part of Europe, entangle our peace and prosperity in the toils of European ambition, rivalship, interest humor, or caprice?[51]

Washington's farewell address (1796) was typified by Wilson, both in his personal character and in his policy. Personally, the process of negotiation and compromise was repugnant to him; whether at Princeton or in the White House, he could not bend, only break, and his characteristic policy was not negotiation, but an appeal to public opinion, over the heads of the opposite government to *their* public. This follows from the abolition of diplomacy.[52] If world public opinion is the greatest international institution, then you break through the cobwebs of diplomacy and frankly appeal to it.

F.D. Roosevelt was not incapable of negotiation or compromise — he was a great 'fixer'. He appealed to world public opinion less than Wilson, less even than Churchill, but there was in him a characteristic distrust of formal diplomacy. Thus he conceived of the Second World War as a purely military act abstracted from any diplomatic context at all, a 'war without diplomacy'. He saw the British concern with the diplomatic context as a concern for subtle intrigue and Victorian imperialism. At Tehran he told Elliot Roosevelt that he was not interested in 'real or fancied British interests on the continent of Europe. We are at war and our job is to win it as fast as possible, and without adventures.'[53] But why did 'we' want to win the war? What were these 'adventures' but measures to create the kind of diplomatic

51. George Washington in Ruhl J. Bartlett, *The Record of American Diplomacy* (New York: Alfred A. Knopf, 1947), pp. 86–8.
52. It is illustrated by Woodrow Wilson in Europe and Rome, December–January 1918–19 and his earlier appeals to the Central Powers, as well as Trotsky as People's Commissar for Foreign Affairs from 1917 onwards.
53. Elliot Roosevelt, *As He Saw It* (New York: Duell Sloan Pearce, 1946), p. 186.

context, or political pattern, he wanted after the war? Another consequence of the Kantian dislike for diplomacy is the devaluation or
demoting of diplomatic activity and of the formal diplomatist. This is
one cause of the decreasing autonomy of the diplomatist today.
Roosevelt was his own Secretary of State: Cordell Hull made trade
treaties but was kept ignorant. US ambassadors were public relations
officers for the American way of life, with no pretence of the slightest
professional competence. And in the Soviet Union the process has
been comparable. Since the Bolshevik Revolution the foreign ministry
has had no independence; Chicherin, Foreign Commissar from 1918 to
1930, was constantly overridden by the Politburo with frequent
competition from the Comintern. Litvinov said: 'You know what I am:
I merely hand on diplomatic documents';[54] Molotov attained the
greatest independence; Khrushchev acted as his own foreign minister,
while Gromyko under him was an official only. In the 1950s the
clearest example of the abolition of diplomacy was Moscow's call to
'the world at large for nuclear disarmament'.

Instead of divide-and-rule or concert the Kantian adopts a stance of
moral isolationism. The Kantian state is the embodiment of pure right,
the vehicle of practical reason; therefore, repudiating diplomacy and
appealing to world public opinion, it must keep itself undefiled by
contrast with other states. In 1848, when Lombardy and Venice rose
against the Austrians, Carlo Alberto published a manifesto of support:
'. . . that God who, with such marvellous impulses, enables Italy to
work out her own salvation.' *Italia farà da se*[55] became the national
watchword till disaster proved it fallacious. There was an intense desire
to owe independence to nobody but themselves. Nehru said in 1949:
'India is an independent country and does not wish to go with a begging
bowl to others.'[56]

That India matured in a short time was seen in her subsequent
readiness to go with a begging bowl for aid, but the vestiges of moral
isolationism were seen as late as Nehru's statement in 1960 when at a
Congress Party conference in Bangalore he said he welcomed the
Chinese challenge in the hope it would shake up people. 'Is India so
weak . . . that ultimately we must appeal to our people to rely on others
to help them? I would sooner this Congress was dead.'[57] He wished for
no alliances: *India farà da se.* In similar vein, the Action Française
slogan in 1940–45 was '*La France seule*', and this was an ingredient in
de Gaulle's position. The Soviet 'Socialism in One Country' also had this

---

54. See Sir Lewis Namier, *Personalities and Powers* (London: Hamish Hamilton, 1955),
pp. 122–3.
55. Bolton King, *A History of Italian Unity* (London: James Nisbet & Co. Ltd., 1899), vol.
I, p. 192.
56. *The Hindu*, 29 March 1949.
57. 'Bangalore Session of the Indian National Congress', Keesing's *Contemporary
Archives*, vol. XII, 1959–60, p. 17288.

Table 1   Machiavellian and Kantian statecraft

	Machiavellian	**Kantian**
Colonial	Divide-and-Rule vertically	Assimilate-and-Rule
International	Balance of Power	Divide-and-Rule horizontally

negative external aspect of moral isolationism till 1934. But is this not simply a version of the Machiavellian principle of self-sufficiency, or a 'go it alone'? It is passive and withdrawn rather than active and aggressive, but perhaps there is not even that distinction.

There are other similarities with Machiavellianism: Kantian statecraft has its own version of divide-and-rule. Appealing over the heads of governments to their peoples is horizontal divide-and-rule instead of vertical; it is divide-and-rule in depth rather than breadth and there is a distinction (see Table 1). One way of measuring the lapse of a revolutionary state from pure Kantianism is to mark the decline in its horizontal divide-and-rule policy. One can enquire further into this similarity: between the Machiavellian go it alone and divide-and-rule, and the Kantian abolition of diplomacy, *fará da se*, and divide-and-rule. It appears that Kantian statecraft approximates to Machiavellian statecraft; indeed in the twentieth-century Grotian statecraft approximates to Kantian and Kantian to Machiavellian. This is an ineluctable drift in the present age. It would seem that the difference between the Machiavellian and the Kantian is insignificant; Stalin and Hitler were both Machiavellians, so why have a third category? Part of the answer is that this is an approximation rather than identity. Kantian politics can surprise the observer who interprets them as Machiavellian, by reverting to their first principles. It is easier to outwit or even check a Machiavellian than a Kantian. For example if Mussolini had been a pure Machiavellian he would have been detachable from Hitler, but he believed in his creed: 'Mussolini the Fascist had conquered Mussolini the Italian.'

Interrelation of the traditions

There is overlapping and indistinctiveness between the three traditions. Each tradition can be subdivided into two or more (see Figure 3), and they dove-tail; thus Grotians and Machiavellians agree in being Realist, in accepting the facts of the world of politics, although they differ in what they bring under the heading of 'fact'. Grotians and Kantians agree in being idealist, in pursuing ideals in the world of politics, although they differ in their estimate of the power of ideals and in their method of attaining them (see Table 2).

MACHIAVELLIAN

Aggressive | Defensive

Revolutionary | Realist

KANTIAN | Evolutionary | Idealist | GROTIAN

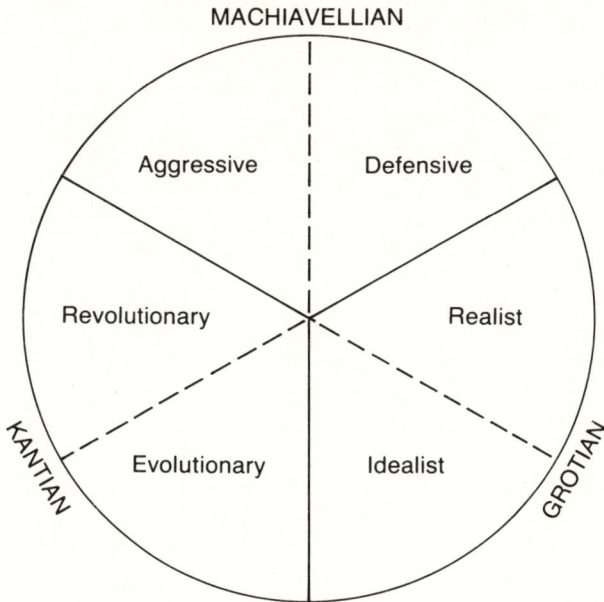

Figure 3   Subdivisions of the traditions

A conflict between the traditions lies in the emphasis placed on the importance of facts as against ideas, and of men as against ideals. The defensive Machiavellian believes that men, not ideas, guide the world. Saburov wrote to Jomini, in May 1880, that politics is the sphere of human passions, the fortuitous clash of wills, and history is the sphere of ideas, producing philosophy retrospectively. 'Ideas are only of service [to men] as munitions. They load telegrams and speeches with them just as you load muskets and cannon with powder.'[58] Mussolini, an aggressive Machiavellian, said with shrewd peasant realism, 'political doctrines pass; peoples remain';[59] and Stalin, a revolutionary Kantian echoed this: 'Only the people are immortal. Everything else is transient. That is why we must be able to value the confidence of the people.'[60]

In contrast, consider the comment of Wilson, an evolutionary Kantian, that 'Men die but ideas live', which he made to Colonel House on his first arrival in Paris in December 1918, when House

---

58. J.Y. Simpson, *The Saburov Memoirs of Bismarck and Russia* (Cambridge: University Press, 1929), p. 136.
59. Quoted in D.A. Binchy, *Church and State in Fascist Italy* (London: Oxford University Press, 1941), p. 353.
60. Quoted in George Plekhanov, *The Role of the Individual in History* (London: Lawrence & Wishart Ltd., 1940), preface, p. 8.

Table 2 Exemplars

	Machiavellian		Grotian		Kantian	
	Aggressive	*Defensive*	*Realist*	*Idealist*	*Evolutionary*	*Revolutionary*
	Cavour early Bismarck	late Bismarck Salisbury	Churchill	Gladstone late Nehru Lincoln	Wilson	Mazzini
					early Nehru	Lenin
	Hitler Mussolini Welensky		Acheson Morgenthau		Dulles Mboya	Hitler Nasser Verwoerd Stalin
					Khrushchev?	

	Idealist	*Realist*
	Mazzini Wilson Nasser early Nehru	Lenin Stalin Hitler

Query: Palmerston?
De Gaulle
Metternich
Dulles

	Machiavellian		Kantian		Grotian	
	Aggressive	*Defensive*	*Revolutionary*	*Evolutionary*	*Revolutionary*	*Idealist*	*Realist*
		Dulles De Gaulle		Dulles		Metternich Palmerston

Note: The names are positioned as in the author's original diagram. Eds.

pessimistically pointed out the obstacles to world security.[61] Similarly, the last words of Sturzo, an ideal Grotian, to the Turin congress in 1923 were: 'Victory belongs to the ideal, not to us; defeat falls on us, not on the ideal.'[62]

Such patterns of dove-tailing and contrasts can be seen in other areas. The Grotian and the Kantian agree that history has a purpose and meaning. The Kantians may regard history as the totality of mankind surging forward and individuals getting trampled underfoot, while Grotians see history as a field in which individuals find their several purposes or meanings and are sceptical about the meaning of the whole; but at least they agree in a sense of history as dynamic, and the individual as having responsibility in it. The Machiavellian however regards history as static or cyclic, and the individual scrapes what corner or burrow in life he can.

Although they disagree in their theory of history, the Machiavellian and Kantian agree that politics have their origin in sin; they believe in the Augustinian doctrine of the state as *'poena et remedium pecati'* — punishment and remedy against sin — like an age-long Borstal or approved school.

Remota itaque justitia, quid sunt regna, nisi magna latrocinia? . . .[63]

In the absence of justice, what is sovereignty but organized brigandage? . . . The answer which a captured pirate gave to the celebrated Alexander the Great was perfectly accurate and correct. When that king asked the man what he meant by infesting the sea, he boldly replied: 'What you mean by warring on the whole world. I do my fighting on a tiny ship, and they call me a pirate; you do yours with a large fleet, and they call you Commander'.[64]

In a secularized version, this comes down to Machiavelli and Hobbes, who find the origin of the state in the badness of men; its essential purpose is to *restrain* men, whether from their greed, violence, or folly. The Machiavellian and Kantian agree in seeing politics as dominated by human rapacity and stupidity, but Kantians see it in a special way, as the rapacity of a special set of men, which explains why 'man is born free but is everywhere in chains' (Rousseau). In other words, Machiavellians believe that the sinful nature of politics is unchangeable, Kantians believe it *can* be changed. Against them both is the Grotian (Aquinas as against Augustine), who believes that

---

61. Thomas Jones, review of Stephen Bonsal, *Unfinished Business* (New York: Double-day, Doran Co., 1944), *Observer*, 15 October 1944.
62. Don Luigo Sturzo, (1871–1959), Sicilian priest and then leader of the 'Populari': the Christian Democrats, quoted in D.A. Binchy, *Church and State in Fascist Italy*, p. 159.
63. St. Aurelii Augustini, ed. J.E.C. Welldon, *De Civitate Dei Contra Paganos* (London: Society for Promoting Christian Knowledge, 1924), vol. I, bk. IV, ch. 4, p. 153.
64. St. Augustine, tr. G.G. Walsh S.J., *The City of God* (New York: Doubleday & Co., 1958), bk. IV, ch. 4, pp. 88–9.

political life is natural to man, and needed for his proper development. As far as international society goes, the Machiavellian and Kantian agree that there is no such thing. The Machiavellian believes that there is not and cannot be one, the Kantian that it must be brought into being. The Grotian however believes the existing diplomatic system is an international society.

There are two familiar criteria of ethical judgement: that based on motive or intention, and that based on consequence or result. (Thus the defenders of the Munich agreement defend Chamberlain's intention, while its critics censure the consequences.) One could argue that politics intrinsically is in the sphere of the ethics of consequence, where 'meaning well' can never be so important as results to others; yet Grotian magnanimity often judges men by their nobility of character rather then their political correctness or success.[65] The Machiavellian and Kantian agree on the whole, however, on judging by consequences. The Machiavellian principle is justification by success, 'getting away with it'; the Revolutionary Kantian principle (not Kant's!) is that the end justifies the means. Does the 'end' mean purpose or conclusion? Both: when it means purpose, the Kantian is nearer the Machiavellian. Whichever it is, 'the end justifies the means' is a version of justification by success; it provides the moral equipment, or technical principle, for achieving success.

Thus the Grotian and Kantian dove-tail in their idealism and their theory of history, whereas the Grotian and the Machiavellian share a certain realism. The Machiavellian and Kantian agree on the origin of politics, on (the absence of) international society, and on the criteria for international morality. Broadly, the Grotian and Kantian approximate over ideals, the Kantian and Machiavellian over methods.

Appendix

Varying relative strength of traditions

1. Machiavellism dominant in late fifteenth century; Grotianism not yet emerged from decadent scholasticism.
2. Doctrinal passions of Reformation aroused religious Kantianism, which rivalled Machiavellism until 1648, and largely fused with it.
3. Grotianism emerged with Vitoria (1480–1546), slowly, and recessive.
4. Machiavellism dominant 1648–1789, Grotianism secondary, Kantianism latent.
5. Kantianism versus Grotianism 1789–1815.

---

65. See Alexander Hamilton, *The Federalist* (London: Dent & Sons, 1934), no. I, and also John Morley, *Edmund Burke: A Historical Study* (London: Macmillan & Co., 1867).

6. Grotianism dominant 1815–48, Kantianism recessive, Machiavellism latent.
7. Kantianism dominant 1848–78, Grotianism and Machiavellism equal second.
8. Grotianism and Machiavellism equal dominant, 1878–1914 Kantianism recessive.
9. Kantianism and Machiavellism destroy supreme Grotian experiment, 1914–39.
10. Kantianism dominant, versus Grotianism recessive, 1939–60 (Machiavellism absorbed into both?).

[The above were as the author listed them. Whether the terminal date of the last phase, 1960, was owing to the Sino-Soviet split, or simply the year the list was compiled, is unclear. It could be argued that phase 10 lasted until 1989 and that we are now witnessing a phase 11: Grotianism resurgent but infused with Machiavellism, Kantianism in temporary eclipse. Eds.]

8: Theory of diplomacy: balance of power

After a discussion of the nature of international society and the basic principles of statecraft, the balance of power comes conveniently next, since for those who believe in this deity, to propitiate it by periodical holocausts, which is called 'maintaining the balance', is itself the fundamental principle of statecraft. The balance of power is a notoriously slippery idea and its consideration involves a linguistic analysis, and an exact study of its political and diplomatic usage. One must ask, 'What does the phrase mean here, in this context?'

Grotian

Grotius himself does not mention the balance of power but there is a conception of it already coming into consciousness before his time, in harmony with his own principles and developed by his formal successors, which may be called the *classic* doctrine of the balance of power. For the Grotian, the phrase 'balance of power' means two things: first, an even distribution of power. This is the basic meaning: equilibrium in the literal, primary sense; a state of affairs in which no power is so preponderant that it can endanger the others. This balance of power is the object of such verbs as maintain and preserve, upset and overturn, redress and restore. Thus Machiavelli said that before the French invasion of 1494, 'Italy was in a way balanced'.[1] Churchill describing Locarno in 1925 wrote: 'Thus there was a balance created in which Britain, whose major interest was the cessation of the quarrel between Germany and France, was to a large extent arbiter and umpire.'[2] Lester Pearson's dictum that 'the

1. Niccoló Machiavelli, *The Prince* (London: Dent & Sons, 1928), p. 169.
2. Winston S. Churchill, 'The Gathering Storm', *The Second World War* (London: The Reprint Society, 1954), vol. I, p. 42.

balance of terror has replaced the balance of power'[3] and the term 'nuclear parity' also illustrate this meaning.

There is an assumption that the even distribution of power is better than any conceivable alternative, so that the phrase passes from being descriptive to normative, and thus to its second meaning for the Grotian: the principle that power ought to be evenly distributed. It is in this sense that the balance of power has been conceived of as a system of international relations, or even a fundamental institution in international politics, and certainly as a basic principle of foreign policy. This was the dominant conception of the balance of power in the 'classical period' of international politics, 1648–1914, and it was spoken of as in some sense providing an unwritten constitution of international society. It was written into the Treaty of Utrecht in 1713 and some argue it became positive law: '. . . in order that the Peace and Tranquillity of the Christian World may be ordered and stabilized in a just Balance of Power (which is the best and most solid foundation of mutual friendship and a lasting general Concord)';[4] and it was cited frequently thereafter down to Bismarck's time. Burke wrote: 'The balance of power had ever been assumed as the known common law of Europe; the question had only been (as it must happen) on the more or less inclination of that balance.'[5]

Thus the balance of power was the constitution of international society in the eighteenth century. The struggle against Revolutionary France and Napoleon was explicitly an attempt to restore the balance; and the principle of the balance of power — that there ought to be an even distribution — was appealed to expressly by the Vienna statesmen (Castlereagh, Metternich, Talleyrand) and formed the basis of the Concert of Europe which was in origin and essence a common agreement on preserving the balance of power. It regained a semi-official currency in the cold war, during the period of the balance of terror, if not in diplomatic documents (which in the twentieth century have evaded political realities more than ever before), at least in the informed commentary of the press and strategic experts. *The Manchester Guardian* wrote, on 21 August 1954, about Attlee's visit to Peking: 'If there is to be coexistence there must be a balance of power, for if power is unbalanced the temptation to Communism to resume its crusade will be irresistible.'[6]

The policy of the balance of power is founded, as Hume says, 'on common sense and obvious reasoning' but the Grotian view of it is not

3. Lester Pearson, speech at San Francisco, 24 June 1955, 'Commemoration of the Tenth Anniversary of the Signing of the UN Charter' (UNP Sales No: 1955 I. 26), p. 215.
4. G. Maccoby and S. Butler, tr., *The Development of International Law* (London: Longmans, 1928), p. 65.
5. Edmund Burke, 'Letters on a Regicide Peace', *The Works of the Right Honourable E. Burke* (London: Samuel Holdsworth, 1842), vol. II, no. 3, p. 333.
6. *The Manchester Guardian*, 21 August 1954, leading article.

exhausted here. For the Grotian it is an expression of justice, of rendering to each power what is owed to it. The Grotian would give three reasons why there should be an even distribution of power. First, to protect the independence of states, the so-called 'liberties of Europe', and the society of nations. The balance of power is 'such a disposition of things that no one potentate or state shall be able, absolutely, to predominate and prescribe laws to the others';[7] it is

that constitution subsisting among neighbouring states . . . by virtue of which no one among them can injure the independence or essential rights of another without meeting with effectual resistance on some side, and consequently exposing itself to danger.[8]

The balance of power in Europe means in effect the independence of its several states. The preponderance of any one Power threatens and destroys this independence.[9]

This conception of the balance of power as a guarantee of national independence sank deep into the European consciousness in the eighteenth century, and although it came under attack in the nineteenth,[10] it was not discredited until Wilson and 1918. The balance of power was seen as a condition, not only of national security, but also of domestic happiness: 'the balance of pow'r?/Ah! till that is restor'd/What solid delights can retirement afford?'[11]

The second reason for an even distribution of power is to consolidate the interdependence of states, to make it manifest and more explicit.

The grand and distinguishing feature of the balancing system is the perpetual attention to foreign affairs which it inculcates . . . the unceasing care which it dictates of nations most remotely situated, and apparently unconnected with ourselves; the general union which it has effected of all the European powers, obeying certain laws, and actuated in general by a common principle; in fine, the right of mutual inspection, universally recognised, among civilised states . . . [12]

Here are the germs of 'peace is indivisible', of the idea of collective security. This is Gladstone's doctrine of concert, the co-operation

7. Emmerich de Vattel, tr. C.G. Fenwick, *Law of Nations*, Washington, DC, Carnegie Endowment (Oxford: Clarendon Press, 1916), bk. III, ch. III, p. 251.
8. F. von Gentz, *Fragments upon the Balance of Power in Europe* (London: Peltier, 1806), ch. I, *ab init.*
9. Lord John Russell in 1859 quoted by H. Temperley & L.M. Penson, *Foundations of British Foreign Policy* (Cambridge: Cambridge University Press, 1938), p. 205.
10. See Viscount Grey of Falloden, *Twenty-five Years 1892—1916* (London: Hodder & Stoughton, 1925), vol. I, pp. 4—6, 10.
11. Isaac Hawkins Browne, *Oxford Book of 18th Century Verse* (Oxford: Clarendon Press, 1926), p. 300.
12. Henry Peter Brougham, *An Enquiry into the Colonial Policy of the European Powers* (London: 1803), vol. II, pp. 210—11.

which neutralizes the selfish aims of power. Quincy Wright has a striking passage in his *A Study of War*.

Whenever maintenance of the balance of power becomes a guide to the policy of a government, that government is on the threshold of conceding that the stability of the community of states is an interest superior to its domestic interests. Doubtless it concedes this only because it believes that stability is a *sine qua non* of its own survival. The concession is, however, an enlightenment of self-interest which approaches altruism or submergence of the self in a larger whole . . . [Here] there are already rudiments of a situation in which law, organisation, and opinion may become more important than military power.[13]

This is highly Grotian, and would be approved by Gladstone or Eisenhower.

The third reason for an even distribution is to make international law possible. Sir Travers Twiss says that the balance of power was recognized as 'a rule of Positive Law' at Utrecht;[14] this is arguable, but there is wide agreement that international law can exist only if there is a balance of power.

If the Powers cannot keep one another in check, no rules of law will have any force, since an over-powerful state will naturally try to act according to discretion and disobey the law. As there is not and never can be a central political authority above the sovereign states that could enforce the rules of the Law of Nations, a balance of power must prevent any member of the Family of Nations from becoming omnipotent.[15]

An equilibrium between the members of the Family of Nations is an indispensable condition of the very existence of International Law.[16]

The balance of power is not a legal principle and therefore not one of international law; but it is a principle of international policy, and one that is indispensable to the existence of international law. And the principle of the balance of power is repeatedly adduced by international lawyers as one of the justifications, if not the main or only one, for intervention.

For the Grotian there follows from this the idea of 'holding' the balance; that is, a power has a special role in maintaining an even distribution. It is irrelevant whether the balance is multiple or simple. This idea was invented by the papacy, and Britain became the self-

---

13. Quincy Wright, *A Study of War*, 2nd edn (Chicago and London: The University of Chicago Press, 1965), vol. II, p. 749.
14. Sir Travers Twiss, *The Law of Nations considered as Independent Political Communities* (Oxford: Clarendon Press, 1844), p. 187.
15. L. Oppenheim, *International Law*, 1st edn (London: Longmans, Green & Co., 1905), vol. I, pp. 73-4.
16. ibid., p. 185.

conscious exemplar; in the Mutiny Act, 1727–1867, the army was
constituted 'for the safety of the United Kingdom the Defence of the
Possessions of His Majesty's Crown, and the Preservation of the
Balance of Power in Europe'.[17] However, the self-satisfied impar-
tiality and inaccuracy of the metaphor becomes apparent: so long as
you hold the pair of scales, you are outside the comparison of weights
and you cannot sit yourself in a scale. This grotesque inaccuracy
covers the Grotian sense of the police-function (or the vigilantes-
function). India saw herself as the holder of the balance when Nehru
in 1955, just before Bandung and Geneva, held that Russia and
America cancel each other out, and form the most perfect balance.
Therefore the non-nuclear countries had more room to manoeuvre
than if one great power was preponderant, and could bring pressure
to bear on both to solve the Korean problem, evacuate China's
offshore islands and ensure disarmament. The *Observer* correspondent
in New Delhi put India's standpoint thus: 'Let us exploit the fact that
people woo us because we constitute a non-aligned force.'[18]

Grotians see the balance of power almost as a political or social law;
they detect an inherent tendency in international politics to produce
an even distribution of power, and see the balance as a general statement of how groupings of powers fall into ever-changing equilibria.
A.J.P. Taylor says the balance of power in the nineteenth century
'seemed to be the political equivalent of the laws of economics, both
self-operating. If every man followed his own interest, all would be
prosperous; and if every state followed its own interest, all would be
peaceful and secure'.[19] However this is not characteristically Grotian;
Grotians do not see international politics in terms of 'laws' (which is
Machiavellian). The balance of power was seen in these terms in the
nineteenth century by Machiavellian statesmen and by the politically
illiterate bourgeoisie, who tended to Cobdenism, wishing to 'let international politics alone'. But the true Grotian always sees a need 'to
take thought for tomorrow', and to take responsible decisions; for him
the balance of power is policy, not 'law'. A good joint Grotian–
Machiavellian definition would be: a multiplicity of sovereign states
tends to fall into unstable equilibrium, striving always for even
distribution, but constantly losing it again.

Machiavellian

The Machiavellian would say that the Grotian analysis is all very well,

---

17. T.J. Lawrence, *The Principles of International Law* (London: Macmillan & Co.,
    1925), p. 128.
18. Philip Deane, *Observer*, 16 January 1955.
19. A.J.P. Taylor, *The Struggle for Mastery in Europe 1848–1918* (Oxford: Clarendon
    Press, 1954), p. xx.

but it remains at a linguistic level; it is unreal and needs to be supplemented by political analysis. The whole Grotian conception of the balance of power as meaning an even distribution of power collapses for three reasons. First, there is no way of measuring relative power to find whether it is evenly distributed. This is why disarmament negotiations fail: there is no common standard of mensuration for battleships and tanks, for divisions and ICBMs, even for divisions and divisions. Secondly, there is no impartial, independent measurer. Measurement is always an estimate, a guess, a suspicion or panic; it is subjective, interested, calculated by parties involved in the dilemma or by one power of its rivals. Thirdly, while it is true that there is an approximation to even distribution sometimes (for example, Locarno, or the nuclear stalemate), all distribution of power is temporary, unstable and inconstant. Consequently the basic fact of foreign policy is that powers usually cannot agree about whether there is an even distribution. Most arrangements of power favour some countries, which seek to preserve the status quo, justifying it as a true equilibrium, and are irksome to other countries which are accordingly revisionist. The balance of power is a useful euphemism so long as it is not taken literally, and does not lead one to suppose that balance is the same as equilibrium.

For the Machiavellian the phrase has a range of meanings. Its basic sense is the existing distribution of power; that is, the distribution that suits the status quo powers. Even revisionists will refer to the existing distribution as a 'balance', not conceding justice to it, but as an accepted diplomatic shorthand. Thus Hitler told Ciano, at Berchtesgaden on 24 October 1936: 'Any future modifications of the Mediterranean balance of power must be in Italy's favour.'[20] During Cripps' mission to Moscow, in July 1940, Cripps told Stalin: 'Both countries ought to agree on a common policy of self-protection against Germany and on the re-establishment of the European balance of Power'; to which Stalin replied that there was no danger of Europe being engulfed by Germany: 'The so-called European balance of power has hitherto oppressed not only Germany but also the Soviet Union. Therefore the Soviet Union will take all measures to prevent the re-establishment of the old balance of power in Europe.'[21] Another example shows Britain as acquiescent [acquiescent in the sense of being compelled to accept the situation at present], but potentially revisionist: 'the balance of sea power has tilted away from us dramatically during the last ten years.'[22] The Grotian response is

---

20. Malcom Muggeridge, ed., Stuart Hood, tr., *Ciano's Diplomatic Papers* (Odham Press, 1948), p. 57.
21. *Nazi Soviet Relations 1939–1941*: Documents from the Archives of the German Foreign Office (Washington, DC: Department of State, 1948), p. 167.
22. L.J. Callaghan presenting Navy estimates in the House of Commons, 12 March 1951, *Hansard's Parliamentary Debates*, vol. 485, col. 1093).

that if revisionist powers are willing to describe the existing distribution of power as a 'balance' this suggests that some degree of objective appraisal *is* possible, that they themselves admit it as a balance while wanting to overthrow it. Revisionists, on the Machiavellian showing, do not speak of 'restoring' the balance when they think the existing balance is unfair to them; thus they resemble gangsters who have declared war on law and order, not revolutionaries who have repudiated law and order as intrinsically unjust. Does not this imply a consensus, including even the revisionists, that a 'balance' actually possesses some intrinsic quality of justice, or of order?

It would seem the Machiavellian has no answer to this. For him, from being the existing distribution of power, the balance of power comes then to mean any possible distribution of power, future, as well as past or present. Churchill said to Eden in 1942: 'No one can foresee how the balance of power will lie or where the winning armies will stand at the end of the war.'[23] Here it means the relationship of power prevailing at a given time; this may be its most frequent usage. 'Balance' has quite lost the sense of 'equilibrium', and implies less stability than change. It is not the object of verbs like 'maintain' or 'resolve', but is more likely to be the subject of the sentence: 'the balance of power has changed; has tilted away', 'a new balance of power is appearing', as if it lies largely beyond human control. The Protean quality, the demonic vitality and changeableness of the balance of power, is seen in the difficulty of giving effect to the principle that power ought to be evenly distributed. The *reductio ad absurdum* is seen in the circumstances of a simple balance, when two powers or blocs are trying to maintain an even distribution by an arms race or struggle for alliances. Here, as is well known, the balance of power is the principle that my side needs a margin of strength to avert the harmful distribution of power. This is where 'balance' acquires the sense of a bank balance; not an equality of assets and debits, but a surplus of assets, a financial margin. At an undergraduate meeting at Oxford in 1913, a cabinet minister (Churchill) told his audience:

'There is just one way in which you can make your country secure and have peace, and that is to be so much stronger than any prospective enemy that he dare not attack you, and this is, I submit to you gentlemen, a self-evident proposition.' A small man [Sir Norman Angell] got up at the back of the hall and said: 'Is the advice you have just given us advice you would give to Germany?' [There was a faint titter but no applause] . . . When the time came for questions and comment, the small man said: 'Our Cabinet Minister tells us in the profundity of his wisdom, that both groups of quarrelling nations will be secure, both will keep the peace, when each is stronger than the other. And this, he thinks, is a self-evident proposition.' [Loud applause this time].[24]

23. Winston S. Churchill, 'The Grand Alliance', *The Second World War*, vol. III, p. 542.
24. C.E.M. Joad, *Why War?* (London: Penguin Special, 1939), pp. 71-2.

Did the young Grotian (Sir Norman) solve this by mere verbal cleverness? Is this not the fundamental conundrum of international politics which has not changed in the slightest from the Anglo-German naval race to the Russo-American nuclear race? Each side wants a balance of power in the sense of a bank balance, a margin of power, to negotiate from a position of strength.

This leads straight on to the question of holding the balance. The Grotian defines this as one power having a special role in maintaining an even distribution, through its ability to contribute decisive strength. The role has been filled most commonly by peripheral powers like insular Britain, flanking Russia, or non-committed India. But this is not adequate for the Machiavellian. To hold the balance is a very equivocal role; if the holder of the balance is weaker than the powers which make the scales, his function will only be as a mediator; if he is as strong as either, or stronger, he will tend to become the arbiter. He may not play this 'special role' in a way which the other powers regard as just; he may be concerned less to maintain an even distribution of power than to improve his own position. On this analysis he is seen not to have a special role or duty in maintaining an even distribution, but a special advantage within the existing distribution. The continental powers always noted about Britain's self-imposed task of maintaining the balance of power in Europe that while she was doing this with her right hand, with her left she was establishing a maritime and colonial hegemony which for two centuries refused to recognize the principle of equilibrium. A basic principle of the Vienna Settlement was the exclusion of colonial issues. At the 1919 Paris Peace Conference, Britain demanded the German fleet to be reduced to a fixed strength and the annexation of the German colonies.

But 'holding the balance' is not confined to special great powers; the Machiavellian democratizes the conception of holding the balance. Most powers have some special advantage, a strategic position, raw materials, or energy and self-confidence, and can contribute some strength to one side or the other, if not a decisive strength. Many a small power likes to think that in some respects it holds a balance, if only between its allies. Holding a balance shades into the ability to contribute *some* strength, into possessing some freedom of action, and this every power wants. In this sense Hume (a Machiavellian) said that the balance of power 'is founded on common sense and obvious reasoning'. Here one can see that holding the balance is simply the policy of divide-and-rule, in Grotian language. It is playing off one side against another: divide and survive, divide and influence. This is true of almost all powers, in the relationship of ally as well as of enemy. De Gaulle said on 10 November 1959: 'France, in equipping herself with a nuclear weapon, will render a service to world equilibrium'.[25] He

---

25. Charles de Gaulle, reported in *The Manchester Guardian*, 11 November 1959.

was concerned not with the NATO-Communist equilibrium but with the equilibrium within NATO itself. One can compare Mussolini's conquest of Albania in 1939 and his intended conquest of Greece in 1940, to preserve the balance against Germany.

This democratization of the concept of the balance of power is the work of the defensive Machiavellian. The aggressive Machiavellian will interpret the phrase monarchically, monopolistically; for him holding the balance involves possessing a decisive advantage, being able to divide-and-rule. Thus Hitler said in 1941: 'What Britain called the balance of power was nothing but the disintegration and disorganisation of the Continent';[26] and Chester Bowles (not an aggressive Machiavellian) used the phrase in this sense when he wrote in 1956: 'the two thirds of the world who live in the undeveloped continents . . . will ultimately constitute the world balance of power.'[27] To have a decisive advantage means having predominance, and this fuses with the idea of the policy of balance as having a margin of strength. Hamilton wrote in 1787: 'We may hope, ere long, to become the arbiter of Europe in America, and to be able to incline the balance of European competitions in this part of the world as our interest may dictate. Our situation invites and our interests prompt us to aim at an ascendant in the system of American affairs.'[28] Bonaparte echoes this in 1797, after the collapse of the First Coalition: 'We hold the balance of Europe; we shall incline it as we wish',[29] and the Kaiser in 1901 announced: 'The balance of power in Europe is me, the British policy of holding the balance is exploded'; 'there is no balance of power in Europe except *me* — me and my twenty-two army corps.'[30]

Here at last the linguistic migration of 'balance' is complete; the word has turned into its opposite: equilibrium has come to mean preponderance, balance has come to mean overbalance; and the verbs governing the phrase pass from possession to identification, from 'holding' and 'inclining' to 'constituting' and 'being'.[31]

26. Adolf Hitler, Speech in the Berlin Sportpalast, 30 January 1941, reported in *The Times*, 31 January 1941.
27. Chester Bowles, 'Why I will vote Democratic', *Christianity and Crisis*, 15 October 1956, p. 137.
28. Alexander Hamilton, *The Federalist* (London: J.M. Dent, 1934), no. xi, pp. 50, 53.
29. '*Nous tenons la balance de l'Europe; nous la ferons pencher comme nous voudrons*', Bonaparte to the Minister of Foreign Relations, 1797, in Albert Sorel, *L'Europe et la Révolution française* (Paris: Plon-Nourrit et Cie, 1906), vol. 5, p. 185.
30. Quoted in H.H. Asquith, *Genesis of the War* (London: Cassell, 1923), pp. 19–20.
31. See also Martin Wight's chapter 'The Balance of Power' in Herbert Butterfield and M. Wight, eds, *Diplomatic Investigations* (London: George Allen & Unwin Ltd., 1966), pp. 165ff.

Kantian

It is easy to see the ingredients which make up the Kantian rejection of the balance of power. There is war-weariness, a sheer disgust with balance of power wars. 'Now Europe's balanc'd; neither Side prevails,/For nothing's left in either of the Scales.'[32]

The Kantian rejects the balance of power also because of its unreliability and unmanageability in practice. Notable examples of this are to be found in the War of the Spanish Succession, when the Archduke Charles's becoming Holy Roman Emperor in 1711 tilted the balance in the contrary direction; the need for Great Britain, Austria and France at the Congress of Vienna to counter with a secret treaty the excessive territorial ambitions of Russia and Prussia; and in 1945 the replacement, following a war fought to restore the balance of power in Europe, of German by Russian predominance.

Kant wrote:

The maintenance of universal peace by means of the so-called balance of power in Europe is like Swift's house, which a master-builder constructed in such perfect accord with all the law of equilibrium, that when a sparrow alighted upon it, it immediately collapsed — a mere figment of the imagination.[33]

Kantians dislike the intellectual sophistry of the idea, its imprecision and paradox, the apparent range of meanings, so that it can justify every policy. Cobden wrote:

The balance of power is a chimera! It is not a fallacy, a mistake, an imposture — it is an undescribed, indescribable, incomprehensible nothing . . . a creation of the politician's brain — phantasm, without definite form or tangible existence — a mere conjunction of syllables, forming words which convey sound without meaning.[34]

Cobden offered three reasons why the theory of the balance of power was wrong. It is chimerical; the exponents of the balance of power say the basis of the system is the 'constitution' or 'union' or 'disposition' of the European powers, but no such state of things ever did exist. Here he alludes to the idea that the balance of power is in some sense the constitution of international society but in an inverted form; that international society has a constitution one of whose expressions is the balance of power. He asserts that there is no international society such that the balance of power is a function of its working; this is a chimera, moonshine. Also it is fallacious. The theory of

---

32. Alexander Pope, *Minor Poems* (Twickenham Edition, 1954), vol. VI, p. 82.
33. Immanuel Kant, *Werke* (Berlin: Academy Edition, 1912–22), vol. VIII, p. 312.
34. Richard Cobden, *The Political Writings of Richard Cobden* (London: William Ridgway, 1868), vol. I, pp. 258–263.

the balance of power contains no definition of standard according to which each state shall be estimated in the balancing of powers, whether it be the extent of territory, the number of inhabitants, or its wealth. This is also a Machiavellian criticism of the Grotian case. Thirdly the theory is incomplete and inoperative, because it neglects, or refuses, to provide against the silent and peaceful aggrandisements which spring from improvement and labour. This is a characteristically Kantian argument: the balance of power deals only with military relations and ignores the effects of progress; that is, moral and material development. It is a quite novel way of looking at international relations, resulting of course from the Industrial Revolution. Consider Denis Healey's Cobdenite observation in *International Affairs*, in April 1958.

In the past it has only been possible to make a big change in the balance of power by gaining resources in territory outside one's frontiers. The sputnik has demonstrated with spectacular effect that it is now possible to produce great changes in the balance of power by making better political and scientific use of the resources inside one's own territories.[35]

To digress a little: this raises the question of how to define a great power, for few changes in the balance of power are more definite than the emergence of a new great power. There are two accepted ways of approaching this question, and one is that a great power is a power that is diplomatically recognized as such. There are certain agreed diplomatic marks of a great power: a permanent seat on the Security Council or the League Council, representation at the Permanent Court of International Justice, or being invited to some *ad hoc* great power conference as when, for example, Italy was invited to the Luxemburg Conference in 1867. The powers which qualify for diplomatic recognition as great powers are those with general interests; they are seen as an élite, responsible aristocracy, who guide international society: the 'great responsibles' as shown in their conduct at the Paris Peace Conference, and the Congress of Vienna.

. . . the government of the world must be entrusted to satisfied nations, who wished nothing more for themselves than what they had. If the world-government were in the hands of hungry nations there would always be danger. But none of us had any reason to seek for anything more. The Peace would be kept by peoples who lived in their own way and were not ambitious. Our power placed us above the rest. We were like rich men dwelling at peace within their habitations.[36]

This accords with Grotian philosophy. But the definition can be

---

35. *International Affairs* (R.I.I.A. Butterworth), vol. 34, no. 2, April 1958, p. 154.
36. Winston S. Churchill on the Tehran Conference 1943, 'Closing the Ring', *The Second World War*, vol. V, p. 300.

chased further. How does a power qualify for recognition as having general interests? Perhaps not by recognition but by self-assertion. Gorchakov wrote of Italy: 'a great power is not recognized, it reveals itself';[37] and Hegel quotes Napoleon before Campoformio: '"The French Republic needs recognition as little as the sun requires it", what his words implied was simply the thing's *strength* which carries with it, without any verbal expression, the guarantee of recognition.'[38]

Khrushchev in August 1958 echoed this in a letter to Third World governments when he said the policy of ignoring China made no sense: 'This great power exists, grows stronger, and is developing independently of whether it is recognised or not by certain governments.'

These definitions are more 'Realistic' and 'Machiavellian', but they are still not quite an adequate answer to the question: 'What powers are able to assert themselves successfully as great powers?' It is clear that some try to assert it without carrying conviction, such as Poland after 1919, perhaps France in the 1950s, and Britain today. Objective, successful self-assertion comes by defeating another great power in war, as Japan did Russia in 1905. If a power has done this, it goes on to assert its universal interests, having a finger in every pie, and diplomatic recognition is quickly conceded. Italy never did this properly, not even in 1918, and China did not in the end defeat the United States in Korea, which was the first Sino-American war. The definition of a great power as one that has defeated another in war is E.H. Carr's definition in *The Twenty Years' Crisis*, and it explains the status, at various times, of England, Prussia, Russia, Japan, and Sweden as great powers (but not Austria, France, the United States, Italy or China). However it plainly carries within itself a logical problem because it involves a finite historical regress. At some point there must have been a great power whose defeat spawned new great powers, but which did not owe its own status to military victory; at some point there must have been a *first* great power.

To return to Cobden's argument: he berates the Machiavellians for concentrating on war and victory as a mark of great powers, and rejects the Grotian emphasis on diplomatic recognition as being legalistic and pettifogging. Great powers can come into existence and alterations can be made in the balance of power, 'by silent and peaceful aggrandisements which spring from improvement and labour'.[39] (Aggrandisement here means growing greater, not aggression). There is a recognition, prior to diplomatic recognition, by the

---

37. Quoted by Otto von Bismarck, tr. A.J. Butler, *Reflections and Reminiscences* (London: Smith, Elder & Co., 1898), vol. I, p. 302.
38. Friedrich Hegel, tr. T.M. Knox, *Philosophy of Right* (Oxford: Clarendon Press, 1949), p. 297.
39. Richard Cobden, *Political Writings*, p. 269.

moral conscience and common sense of mankind, not of military strength but of moral and material growth, which makes a power a great power. Take the example of the United States. When did it become a great power? It quietly grew into such, and was seen as such, without diplomatic recognition or military violence.[40] The Machiavellian answers the question of when the United States became a great power by citing the Spanish–American War; the Civil War; its army of a million men; perhaps the expulsion of the French from Mexico. But still, the United States remains anomalous. So does China; Raymond Aron wrote that the 'Communist victory in China . . . has upset the world balance of power.'[41] Was it not obvious that the largest nation on earth, once it had strong effective government, must by its mere existence alter the balance of power? Bright argued in 1854 that if disturbing the balance of power was a legitimate cause of war then Austria had a cause of war against Britain. England compared with Austria was three times as powerful as thirty or forty years before; Austria was politically divided and bankrupt, England was united and its wealth and productive power were steadily increasing.

Might not Austria complain that we have disturbed the balance of power because we are growing so much stronger from better government, from the greater union of our people, from the wealth that is created by the hard labour and skill of our population, and from the wonderful development of the mechanical resources of The Kingdom?[42]

The Machiavellian criticized the Grotian principle of an *even* distribution of power on the grounds that there is no way of measuring relative power. The Kantian goes further and argues that there is no agreement or clear-sightedness about what one is meant to be measuring. If a balance of power theorist knew his business, he would try to measure, not simply power, but relative national growth in all spheres, which is absurd. To this the Machiavellian has two answers: first it is not absurd; it is what an analysis of the balance of power today actually does. It is clear that military power involves not only men under arms, or a stockpile of atomic bombs, but also the production of machine-tools and reserves of petroleum. Secondly, there is a fairly definable point where national growth becomes militarily relevant; where silent and peaceful improvements can be seen to have power-political consequences. To take Healey's argument: sputnik had obvious military implications, and can be compared to Germany's decision to build a great navy. Soviet Russia's sally into space and

---

40. ibid., pp. 279—83. See also: *Speeches by Richard Cobden*, ed. John Bright, Cobden's castigation of British ignorance of the USA (London: Macmillan & Co. 1880), pp. 361, 491, and John Bright 'War with Russia', 31 March 1854, *Speeches*, (London: Macmillan & Co., 1898), p. 233.
41. *The Manchester Guardian*, 23 January 1951.
42. John Bright, *Speeches*, p. 233.

Imperial Germany's on to salt-water before the First World War did immediately begin inclining the balance of power, although one could describe them both as making use of growing domestic resources. The Meiji revolution of the 1870s in Japan did not affect the balance of power; the Communist conquest of China did so because it carried China, now under strong centralized government, from one camp to the other in the ideological conflict.

Kantians have a great emotional revulsion against the idea of the balance of power. This is best expressed by John Bright showing radical penetration:

The more you examine this matter, the more you will come to the conclusion which I have arrived at, that this foreign policy, this regard for 'the liberties of Europe', this care at one time for 'the Protestant interests', this excessive love for the 'balance of power', is neither more nor less than a gigantic system of out-door relief for the aristocracy of Great Britain.[43]

The basis of this emotional revulsion is not only that wars fought to preserve the balance pander to the military proclivities of the ruling classes, but that the policy offers no permanence, and is a bar to progress. Its lack of permanence can be seen in Britain's history. We have, says Bright, been at war with, for, and against every nation in Europe; we have fought with Russia against France, and pledged ourselves against another Bonaparte on the throne of France; and now we are with France against Russia. He goes on: 'The balance of power is like perpetual motion or any of those impossible things which some men are always racking their brains and spending their time and money to accomplish.'[44] Bright also pointed out how the balance of power obstructs progress: 'If this phrase of the "balance of power" is to be always an argument for war, the pretence for war will never be wanting, and peace can never be secure.' And again he wrote:

In pursuit of this Will-o'-the-wisp (the liberties of Europe and the balance of power) there has been extracted from the industry of the people of this small island no less an amount than £2,000,000,000 sterling . . . I behold the hideous error of your Government, whose fatal policy consumes in some cases a half, never less than a third, of all the results of the industry which God intended should fertilise and bless every home in England, but the fruits of which are squandered in every part of the surface of the globe, without producing the smallest good to the people of England.[45]

One can compare the position of the average isolationist Congressman. It is worth noting that Kant, making a second reference to the balance of power, sees it as a necessary step in progress (see p. 173 above for the first). The state of international anarchy and a

---

43. ibid., p. 470, see also pp. 330–2.
44. ibid., p. 469.
45. ibid., pp. 232, 469.

constant readiness for war retard the capacities of mankind in their progress, but these evils evoke their own antidotes.

A law of Equilibrium is discovered for the regulation of the really wholesome antagonism of contiguous States as it springs out of their freedom; and a united Power giving emphasis to this law, is constituted whereby there is introduced a universal condition of public security among the Nations.[46]

Here the balance of power is a step towards a cosmopolitan world republic, or league of republics.

These are the reasons, analytically, for the Kantian rejection of the balance of power. One can also trace the assault upon it historically, from the importance of the balance of power during the *ancien régime*, through its rejection, as democracy grew. The Jacobins in France completely rejected it:

As for the balance of power, it was so far from being admitted by France . . . that in the whole body of their authorised or encouraged reports and discussions on the theory of the diplomatick system, they constantly rejected the very idea of the balance of power, and treated it as the true cause of all the wars and calamities that had afflicted Europe . . . exploding, therefore, all sorts of balances, they avow their design to erect themselves into a new description of empire, which is not grounded on any balance, but forms a sort of impious hierarchy, of which France is to be the head and the guardian.[47]

The revolutionary Kantian aims at a revolutionary state to which the balance of power is the chief obstacle (the Bolsheviks denounced 'imperialist diplomacy' rather than the balance of power). This rejection of the theory of the balance of power can be traced from Cobden and Bright and their influence on the United States, to Wilson and the League. Wilson declared: 'Peoples and provinces are not to be bartered about from sovereignty to sovereignty as if they were mere chattels and pawns in a game, even the great game, now for ever discredited, of the balance of power.'[48] He advocated 'not a balance of power, but a community of powers; not organized rivalries, but an organized common peace'.[49] Thus 'balance of power' became a dirty word, and dropped out of diplomatic language. Historians referred to it as obsolete, as the 'eighteenth-century' conception.

By coincidence in 1932 two books appeared: one was by M.H. Cornejo, *The Balance of the Continents*:

The balance of the continents signifies the intervention of factors which history has developed in different regions and which events have stirred to

46. W. Hastie, *Kant's Principles of Politics* (Edinburgh: T. Clark, 1891), pp. 19–20.
47. Edmund Burke, 'Regicide Peace', *Works*, vol. II, pp. 333–4.
48. Woodrow Wilson, Address to a Joint Session of Congress, 11 February 1918, 'Four Principles Speech', *The Papers of Woodrow Wilson* (Princeton, NJ: Princeton University Press, 1984), vol. 46, pp. 322–3.
49. ibid., Address to the Senate, 22 January 1917, p. 351.

reciprocal action — to carry out a work of universal cooperation. This balance of essentially peaceful interests will not be, as is that of states, a balance of antagonism . . . The continents are impelled to establish the equilibrium by economic interests and juridical ideals . . . it is the balance of cooperation, spiritualized social elements seeking a universal rhythm.[50]

These are Kantian ideas in fulsome Latin American rhetoric; the balance of power is spiritualized into a rhythm of co-operation. The other book was by Valentine de Balla, *The New Balance of Power in Europe*:

The present study is an attempt to describe the formation of a new European balance of power . . . two political groups are racing to attain military supremacy — one seeks to maintain the political structure of Europe, the other strives to change it.[51]

(This is the Machiavellian 'balance', meaning any distribution of power.) Those who regard the first book as waffle are Machiavellian; those who consider the second myopic, concentrating on the trees and not the wood, are Kantian.

In the 1930s Europe became increasingly inclined to see the balance of power principle re-emerging from the depths. It had vanished largely because of the peculiar circumstances of 1919: the Allied monopoly of power; the German defeat and Austrian and Ottoman disintegration; and the United States and Soviet withdrawals from Europe. But now the pattern had simplified into the League of Nations against the Axis powers. Russia was first with the League until Munich, and then holding the balance, while America was drawing towards the League powers. After the Second World War old arguments revived, but with less assurance. The United Nations was based on a different principle from the balance of power: 'collective security'. The Yugoslav delegate at the Preparatory Commission in December 1945 asked whether the United Nations headquarters should be in the territory of a great power, and most of the arguments against appealed to the balance of power. Bevin said in 1948 that the 'old-fashioned conception of the balance of power' must be discarded in favour of a European union, but he then championed it manfully, in the Marshall Plan and NATO.[52] The 'balance of terror' caused by nuclear parity revives the Grotian concept at its simplest. However the neutralism of the non-aligned nations continues the Kantian critique of it, as they keep out of alliances and pacts, the 'web of power politics'.

---

50. M.H. Cornejo, *The Balance of the Continents* (London: Oxford University Press, 1932), p. 206.
51. Valentine de Balla, *The New Balance of Power in Europe* (Baltimore, Johns Hopkins Press, 1932), preface, see also Martin Wight, 'The Balance of Power', *Diplomatic Investigations*, pp. 172 – 3.
52. *Hansard's Parliamentary Debates*, vol. 446, col. 388.

9: *Theory of diplomacy: diplomacy*

Grotian

In the book *Diplomacy*, by Harold Nicolson, the author describes what he calls 'diplomacy' as if it is the only form of diplomacy (just as one might talk of 'civilization' rather than civilizations). But Nicolson's book itself shows the limits of this exclusive conception of diplomacy. It appears that what he means by the word is 'British diplomacy', and against it can be distinguished, for example, German diplomacy ('heroic' or 'warrior'), or Italian diplomacy ('mobile' or 'opportunist'). So different types of European diplomacy do exist, and there is moreover a distinction between 'old' and 'new' diplomacy. The 'diplomacy' which is British diplomacy does have some claim to be called 'classic diplomacy'. Nicolson describes it in various ways:

Diplomacy . . . in its essence is common sense and charity applied to International Relations; [it is the] application of intelligence and tact to relations between governments . . .
It is not religion that has been the main formative influence in diplomatic theory; it is common sense.
The worst kind of diplomatists are missionaries, fanatics, and lawyers; the best kind are reasonable and humane sceptics.
The art of negotiation is essentially a mercantile art.
The foundation of good diplomacy is the same as the foundation of good business — namely, credit, confidence, consideration and compromise.[1]

This is the central or 'classical' view of diplomacy and it is explicitly Grotius's. This Grotian diplomatic theory, which hooks on conveniently to the Grotian theory of the balance of power, presupposes or requires certain objective conditions for successful diplomatic negotiation. These conditions are two: first the material or physical, the possibility for the parties of dealing on equal terms; and secondly the

---

1. Harold Nicolson, *Diplomacy* (London: Thornton Butterworth Ltd., 1939), pp. 50, 132, 144.

moral, the possibility for the parties of mutual confidence.

The need for the possibility of dealing on equal terms can be linked directly with the theory of the balance of power; that is, the material or physical condition of diplomacy is the existence of a balance of power. Indeed, the balance of power theory is at the foundation of the Grotian, or classic, conception of diplomacy. Now, when anti-colonialism is orthodoxy, and there is a consciousness of how Western civilization trampled on the face of non-Western civilizations, the beginning of the story is often forgotten: the impossibility of diplomacy with the Mogul Emperor, Jahangir, in the seventeenth century,[2] or with the Manchu Ch'ien Lung in the eighteenth century.[3] These potentates could not believe there were states with whom they might deal on terms of equality; they did not recognize the principle of the balance of power. However in this context the phrase would mean the balance of *bargaining* power, which is different from the balance of *general* power. It involves the possibility of give and take, mutual concession, and the even distribution of bargaining assets. There may be no even distribution of power in general between a United States and a Cuba, or a Britain and an Iceland, but there can be an even distribution of bargaining assets. A third-rate power can even take action which is strictly aggressive against a great power, and obtain a strong bargaining position by doing so.

Diplomacy requires, then, the ability to deal on even terms, the possibility of give and take, where either side can make concessions while leaving the substance of its interests intact, or else the side making the greater concessions receives compensation. This is the original meaning of 'negotiating from a position of strength'. The phrase, or idea, is traceable back to Dean Acheson, in his address to the Advertising Council, in the White House, on 16 February 1950: 'The only way to deal with the Soviet Union, we have found from hard experience, is to create situations of strength.'[4]

The defensive posture in Acheson was a desire, not so much to out-strip Russia, as to level up to her position, to restore an even distribution of bargaining assets. Another example comes from before the Geneva Conference in 1954, when it became a matter of diplomatic concern and calculation for the Western powers that France should strengthen her military position in Indo-China against the Vietminh, not so that she should be able to recognize Indo-China but so that she should be able to abdicate. She could only make a respectable withdrawal if her

---

2. Sir Thomas Roe was sent to the Emperor's Court in 1615 by James I as ambassador; he stayed for about three years.
3. See Arnold J. Toynbee, *A Study of History* (London: Oxford University Press, 1935), vol. I, p. 161.
4. Dean Acheson, 'The Task of Today's Diplomacy', summary of remarks made at a meeting of the Advertising Council, White House 16 February 1950, released to the press 9 March 1950. In Coral Bell, *Negotiation from Strength* (London: Chatto & Windus, 1962), p. 13.

military situation were improved. As Eden observed, 'military success had to precede negotiation'.[5] At least they had to hold their ground militarily, so that their bargaining position at Geneva should not be weakened.

The balance of bargaining power, as a necessary material condition of negotiation, means that each side has the possibility of coercing the other side, either by withholding concessions, or by driving an unfair bargain such as exploiting some immediate advantage in order to sell its concessions too dearly, in which case there is an element of unbalance. Also the balance of bargaining power may be altered by some action outside the conference room (for example, Germany's conclusion of the Rapallo Treaty with Soviet Russia in 1922). In general, Grotian theory condemns these manipulations of the balance of bargaining power.

There is a good example of the exploiting of an immediate advantage in the dispute over Trieste after the Second World War. The Italian Peace Treaty of 1947 made Trieste a free territory, but the disagreement between the great powers about the governor left it partitioned in fact between the occupying powers; the north taken by the British and Americans, the south by the Yugoslavs. Italy claimed all Trieste, and all Italian opinion was inflamed about it except for the Communist party under Togliatti which could not appeal to national sentiment but supported the Cominform. As the election of 1948 approached, which the Communist party might have won, the Western powers decided to exploit this circumstance. Shortly before the elections they proposed in a tripartite declaration a drastic revision of the Italian Peace Treaty giving the whole of Trieste — both zones — to Italy. This was done to embarrass Communists everywhere and influence the Italian elections. The Tripartite declaration delighted Italians and helped a sweeping Christian Democrat victory at the polls. It was irrelevant to the dragging negotiations with Russia over Trieste, because Soviet consent was needed to revise the Peace Treaty and this would not be given. It was a smart trick. Eden comments: 'Later events cast doubts on the wisdom of this Western initiative. In the most tangled diplomatic problems it seldom pays to snatch a short-term advantage, especially if this limits the area of manoeuvre, as in this instance.'[6]

The Geneva Conference of 1954 gives an example of a country trying to change the balance of power during negotiations. In the middle of the conference, Eden read in the papers of the Franco-American discussions for immediate United States military intervention in Indo-China (of course Eden had not been informed by Dulles):

I was relieved when Bidault informed me that France would make no request

---

5. Sir Anthony Eden, *The Memoirs of The Rt. Hon. Sir Anthony Eden, Full Circle* (London: Cassell, 1960), p. 84.
6. ibid., pp. 178–9.

for intervention while the conference was still in session. Nevertheless, the episode had its dangers. It was not that I minded 'noises off'. They could be helpful, but only under certain very definite conditions.[7]

Later Bidault told him that if agreement at Geneva was not reached America would send in three divisions. 'He added that he regarded this as distant thunder which might help the conference.'[8]

These are illustrations of how, in a balance of bargaining power, either side has the possibility of coercing the other. These means of exerting pressure, these inherent possibilities of coercion, are well known to all concerned; they are inherent in international politics, and in much domestic politics too. The Grotian disapproves of snatching advantages, rocking the conference boat, noises off, but to say this is not enough; his attitude to such possibilities of coercion in general is important, subtle, even paradoxical. While the balance of bargaining power is not in doubt, both sides know that coercion lurks in the background, but they avoid reference to it. They know that 'coercion' in its extreme form means war, but this must not be mentioned; in the last resort war may be threatened, but it is understood that this is a statement of moral inflexibility and different from actual war. [e.g. Lloyd George threatening war on Ireland in order to secure the Treaty, 1921. Eds.] However if the balance of bargaining power seems endangered, it at once becomes necessary to speak plainly and firmly.

As long as the possibility of give-and-take remains clear, there is a duty of reticence about the coercive aspects of the balance of bargaining power. War in international affairs, like death in private affairs, is not normally a subject of decent conversation; every responsible person knows they are there in the background but does not speak of them. 'Metternich at a conference, when the word "war" was used, held up his hands in horror: Hush! War is an obscene word; never to be used, lest using it one makes the idea of it more possible.'[9] Similarly Burke, talking of the English admirers of the French Revolution, commented:

I never liked this continual talk of resistance, and revolution, or the practice of making the extreme medicine of constitution its daily bread. It renders the habit of society dangerously valetudinary; it is taking periodical doses of [stimulating drugs] to our love of liberty.[10]

---

7. ibid., p. 120.
8. ibid., p. 127.
9. Sir Frank Fox, *The Mastery of the Pacific* (London: The Bodley Head Ltd., 1928), p. VI.
10. Edmund Burke, 'Reflections on the Revolution in France', *The Works of the Right Hon. Edmund Burke* (London: Samuel Holdsworth, 1842), vol. I, p. 405.

So far can the effects of this reticence go, that it can become generally understood that a threat of war — if such becomes necessary — is generically different from actual war, although it has to be taken with utmost seriousness. In 1840 during the Mehemet Ali crisis, Louis-Philippe told Bulwer, the British Ambassador: 'M. Thiers is furious with me, because I was not willing to go to war. He tells me that I talked about going to war — but to talk of going to war, and to go to war, are two things very different.' Bulwer commented: 'One is not obliged in diplomacy to consider every menace of war as actual war'.[11] Perhaps the reasoning behind this is that the intention or desire for war is absent, but things may get out of control; it is a threat of a generalized contingency. Eden's *Memoirs* illustrate how it is done. On 5 May 1954 at Geneva, Molotov and Gromyko dined with Eden and they talked over the entire situation;

Towards the end of our conversation, I said that I would speak very frankly. If the Indo-China situation was not effectively handled here at Geneva, there was a real danger that the supporters of each side would go on increasing the degree of their participation, until finally there was a clash between them. If it happened, I continued, it might well be the beginning of the third world war. Molotov fully agreed with this assessment.[12]

Eden was not saying in certain circumstances I and my allies will go to war with you and yours; but: in certain circumstances a situation may arise, beyond our control which, as we talk together here now, we should all deplore.

These points illustrate the theoretical basis of the graded formulae of diplomatic language; the guarded understatements and conventional phrases with known currency value.

Thus 'My Government cannot remain indifferent to . . .' means it will intervene;
'my Government views with concern . . .' means it is going to take a strong line.
'In that event, my Government will be obliged to consider its own interests' indicates that it will break off relations, and if something 'will be regarded as an unfriendly act' it would lead to war.[13]

Metternich's outburst on war, as mentioned above, and Louis-Philippe's caution during the Mehemet Ali crisis, are two illustrations from the period 1815–48, one of the most Grotian in international politics, when the Holy Alliance and revolutionary nationalism were in an uneasy equilibrium, and the Concert of Europe flourished.

---

11. H.L. Bulwer, *The Life of Henry John Temple, Viscount Palmerston* (London: Richard Bentley, 1871), vol. II, p. 352.
12. Sir Anthony Eden, *Full Circle*, p. 117.
13. Harold Nicolson, *Diplomacy*, pp. 227–8.

Compare the analogue period after 1945, with its balance of terror and nuclear parity, when once again it is agreed that one does not threaten war and that the threat of war, if it has to be made, is a different matter from actual war. One of the main threats of war in this period — described as 'nuclear blackmail' — is in Bulganin's letter to Eden of 5 November 1956 at the height of the Suez crisis. British commentators agreed to regard this as a threat of war, generically different from actual war.[14] [There was also Eisenhower's threat to China in 1953 to end the Korean War — revealed long after. Eds.]

The duty of reticence lasts only while there is a possibility of dealing on equal terms; if the balance of bargaining assets is deliberately upset or endangered, then a duty of frankness emerges. There is a need to make the consequences of the other party's action perfectly plain. This is the foundation of the Grotian attitude towards aggression and the preservation of international security, and it will be elaborated and illustrated in that chapter.

The normal duty of reticence and the contingent duty of frankness are, so to speak, the moral consequences of the material or physical condition for diplomacy; that is the possibility of dealing on equal terms. The moral condition for diplomacy is mutual confidence, but this is not quite straightforward; it is two-sided, involving reciprocity and mutuality: what you owe to me as well as what I owe to you. Eden wrote about the Iranian oil dispute in July 1952: 'We are ready at any time to negotiate a settlement, but, in order that there may be negotiations it is essential that there should be two parties who are prepared to negotiate.'[15]

First, the opposite number must prove his readiness to negotiate; he must create confidence on the other side. It may exist already (if the two parties are friends) and then the need does not arise, but if it does not exist, something must be done to inspire it. In April 1953, after Stalin's death, Eisenhower appealed to the new leaders of the Soviet Union to give tangible evidence of their desire for peace which could lead to a reduction in armaments: 'We care only for sincerity of peaceful purpose, attested by deeds. The opportunities for such deeds are many.'[16] It is the situation in which a gesture from the other side is demanded. India, before Khrushchev and Bulganin's visit in November 1955, took the position that if there were to be negotiations with China, the next move must come from Peking, and it must be conciliatory enough to inspire confidence that China really wanted a settlement.

Underlying this is the doctrine that the principles of a case are more important than the facts of it. In January 1960 Mr Justice Cassels, in

---

14. Sir Anthony Eden, *Full Circle*, p. 554; see also Guy Wint and Peter Calvocoressi, *Middle East Crisis* (London: Penguin Books, 1957), p. 82.
15. Sir Anthony Eden, *Full Circle*, p. 205.
16. Dwight D. Eisenhower quoted in Sir Anthony Eden, *Full Circle*, p. 50.

the Court of Criminal Appeal, quashed the convictions of three men found guilty at the Nottingham Assizes where Mr Justice Stable had told the jury to come to a verdict in twenty minutes; Cassels enunciated the doctrine that the abstract principle of justice is more important than the justice of the case itself. In the same vein, Nehru in August 1959 said: 'It does not make very much difference physically to China or India whether a mile or two in the high mountains belongs to them or to us. It does matter very much if a treaty is broken or an aggressive attitude is taken.'[17]

This is not just petty legalism or moralism: a gesture must be made to prove that both sides respect the same principles of negotiation. There is an obverse to this: if an antagonist will prove his readiness to negotiate, then one must not humiliate him in advance. In the preparations for the Geneva (Indo-China) conference in 1954 the United States wanted retaliation against China to make her withdraw aid from the Vietminh. Eden commented:

There is a distinction between warning China that some specified further action will entail retaliation, which might be an effective deterrent, and calling upon her to desist from action in which she is already engaged. I cannot see what threat would be sufficiently potent to make China swallow so humiliating a rebuff as the abandonment of the Vietminh without any face-saving concession in return.[18]

He added that China would not yield to threats, in which event the Western powers must either retreat ignominiously or embark on war against her; in effect, do not humiliate in advance.

Once your opponent has shown his readiness to negotiate, then you must do so also. If these objective conditions are granted, if there is some balance of bargaining power and a possibility of dealing on equal terms, and if your antagonist has won your confidence by proving his readiness to negotiate, then you can do your part and deserve his confidence by advancing with a gleaming smile and an outstretched hand. It is then that the principles of classic diplomacy can bear fruit, conferences and summit meetings come into their own and have a chance of being something more than a source of disillusionment for the simple-minded or of cynical wit for the politically sophisticated.

'Is there anything in the world today which can take the place of ink, pens, a conference table with its green cover, and a few greater or smaller burglars?' (Metternich at Laibach, 1821). There is no alternative to negotiating.

The principles of classic diplomacy can be enumerated. First there is honesty or truthfulness ('credit'). Don't tell lies or break promises,

---

17. Jawaharlal Nehru quoted in *The Guardian*, 10 November 1959. See also J. Nehru, *India's Foreign Policy* (Delhi: The Publications Division, Ministry of Information and Broadcasting, Government of India, 1961), pp. 338, 349, 354.
18. Sir Anthony Eden, *Full Circle*, p. 93.

it does not pay and brings its own retribution; establish a reputation for straight dealing.[19] Talleyrand in his last address to the Académie des Sciences Morales et Politiques declared that diplomacy was not the art of duplicity and deceit. If ever there is a need for good faith, it is in politics: only that can make our transactions durable and reliable.

The second principle is that of moderation and restraint, keeping a sense of proportion. It requires the absence of assertiveness or national (and personal) egotism, and a readiness to make concessions, to give way on unessentials. Eden commented on the Berlin Conference in January 1953: 'A tiresome argument with the Russians about which building to use provided a discouraging prelude for our conference. It is usually prudent to be conciliatory on matters of secondary importance, though in dealing with the Russians these can add up to quite a bill.'[20] Eden, Dulles and Bidault agreed together to avoid a prolonged wrangle about Molotov's proposed agenda, so as to get down to the discussion of Germany and Austria. Eden noted: 'by accepting the Soviet agenda we have saved much haggling and gained world good will. We shall need it.'[21]

There is courtesy: seeking not diplomatic 'victories', 'triumphs', or 'successes', all of which imply a defeated antagonist, but 'agreements', which suggests common achievement; or perhaps seeking 'victories' which come without being noticed. The art of diplomacy is to conceal the victory: 'The best diplomacy is that which gets its own way, but leaves the other side reasonably satisfied. It is often good diplomacy to resist a score.'[22] Leave your antagonist a line of retreat but studiedly ignore whether he is taking it.

The fourth principle is respect for the other side: this involves both thinking the best of people, and trying to share their point of view, understand their interests. Palmerston wrote to Arthur Aston, the secretary in the Paris embassy in 1836, when the Entente Cordiale between Whig Britain and Louis-Philippe was crumbling, each suspecting the other of disloyalty or treachery over Spain and Portugal:

But what a little and narrow-minded policy and view of international affairs that must have been, which led the French Government to exhaust against their dear friend and ally all those resources of intrigue and diplomacy which, if well applied, might have produced some results honourable to them and beneficial to Europe! However, so goes the world, and one must take men as one finds them, and make the best of what is, shut one's eyes to failings and faults, and dwell as much as one can upon good points . . .

---

19. See Harold Nicolson quoting De Callières (1645–1717), *De la manière de négocier avec les souverains* (Paris: Brunet, 1716) in *Diplomacy*, pp. 108ff.
20. Sir Anthony Eden, *Full Circle*, pp. 61–2.
21. ibid., p. 65.
22. ibid., pp. 356–7. The neatest definition once appeared on the back of a matchbox: 'Diplomacy is allowing somebody to have your way.' Eds.

and again, this time to H.L. Bulwer: 'We must take people as they are, and make the best of their good qualities, without dwelling too much on their bad' ('A phrase Lord Palmerston frequently repeated').[23] Eden's *Memoirs* are full of examples of his capacity to get inside the mind of his opposite party and understand their interests.[24]

All these principles slide into one another, and are facets of the same thing. It begins to sound like a course in moral theology — honesty, moderation, courtesy, sympathy for others — and one sees that Nicolson's dictum, 'diplomacy . . . in its essence is common sense and charity applied to international relations',[25] is not exaggerated. It might be summed up as a reconciliation of interests, a composing of differences, even, perhaps, creating a common interest. Webster says of Castlereagh that he

had the great gift of obtaining what he wanted in such a manner that others came to want it also, [he] was very successful at persuading others that his plans were the same as theirs, or at the worst that they had gained the major part in the compromises which he was so expert in framing.[26]

Thus Eden at Geneva in 1954 strove to unite the interests of the West, the Communist powers, and the uncommitted nations; it was essential, in his view, to secure the benevolence or participation of India.

If one tries to assemble the elements of a Grotian view of international politics it is here, having delineated the principles of diplomacy, that one is most aware of a theory constructed in terms of tension, balanced opposites, political factors interpenetrated by moral ones, and power harnessed by purpose. And the easiest way to understand the other traditions concerning diplomacy is by seeing them tearing the arch apart, relaxing the intellectual tension; the Kantian going off with the moral element, disentangling it from objective conditions of negotiation, and the Machiavellian going off with the power element and releasing it from moral controls.

Machiavellian

It is easy enough to see how a Realist or Machiavellian critique will dissolve the Grotian synthesis that has been sketched; at many points this synthesis was open to attack. The Machiavellian would cast doubt

23. H.L. Bulwer, *The Life of Henry John Temple, Viscount Palmerston*, vol. II, pp. 239, 285.
24. Sir Anthony Eden (of the Soviet leaders before the Berlin Conference of 1953, Bulganin and Khrushchev in Britain in 1956, the Chinese during the Geneva Conference of 1954, and the Yugoslavs over Trieste 1954). *Full Circle*, pp. 58ff., 359, 93 and 123, 184.
25. Harold Nicolson, *Diplomacy*, p. 43.
26. C.K. Webster, *The Foreign Policy of Castlereagh 1812–1815* (London: G. Bell & Sons Ltd., 1931), vol. I, p. 487.

on the existence or even the possibility, of the Grotian 'objective conditions' of negotiation, at least as formulated by the Grotian. Equal terms, the balance of bargaining power, never exist any more than does the balance of power; the Grotian appears to the Machiavellian like one who should say, 'the condition for navigation is a calm sea'. But this is politically childish, he who cannot navigate except when the equilibrium of the sea's surface is not destroyed and agitated by winds is not a navigator, since navigation consists in conquering or outwitting the weather and getting from one's sailing-point to a destination. Also, mutual confidence never exists, fully; and the distinction between material and moral conditions is unreal; it was continually breaking down even as the Grotian tried to explain it. Diplomacy is for the Machiavellian the intelligent application of pressure or inducement in pursuit of one's own interests in such a way as to make the full exertion of one's power unnecessary. The only moral condition of diplomacy is the existence of sufficient intelligence, discretion and technical skill in applying material force and offering material favours.

The Machiavellian conception of diplomacy can be organized under four heads: flux or change; fear and greed; negotiation from strength; and the technique of bargaining. Flux, or change, is the great 'objective condition' of diplomacy; the endless flux of political life is the raw material which the diplomatist must fashion. It is what Machiavelli himself called *fortuna*. The Machiavellian attitude to political change might be traced through four words: adapt, forestall, facilitate and control.

Adaptability to change is the basic quality required of the diplomatist; he must be able to adapt himself to the changing surface of the sea, to take the rough weather with the smooth. 'The evils by which the body politic is threatened are in a state of constant change, and with them the remedies by which those evils must be cured'[27] (Salisbury on Pitt). In politics there is only one mistake more foolish than assuming that what happens now will go on happening for ever; that is, obstinately trying to make sure that it does. This fundamental quality of adaptability, the capacity for modifying objectives in mid-negotiation, was present in Eden's successes. (He skilfully used the technique over the Iranian oil crisis, the settlement of Trieste, the partition of Indo-China, independence for Cyprus, and German participation in the defence of Europe, as later did Macmilian in his weathercocking to the 'wind of change' in Africa.) Salisbury wrote to Lytton in May 1877;

The commonest error in politics is sticking to the carcasses of dead policies. When a mast falls overboard, you do not try to save a rope here and a spar there, in memory of their former utility; you cut away the hamper altogether.

---

27. *Essays by the Late Marquess of Salisbury* (London: John Murray, 1905), p. 121.

And it should be the same with a policy. But it is not so. We cling to the shred of an old policy after it has been torn to pieces; and to the shadow of the shred after the rag itself has been torn away.[28]

This was true, perhaps not of Britain in Africa in the later 1950s, but probably of Britain in the Middle East.

The capacity to adapt oneself to change is the minimum diplomatic requirement. A higher achievement is to anticipate change, to see the dirty weather ahead and avoid it or outflank it. It was the essence of the great Lord Salisbury's diplomatic philosophy: 'His own conception of a perfect diplomacy was always of one whose victories come without observation.'[29] Webster, a Grotian, applies this to Castlereagh as if it describes 'courtesy', concealing a diplomatic victory in mutual congratulations on a common achievement of agreement;[30] but in its place in Lady Gwendolen Cecil's *Life* [of Salisbury] it clearly describes something different, this Machiavellian quality of forestalling change. Salisbury's handling of the Eastern Crisis in 1878 is usually regarded as his supreme achievement. He thought the opposite: 'I never wish for my foreign policy to be judged by my action in '78. I was only picking up the china that Derby had broken.'[31] British policy should have been decided in 1875, when the crisis began, and pursued steadily; he had to do in three months what ought to have taken three years. 'Long-prepared and concentrated purpose was of the essence of his policy.'[32]

The 'victories without observation' of diplomacy are not the concealed victories in the Grotian sense, but the changes forestalled, the crises foreseen and averted. This leads to the view put forward by modern Machiavellians like Carr and Butterfield, that the height of diplomatic skill would be to anticipate change by such skill in granting peaceful change, that the powers desiring change would not need to display violence to put their complaints on the agenda.

'The English aristocracy . . . have on occasion been able to forestall that resort to violence which would have released a flood of uncontrollable change. And this, too, is a form of diplomacy — a victory of the human intelligence in its perennial conflict with force and chance.'[33] It was to be seen, too, in the case of Macmillan's speech to the South African parliament in Capetown in February 1960 about a 'wind of change' in Africa.

When change is thought of as something to be adapted to, to be

---

28. Lady Gwendolen Cecil, *Life of Robert Marquis of Salisbury* (London: Hodder & Stoughton, 1921), vol. II, p. 145.
29. ibid., p. 232.
30. C.K. Webster, *The Foreign Policy of Castlereagh 1812–1815*, vol. I, p. 478.
31. Lady Gwendolen Cecil, *Life of Robert Marquis of Salisbury*, vol. II, pp. 231–2.
32. ibid., p. 232.
33. Herbert Butterfield, *Christianity, Diplomacy and War* (London: The Epworth Press, 1953), p. 69.

outwitted or forestalled, it is seen as hostile and inimical to the status quo, but the practised Machiavellian thinker can come to conceive of change that is inevitable as a process which can in some degree be directed. Thus Machiavelli himself imagined *fortuna* not only as a mysterious process to be watched with a cautious eye, but also as something which could be seized and mastered by the adventurous, violent, or audacious. The most eloquent contemporary exponent of the view that the function of diplomacy is to assist change is G.F. Kennan.

The function of a system of international relationships is not to inhibit this process of change by imposing a legal straitjacket upon it but rather to facilitate it; to ease its transitions, to temper the asperities to which it often leads, to isolate and moderate the conflicts to which it gives rise, and to see that these conflicts do not assume forms too unsettling for international life in general. But this is a task for diplomacy, in the most old-fashioned sense of the term.[34]

The task of international politics is not to inhibit change but to find means to permit change to proceed without repeatedly shaking the peace of the world.[35]

Salisbury writes in 1880, of the Near East, in words which could apply to Asia or Africa since the war:

It is a fallacy to assume that within our lifetime any stable arrangement can be arrived at in the East. The utmost we can do is to provide halting-places where the process of change may rest awhile. But what we have to do is rather to assume the probability of change, and so shape our precautions that it shall affect no vital interest of ours.[36]

Here control means something like the control of a river, building dykes to contain it so that it does not flood your property; but the conception of 'control' could go farther. Can change not be diverted and directed? Might it not be possible, to change the metaphor, to ride the tiger? If there is a Machiavellian who abets and facilitates change in order to control it, and understands 'controlling' as directing, then he is half-way round the political circle, at the point where aggressive Machiavellianism meets revolutionary Kantianism. This is the realm of Stalin or of Hitler, who simply manufactured change by arousing irredentist movements hitherto quiescent.

As perpetual change is the material objective condition of diplomacy,

---

34. George F. Kennan, *American Diplomacy 1900–1950* (New York: The New American Library by arrangement with the University of Chicago Press, 1955), p. 96.
35. George F. Kennan, *Realities of American Foreign Policy* (London: Oxford University Press, 1954), pp. 35–6.
36. Lady Gwendolen Cecil, *Life of Robert Marquis of Salisbury*, vol. II, p. 377.

corresponding to the Grotian's 'equal terms', so the moral objective
condition corresponding to the Grotian's 'mutual confidence', is fear.
Here 'objective condition' acquires a different meaning; the Grotian
uses it as if to describe the *sine qua non* of diplomacy: if the condition
is not granted there can be no negotiation. For the Machiavellian this
is quite unreal. 'Objective conditions' have to be recognized, in the
sense of objective circumstances; whether welcome or not, they form
the groundwork of all policy. Diplomacy, as Butterfield has said, functions in cases where wills are in conflict and power is involved, so
that, if there were not negotiation, there would be a direct appeal to
force. The force may be muffled or transmuted into a kind of bargaining power, but it is ineradicably there. Thus, 'diplomacy is potential
war',[37] and 'diplomacy in practice, is mutual instruction through fear'
(Baron von Humboldt).[38]

When stripped of the niceties of protocol, diplomacy is seen to
proceed by coercion and bribery, by stick and carrot. These pressures
and bribes can be economic, political, or military. Consider the hold
that the United States has had on King Hussein, the Shah, King Saud
of Arabia, and they on the United States; or that the Soviet Union had
on Gomulka and Ulbricht, and they on it. Powers are held to one
another by fear of the consequences of a breach, and, in Walpole's
definition of the gratitude of place-expectants, by 'a lively sense of
future favours'.

Influence abroad is to be maintained only by the operation of one or other of
two principles — hope and fear. We ought to teach the weaker Powers to
hope that they will receive the support of this country in their time of danger.
Powerful countries should be taught to fear that they will be resisted by
England in any unjust acts either towards ourselves or towards those who are
bound in ties of amity with us'.[39]

Kennan wrote that he viewed with scepticism America's chances of
exerting useful influence unless she learned to create as much respect
for her disfavour as for her possible favour. American policy towards
the uncommitted world must embrace, 'for all to see', the harsh as
well as the mild elements, with the possibility of their being applied
flexibly, interchangeably, even simultaneously. He wanted to find
ways in which the denial of American favour 'can be made to bring
other people to respect the seriousness of our purposes and the dignity
of our position in the world'. And he quotes Jefferson to make his
point.[40]

---

37. R.G. Hawtrey, *Economic Aspects of Sovereignty*, p. 107, quoted by Palme Dutt,
    World Politics 1918—1936 (London: Gollancz, 1936), p. 26.
38. Quoted by E.L. Woodward, *War and Peace in Europe 1815-1870*, (London:
    Constable & Co. Ltd., 1931), p. 12.
39. Lord Palmerston in the House of Commons, 17 August 1844, *Hansard's
    Parliamentary Debates*, LXXVI, col. 1873.
40. G.F. Kennan, *Realities of American Foreign Policy*, pp. 58—9.

The diplomatist has to recognize his own objectives and limitations; there are certain things he wants, certain consequences he fears, and certain things he cannot do because his power reaches its limits. Thus one arrives at two conclusions. The first was expressed in an extraordinary sentence by E.H. Carr: 'A successful foreign policy must oscillate between the apparently opposite poles of force and appeasement.'[41] The second is that the wider object of diplomacy is to establish balanced antagonisms, controlled international tensions, so as to gain the maximum influence with the minimum obligation. The ideal of removing these tensions, of educing some common interests, is quite chimerical; Gladstone, for example, believed in such an ideal, Bismarck did not.

Given these objective conditions, the rule of one's own diplomacy must be to negotiate from strength, and this in the accepted sense of the phrase. It is all very well to say that Acheson originated this phrase as meaning attaining parity of bargaining power, or a levelling up, but would the Russians have concurred with his use of the phrase in this sense? of course not. This is the old argument about the balance of power in the sense of the even distribution of power: if the distribution suits you, you call it even, if it does not suit you, you deny its evenness. It is not an accident or perversion of language that 'negotiating from strength' has come to mean negotiating from a preponderance of strength, or 'having an edge'. This is language conforming to political reality. Thus Dr Raghuvira, telling the Indian Council of States on 8 March 1960 that he had information that China would test an atom-bomb on the 28th, said this date had been chosen to enable Chou En-lai to speak from a position of strength when he visited India in April.[42] 'Walk softly and carry a big stick,' as President 'Teddy' Roosevelt said.

There are three corollaries of this position, which the Grotian would not accept. First, improve your position and increase your strength as the opportunity offers; Grotian moral arguments boil down to the opposite, that only restraint is prudential; (thus Nicolson condemned as 'sudden diplomacy' Aerenthal's seizure of Bosnia-Herzegovina (1908)). But for the Machiavellian the only test is success. De Gaulle's diplomacy illustrates this: 'As a soldier [he is] convinced that attack is the best means of defence. His experience during the Second World War has taught him that future power can be successfully used like present power if this is done with boldness, imagination and utter intrepidity.'[43] He 'blackmailed the United States' in 1966 by ejecting the NATO bases and raising the price of his friendship because he could not be quite confident of America.

---

41. E.H. Carr, *The Twenty Years' Crisis 1919–1939* (London: Macmillan Co. Ltd., 1939), p. 284.
42. Victor Zorza in *The Guardian*, 9 March 1960.
43. Sebastian Haffner in the *Observer*, 6 December 1959.

A second corollary is brinkmanship; the belief that threats of the final coercion are not out of place. Taking the calculated risk of war is often necessary. 'Some say that we were brought to the verge of war. Of course we were brought to the verge of war. The ability to get to the verge without getting into war is *the necessary art*. If you cannot master it . . . if you are scared to go to the brink, you are lost' (Secretary of State J.F. Dulles January 1956).[44] These notions are only remarkable because they came from a leading Presbyterian member of the ecumenical 'Commission on a just and durable Peace'.

The third corollary is firmness through fatalism. One who is confident of negotiating from a preponderance of strength, and who is prepared to face war, acquires a fatalistic freedom from fear. 'My opinion . . . is now what it has been all along, that, till France is ready, *nothing will provoke* her to quarrel with us; and that, when she is ready, *nothing will prevent* it.'[45]

If Stalin wants war there will be war. If he does not want it he is not going to be provoked into starting it first because the US have decided to keep Formosa on our side of the barricade.

There is little reason to believe that a landing of British troops in Persia would lead to a third world war. If Stalin wants war there will be war, with or without a pretext. But he is certainly not going to be driven into starting one simply because we decide to take strong action to protect vital British interests.[46]

Sir John Slessor argued in 1954 that 'if the Russians wanted war, they would not worry about waiting to be provoked; and we should not allow our strategy to be deflected by weak-kneed fear of provoking them, or refrain from the use of force for fear of it leading to general war'.[47]

This is the obverse of the Grotian's attempt to get inside and appreciate the other man's interests. It assumes a hostility and irreconcilability of views, discounting the other side's views in advance.

The criterion of one's own policy becomes the hostility it arouses in a potential enemy. Here disregard for the other power's point of view passes over into reasoned antagonism, and the full consequence is drawn from irreconcilable interests. '. . . an *English* Ministry never need desire a greater eulogism of their conduct, than the being cried down and disapproved by that of *France*.'[48]

---

44. Secretary of State J.F. Dulles, interview in *Life Magazine*, 11 January 1956, reported in *The Times*, 12 January 1956.
45. Third Earl of Malmesbury, ed. Harris to Carmarthen from Hague, 1786, *James Harris, First Earl of Malmesbury, Diaries and Correspondence* (London: Richard Bentley, 1845), vol. II, pp. 201–2.
46. Julian Amery, letter to *The Times*, 24 July 1950, and to the *Observer*, June 1951.
47. Sir John Slessor, *Strategy for the West* (London: Cassell & Co., 1954), p. 58.
48. Third Earl of Malmesbury, ed., Harris to Fox, from St. Petersburg, 1783, *James Harris, First Earl of Malmesbury, Diaries and Correspondence*, vol. I, p. 524.

It is likely to become a firmer principle as one passes round the political circle from aggressive Machiavellianism to revolutionary Kantianism. In ideological warfare, or cold war, the assumption that what your enemy dislikes must be virtuous and advantageous to you is built-in. Aneurin Bevan continually attacked this assumption: 'It will be fatal to judge every diplomatic move we make by the simple test of whether or not it wounds the Communists.'[49]

So far 'diplomacy' in Machiavellian theory tends to slide away from the narrow sense of negotiation to the wider sense of 'policy'; but the Machiavellian does not neglect the art of negotiation; he studies all its tricks. Here he has much common ground with the Grotian, though the Grotian sees these technicalities as subject to moral restraint, while the Machiavellian sees them as open to exploitation. There are two or three ground rules to be remembered for successful negotiation. In all bargains the man most warmly bent on obtaining the object of discussion is inevitably the weaker; his eagerness drives the price of agreement up in exact proportion. Thus Hitler constantly raised the price of peace which the League powers so anxiously desired. The Machiavellian will resort to the technique of the special train; steam up, ready to depart!

The Duce insisted that the Axis Powers should make a gesture which would reassure people of the peaceful intentions of Italy and Germany [an international conference was to be proposed]. Ciano said that the Duce considered that the party would win at a conference which was ready in certain circumstances to allow the conference to fail and take into account the eventuality of war as a result of failure.[50]

There is always an advantage in framing the issue; as Lloyd George is reported to have said: 'Never negotiate on the other fellow's draft.' Acheson put it to the NATO Parliamentary Conference in Washington in November 1959, 'that the man who could frame the issue had gone far towards a successful conclusion of it'.[51] Another rule or trick of negotiation is to proceed from small to big issues. Eden told the UN General Assembly in Paris in 1951: 'On both fronts, political and economic, let us grasp definite and limited problems, and work for their practical solution . . . Preparation, conference and agreement: starting from small issues and working to the great.'[52] Khrushchev echoed this when talking to NATO ambassadors at a cocktail party in February 1958: deputations should start with simple issues before coming to the more difficult, 'it is like a meal. First you have

49. Aneurin Bevan quoted in 'Sayings of the Week', the *Observer*, 27 January 1957.
50. Count Galleazzo Ciano: Hitler talks, 12 August 1939, *Nazi Conspiracy and Aggression* (Washington, DC: US Printing Office, 1946), vol. VIII, Document TC77, pp. 523–4.
51. Reported in *The Guardian*, 20 November 1959.
52. Sir Anthony Eden, Full Circle, p. 11.

appetizers. Then soup and fish. Then, the main course.'[53] This
describes either the stages of approach to a Grotian agreement, or the
stages of a Machiavellian softening-up operation.

Kantian

While the Machiavellian runs off with the physical elements in the
Grotian synthesis, the Kantian moves in the opposite direction with
the moral elements. The position of the Kantian is perhaps more
difficult to formulate than the other two, because he does not really
believe in diplomacy, except under protest. His position appears more
fragmentary than theirs, as if it is just disconnected protests against the
predominant view, but this may be an optical illusion suffered by the
politically sophisticated. For on the whole this moral position is not
the statesman's or diplomatist's philosophy but the private person's
(letters to the press), or the armchair philosopher's (Cobden). Few
with practical experience of international politics and diplomacy have
been Kantians, or remained it. Revolutionary Kantians tend to slide
into Machiavellianism, or to moderate into Grotianism (Khrushchev is
possibly an example of this). Evolutionary Kantians in power have
been few (Wilson and Eisenhower are examples).

As with other traditions, one can distinguish between objective
conditions of diplomacy and principles to be followed in these conditions. The Grotian objective conditions are equal terms (the material
objective condition) and mutual confidence (the moral objective
condition); the Machiavellian equivalents are political change (the
material) and fear and greed (the moral objective condition).

Although apparently paradoxical, one can set against these the
Kantian objective conditions: reduction of tension, and open
diplomacy. Perhaps it is paradoxical to suggest that the relaxation of
tension is an equivalent of the material objective conditions of equal
terms and political flux. It must be remembered of course that
Kantian theory emphasizes moral factors at the expense of material
ones; indeed it so consistently depreciates material factors that not
one could be singled out to make a heading for a subdivision of the
theory. And two things need to be noted about the Kantian's conception of international tension; first, it is generalized, absolute,
unqualified, rather than specific or qualified; and it is usually stated
generally, not as a particular tension between, for example, England
and France, or the West and the East. Secondly, the concept is
negative, and it is more often found stated negatively, 'reduce
tension', than positively, 'create confidence'. The negative formulation is predominant in Cobden's pamphlet *The Three Panics*
(published 1862) which describes the three anti-French panics of

---

53. Reported by Walter Lippmann in *The Manchester Guardian*, 4 February 1958.

1847–8, 1851–3 and 1859–61, and their attendant naval races. Cobden refers to 'these great political delusions', to 'alarmists', and to 'panics'.[54] It is a conception of international pathology, not of moral philosophy.

International tension is indeed, then, the Kantian obverse of the Machiavellian political flux. The Kantian, too, sees this endless sequence of political change (many Kantians start from the Hobbesian view of the political state of nature). But he sees it in psychological terms, as the ebb and flow of pointless rivalries, the vicious spiral of reciprocal fears and defiances, and panics which mount and can sometimes issue in war over trifles, but sometimes burst like bubbles, and in either case are deplored by the reflective mind and the retrospective historian. The Kantian might be thought to have a particular antiseptic function in pointing out the ridiculousness and futility of so many of the changes in international politics. Cobden wrote of the end of the 1851–3 panic: 'The sudden change which was now to be witnessed in the temper of the public and the action of the Government was so unlooked for, and so utterly beyond all rational calculation, that it might be compared to the shifting of the view in a kaleidoscope.' So in February 1853 the English fleet was preparing for a French invasion; in August of that same year the 'English and French fleets are lying side by side in Besika Bay', having entered into an alliance, and about to go to war against Russia.[55]

Recent examples are not difficult to find. The disarmament and demilitarization of Germany in 1945 was followed by the rearmament and remilitarization of a largely reluctant Germany in 1954, to bring her into NATO. In 1947 the Americans imposed a constitution on Japan including an article renouncing war and the right to possess armed forces; there was a peace treaty in 1950, and in 1951 Dulles, in Tokyo, said Japan not only had the right but the duty to rearm to play her part in collective security. In 1949 Britain sent an ultimatum to Israel that if Israeli troops were not withdrawn from Sinai within forty-eight hours Britain would enter the war against Israel on the side of Egypt; in 1956 Britain took advantage of the Israeli attack on Sinai to attack Egypt. Selwyn Lloyd, in October 1956, said: 'For us in Europe it is a matter of vital importance to maintain the canal as an international waterway'; and in May 1957: 'one of the practical lessons we have learned as a result of the canal being closed, is that it is a wasting asset.'[56]

These ironies (and peripatetics) are agreeable to the non-Kantian, but they make the Kantian angry; he condemns the folly and passion which they illustrate. Cobden describes 'the manner in which panics

---

54. Richard Cobden, *The Political Writings of R. Cobden* (London: William Ridgeway, 1867), vol. II, pp. 224, 225.
55. ibid., pp. 268, 269.
56. See *House of Commons Debates* on Suez of 23 October 1956 and 1 May 1957.

are created and sustained':

A Government proposes a large expenditure for armaments, on the plea that France is making vast warlike preparation; and the public, being thereby impressed with a sense of impending danger, takes up the cry of alarm: when the Minister quotes the echo of his own voice as a justification of his policy, and a sufficient answer to all opponents.[57]

A hundred years later it is not so much that government manufactures public opinion which it then says it must follow, as that the government withholds information [is 'economical with the truth', Eds], conceals the truth, disinforms, and fails to inform public opinion in essential matters of defence and foreign policy, so that it cannot make an instructed judgment on government policy and accepts what is done *faute de mieux*. This is the current Kantian protest.

The Kantian believes that something ought to be done and can be done to reduce tension. If you ask, what?, the answer is, *make a gesture*. This can take the form of a collective, or an individual gesture. An example of the former would be to propose a dramatic reduction in armaments, or the withdrawal of troops in equal proportions from Central Europe. The aim of this has nothing to do with security but to gain the psychological improvement of an atmosphere of lessened tension. The Soviet Union has continually resorted to such proposals (for example, the proposal for an immediate convention for the prohibition and destruction of all atomic weapons, recurring since 1947; for a one-third cut in the forces of all states, since 1948; for an immediate cessation of nuclear tests since 1956; and for total disarmament, 1959), and while they are propaganda gambits, and carefully related to the realistic appraisal of Russia's defensive or aggressive requirements, they seem to stem, nevertheless, from this fundamental Kantian belief that international tension is an irrational obstacle to the fulfilment of human potentialities and ought to be reduced; in other words, they are 'sincere'.

One can also make an individual gesture, or a unilateral move, as a contribution towards the collective gesture; and this is the opposite of the pedantic legalistic Grotian insistence that the other fellow must make a gesture first, to prove *his* sincerity and readiness to negotiate. Thus, in the 1956 presidential election campaign, for example, Stevenson proposed that the United States should suspend nuclear tests, a suggestion met with howls of execration, as showing his unfitness for political responsibility, and so in 1957 the Soviet Union had the tactical advantage of suspending her own first. The Machiavellian will say that no power makes an individual gesture which is not calculated to benefit the national interest, or at least calculated not to harm the national interest, but this is somewhat dogmatic, a priori, and each case would have to be examined on its merits. It is possible that a

---

57. Richard Cobden, 'Third Panic', *Political Writings*, vol. II, p. 385.

power, recognizing that absolute security is always impossible, may consider a moral gesture within the scope of its policy. Cobden liked to quote Peel's speech in 1850: 'I believe that, in time of peace, we must, by our retrenchment, consent to incur some risk.'[58] Is it possible that, in Kremlin discussions on the reduction of Soviet armed forces, Nikita Krushchev spoke thus? [and Gorbachev a generation later? It also recalls Labour apologists for unilateralism in the 1980s. Eds].

Open diplomacy can be taken as the Kantian's moral objective condition for diplomacy. Wilson addressed Congress, on 8 January 1918:

The programme of the world's peace, therefore, is our programme; and that programme, the only possible programme, as we see it, is this: *One*. Open covenants of peace, openly arrived at, after which there shall be no private international understandings of any kind but diplomacy shall proceed always frankly and in the public view.[59]

Article 18 of the Covenant of the League of Nations says that no treaty is binding until registered with the Secretariat; and in the Charter of the United Nations, Article 102 states that no treaty not registered may be invoked before any organ of the United Nations.[60]

The principle of open diplomacy was in fact invented or discovered by Kant himself and is laid down in *Perpetual Peace*. It ends with two long appendices which are the profoundest part of the pamphlet; the first is: 'On the Disagreement between Morals and Politics in relation to Eternal Peace', a super-Hobbesian analysis of actual international politics; the second: 'On the Agreement between Politics and Morals according to the Transcendental Idea of Public Right and Law' (Kantian jargon for 'according to an ideal state of affairs' or 'in theory' 'transcendental' meaning a priori, ideal, or non-empirical). Here Kant shows how politics and morals must be harmonized. Kant says that public right (which means ideal law, or justice) has matter or content on one side and form on the other, and he equates its form with publicity: 'without publicity there cannot be justice, which can only be thought of as capable of being made public.'[61] Thus publicity becomes a criterion of right and he formulates a proposition which he calls 'The Transcendental Formula of Public Right': 'All actions which relate to the right of other men are contrary to right and law, if their maxim does not permit publicity.'[62]

---

58. ibid., p. 425.
59. Ruhl I. Bartlett, ed., *The Record of American Diplomacy* (New York: Alfred A. Knopf, 1947), pp. 459–60.
60. See also Jeremy Bentham, *Plan for an Universal and Perpetual Peace*, Grotius Soc. Publications No. 6 (London: Sweet & Maxwell Ltd., 1927), pp. 31ff.
61. Carl I. Friedrich, *The Philosophy of Kant* (New York: The Modern Library, 1949), p. 470.
62. ibid., p. 470.

A maxim or principle of conduct cannot be right if it has to be kept secret in order to succeed, if its public confession would arouse the resistance of all men against its purpose. If to declare the principles on which you act would arouse universal hostility against you, this can only be because your principle is unjust and threatens everybody. Hitler, for this reason, could not have openly avowed his principles and aims. Leaving aside *Mein Kampf* as an early indiscretion, which happily for him few people noticed, his speeches after 1933 appealed to the Wilsonian principle of self-determination from 1919, and gained their success thereby on the principle of the big lie. There is a distinction here between National Socialism and Communism, which does not conceal its aims at all, although it may describe them in terms its opponents cannot accept, and pursue them by tactical deviousness its opponents denounce as dishonest; but no bourgeois nationalist such as Nasser or Nehru, who accepts Soviet help, has any reason to be in doubt about the intended end.

Kant gives examples of the applicability of his principle that what is not compatible with publicity is unjust. In constitutional law, or the public right of the state, there can be no right of rebellion against a tyrant. True, tyranny violates the rights of people, and dethronement would be no injustice to the tyrant; but the people could not before the social contract announce that they reserved the right to an occasional insurrection. This would arrogate to themselves the right of power over the supreme authority and would contradict the purpose of the social contract. Thus the maxim on which rebellion would proceed, if publicly professed, would make its own purpose impossible, and is therefore unjust.

In international law, a state may not violate its undertakings and promises on the grounds that the sovereign's responsibility to his subjects (in whose name he makes the agreements) may override his position as the highest state official responsible for the state's interests and undertakings, because if a ruler *avowed* such a maxim publicly, other states would avoid making treaties with him or would unite to overthrow him. Similarly, preventive war is not permissible, because a state which proclaimed the maxim that you may attack a powerful neighbour simply because its power arouses apprehension, and before any injury is actually received, would bring about the evil that is dreaded, for the power feared would anticipate the intended attack on it. Nor is it permissible for a great power to annex a small power whose geographical position is a nuisance to it. If a great power published such a maxim of policy, either small powers would combine against it or jealous fellow great powers would fight it for the prize, and the maxim would make itself impracticable by its publicity. Thus the incompatibility of certain maxims of international policy with publicity furnishes a good criterion of the non-agreement of politics with morals.

But Kant goes on to state a transcendental affirmative formula: 'All maxims which *require* publicity in order not to miss their purpose agree with right, law and politics.'[63] But, he says, the bare converse of this, that maxims *allowing* publicity are for this reason just and right, cannot be inferred, for the simple reason that a man or state with decided superiority of power does not need to conceal his maxims. If these maxims can *only* attain their end by publicity, they must be in agreement with the general purpose of mankind, that is, happiness, and they must be in harmony with the rights of mankind. Here the argument ends: only those political principles that *need* to be published in order to be effective are in accordance with human happiness and human rights.

Kant gives no examples of his affirmative formula, and it seems to be difficult to think of a political principle that *needs* to be made public in order to become effective except a statement which formulates the rights of man or of states. For example: every man and woman has an equal right to life, liberty, and the pursuit of happiness, and a voice in choosing his or her own government. This is the principle which would be ineffective unless it was made public; by publishing it you tell men and women something about themselves they may not have recognized and tell them how they are expected to behave. Publication starts the process of social and political ferment which it is intended to start. The statement that every group-conscious people has the right to national self-determination and to form its own state is likely, similarly, to cause the intended ferment; and the statement that every state, great and small, has equal rights in international law and in international society generally will encourage small powers to assert themselves (for example, as they did at San Francisco in 1945, when they complained and protested — but in vain — against the Security Council voting procedure). The assumption behind the transcendental formula of international right is a highly Kantian one: that all men are by right equal and free and the only way to teach them the right use of freedom is to grant it and let it *be used*; freedom is learned by practice.

This might be taken as the statement of principle of Popper's 'Open Society', a society 'in which men have learned to be to some extent critical of taboos, and to base decisions on the authority of their own intelligence.'[64]

It is the opposite of a Platonic society, where political wisdom and political principles have to remain esoteric, unpublishable, because only rulers (philosophers) are capable of handling them and the people at large would not understand them. Wilson added two further deductions or applications: every people has the right to know the international engagements entered into in their name by their governments ('open covenants'); and every people has the right to follow the

---

63. ibid., p. 476.
64. K.R. Popper, *The Open Society and its Enemies*, 1st edn., (London: Routledge & Kegan Paul Ltd., 1949), vol. I, note to the introduction, p. 178.

process by which international engagements are entered into ('openly arrived at'). These two applications of the transcendental affirmative formula are the Wilsonian doctrine of open diplomacy; they were maxims that would not have been wholly effective without being published in the Fourteen Points, and their publication tended to make people insist that they should be carried out. The fear of 'secret understandings' has taken deep root in the West and offers an explanation of the state of the world more comforting than the facts of power.

Eden records that in 1942 he talked with Roosevelt in the White House about the post-war world and they discussed the greatness and failure of Wilson, and how they might learn from his tragedy. 'I hope we might reach open covenants secretly arrived at. The President laughed and agreed.'[65] This is the position, too, of Nicolson, who also distinguishes between policy and negotiation.[66] One might put the distinction crudely: the Kantian believes in open covenants openly arrived at, the Grotian in open covenants secretly arrived at, and the Machiavellian in secret covenants secretly arrived at. It is now widely agreed that in practice the principle of 'openly arrived at' is on the whole not a success. The maxim that all negotiation ought to be public has defeated its own purpose by reducing the agreements so arrived at to empty insincere platitudes and debasing the verbal currency of diplomacy, and by compelling governments to return to secret negotiations. (Does this show that the maxim that all negotiation ought to be public was itself incompatible with publicity, and therefore condemned by the negative transcendental formula of public right?)

Given these Kantian versions of the objective conditions of reduced tension and open diplomacy, we might sum up the principle of Kantian diplomacy corresponding to the Grotian's reconciliation of interests and the Machiavellian's negotiation from strength, by the phrase 'moral suasion'. Cobden said in a debate in the House of Commons:

I hope to see the day when the intercourse of nations will exhibit the same changes as those which have taken place in the intercourse of individuals [and as in private life we no longer carry weapons, and duelling is dead], something should be done to carry the same spirit into the intercourse of nations. In domestic life, physical correction is giving way to moral influence. In schools and lunatic asylums this principle is successfully adopted, and even the training of animals is found to be better done by means of suasion. Cannot you adopt something of this in the intercourse of nations?[67]

---

65. Sir Anthony Eden, *Full Circle*, p. 175.
66. See Harold Nicolson, *Diplomacy*, p. 84.
67. John Bright, ed., debate on the Don Pacifico case 28 June 1850, House of Commons, *Richard Cobden's Speeches* (London: Macmillan & Co., 1880), p. 424.

One of the transformations of the principle of moral suasion is: always negotiate, and do so without the conditions and qualifications with which the Grotian hedges the process. Negotiation is always better than non-negotiation, or any other alternative, so keep on talking, lest you do something worse. It is paradoxical of the Kantian position that it both repudiates diplomacy in general and puts the greatest weight on pure diplomacy: negotiation abstracted from coercion and bribery, to preserve peace. Also, negotiation does produce results: 'Talk it out round a table.' This was Eisenhower's simple belief, that if people of differing views and opposed emotions only sit round a table and are made to discuss, the best solution will automatically result. A caustic critic has analysed this belief in negotiation into three models: first, that of the college debate, an exercise in histrionics and logic where the decision goes to the case presented best. Thus at a certain point Khrushchev says to Eisenhower, 'all right, you've got me! I can't answer that one. So what are your terms?' The second model is a business deal or haggling, the Yankee trader theory. Eisenhower visits Khrushchev's store: 'Any Berlin settlements in stock?'; they argue about prices and quality, Eisenhower makes for the door in scorn, Khrushchev puts the goods back on the shelf with a shrug, each turns back, and at last the right price is reached. The third model is that of a Quaker meeting; it is the inspirational theory: the spirit of togetherness descends, souls are in propinquity, and new insights, new understanding, and a spirit of reconciliation emerge.

'Moral suasion' tries to cultivate international understanding. If negotiation does not produce the hoped for results, people are encouraged to get to know each other, and talk together. 'People all over the world want peace so much that governments had better get out of the way and let them have it,' said Eisenhower in a TV programme with Macmillan on 31 August 1959. If half the money wasted on obsolescent armaments was spent in explaining our situation to the peoples behind the Iron Curtain, and securing closer contact and more mutual understanding, it might well make it impossible for a Communist aggressor to secure the necessary minimum of public support for starting a war. But how can 'we' do this, if not through our governments? The answer is that 'we' in fact will not do it, but our governments will do it for us, in our name. This is where moral suasion transforms from evolutionary to revolutionary Kantianism. The yearning of people to speak to people over the heads of their governments is replaced by the skill of governments in speaking to peoples over the heads of other governments.

There are different forms of this. One is 'new' diplomacy, which goes back at least to the French Revolution. When Malmesbury was negotiating with the Directory in 1797,

the Directory published his confidential memorial, and their answer to it with comments in the *Redacteur*. When Lord Malmesbury remonstrated against this unfair and unjustifiable appeal to the passions of the people during a transaction of this nature, it was defended by M. Delacroix 'as indispensable in the present responsible situation of the Directory'.[68]

But apparently the name 'new diplomacy' became current in England to describe the Machiavellian procedure of Joseph Chamberlain; it was the Liberals' name for his conduct of negotiations preceding the South African War. The object of the old diplomacy was secrecy; of the new, publicity. Chamberlain said that in dealing with the Transvaal he communicated what was happening to the world 'not week by week but moment by moment'. The earliest complaint of it was of the despatch to President Krüger in 1896, which Chamberlain published before it could reach Pretoria; it was an invitation to visit Britain. Jingoes called it 'superb arrogance'; radicals thought it provocative and that it had prevented Krüger from accepting.[69] Chamberlain's practice was not confined to colonial diplomacy; he introduced it into foreign affairs too, believing there was no longer room for the mysteries and reticences of traditional diplomacy. 'Ours is a democratic Government; we gain all our strength from the confidence of the people, and we cannot gain strength or have that confidence unless we show confidence in turn.'[70]

Whether this is an example of genuine Kantianism or of unscrupulous Machiavellian flexibility depends on how much you think Chamberlain was just a cad and a bounder and how much an idealist; he was both. Anyway 'new diplomacy', in this limited sense of violating the privacy of confidential diplomatic communication, became general after 1918, especially in Soviet diplomacy, and also Hitler's. Its purpose is to bring external pressure to bear on the government with which negotiations are taking place, in the very process of negotiating; the pressure that is of its own, and others', public opinion. As was once said: 'The new fad in diplomacy is to release the text of the international communication before it is sent. This saves time by allowing the recipient to get sore about the letter before he even gets it.' (Arguably, with more 'mature' Western publics, this process is ineffective.)

Connected with 'new diplomacy' is conference diplomacy, which maximizes publicity and generalizes the propaganda-effect. Machiavellians prefer bilateral diplomacy (apart from Munich, Hitler always avoided conferences), but Russia since 1934 has utilized multilateral diplomacy especially in the League and United Nations, largely if not wholly as a propaganda forum. Khrushchev said he liked conferences: they confuse opinion, postpone decisions, and tend to cause friction in the Western alliance.

---

68. Third Earl of Malmesbury, *Diaries and Correspondence*, vol. III, p. 282n.
69. Alexander Mackintosh, *Joseph Chamberlain* (London: Hodder & Stoughton, 1906), pp. 236-7.
70. ibid., p. 248.

Inflammatory propaganda is another way of appealing to people over the heads of their governments. Possibly all forms of moral suasion, all such appeals over the heads of governments are incitements to disaffection or even rebellion. Thus diplomatic negotiations with Egypt were made against the background of Cairo radio; those with Greece over Cyprus against that of Greek radio urging the people of Cyprus to rebel. Agitators in a quiet safe studio can now incite people on another continent to commit murder, arson, or insurrection. The BBC did this with superb effect to occupied Europe during the war, but has since become mildly Grotian, as complaints in the *Spectator* about the Russian and Yugoslav services showed. Moscow Radio does it discreetly and probably with greater long-term effect.

At this point the transformations of moral suasion might be thought complete; it has been transmuted into ideological coercion or doctrinal warfare. This illustrates the vitality and ambiguity of Kantianism, the capacity for metamorphosis and the protean quality in all messianic, millenarian, utopian creeds. At the heart of Kantianism, underlying even its philosophical, 'enlightened', rationalistic manifestations in Bentham or Bertrand Russell is a religious element: the desire to convert the world, to save mankind from the wrath to come. But the supreme test of religious emotion is how it responds to a situation where it is clear that a large proportion of mankind is obstinately uninterested in being converted. Here religious emotion easily swings over from the yearning to convert the world into the impulse to condemn the world; with Christianity especially this has been true. This is the root of the revolutionary Kantian's ideological division of the world into the saved and the damned, the orthodox and the heretic, the virtuous and the corrupt. It explains such infelicities of feeling and expression as when Dulles told a Congressional Committee in August 1957: 'If making of loans to underdeveloped countries keeps a country from Communism, I do not care whether they like us or not . . . Whether we make friends I do not care. I do not care whether they like us or hate us.'[71] (He at one time represented American Christendom on the World Council of Churches.) It also explains the diplomatic principle that 'He who is not with us is against us'. This is a Stalinist maxim, and McCarthyite too: you are not pro-American unless violently anti-Russian. It is reflected in Dulles's belief that neutrality was a kind of treason in the war to preserve civilization. Both the West and Russia have retreated a little from this position, which came to be adopted passionately by the anti-colonialists.

---

71. Reported in *The New York Times*, 11 August 1957; see also Milton Mayer, 'The American Spirit', *The Progressive*, January 1959, p. 65.

10: Theory of war

War is the central feature of international relations, although in academic study this is sometimes forgotten. If this is too Realist a statement, one can say instead that war is the ultimate feature of international relations, as revolution is the ultimate feature of domestic politics. One test of the profundity and insight of an international theorist is what he has to say about war; but there are two distinct theoretical enquiries: the character, or nature of war as a phenomenon, and the conduct and purpose of war as a policy.

Character of war

Rationalists

There are two basic tenets to the Rationalist theory of war. The first is that the object of war is peace, not vice versa. Peace is the norm, and war the violation or exception; peace is logically prior to war. There is a classic statement of this in *De Civitate Dei*:

Whoever gives even moderate attention to human affairs and to our common nature, will recognise that as there is no man who does not want to be joyful, neither is there anyone who does not wish to have peace. Even those who make war desire nothing but victory, desire, that is to say, to attain peace with glory . . . Wars are waged with the desire for peace, even by those who take pleasure in exercising their warlike nature in . . . battle. So it is obvious that peace is the end sought for by war. Everybody seeks peace by making war, but nobody seeks war by making peace. Even those who interrupt the peace in which they are living, have no hatred of peace, but only wish it changed to a peace which suits them better. They do not therefore wish to have no peace, but only one more suited to their mind.[1]

The second tenet of the Rationalist is that war is a necessary evil, to be minimized as far as possible. It is necessary, because it is the only

---

1. St. Augustine, ed. J.E.C. Welldon, *De Civitate dei Contra Paganos* (London: Society for Promoting Christian Knowledge, 1924), vol. II, p. 482. English tr. John Healey, *The City of God* (London: J.M. Dent & Sons Ltd., 1934), p. 140.

means of justice when there is no political superior. Burke expressed this:

As to war, if it be the means of wrong and violence, it is the sole means of justice amongst nations. Nothing can banish it from the world. They who say otherwise, intending to impose upon us, do not impose upon themselves. But it is one of the greatest objects of human wisdom to mitigate those evils which we are unable to remove.[2]

Grotius, too, is concerned to map out this middle line between accepting war as inevitable, and limiting or restricting it as hateful. At the end of *Prolegomena* he says:

I observed everywhere in Christendom a lawlessness in warfare of which even barbarous nations would be ashamed. Nations would rush to arms on the slightest pretext or even without cause at all. And arms once taken up, there would be an end to all respect for law, whether human or divine, as though a fury had been let loose with general licence for all manner of crime.[3]

He goes on to say that this barbarity has led some thinkers (for example his fellow-countryman Erasmus) to the pacifist conclusion that all arms should be forbidden to a Christian. Grotius, who is the most common-sensible of thinkers, believes this is going too far in the other direction. 'I believe they [incline to this opinion] on the principle that to straighten a bent stick one must bend it strongly the other way.' But this will do more harm than good: 'A remedy must . . . be found for both schools of extremists — for those that believe that in war nothing is lawful, and for those for whom all things are lawful in war.'[4] And this is the task Grotius himself undertakes.

It is not characteristic of the Rationalist tradition to speculate about the 'causes of war'. Such an intellectual exercise is characteristic of the twentieth century, which is the first time war has been regarded as unnatural, and therefore requiring special investigation. This century is infected by Inverted Revolutionism. Rationalist thought about the character of war tends to accept it as a normal expression of human nature, although also a detestable one, and to engage in a consideration of how it can be mitigated and limited. The rationalist has an empirical and reformist temper; there is an implicit belief that much mitigation and limiting is possible. The inherent social co-operativeness of men, which has banished war from municipal society, may restrain war in international society.

The belief that war is a necessary evil is seen also in Lincoln.

---

2. Edmund Burke, 'Regicide Peace', *The Works of the Right Hon. Edmund Burke* (London: Samuel Holdsworth, 1842), vol. II, p. 299.
3. Hugo Grotius, tr. F.W. Kelsey, *Prolegomena* (Indianapolis and New York: Liberal Arts Press Book, H. Jonas Co. Ltd., 1957), para. 28.
4. ibid., para. 29, pp. 35–6.

Although the political unit against whom he conducted the war (a war, incidentally, which was a flat rejection of the principle of self-determination) never achieved international personality and statehood, his theoretical position is identical to Burke's. His philosophy of war was first sketched in the extraordinary meditation he wrote for himself in September 1862, which John Hay found among his papers, and was later expressed with great profundity in the Second Inaugural:

Fondly do we hope — fervently do we pray — that this mighty scourge of war may speedily pass away. Yet, if God wills that it continue, until all the wealth piled by the bond-man's two hundred fifty years of unrequited toil shall be sunk, and until every drop of blood drawn with the lash, shall be paid by another drawn with the sword, as was said three thousand years ago, so still it must be said 'the judgements of the Lord, are true and righteous altogether.' . . .

With malice towards none; with charity for all; the firmness in the right, as God gives us to see the right, let us strive on to finish the work we are in; to bind up the nation's wounds . . . to do all which may achieve and cherish a just, and a lasting peace, among ourselves, and with all nations.[5]

Realists

It is Realists who, because of their interior acceptance of international anarchy, let their minds speculate with most freedom and fascination about the character of war. For them, man is an irrational, fighting animal; 'you cannot change human nature', and war is natural and inevitable. This is an inversion of the Augustinian position which asserts the primacy of peace. For the Realist peace is the laboratory of war. The French Communist slogan against NATO was: 'The inevitability of war, *la fatalité de la guerre*, is the Fascist doctrine'; for 'Fascist' read 'Realist'. The extreme of Realist doctrine is militarism, the assertion that war is not only inevitable but good, that it brings out the finest side of human nature. Francis Bacon wrote:

Nobody can be healthful without exercise, neither natural body nor politic; and certainly, to a kingdom or estate, a just and honourable war is the true exercise. A civil war, indeed, is like the heat of a fever; but a foreign war is like the heat of exercise, and serveth to keep the body in health; for in a slothful peace, both courages will effeminate and manners corrupt. But howsoever it be for happiness, without all question for greatness it maketh to be still for the most part in arms . . .[6]

---

5. Abraham Lincoln, *The Collected Works of Abraham Lincoln* (New Brunswick NJ: Rutgers University Press, 1953), vol. VIII, p. 333.
6. Francis Bacon, 'Of the True Greatness of Kingdoms', *Essays* (London: Dent & Sons, 1939), p. 95.

(Note the switch from 'just and honourable' in the first sentence to 'foreign' in the second.) This is the medical theory of the state; and Hegel also uses the metaphor of hygiene: by war, 'the ethical health of peoples is preserved in their indifference to the stabilization of finite institutions'; just as the blowing of the winds preserves the sea from the foulness which would be the result of a prolonged calm, so also corruption in nations would be the product of prolonged, let alone 'perpetual', peace.[7] The famous letter of the great Moltke echoes this:

Perpetual peace is a dream — and not even a beautiful dream — and War is an integral part of God's ordering of the Universe. In War, Man's noblest virtues come into play: courage and renunciation, fidelity to duty and a readiness for sacrifice that does not stop short of offering up Life itself. Without War the world would become swamped in materialism.[8]

There is a mystique of war expressed in Prussianism and Fascism, in d'Annunzio and Mussolini. More soberly, Walter Bagehot provides a good example of the biological theory of Realism, international Darwinism. In a chapter of *Physics and Politics* entitled 'The Use of Conflict' he says:

Three laws, or approximate laws, may, I think, be laid down . . . First. In every particular state [i.e. condition] of the world, those nations which are strongest tend to prevail over the others; and in certain marked peculiarities the strongest tend to be the best. Secondly. Within every particular nation the type or types of character then and there most attractive tend to prevail; and the most attractive, though with exceptions, is what we call the best character.

(Thirdly, both these competitions are intensified at the present day.)

These are the sort of doctrines with which, under the name of 'natural selection' in physical science, we have become familiar; and as every great scientific conception tends to advance its boundaries and to be of use in solving problems not thought of when it was started, so here, what was put forward for mere animal history may, with a change of form, but an identical essence, be applied to human history.[9]

He says later:

---

7. Friedrich Hegel, tr. T.M. Knox, *Philosophy of Right* (Oxford: Oxford University Press, 1958), para. 324, p. 210.
8. Bismarck's criticism of Moltke's 'love of combat and delight in battles' forms an interesting Rationalist contrast. See 'Letter to Bluntschli', 11 December 1880, in Arnold J. Toynbee, *A Study of History* (London: Oxford University Press, 1939), vol. IV, p. 643.
9. Walter Bagehot, *Physics and Politics* (London: C. Kegan Paul & Co., 1881), pp. 43, 44.

Conquest is the premium given by nature to those national characters which
their national customs have made most fit to win in war, and in most material
respects these winning characters are really the best characters. The characters
which do win in war are the characters which we should wish to win in
war.[10]

'These are the sort of doctrines with which, under the name of
"natural selection", we have become familiar,' wrote the Victorian
editor of the *Economist*. We have indeed:

The idea of struggle is as old as life itself, for life is only preserved because
other living things perish through struggle . . . In this struggle, the stronger,
the more able, win, while the less able, the weak, lose. Struggle is the father
of all things . . . If you do not fight for life, then life will never be won.[11]

This doctrine of Hitler's is expounded at tedious length in *Mein
Kampf*, but it is stating what is a fundamental truth. All states and
nations, even welfare states, have been built by struggle and war.
Hence the radical ambiguity of a position like that of the Western
powers after 1919, who after a successful career as burglars tried to
settle down as country-gentlemen making intermittent appearances on
the magistrate's bench. One can ask whether they ever found the
theoretical, moral answer to the Realist critique levelled at them by
Axis propaganda: that they had got where they were by struggle; that
they could not contract out of the struggle at a moment that happened
to suit them; and still less could they justify and protect themselves in
an attempt at contracting out of it by appealing to sets of moral principles which they had ignored when they were committed to the
struggle. It is arguable that the only way in which they could have met
the moral challenge of the Axis would have been by voluntarily
abdicating all that they had previously won by struggle, and that their
moral inability to do this, their lack of moral justification, takes one
to the heart of the difference between personal and political morality.

The contrast between Rationalist and Realist attitudes can be
illustrated from two classical writings on international theory of nearly
equal date: *The Federalist* (1787–8) and *Letters on a Regicide Peace*
(1796), in their respective answers to the question: does vicinity, or
adjacency, make for war?; it depends on the circumstances. Are there
general, universal, normally obtaining reasons to explain why India
and Pakistan, or Israel and the Arab states, are in conditions of chronic
bad relations, while on the other hand Western European countries are
not? Hamilton was a Realist, and perhaps the most civilized of the roll-
call. That was why opponents of the League of Nations' type of inter-
nationalism, the Lionel Curtis imperialists, adopted him as their patron

---

10. ibid., p. 215.
11. Adolf Hitler, Speech at Kulmbach, 5 February 1928; quoted in Alan Bullock, *Hitler:
    A Study in Tyranny* (London: Odham's Press, 1952), p. 31.

saint after 1919. In *The Federalist* he wrote:

So far is the general sense of mankind from corresponding with the tenets of those who endeavour to lull asleep our apprehensions of discord and hostility between the [not yet United] States, in the event of disunion, that it has from long observation of the progress of society become a sort of axiom in politics, that vicinity, or nearness of situation, constitutes nations' natural enemies.[12]

Hamilton continues, quoting l'Abbé de Mably:

'neighbouring nations [says he] are naturally enemies of each other, unless their common weakness forces them to league in a *Confederate Republic*, and their constitution prevents the differences that neighbourhood occasions, extinguishing that secret jealousy which disposes all states to aggrandise themselves at the expense of their neighbours.' This passage, at the same time, points out the *evil* and suggests the *remedy*.[13]

Contrast this with the splendid passage in *Letters on a Regicide Peace*, less well known than it might be, in which Burke expounds his conception of the Commonwealth of Europe, the civilized society of states, which the Jacobins had repudiated and assaulted in arms. He distinguished between the three elements that bind the commonwealth of states together:

in the first place the Law of Nations, the great ligament of mankind; secondly, the Law of Treaties, which is the public law of Europe; and thirdly, the 'Law of Civil Vicinity', the Law of Neighbourhood, which determines the rights and duties of states according to their mutual geographical relations, and is a law existing in nature, tradition and custom.[14]

Hamilton's 'law of vicinity' was mutual conflict; Burke's was the foundation of what today would be called regional associations of organic historic and cultural communities, like, for example, Western Europe, or the Arab League. These regional associations are all susceptible of Realist analysis: why are they formed, and whom are they directed against? (Western Europe versus Russia; the Arab League versus Israel); but an analysis of Burke's 'law of civil vicinity' finds him talking on a different plane: he would not deny the validity of the Realist critique, but would say that by itself it was not enough. It does not invalidate the assertion that vicinity, and the historical bonds which accompany it, form a particular community and interdependence of rights and duties:

---

12. Alexander Hamilton, *The Federalist or the New Constitution* (London: J.M. Dent, 1934), no. VI, p. 25.
13. ibid., p. 25.
14. Edmund Burke, *The Works of the Right Hon. Edmund Burke*, vol. II, p. 300. See also C. Dawson, *Understanding Europe* (London: Sheed & Ward, 1952), p. 58.

Men are not tied to one another by papers and seals. They are led to associate by resemblances, by conformities, by sympathies. It is with nations as with individuals. Nothing is so strong a tie of amity between nation and nation as correspondence in laws, customs, manners, and habits of life. They are obligations written in the heart. They approximate men to men, without their knowledge, and sometimes against their intentions. The secret, unseen, but irrefragable bond of habitual intercourse holds them together, even when their perverse and litigious nature sets them to equivocate, scuffle, and fight, about the terms of their written obligations.[15]

These words might be written over the entrance of the Maison de l'Europe, in Strasbourg. When Burke writes like this he seems to be endeavouring to describe the moral nature of things, the inherent nature of international vicinity, deeper than the sociological generalization that vicinity makes for war. He is, in fact, speaking ontologically.

Revolutionists

In their respective positions regarding the theory of power the Revolutionists resemble the Rationalists in not holding power to be self-justifying; similarly here, they resemble the Rationalists in holding war not to be self-justifying. Like them, they say that peace is prior to war, and war is a necessary evil, but they say each with a distinct emphasis. Whereas the Rationalist tends to think of single individual wars, which are waged to restore the balance of power, to free certain subjugated countries, or to restore a status quo, the Revolutionist thinks of a series of wars which are directed, consciously or unconsciously, towards an ultimate future peace. The peace is identical with the reconstitution of international society, not a restoration of the balance of power or the status quo, but a revolutionary new state of affairs. As for the dictum that war is a necessary evil, the Rationalist emphasizes the noun, evil ('war is an inescapable evil'), while the Revolutionist emphasizes the adjective necessary ('war is a regrettable necessity'). These differences, especially the latter, spring from a deeper difference in the theory of politics. For the Rationalist, politics are for the sake of the good life, which means for the sake of the individual. 'Good life' is the goal, not of the state, nations, the 'free world', or similar abstractions, but of ordinary people, the man in the street. (A nation may have a goal of a *standard of life* but that is something quite different from the good life, and it is moral illiteracy to confuse them, however common it may be.) For the Revolutionist politics are for the sake of immanent social development, as propounded by the given doctrine. There is less emphasis on the individual, and more on the movement of society, and in the extreme

---

15. ibid., vol. II, pp. 298–9.

case the individual is regarded as expendable in the cause of moving society. So the fundamental Revolutionist tenet about the nature of war, answering the double tenet of Rationalism that war is a means to peace, and a necessary evil, is that war is the agent or instrument of history.

In the older Christian language of the Christian proto-revolutionists, war is the scourge of the Lord, for chastizing the sins of his guilty people. It is the flail, the instrument of the thresher, the tool with which the grain is beaten out of the ear. War is the means by which the Lord threshes out the historical wheat from the historical chaff. There is a good deal in the Old Testament to feed this conception of war, which was a powerful influence in the sixteenth and seventeenth centuries. There is Isaiah's tremendous picture:

Who is this that cometh from Edom, with dyed garments from Bozrah? this that is glorious in his apparel, travelling in the greatness of his strength? I that speak in righteousness, mighty to save.
Wherefore art thou red in thine apparel, and thy garments like him that treadeth in the winefat? I have trodden the winepress alone, and of the people there was none with me: for I will tread them in mine anger, and trample them in my fury, and their blood shall be sprinkled upon my garments, and I will stain all my raiment. For the day of vengeance is in mine heart, and the year of my redeemed is come.[16]

This was the conception of Cromwell's Ironsides in the English Civil War, as Macaulay depicts them at Naseby:

Oh evil was the root, and bitter was the fruit,
And crimson was the juice of the vintage that we trod;
For we trampled on the throng of the haughty and the strong,
Who sate in the high places, and slew the saints of God.

Down, down, for ever down with the mitre and the crown,
With the Belial of the Court, and the Mammon of the Pope;
There is woe in Oxford halls: there is wail in Durham Stalls:
The Jesuit smites his bosom: the Bishop rends his cope.[17]

and it was the Abolitionists' conception of the American Civil War two hundred years later:

Mine eyes have seen the glory of the coming of the Lord:
He is trampling out the vintage where the grapes of wrath are stored;
He hath loosed the fateful lightning of his terrible swift sword:
His truth is marching on.[18]

---

16. Isaiah, ch. 63, verse 1–4, King James' Version.
17. T.B. Macaulay, 'The Battle of Naseby', verses 2, 14, *Lays of Ancient Rome* (London: J.M. Dent, 1968), pp. 493, 494.
18. Julia Ward Howe, 'Battle Hymn of the Republic', *The Patriotic Anthology* (New York: Doubleday, 1945), p. 196.

The Abolitionists were the Revolutionists of American society.

When men ceased to believe in a Lord with a scourge or flail, or trampling the winepress, they saw war as the agent of history in a new way. As quoted before, Marx said: 'Force is the midwife of every old society pregnant with a new one.'[19] This meant that war, the most effective and satisfactory mode of force, could be such a midwife. Instead of war, the scourge of the Lord, there is war, the midwife of society. 'Let an impure blood water our furrows,' cries the 'Marseillaise'. Stalin wrote, in justification of war: 'The Bolsheviks were not mere pacifists who sighed for peace and confined themselves to the propaganda for peace . . . The Bolsheviks advocated an active revolutionary struggle for peace, to the point of overthrowing the rule of the bellicose imperialist bourgeoisie.'[20]

The conception of war as the instrument of history can be rounded out by another, that summed up by the Allied slogan of the First World War: 'The war to end war.' This was equally a Revolutionist notion; war was to be an agent of history, not simply to restore peace, but to *end wars*. War was to end history in its war-making aspect, and to make the world safe for non-war, for democracy, for Communism. It does not matter much what a war is considered to be making the world *safe for*. The formula is a Revolutionist one because it conceives of war not as an ugly political instrument but as a vehicle of an historical apocalypse. This was the dominant idea in Allied countries about the First World War. The literature of that war, both the political speeches and the pure literature, is full of figures of speech and metaphors which mingled the old Revolutionist idea of war as God's purifying process, with the newer one of war as the final liberating cataclysm.

Holmes pointed back to the moonlit sea, and shook a thoughtful head.
'There's an east wind coming, Watson.'
'I think not, Holmes. It is very warm.'
'Good old Watson! You are the one fixed point in a changing age. There's an east wind coming all the same, such a wind as never blew on England yet. It will be cold and bitter, Watson, and a good many of us may wither before its blast. But it's God's own wind none the less, and a cleaner, better, stronger land will lie in the sunshine when the storm has cleared.'[21]

Conan Doyle was a very representative Englishman in his prejudices and limitations.

---

19. See above 'Theory of National Power', p. 107, *Handbook of Marxism* (London: Victor Gollancz, 1935), p. 391.
20. Josef Stalin, *History of the Communist Party of the Soviet Union* (Moscow: Foreign Languages Publishing House, 1945), p. 167.
21. Conan Doyle, 2 August 1914, in *His Last Bow* (London: Grafton Books, 1988), p. 224.

Two questions about the Revolutionist theory of war must now be asked: one concerning Communism and the other Fascism. Revolutionists agree with Rationalists that peace is logically prior to war, although with a different emphasis. But is this true of Marxists? For them, peace is certainly the *end* (τέλος) of war (in which they differ from Fascists), but this does not mean necessarily that they hold peace to be prior to war. A Marxist would probably not allow himself to be cornered in such political metaphysics, but the question is worth asking. The Rationalist thinks peace is the object of war because he has some conception or assumption of a primal unity or harmony, which has been temporarily shattered by folly and badness, but which normal 'post-war' political society can approximate to again. The Marxist–Leninist has, almost certainly, no such assumption. Whether the word 'primal' is used historically, of primordial peaceful society, or logically, of first principles, Marxism does not see unity and harmony, but conflict, as primal.

The second law of dialectics asserts the unity of opposites, the essentially contradictory character of Reality, containing opposites which conflict yet interpenetrate. It is a Marxist controversy whether the reconciliation of opposites, or their struggle, should be emphasized. Lenin laid down: 'the unity of opposites is conditional, temporary and relative. The struggle of the mutually exclusive opposites is absolute, as movement and evolution are.'[22] It seems that in some sense struggle and conflict are absolute, while harmony and unity are only relative. If reconciliation and unity were emphasized, there would be a danger of slipping into a static conception of nature and history, whereas dialectical materialism is essentially a dynamic philosophy of nature and history. The forward movement of affairs requires the postulate of the primacy of the conflict of opposites. Thus Isaiah Berlin presenting Marx's view of the dialectic says: 'Genuine progress is constituted not by the triumph of one side and the defeat of the other, but by the duel itself which necessarily involves the destruction of both.'[23]

Therefore Lenin may share the doctrine of Augustine, that war aims finally at peace, but he repudiates the doctrine that this peace reflects a stable harmonious order which is the ground of all human experience, the nature of things. Indeed it is arguable that the disagreement outweighs the agreement, and that at the deepest level, of philosophical premises, Lenin is nearer to Hobbes or Machiavelli.

The second question, concerning Fascism, is whether Fascists are Realists or counter-Revolutionists. One can only answer that, prima facie, they are both; they show characteristics of both ways of thought.

---

22. David Guest, *A Text Book of Dialectical Materialism* (London: Lawrence & Wishart Ltd., 1941), p. 76.
23. Isaiah Berlin, *Karl Marx* (London: Oxford University Press, 1948), p. 116.

At this point in the political spectrum infra-red merges into ultra violet. It is a question worth looking into, whether counter-Revolutionism has always tended to be more Realist than Revolutionist. Fascism is more Realist, further from Rationalism, than Communism. And equally, were not Metternich and Nicholas I intrinsically more Realist, further from Rationalism, than the Jacobins?

To illustrate the counter-Revolution in a single figure, one would choose Joseph de Maistre (1754–1821), the most prominent Catholic political writer of the early nineteenth century. A Savoyard, educated by the Jesuits, and later a diplomat in St. Petersburg, he was a classic reactionary and he hated Rousseau, Voltaire and all liberals. His major works were: *Considérations sur la France* (1796); *Du Pape* (1817) — he saw the Pope as the best focus for counter-revolution; and *Soirées de St. Pétersbourg* (1817). He develops a theory of war, and in the *Soirées* asks by what mysterious magic men go off to kill others, and why, whereas the executioner is universally execrated, the soldier is universally admired. He concludes that this reflects a deep spiritual law, 'the great law of the violent destruction of living beings', 'the occult and terrible law'.[24] He contemplates 'Nature red in tooth and claw' but this is not Darwinian, biological, struggle-for-existence, Realism. His theory is altogether profounder than that. He asserts that war is divine and has a supernatural significance; it is the punishment for original sin: 'The exterminating angel revolves like the sun around this unhappy planet, and only lets one nation relax temporarily in order to smite another . . .' [At the moment when men, rulers, for their own temporal reasons, good or bad, just or unjust, begin a war] 'God advances to avenge the wickedness which the inhabitants of the world have committed against Him.'[25] War is the purifying process applied by Providence to the human race; it does not merely pose the problem of evil, it gives the answer: 'the whole earth, continually drenched with blood, is nothing but an immense altar where all living things must be sacrificed without end, and without limit, and without ceasing, until the consummation of all things, until evil is extinguished, and until death itself is dead.'[26]

De Maistre's blood-consciousness is not obsessive in his writings, rather it reflects a clear apprehension of facts which pose an intellectual problem. He states categorically that it is impossible to form an international society (disassociating himself from Suarez and Kant's international social contract). He had an influence upon Tolstoy and upon later heterodox French Catholic writers like Léon Bloy and George Bernanos. In his premises, arguments and conclusions he seems the opposite of Kant.

---

24. de Maistre, author's tr., *Les Soirées de Saint Pétersbourg* (Lyon, Paris: Librairie Catholique Emmanuel Vitte, 1924), vol. II, p. 14.
25. ibid., pp. 25, 27.
26. ibid., p. 25.

Purpose and conduct of war

Rationalists

The centre of the Rationalist theory of the purpose and conduct of war is occupied by the doctrine of the just war. Aquinas laid down three criteria for a just war: it must be declared by the proper authority (this was a provision against feudal licence); it must have a just cause, for example defence, or to remedy injustice; and it must be fought in the right frame of mind. It is the starting point of a theory of personal military obligation, which is well expressed in *Henry V*.[27] The King talks with his soldiers the night before Agincourt, when the need for each soldier to 'wash every mote out of his conscience' is discussed, and the King ponders his own heavier and representative responsibility for all his men. Additional criteria for a just war are found in the neo-scholastics: it must be fought by just means, with respect for the distinction between combatants and non-combatants; and the evil caused and the harm wreaked by the war must be less than the evil which the war is intended to control or destroy. (In other words, war must be considered in terms of consequential ethics). Now these criteria are not only related to a feudalism which is obsolete in the twentieth century, they are also highly subjective. Indeed, as with much medieval thought, they appear largely tautologous. War must have a just cause, be fought by just means, be fought in the right frame of mind; this is very nearly the same as saying that the criterion of a just war is that it should be just. Bentham makes a similar criticism of Vattel (and it would apply with as much or as little force to Grotius and others): Vattel's propositions are 'old-womanish and tautological'; he builds castles in the air, and has so dull a perception of the princi-ple of utility that his statements resolve themselves into formulae like 'it is not just to do that which is unjust'.[28] The vagueness of these criteria makes a debasement of the just war theory very possible, and allows for endless argument and complex casuistry. Nevertheless the theory remains embedded in Western tradition.

There has been a threefold development of the doctrine of the just war. First, it has been transposed into the secular key. Before, 'justice' was defined by ecclesiastical authority, in the Crusades for example. Grotius' whole work was an attempt to restate and revive the criteria of just war. This inaugurated the modern development of international law, which has tended increasingly to seek legal criteria for a just war, as the legal framework of international society has developed and grown complex. From this came the inter-war belief that aggression

---

27. William Shakespeare, *Henry V*, Act IV, Scene I, line 180.
28. *Works of J. Bentham*, vol. X, p. 584, quoted in E. de Vattel, tr. C.G. Fenwick, *The Law of Nations or The Principles of Natural Law* (Washington, DC: Carnegie Institution of Washington, 1916), vol. III, p. xliv.

could be legally defined, and war reduced within legal categories, which would provide juridical norms for war. For example, the United Nations' condemnation of China as an aggressor in 1950 was an assertion, in secular legalized form, that China was engaged in an unjust war. Moreover, besides the definition of a just or non-aggressive war, there has been a steady attempt to impose restraints on the methods of war, in, especially, the Geneva Conventions. The theory of limited war is Rationalist:

> The object in war is to obtain a better peace — even if only from your own point of view. Hence it is essential to conduct war with constant regard to the peace you desire . . . A State which expands its strength to the point of exhaustion bankrupts its own policy, and future.
> If you concentrate exclusively on victory with no thought for the after-effect . . . it is almost certain that the peace will be a bad one, containing the germs of another war . . .

concludes Liddell Hart in *The Strategy of Indirect Approach*.[29] There are certain things in war one may not do. 'The Bishop of Chichester [George Bell] said when planning the establishment of an International Authority we should come to grief again unless there was a moral standard for international conduct which nations imposing that authority were prepared to accept.'[30] The theory of graduated deterrents and the demand for military prudence and morality is also Rationalist.[31]

Secondly, the just war doctrine has been abandoned by its original sponsors, the Church, and is theoretically obsolescent in its old form. It is virtually as obsolete as the doctrine of usury, the condemnation of which was never revised or repealed in the light of capitalist society. The doctrine of just war has similarly not been refurbished in modern international society, although there were faint attempts to restate it, notably by Taparelli d'Azeglio S.J., a piece of nineteenth-century medievalism.[32] At an unofficial conference of Catholic clergy at Freiburg in 1931 the doctrine was condemned as outmoded. No modern war can be just, because of the methods used, which erase the distinction between combatants and non-combatants, and because it does more harm than good.[33] However, popular opinion judged differently: 'The cause for which we had taken up arms [in 1939] was alone sufficient to make our war a just war in the eyes of all men

---

29. B.H. Liddell Hart, *The Strategy of Indirect Approach* (London: Faber & Faber, 1941), pp. 202–3.
30. See *The Times*, 15 April 1943, House of Lords Report.
31. Thomas Murray in 'The Atomic Energy Commission Report to the Sub-committee of the U.S. Senate Foreign Relations Committee in Washington', reported in *The Times*, 13 April 1956.
32. J. Eppstein, *The Catholic Tradition of the Law of Nations* (London: Burns & Oates, 1935), pp. 130ff., see also pp. 266–72.
33. ibid., pp. 138ff.

acknowledging a law which is the Law of God.'[34] The Anglican report *The Church and the Atom*[35] to the Lambeth Conference 1948, recognized the distinction between combatants and non-combatants; military and non-military objectives; and 'strict necessity' and its abuse. But this assumes a moral climate which no longer existed. A moral theology of war is needed. Meanwhile, the report condemned the past but licensed the future: it issues a retrospective condemnation of obliteration bombing and Hiroshima, but sanctioned the atomic bomb as a 'deterrent' and justified its future use in reprisal.

Thirdly, the doctrine of just war has permeated Western thought and although dead it will not lie down. The idea that war needs to be justified has become indissolubly combined with civilized Western tradition, so that it is thoroughly saturated with Rationalism. Grotius said: 'War is not one of the social arts. Rather, it is something so horrible that only sheer necessity or perfect charity can make it lawful.'[36] And this remains what the democratic powers, the Western Allies, like to think is their doctrine of war. To a remarkable extent it actually is. This is illustrated by the widespread belief in limited warfare: economy in the methods of war, and limits to the principle of necessary severity. Clausewitz's dictum that the purpose of war is to persuade the enemy to accept your will, to convert him, is incompatible with knocking him to pieces in the effort to achieve a simple military victory. There was much soul-searching about the justification of using the atomic bomb against Japan, as well as protest against the strategic bombing of Germany.[37] (It is interesting here to consider whether the Rationalist principle of economy in the methods of warfare is only valid when the enemy is actuated by Rationalist principles too.)

There remains also in the Western powers' attitude to war the ghost of Aquinas' criterion that a just war must be declared by the proper authority. The Anglo-French position in 1939 would have been morally stronger if they had mobilized the League machinery to declare a punitive war on Germany, or so Churchill suggested retrospectively. The war in 1939 was not declared in defence of the Covenant or on the recommendation of the Council of the League: that is, through those procedures which, after 1919, constituted the declaration of war by proper authority. The war was an old balance-of-power war, like all its predecessors, and in some eyes this impaired the justice of the Allied cause. Partly for this reason, the United States from 1950 onwards took great pains to obtain United Nations

---

34. *The Tablet*, 12 May 1945, p. 217.
35. The report was commissioned at the request of the Church Assembly to comment on the study *The Era of Atomic Power* (London: British Council of Churches), see *International Affairs*, vol. XXV, 1949 (London: R.I.I.A.), p. 74.
36. Hugo Grotius, Selections tr. W.S.M. Knight, *The Law of War and Peace* (London: Peace Book Company, 1939), bk. II, ch. IX, p. 71.
37. For example the Bishop of Chichester's letters to *The Times*, spring 1943.

authorization for its war in Korea. This was not only to gain allies, but more importantly to gain moral sanction from the 'proper authority'.

Realists

Realists of course have no use for a doctrine of just war; they negate, or erect a critique of, the moral propositions of the Rationalists. In Realist doctrine, war, as Clausewitz said, is 'the continuation of policy by other means'. This implies that war is an instrument rulers will use without any scruple or specific moral repugnance, and contrasts with the Rationalist doctrine that war is the breakdown of policy. R.G. Collingwood, in *The New Leviathan*, says: 'not war, but peace, is the extension of policy: war is the breakdown of policy.'[38]

There are three particular facets of the Realist doctrine of the conduct of war which can be touched on. The first is the belief in preventive war. For the Realist there can be no rules about starting war; there is no point in being handicapped. Assume the enemy will attack as soon as suits him, so strike first. 'Twice is he blest who had his quarrel just, but thrice is he who gets his blow in first.' Bacon wrote: 'Neither is the opinion of some of the schoolmen to be received, that a war cannot justly be made but upon a precedent injury or provocation. For there is no question but a just fear of an imminent danger, though there be no blow given, is a lawful cause of a war.'[39] Admiral Fisher suggested to the King in 1908 that the German Fleet should be 'Copenhagened' — he meant sunk inside Kiel harbour: 'Why should we wait for Germany to have the advantage of choosing her own moment for attack? Why not ourselves find the pretext and attack her?'[40] Contrast Grotius: 'This is a doctrine contrary to every principle of equity that justice allows us to resort to force in order to injure another merely because there is a possibility that he may injure us.'[41]

The second facet of the Realist doctrine is the acceptance of unlimited war, of the maximum exercise of strength. (This is the opposite of the belief in economy of methods of the Rationalists.) War is inherently illimitable and uncontrollable; 'laws of war' and any attempt to restrict or alleviate its damage are inconsistent; and talk of 'methods too horrible to employ' is sentimental nonsense; frightfulness pays in the long run. Superior force, be it air-power, atomic bombs or other technical advantages should be used with no

---

38. R.G. Collingwood, *The New Leviathan* (Oxford: Clarendon Press, 1944), p. 237. See also G.F. Kennan, *Realities of American Foreign Policy* (London: Oxford University Press, 1954), pp. 81ff.
39. Francis Bacon, 'Of Empire', *Essays*, p. 59.
40. See R.H. Bacon, *The Life of Lord Fisher of Kilverstone* (London: Hodder & Stoughton, 1929), pp. 74ff.
41. Hugo Grotius, *The Law of War and Peace, 1625*, p. 57.

consideration except their military effectiveness. Ruthlessness is the ultimate kindness. 'Leave them with nothing but their eyes to weep with,' said Sheridan to Bismarck (1870).[42] Sherman's capture of Atlanta and march through Georgia, destroying factories and public stores, during the American Civil War, showed the same attitude: 'If the people raise a howl against my barbarity and cruelty, I will answer that war is war, and not popularity-seeking. If they want peace, they and their relatives must stop the war.'[43]

It should be noted that the argument that the maximum deployment of strength will shorten a war and save lives in the end, as was used to justify the dropping of the atomic bomb in 1945, is a proposition in utilitarian ethics, involving the calculus of speculative consequences. It is frequently answered retrospectively by the counter-assertion that the exercise of strength was unnecessary even for its prime purpose of securing victory: Fleet Admiral King asserts in his memoirs, *A Naval Record*, that Japan could have been compelled to surrender by a naval blockade alone.[44]

The third aspect of Realist doctrine is the destruction of the enemy as the goal of war. There can be no compromise with the enemy while fighting him, and no conciliation of him after victory is won. The twin conceptions of unconditional surrender and a Carthaginian peace are Realist.

Revolutionists

Again, the Revolutionists seem to combine features of both the Rationalist and the Realist theories of the purpose and conduct of war. Communists, for example, seem to combine Rationalist theory, since they talk in terms of just war, with Realist practice and method, since though they believe sometimes in winning over the conquered and 'converted' populations by kindness, they more often display a terror and ruthlessness of method comparable to the Realists. The Communist theory of the just war is expressed in the *History of the C.P.S.U.*:

It was not to *every kind* of war that the Bolsheviks were opposed. They were only opposed to wars of conquest, imperialist wars. The Bolsheviks held that there are two kinds of war:
a) *Just* wars, wars that are not wars of conquest but wars of liberation, waged to defend the people from foreign attack and from attempts to enslave them,

---

42. Dr Moritz Bush, *Bismarck: Some Secret Pages of His History* (London: Macmillan, 1898), vol. I, p. 171.
43. Quoted in F.L. Paxson, *The American Civil War* (London: Williams & Norgat), p. 227.
44. E.J. King and W.M. Whitehill, *Fleet Admiral King. A Naval Record* (London: Eyre & Spottiswoode, 1953).

or to liberate the people from capitalist slavery, or lastly, to liberate colonies and dependent countries from the yoke of imperialism; and

b) *Unjust* wars, wars of conquest, waged to conquer and enslave foreign countries and foreign nations. Wars of the first kind the Bolsheviks supported. As to wars of the second kind, the Bolsheviks maintained that a resolute struggle must be waged against them to the point of revolution and the overthrow of one's own imperialist government.[45]

This is the language of the just war, but it is not quite the same as Rationalist doctrine. Stalin said: 'We are not against all wars. We are *against* imperialist wars, as being counter-revolutionary wars. But we are *for* liberating, anti-imperialist, revolutionary wars . . .'[46] and Lenin: 'we have always declared it to be absurd for the revolutionary proletariat to forswear revolutionary wars.'[47]

Here we have quite different language from that of Grotius, when he talked of war not being one of the social arts, but so horrible that only sheer necessity can justify it. For the revolutionary, war has to be one of the social arts. 'Force is the midwife of society,' said Marx;[48] war is the midwife of the regenerated international society. All rationalist casuistry about degrees of necessity, state of mind, and so on is irrelevant, and swept away. The criterion of the just war is ideological (which is even more subjective than the ethical criteria the Rationalist tradition pretends to offer). Legal definitions of war are nonsense.

Now this doctrine, if its characteristics have been distinguished rightly, is not that of the just war, but something else, quite distinct and equally ancient. In two other Communist statements about war, the language gives a clue: first, Lenin:

The class character of the war is the fundamental question that confronts a socialist (if he is not a renegade). If war is waged by the proletariat after it has conquered the bourgeoisie in its own country and is waged with the object of strengthening and extending socialism such a war is legitimate and 'holy' . . .

and secondly, Moscow radio, on the 16 February 1948, talking of the glories of the Soviet Army: 'In the course of all its glorious history it has not raised and could not have raised its arms for the sake of unjust aims. The wars it has waged have been just and sacred.'[49]

Legitimate and *holy*, just and *sacred*; here, beneath the language of the just war doctrine, we see the language of the doctrine of the holy

---

45. *History of the Communist Party of the Soviet Union*, pp. 167–8.
46. Josef Stalin, Letter to Gorki, 17 January 1930, *Works* (Moscow: Foreign Languages Publishing House, London: Lawrence & Wishart Ltd., 1955), vol. XII, p. 182.
47. V.I. Lenin, quoted by Mark Wardle in a letter in *The Listener*, 6 November 1952, p. 767.
48. Karl Marx, 'Das Kapital', *A Handbook of Marxism*, p. 391.
49. Both quoted by Mark Wardle in a letter in *The Listener*, 6 November 1952, p. 767.

war. Zinoviev, in his opening speech to the Baku Congress of Eastern Peoples in 1920, said:

Comrades! Brothers! The time has come when you can start on the organization of a true and holy people's war against the robbers and oppressors . . . The Communist International turns today to the peoples of the East and says to them: 'Brothers we summon you to a holy war, in the first place against English imperialism'.[50]

The doctrine of the holy war has a Muslim origin; it is possibly Jewish also. The injunctions for occupying the land of Canaan issued by Moses in *Deuteronomy* suggest a holy war, a war of extermination.

When the Lord thy God shall bring thee into the land
whither thou goest to possess it, and hath cast out many
nations before thee, . . .

And when the Lord thy God shall deliver them before thee;
thou shalt smite them, and utterly destroy them; thou
shalt make no covenant with them, nor shew mercy unto them: . . .

For thou art an holy people unto the Lord thy God:
the Lord thy God hath chosen thee to be a special people
unto himself, above all people that are upon the face of
the earth.[51]

It is echoed in Psalm 149:

Let the high praises of God be in their mouth,
and a two-edged sword in their hand;
To execute vengeance upon the heathen,
and punishments upon the people;
To bind their kings with chains, and their nobles
with fetters of iron; . . .

This is good hot stuff, and was chanted with Revolutionist intent by Cromwell's Ironsides as they went into battle against the Cavaliers. Voegelin, however, in *Order and History* denies that the original Hebrew theory was one of holy war.[52]

It is Muslim theory that gives a fully developed doctrine of the holy war, which has dominated — the word is scarcely too strong — Western international theory ever since (and which is also relevant to Israel and the Arab states). In Islamic constitutional law the whole world is divided into Dar-al-Islam, the abode of Islam (Islam means 'submitting oneself to God'; the word was chosen by Muhammad for his faith); and Dar-al-Harb, the abode of war; and this latter is that part

---

50. G.E. Zinoviev quoted in E.H. Carr, *The Bolshevik Revolution* (London: Macmillan & Co., 1953), vol. III, p. 261.
51. *Deuteronomy*, VII, verse 1, 2 and 6, King James' Version.
52. See Erich Voegelin, *Order and History* (Louisiana: State University, 1956), vol. I, p. 209.

of mankind which has not accepted Islam, and where war reigns, actually or potentially, until by conquest it is absorbed in Dar-al-Islam. Among the religious duties inculcated on Muslims by the Koran is the Jihad, the duty of waging war on those who do not accept the doctrines of Islam. Death in such a war brings the glory of martyrdom, immediate entry into paradise, and peculiar privileges there. Thus Jihad is the duty of waging a war which is perpetually latent. In a modern interpretation of the doctrine, Jihad is explained in terms of spiritual life. The last declaration of Jihad was in November 1914 in the Ottoman Caliph's (or Sultan's) name. It called on all Muslims, in the Entente or neutral countries, to fight together with the Ottoman Muslims.[53] The result was not encouraging, its immediate and direct effect was negligible. Although Jihad as a formality is defunct, as an idea it has potency in contemporary Islamic radicalism and is often employed by Muslim terrorists [and indeed rulers — Eds].

The idea of the holy war was transposed from Islam to Christendom in the shape of the Crusade. A Crusade was not just a war for the liberation of holy places, or simply a war against infidels, but a war undertaken as a penance. It was 'a new path to heaven' which gave forgiveness of sins, a penitentiary pilgrimage. The crusading idea was rapidly debased, but was still alive with President Eisenhower and Dulles. Secularized, it has become characteristic of the Revolutionist doctrine of war. The Jacobins of the French Revolution, and the Communists (on a parallel with Islam), divided the world into Dar-al-Islam and Dar-al-Harb.

Holy war is parallel to the Realist doctrine of war in embracing the principles of preventive war, and the total, ruthless, unlimited war; but the unconditional surrender demanded by the Realists is extended into a demand for revolution as a condition of granting peace to the defeated enemy. For example, Bonaparte, the victorious Republican in Italy, wished to negotiate only with Republican governments, and Wilson in 1918 wanted to negotiate only with democratic governments; so Stalin in 1943 would not recognize Poland, and others, without a 'friendly' government. Another characteristic of holy war doctrine is that it entails a horizontal division of mankind and international society, overriding state-frontiers, into two classes, the good and the bad. One example may suffice: '*Il n'existe que deux partis: celui des hommes corrompus et celui des hommes vertueux. Ne distinguez pas les hommes par leur fortune et par leur état mais par leur charactère*' (Robespièrre). (There are only two kinds of men, the corrupt and the virtuous. Do not judge men by their fortune or wealth but by their character.)[54] For the Calvinists: the elect and the

---

53. *Survey of International Affairs 1925* (London: Oxford University Press, 1927), vol. I, pp. 43–4.
54. Martin Wight's notes on lectures on 'the French Revolution' delivered by C.R.M.F. Cruttwell in Oxford 1932–3, p. 76.

reprobate; the Jesuits: Catholics and heretics; Jacobins: virtuous and corrupt; Communists: proletariat and bourgeoisie. There is a short step from this doctrine to the idea of being in a state of permanent war — latent or open — 'cold war' or co-existence: 'the Communist is always at war.'

The fundamental idea in the Revolutionary theory of the nature of war is that war is the agent of history, it makes the world safe for the doctrine, war is fought to end war. But particular wars differ in their susceptibility to such interpretation, or can be seen with differing degrees of philosophical abstraction. Not all wars are equally valid agencies of history, or equally relevant to the Revolutionists' purposes. If a war is only indirectly relevant to the purposes of history, the Revolutionist will probably experience a sense of duty to transform it into a directly relevant instrument. Thus Lenin saw the First World War (while he was still in Switzerland) on two planes simultaneously. In the long run it would serve the historical process by hastening the breakdown of capitalism, intensifying the suffering of the masses and creating an objective revolutionary situation; in the short run, it was a criminal and reactionary undertaking, with the bourgeoisie in every country pursuing their predatory aims under the cover of 'nationalist' ideology. It is necessary to hasten the long run and obliterate the short run: 'The only correct expression of this task is the slogan, "Turn the imperialist war into civil war"',[55] and turn the proximately relevant into immediate relevance.

The extreme point of the Revolutionist theory of war is found in the principle of extermination. The word 'principle' is used advisedly. Revolutionists are those who use extermination not just as an instrument of policy, but as a matter of principle: earlier Revolutionists would have said, as a matter of duty; contemporary ones would say, 'scientifically'. To go back to the Albigensian Crusade, the first crusade turned against Christendom itself; at the Sack of Beziers in 1209, the cry was: 'Kill them. For God will know his own.' This terrible saying has echoed down the centuries, with different variations of the same theme. The Papal Inquisition was founded after the Albigensian Crusade for the 're-education' of southern France; impenitent heretics were to be exterminated in a literal application of: 'If a man abide not in me, he is cast forth as a branch, and is withered; and men gather them, and cast them into the fire, and they are burned',[56] and John Henry Newman in the nineteenth century said:

[The Church] regards this world, and all that is in it, as a mere shadow, as dust and ashes, compared with the value of one single soul . . . She holds that it were better for the sun and moon to drop from heaven, for the earth to fail, and for all the many millions who are upon it to die of starvation in extremest

---

55. V.I. Lenin, 'Socialism and War', *A Handbook of Marxism*, pp. 679, 683.
56. St. John, ch. 15, verse 6, King James' Version.

agony, so far as temporal affliction goes, than that one soul, I will not say, should be lost, but should commit one single venial sin, should tell one wilful untruth, though it harmed no one, or steal one poor farthing without excuse.[57]

This is theologically faultless, granted its premises, and is notable only in expressing theological statements in dramatic language with unmuffled logic. But one can see the way men less gentle and more ruthless than Cardinal Newman might apply it, in circumstances in which the sin in question was not stealing one poor farthing, but heresy and infidelity. Norman Cohn, in *The Pursuit of the Millennium*,[58] traces heretic antecedents of modern totalitarianism; but there are also orthodox ones.

In July 1936 Franco gave an interview to a *News Chronicle* correspondent at Tetnan. The Nationalists had carried out systematic massacres of Reds.

'How long . . . is the massacre to go on?' . . .
'There can be no compromise, no truce. I shall go on preparing my advance to Madrid. I shall advance, I shall take the capital. I shall save Spain from Marxism, at whatever cost,'
'That means you will have to shoot half Spain,'
'I repeat, at whatever cost.'[59]

The correspondent was Arthur Koestler.

The terror is the modern secular equivalent of the Inquisition, and it has broken out at least three times in modern European history: during the French Revolution, under the Nazis, and under the Communists. In France, St. André, a former Protestant pastor who supervised the navy in the Committee of Public Safety said: 'To establish the foundations of the Republic securely we should I think reduce the population by more than a half.' He was not alone; St. Just: 'By a Republic I mean the total destruction of everything opposed to it'; and Carrier, conducting the Terror in the provinces, declared: 'In Lyons there are not 10,000, — I will not say good citizens, — but such as may be spared.' The Jacobins were consistent and clear-minded about this theory of depopulation: 'We would rather make a cemetery of France than fail to regenerate it after a fashion.'[60] [Pol Pot and other Khmer Rouge leaders were educated in Paris: the last of the Jacobins? Eds.]

Nazi terror theory was not much different:

---

57. John Henry Newman, *Certain Difficulties felt by Anglicans in Catholic Teaching* (London: Burns & Oats, 1879), vol. I, p. 240.
58. Norman Cohn, *The Pursuit of the Millennium* (London: Secker & Warburg, 1957).
59. 'Our Special Correspondent', *News Chronicle*, 29 July 1936.
60. Martin Wight's notes on lectures on 'the French Revolution' delivered by C.R.M.F. Cruttwell in Oxford 1932-3, pp. 25, 77.

What happens to a Russian or a Czech does not interest me in the slightest . . . Whether nations live in prosperity or starve to death interests me only in so far as we need them as slaves for our Kultur. Whether 10,000 Russian females fall down from exhaustion while digging an anti-tank ditch only interests me insofar as an anti-tank ditch for Germany is finished . . .

said Himmler in 1943,[61] and Hans Frank, Governor General of occupied Poland, remarked in his diary a little earlier:

8.3.1940; Wherever there is the least attempt by the Poles to start anything, an enormous campaign of destruction directed against them will follow . . . 24.8.1942; It is much better when a Pole breaks down than that a German succumbs. That we sentence one point two million Jews to die of hunger should be noted only marginally.[62]

The theory of the Communist terror is a variation on the same theme: 'He (Stalin) was one of those rare and terrible dogmatists capable of destroying nine-tenths of the human race to "make happy" the remaining tenth' (Djilas, in *Conversations with Stalin*),[63] and Lenin: 'To conceal from the masses the necessity for a desperate sanguinary war of extermination as the immediate task of future revolutionary action means deceiving both ourselves and the people.'[64] This is the principle of mass terror for the liquidation of class enemies. Khrushchev in his speech to the twentieth Party Congress, charged that Stalin had applied the principle 'incorrectly', because after the exploiting classes had already been liquidated, mass terror was turned inwards against the Party itself. Lenin had used the weapon 'correctly'.[65]

The word 'liquidate' has become familiar as a cliché, but in its original usage 'liquidate' was a verb governing a plural or collective noun. It was not individuals who were liquidated, but classes: the exploiting bourgeoisie, class enemies of the workers. In a famous phrase at the time of Brest-Litovsk, in March 1918, Lenin said: 'Politics begin where the masses are, not where there are thousands, but millions, that is where serious politics begin.[66] This can be adapted to 'liquidation begins where the masses are'. Bernard Shaw, who liked to

61. Heinrich Himmler quoted by Mr Dodd (USA) at the Nuremberg Trial, 11 December 1945, *Manchester Guardian*, 12 December 1945, report of trial.
62. *Nazi Conspiracy and Aggression* (Washington, DC: US Government Printing Office, 1946), vol. IV, doc. 2233-M-PS, pp. 900, 906.
63. Milovan Djilas, *Conversations with Stalin* (London: Rupert Hart Davis, 1962), p. 171.
64. V.I. Lenin, 'The Lessons of the Moscow Uprising', *Selected Works* (Moscow, Leningrad: Co-operative Publishing Society, 1934), vol. III, p. 349.
65. N. Khrushchev, ed. Thomas P. Whitney, *Khrushchev Speaks* (Ann Arbor: University of Michigan Press, 1963), p. 217.
66. V.I. Lenin, 'Report on War and Peace to the 7th Congress of the R.C.P. (Bolshevik) 7 March 1918', *Selected Works*, vol. VII, pp. 295–6.

pose as an apologist for totalitarianism said: 'If we desire a certain type of civilization and culture, we must exterminate the sort of people who do not fit into it.'[67]

There are various Anglo-Saxon approximations to the theory of depopulation: Cromwell's policy in Ireland, and notably the massacre at Drogheda (1650) and the massacre at Glencoe instigated by the Scottish advisers of William III (1692) are two examples. Dr Thomas Arnold's belief in the necessity of emigration to remove the surplus population, and of transportation of criminals, is another.[68]

In 1948 the General Assembly of the United Nations adopted the Convention on the Prevention and Punishment of Genocide. It was signed by fifty-two states including the Soviet Union, and is now in force.[69] Genocide is defined as

acts committed with intent to destroy, in whole or in part, a national, ethnical, racial or religious group such as killing or causing serious bodily or mental harm to members of the group; deliberately inflicting on the group conditions of life calculated to bring about its total or partial destruction.[70]

It is a crime under international law, whether in peace or war. This registers a Rationalist reaction of international conscience, if there be such a thing. The crime of 'genocide' was framed or defined on the model of Hitler's treatment of the Jews, and it would cover the Albigensian Crusade, which, as the destruction of a religious group, was a notable early act of genocide in Western European history. It does not however seem to cover the liquidation of classes.

In 1948, when the Convention was adopted, Stalin's deportation of the Estonians was in full swing, and this approximated to genocide; Khrushchev said that Stalin was contemplating similar treatment of the Ukrainians. In 1955, it was being said of General O'Daniel, the head of the United States military mission to Vietnam, that his policy was contained in this command: 'Paint the good white and the bad red, and kill all the red',[71] which expresses very simply the Revolutionist principle of holy war: divide mankind into good and bad on a criterion provided by your doctrine, and then kill all the bad. This is an abiding theme in Revolutionist doctrine.

Revolutionist extermination is quite distinct from Realist extermination, because it is conducted *on principle*. Of course, history is a

---

67. Raymond Mortimer quoting GBS in a review of *Bernard Shaw* by St. John Ervine, *Sunday Times*, 29 July 1956.
68. See Thomas Arnold's letters to the *Sheffield Courant*, and T.W. Bamford, *Thomas Arnold* (London: Crescent Press, 1960), pp. 46 and 109–10.
69. See *UN Review*, June 1956, vol. II, no. 12, p. 16.
70. L. Oppenheim, ed. H. Lauterpacht, *International Law* (London: Longmans, 1955), 8th edn, vol. I, para. 340, p. 750.
71. Robert Guillain, 'The Tragedy of Vietnam', *The Manchester Guardian*, 27 May 1955.

record of massacres (Marlowe's *Tamburlaine the Great* is a portrayal, in splendid rhetoric, of a ruler intoxicated by power), and the Realist tendency towards ruthlessness and unlimited means will produce massacres, but these are usually governed by a principle of utility. Extermination in order to eradicate heresy, to purify society, for scientific social engineering, for the sake of the cause, is something different.

Islam may have invented the holy war, but it did not exterminate. Moreover, this kind of extermination is something specifically Western, as Revolutionism is specifically Western. The West has invented the steam-engine, differential calculus, nuclear physics, the cathedrals and the orchestral symphony, but also doctrinal extermination. [The Turkish massacre of the Armenians in 1916 may be cited as an example of non-Western genocide, but the philosophy of nationalism which lay behind this atrocity was itself Western in origin. Eds.]

Addendum: the nuclear dimension

It has been suggested that much of what has been said about the theory of war has been rendered obsolete by the advent of nuclear weapons, because it is no longer realistic to use war as an instrument of policy. A word ought to be said about this in the hope of clearing up misconceptions.

First a verbal point: it is loose talking, imprecise thinking, to say that political Realism is obsolete because war is no longer realistic. 'Realist' is not the same as 'realistic'. The word Realist has, so to speak, hitherto been used with a capital 'R' in an attempt to elucidate the main features of a political tradition which embraces Machiavelli, Hobbes, Hegel and Morgenthau. Such people as these are generally described as Realist and so the label has here been adopted. This does not mean any inference or assumption that what Realists say is realistic. (Hobbes' theory of social contract may seem unrealistic, but Hobbes remains a Realist.) For example, it has been suggested above that a characteristic Realist doctrine of war was one of ruthlessness, or by using maximum force to compel surrender and that this was exemplified by the Anglo-American decision to use atomic bombs against Japan in 1945; the reader was then reminded that there was room for argument whether this Realist decision had been a *realistic* one, whether in fact it had not been regrettably short-sighted.

What does 'realistic' mean? The opposite, in the last sentence, of 'regrettably short-sighted'. This is one kind of connotation we give to 'realistic': seeing reality clearly, therefore seeing further than others. But 'realistic' is also a word of approval, used of a kind of thinking which looks in the same direction as we look, and as far as we look, or of a kind of action which aims at the ends we think admirable. Thus, the criticism of the use of the atomic bomb against Japan in

1945 is of course a Rationalist criticism. It argues that it was *unrealistic* to think merely of ending the war against Japan quickly and so saving the lives of one million Americans likely to have been lost in storming the coasts of Japan, without thinking also of the long-term effects of using this weapon, of the effects on our ally Russia and Asian opinion, and of the moral effects. The Rationalist holds that he is really more realistic than the Realist because deep moral truths and principles which are the Rationalist's stock-in-trade are more real, more effective, more potent, than equations of power which are the Realist's stock-in-trade.

The Revolutionist holds that *he* is really more realistic than either Realist or Rationalist because he is in possession of the doctrine, the idea, which enables him to conform his action to the movement of history without which clue all political action is sterile and self-defeating.

The second point is one of fact: there can be no doubt that the possibility of general war still enters into political calculations. It may be the case that nuclear weapons have made war between the major powers impossible or obsolete, but to assert this now is simply a wishful assertion of hope. If in a hundred years' time there has been no major war it might reasonably be said the balance of terror has stood the test of time and eliminated war of this character. But the hope that nuclear weapons have made war impossible is a very limited hope. Strictly it means, or should mean, that nuclear weapons have made nuclear war between nuclear powers impossible. To hope that nuclear weapons will not be used is not the same as the hope that war is obsolete. Indeed not only has conventional war been frequently engaged in since the birth of the atomic age, but nuclear powers have themselves occasionally threatened nuclear war: Russia against Britain and France in the Suez crisis; the United States against China and North Korea in 1953,[72] and again in the Syrian crisis of 1957. The Sixth Fleet was armed with atomic artillery, and was 'ready for anything from a brush fire to full scale war'. These threats may have been bluff: the point is that they brought the possibility of war into political calculations.

Not only does the possibility of war still enter political calculations, as it has always done, but one can go further and say that every power still regards war, in the last resort, as a lesser evil than defeat. Nuclear powers to begin with regarded nuclear war as preferable to capitulation. The British White Paper on Defence of 1955, said:

Nevertheless, in the last resort, most of us must feel that determination to face the threat of physical devastation, even on the immense scale which must now be foreseen, is manifestly preferable to an attitude of subservience to militant

---

72. [The United States nuclear threat against China and North Korea in 1953 was not revealed until later — Eds.]

Communism, with the national and individual humiliation that this would inevitably bring.[73]

Mutatis mutandis, this is true of virtually every power today, and certainly of all great powers. It has always been an axiom of international politics. President Cleveland, in his message to Congress on the last occasion on which Britain and the United States contemplated war with one another, over the Venezuelan crisis in 1895, enunciated the same axiom, that war is a lesser evil than defeat: 'There is no calamity which a great nation can invite which equals that which follows a supine submission to wrong and injustice and the consequent loss of national self-respect and honor beneath which are shielded and defended a people's safety and greatness.'[74] This axiom has not been refuted by the advent of nuclear weapons. Individuals may wish that it had, but no *peoples* have yet embraced such a revolution of values.

If the possibility of war still enters into the political calculations of every power, then the political theories of war are as relevant as ever. That is, theories of war still influence policy, and policies can be studied in terms of the theories that inspire them. In terms of theory, the current anxiety about nuclear weapons has caused a revival of, or reversion to, Rationalist doctrines of war, particularly the doctrine of limited war. It has never been dead, and has now acquired a new cogency, and become correspondingly fashionable. Western society, like a drunkard at the onset of delirium tremens, has reverted to some of its oldest moral principles, and one can only hope that it is a real *conversion*, not just a panic *reversion*. But one of the practical difficulties about Rationalist principles is whether one side can hold to them when it is not quite certain whether its adversary shares them. The balance of terror seems to be as unstable as the balance of power, as one so-called 'ultimate weapon' succeeds another almost every year. A temporary technological ascendancy cannot fail to encourage a Realist line of thought, and consideration of the advantages of preventive war, the knock-out blow such as Pearl Harbor.

The anxiety among Western nuclear powers lest nuclear weapons will become diffused among small powers is precisely an anxiety lest small powers may not be guided by Rationalist principles but pursue their private quarrels along Realist lines. Malenkov, when he said that a nuclear war would destroy Communist and capitalist society alike, seemed to be displaying Rationalist premises, but he was speedily disgraced; and when Khrushchev repeated time and again that a nuclear war would smash capitalism for good, but not Communism, he was talking in Revolutionist terms, foreseeing a war that would

---

73. *Parliamentary Papers* (London: HMSO, 1954/55), vol. X, Cmd. 9391, para. 24.
74. S.G. Cleveland in R.J. Bartlett, ed., 'Message to Congress', 17 December 1895, *Record of American Diplomacy* (New York: Alfred A. Knopf, 1947), pp. 351–2.

finally exterminate or enslave the unbeliever.

It is true that he spoke also of peaceful co-existence and peaceful competition, and sometimes seems to have revised Lenin's doctrine of an inevitable armed clash between the two camps, but this is not incompatible with the other. It would be good Marxist principle, as well as good Russian tradition, not to start a war between the great powers; to proceed, as Palmerston said of Russian policy in the 1830s, by sap rather than by storm; and to wait for a great war to come, if come it shall, through the initiative of others, and then to turn it to advantage. That was the Soviet position in the 1950s. It is worth remembering that Soviet policy under Stalin was restless and aggressive in appearance, at the time when America had the atomic monopoly and (for what it is worth) managed the United Nations. Since Russia has developed the H-bomb, and the Third World states are the dominant voice in the United Nations, Soviet policy has become bland and co-existential, and anxiety has given place to confidence.

11: Theory of international law, obligation and ethics

There are three depths of enquiry, three superimposed paradigms which correspond to the related theories of international law, obligation and ethics.

International law

The three old traditions or schools of international law, the Grotians, naturalists, and positivists, are relevant to this classification but do not exactly correspond. Naturalists affirmed that there is no international law except what is found in natural law, they denied any positive law of nations, but their natural law was that of Hobbes, the law of anti-social liberty. (Pufendorf, the founder of the naturalists, was Hobbes' first international pupil.) They tended to work deductively and be realistic.

Positivists affirmed that there is no international law except what is found in custom and treaties, that is, what is based on common consent. Some denied the existence of a law of nature, and seem to be the 'antipodes of the naturalists'.[1] But extremes meet, and the positivists were inductive Realists.

Rationalists

The Grotians are normally described as being midway between the others, the judicious mean who derive international law equally from the law of nature and from existing practice and agreement among nations. They are the predominant and orthodox school of the seventeenth

---

1. L. Oppenheim, ed. H. Lauterpacht, *International Law* (London: Longmans, Green & Co., 1966), vol. I, 'Peace', p. 96.

and eighteenth centuries, and the bearers of the Rationalist tradition. Their Rationalism, however, resides not in their being midway, but in their holding the pre-Hobbesian traditional doctrine of natural law, as Grotius did (though not all of his successors).

The naturalist tradition has two fundamental doctrines. The first is that the sovereignty of states in the international community and the absence of any common superior does not involve pure anarchy, because prior to all political organization there still exists law, based on reason and the nature of man as a social being. The second doctrine is that the primary evidence of what that law is is custom, the existing practice of all nations. The first doctrine relates to the law of nature, the second to the Roman *jus gentium*, which Grotius laid together as the foundations of modern international law, and this is the characteristic Rationalist approach to it.

Natural law has been widely abandoned and discredited in its ancient form, but the central tradition of international jurisprudence still makes two assertions which are derived from it. First, where there are no treaties or judicial decisions, international law must be sought in the customs and usages of civilized nations, and, as evidence thereof, in the works of jurists and commentators. This body of customs and usages, the existing practices of nations, is not simply a codification of the law of the stronger, because it embodies compromises between conflicting interests of different states at different periods. It has given rise to an impressive catalogue of arbitral settlements, effectively observed by great powers as well as small, and to valuable work by international commissions (and the work of the Permanent Court of International Justice between the Wars). The second assertion is that this body of custom and existing practice, which is international law, does reflect and derive its authority from the recognition of what C.A.W. Manning has called a law behind the law. The element of *jus gentium* has come to predominate over that of *lex naturae*, but the recognition of a law behind the law remains: there are fundamental or natural norms, even though the way in which they are conceived, and the nature of the appeal to them, may change.

Oppenheim divides modern international lawyers into two schools, the legal and the diplomatic.[2] The legal school wants international law to develop along the lines of municipal law. It aims at the codification of decisive rules of international law and its administration by effective international courts. This is the Grotian, or Rationalist tradition. The diplomatic school thinks of international law not as a body of firm rules but as one of elastic principles. Instead of international courts it advocates diplomatic settlement of disputes, or arbitration, because these methods may work, but international courts have been proved ineffective by history. These are the Realists.

---

2. ibid., vol. I, pp. 87–8.

Realists

Positivists discount the natural law tradition wholly: one can know nothing of any metaphysical law behind the law, and such speculations do not affect the actions of states; and they emphasize the absolute sovereignty of the members of a comity of nations, for these are the only sources of power, and law is derived from power. Positivists assert, therefore, a consensual theory of international law. 'International Law is the sum of the rules by which states have *consented* to be bound, and nothing can be law to which they have not consented.'[3]

International law is simply the sum of treaties, and its only source is the precedents of state practice. Arbitral settlements, international commissions, the Permanent Court, have all achieved little, and only in the interstices of international relations where vital interests are not concerned. Interstitially, the consensual theory may be mitigated by the principle of 'tacit consent', but this is in relation only to the subsidiary and marginal interests of states. This doctrine is a characteristically Realist analysis; and its most interesting exponent in this context is Treitschke:

The existence of international law is always precarious. It always must remain a *lex imperfecta*, because no power higher than the states themselves can be called upon to arbitrate . . . In order to make no mistake as to the real meaning of international law, we must always remember that it must not run counter to the nature of the State. No State can reasonably be asked to adopt a course which would lead it to destroy itself. Likewise every State in the comity of nations must retain the attributes of sovereignty whose defence is the highest duty even in its international relations. We find the principles of international law most secure in that department of it which does not trench upon questions of sovereignty; that is in the domain of etiquette and of international civil law.[4]

In other words, international law operates in the domain of subsidiary importance. The state is prior to international law, both logically and historically.

Revolutionists

Where do we look for a Revolutionist theory of international law? There are probably the rudiments of one among the publicists of the Counter-Reformation, the Calvinists and the Jesuits; the Jacobins scarcely had one: they were never at peace. It is the Marxists who

---

3. J.L. Brierly, *The Law of Nations* (London: Oxford University Press, 1938), p. 42.
4. H. von Treitschke, tr. A.J. Balfour, *Politics* (London: Constable & Co., 1916), vol. II, pp. 591–5.

have had the leisure to develop one and the Soviet theory of international law is interesting. The standard definition of international law, originating with A.Y. Vyshinsky and enlarged by F.I. Kozhevnikov, is that:

International law may be defined as the will of the ruling classes expressed in the sum total of the norms, conventional or customary regulating the legal relations among states, which arise in the process of their struggle and cooperation, and secured by individual or collective state coercion.[5]

This definition is positivist in character: international law is the sum of existing treaties and customs; there are no natural or fundamental norms, no law behind the law. It describes international law as recording the conflicts of states as well as governing their co-operation, indeed, it gives their 'struggle' priority over their co-operation; and it describes the sanction of international law as coercion exercised by states individually or collectively. Such a view might be related to the Realists' conception of a *bellum omnium contra omnes*, or to the Revolutionists' conception of a perpetual latent holy war. But there is a more important characteristic of this definition to notice: it begins by defining international law as the will of the ruling classes of the states it binds. It assumes that law is a product of social systems and defines international law accordingly. In effect, it defines it ideologically, in terms of Marxist sociology, and this is a specific difference from naturalist and positivist conceptions of international law.

These are perhaps pointers to a Revolutionist theory of international law, as seen in the standard Soviet definition, and they are confirmed by a further examination of the Soviet conception of international law. For example, Soviet jurists have a special notion of the *function* of international law. Kozhevnikov attempted to explore Soviet practice in terms of international law in his textbook on the subject:

The political, economic and other relations between states may have the character of *struggle* as well as the character of *cooperation*. Struggles among states in widely varying spheres of international life may find expression also in the forum of international law; in other words, the institutes of international law are used by states as a means of struggle for their political and economic interests. International law is used as a form of consolidation and legalization of successes achieved as a result of political struggles. International law regulates and consolidates relations arising in the process of *struggle* of states as well as in the process of their cooperation.[6]

---

5. F.I. Kozhevnikov, *A Textbook on International Law*, publ. 1947, quoted by O.J. Lissitzyn in 'Recent Soviet Literature on International Law', *The American Slavic and East European Review*, vol. II, no. 4, December 1952 (Columbia University Press), p. 259.
6. ibid., (emphasis in the original), p. 262.

The Soviet conception of international law is highly pragmatic; it is seen as an instrument of policy and accepted to the extent it serves the interests of the Soviet state. Originally its whole fabric was repudiated by the Soviet state, just as it was by the Jacobins (which evoked Burke's philippics): the Revolutionaries and the virtuous state *contra mundum*. Later, as the Soviet Union resumed the role of a great power in international relations, its attitude to international law changed. Since 1934, its defensive value has been found and exploited, as a bulwark against the imperialist aggression, first of Germany, then of the United States. Thus technically 'conservative' doctrines of international law are espoused to protect the interests of the revolutionary state in the period of its consolidation of power; a cardinal Soviet doctrine is the priority of municipal over international law, and the sovereignty and equality of states is emphasized as an obstacle to imperialist aggression. Also, the appeal to international law itself has value as an ideological weapon. Western imperialist states can be branded as law-breakers, violators of the Charter. There is an apparent inconsistency, in that international law, in the Soviet view, 'legalizes' the successes achieved in international struggle but there are no fundamental norms, no law behind the law, by which to adjudge the legalized successes of the United States as ultimately illegal and unfair to the Soviet Union, except, of course, the revolutionary messianic vocation of the latter.

Thus the Soviet theory of international law has two characteristics, closely related. First it is, seen objectively, uncertain, ambiguous and arbitrary. Any traditional rules of international law which are incompatible with the basic notions of Soviet policy and ideology may be arbitrarily set aside. The validity of international law is qualified by its compatibility with the concepts of a particular country. This is a truly revolutionary doctrine. It is a persistent Soviet contention that the Soviet Union is free to reject norms and institutions which are unacceptable to it as a socialist state. The second characteristic is that, seen subjectively, from inside, the Soviet theory of international law makes it flexible, and open to many opportunist and casuistical possibilities. (A new type of international law is said to be emerging in theory in inter-Communist state relations, but is not yet much explored.)[7]

To conclude, in the Rationalist tradition, international law is conceived as the existing practices and treaties of states, constantly refined by references to certain fundamental standards and norms of which they are the imperfect expression. In the Realist tradition, it is conceived as the sum of treaties agreed to by sovereign states who *ex*

---

7. See J.N. Hazard, 'The Soviet Union and International Law', *Soviet Studies*, vol. I (Oxford: Blackwell, January 1950), pp. 189ff., and O.J. Lissitzyn, 'Recent Soviet Literature on International Law', *American Slavic and East European Review*, December 1952, pp. 257ff., and Ivo Lapenna, *Conceptions soviétiques de droit international public* (Paris: Pédone, 1954).

hypothesi will abate no essential of their sovereignty; and in Revolutionist tradition, it is an ideological weapon for the prosecution of holy war by the Revolutionist state.

International obligation

Here the paradigm can be taken a stage deeper, to consider the theories of international obligation underlying these contrasted conceptions of international law.

Rationalists

For the Rationalists, the foundation of all international intercourse is the sanctity of international obligations, the inviolability of promises, and the binding character of treaties. This needs no elaboration: it can be summed up in the maxim, *pacta sunt servanda*. But why must agreements be observed? Utilitarian reasons may be adduced as the sources of authority for this principle, but the oldest and profoundest answer is that the observance of agreements represents an ethical norm; it conforms to an inherent standard of justice.[8]

'The quest for the reason of validity of a norm is not — like the quest for the cause of an effect — a *regressus ad infinitum*; it is terminated by a highest norm which is the last ground of validity within the normative system'. In other words, the basic norm is the necessary hypothesis on which the jurist sets to work.[9]

Realists

If the Rationalist principle of international obligation can be summed up by '*pacta sunt servanda*', the Realist principle can be conveniently counter-summarized by '*rebus sic stantibus*'. This is the ablative absolute: 'things remaining as they are', 'while conditions remain the same', the doctrine of changed circumstances. Treitschke said:

All the restraints to which states bind themselves by treaty are voluntary, and . . . all treaties are concluded on the tacit understanding *rebus sic stantibus*. No state ever has existed, or ever will exist, which is willing to hold to all eternity to the agreements which it signs.[10]

---

8. See A.P. D'Entrèves, *Natural Law* (London: Hutchinson, 1951), p. 77.
9. ibid., p. 106.
10. H. von Treitschke, *Politics*, vol. II, pp. 595-6.

Treaties are inherently temporary, and their observance is inherently conditional on their continuing to serve the vital interests of the state.[11]

It was only quite late, in the nineteenth century, that this principle, like the positivist theory of international law, came to be consciously accepted and acted on, and this illustrates the drift away from Rationalism towards Realism. Early treaties were almost always made without limit of duration: they were the 'perpetual treaties' and 'eternal peaces' of the sixteenth and seventeenth centuries, and all engagements were of indefinite duration.[12] Defining the duration of treaties became common only in the second half of the nineteenth century; for example the Austro-German alliance of 1879 was drawn up for five-year periods and renewed. At the same time the tacit acceptance of the doctrine of *rebus sic stantibus* became prevalent. Such a doctrine can of course lead, in extreme cases, to complete opportunism and diplomatic egotism: Hitler told the conference of supreme commanders on 23 November 1939: 'Moreover, we have a pact with Russia. Pacts, however, are only held as long as they serve the purpose. Russia will hold herself to it only so long as Russia considers it to be to her benefit. Even Bismarck [in the nineteenth century] thought so.'[13]

Revolutionists

It is not easy to find a specific Revolutionist theory of international obligation to set against the clear-cut Rationalist and Realist theories. It was said that one main characteristic of the Soviet theory of international law was its flexibility, and opportunist possibilities. In his book mentioned earlier, Kozhevnikov emphasizes that the norms of international law are not to be interpreted in an 'abstractly dogmatic' fashion: 'The socialist principle of respect for international treaties . . . must not be understood . . . abstractly-dogmatically in the sense of absolute inadmissibility, under all circumstances, of changes in international treaties.'

An abstractly-dogmatic understanding of the principle '*pacta sunt servanda*' would close the road to any development in the field of international relations. Lenin said that to deny in principle the possibility of changes in the status quo would be highly reactionary, and a mockery of the fundamental concepts of historical science, that

---

11. See H.J. Morgenthau: Treaties last only while they continue to express the interest of the signatories, *In Defense of the National Interest* (New York: Alfred A. Knopf, 1951), p. 147.

12. G. Butler and S. Maccoby, *Development of International Law* (London: Longman, Green & Co. Ltd., 1928), pp. 518ff.

13. *Nazi Conspiracy and Aggression* (Washington, DC: US Government Printing Office, 1946), vol. III, p. 575.

is, of Marxism. This amounts to a convenient flexibility of interpretation: arbitrary denunciation of treaties is inadmissible but not every denunciation of treaties is arbitrary. The corollary is that denunciation of treaties by the Soviet Union is never arbitrary — no Soviet publication will admit that the Soviet state has ever violated international law, or even that its actions have been legally questionable.

The same rule of avoiding 'abstractly-dogmatic' interpretations (that is, the same convenient flexibility in interpretation) applies to the question of territorial change. The Communist Party always claims that it is against annexation, meaning the seizure of others' lands, because, as Lenin said, such seizure violates the self-determination of nations. But this does not preclude any changes in territorial status, for the recognition of an abstract stability in the territorial status quo is alien to the principles of Leninist–Stalinist policy. According to Lenin, not every military incorporation is annexation, because socialists cannot reject violence and war which are in the interests of the majority of the people. Soviet doctrine therefore admits of territorial changes on the basis of law and justice. Indeed, the expansion of territory is not alien to the Soviet Union.[14]

The Revolutionist theory in international obligation may be summed up as an avoidance of an 'abstractly-dogmatic' interpretation of the Rationalist principle of *pacta sunt servanda* which is limited, not by a time-clause as with the Realists, but by an implicit clause which discriminates between the status of those who give the promise and those who receive it. The theory also subordinates this principle to the dictates of ideological necessity; in the Soviet case, the interests of international revolution. In other words, the time has not yet come when political obligation can be fully actualized, when treaties become sacred and promises inviolable: that will come only with the fulfilment of the revolution. Meanwhile, the violation of treaties and annexation of territories is sometimes permissible and necessary, when these actions are taken against those who obstruct the fulfilment of revolution.

Here we come upon an ancient political principle of European history: the principle that faith need not be kept with heretics. This was first enunciated at the time of the Albigensian Crusade, by Innocent III, the greatest of medieval pope legislators, in his Bull of 1208 deposing the Count of Toulouse ('faith need not be kept with those who do not keep faith with God'). The Bull released subjects from their allegiance to the heretic prince.[15] But the principle applied with equal force the other way and could be construed in wider senses. It

---

14. F.I. Kozhevnikov, 'Stalin's speech in praise of Lenin at the Second Congress of Soviets', in *The History of CPSU* (Moscow: Foreign Languages Publishing House, 1945), p. 269.
15. See R.W. Carlyle, *A History of Medieval Political Theory in the West* (Edinburgh and London: William Blackwood & Sons Ltd., 1950), vol. V, pp. 181-2.

was invoked at the Council of Constance concerning the reformer, Hus; the Council declared that no promise is binding which is against the interests of the Catholic faith. Hus had been granted safe conduct by King Sigismund, was imprisoned soon after his arrival and burnt a few months later (6 July 1415).[16] The principle became widely quoted and generally acted upon by the Revolutionists, Catholic and Protestant, of the sixteenth century, and it has become the fundamental principle of obligation of their secularized Jacobin and Communist successors. In the case of the latter, one may cite both Stalin's arrest, in 1945, of Polish resistance leaders after inviting them to Moscow to discuss the formation of a new government, and the arrest and prompt execution of Imre Nagy, Hungarian premier in the brief rising of 1956, after promising him safe conduct from the Yugoslav embassy in Bucharest to Yugoslavia. It is a principle of differential morality, of selective moral commitments. Obligation is determined by the ideological compatibility of the other party.

Thus the three theories of international obligation can be summed up:

Rationalist: *Pacta sunt servanda*
Realist: *Rebus sic stantibus*
Revolutionist: *Cum haereticis fides non servanda*

International ethics

The ethical principles underlying the contrasted conceptions of international obligation have now to be considered. There are two questions to be asked: 'What is the nature of political morality?' and, 'How is political morality applied?' The answers lead to a theory of the double standard of morality, and a theory of political compromise.

Rationalists

The Rationalist tradition has two connected features, both of which can be related to the specific Rationalist conception of man as an ambiguous being, a being embodying a tension; not simple, as in the Realist view; but complex, and with a complexity not distributed vertically between the two divisions of the human race as the Revolutionists see it, but horizontally, among all mankind.

The first facet of the Rationalist tradition is that politics is the order of justice, and personal life is the order of charity (love). It is the Christian and Stoic tradition that politics, the affairs of collections of

---

16. See K. Krofta in *The Cambridge Medieval History* (Cambridge: At the University Press, 1936), vol. VIII, pp. 58–9.

men and women, must be governed by a different principle from that which governs private relations. Justice is the principle governing the actions of men when they are acting on behalf of other men, as when a representative is acting on behalf of his constituents. There is an implicit conflict of rights between him with whom the representative is dealing, and those whom he is representing, and so his task is to adjudicate, to decide what proportion of rights is due to each. Aristotle's definition of justice was 'giving to each that which is due'.

In the Rationalist view, it is not true that the ethics of private life have *no* applicability in political and international transactions, but the applicability needs to be accurately understood. The analogue of international relationships in private life is not the conduct of single individuals acting towards one another for themselves, but the conduct of trustees. It is admirable for an individual to give away his money for philanthropic purposes, but not for a trustee to give away the money of his ward. The trustee should not be indifferent to the rights of others besides his ward, and it would be wrong for him to seek to gain more than the ward is entitled to in strict justice; but it would be wrong for him not to insist on all that his ward is entitled to in strict justice. In his dealings with others on behalf of his ward he goes by the law of justice, not of charity.

The action of states is that of the governments of those states, and they are in the position of trustees. They are there to secure the interests of the people they serve; they should respect the rights of other states and not seek to gain more for their people than is just, but they are bound also not to give away anything that their people may in justice claim. Governments cannot be expected to act continuously on any other grounds than national interest tempered by justice, and they have no right to do so, being agents and not principles. Hence it follows that the Rationalist tradition affirms a double standard of morality: the ethic of charity in private morality; the ethic of justice in state morality. This is not to say that private morality is moral and state morality is immoral; the validity of the ethical is maintained in both fields.

A subsidiary question, however, arises: 'What is the content of political morality?' And here we may note the debate between Rationalists and Revolutionists on whether a political motive is to be found either in gratitude or in guilt-and-reparation.

The second facet of the Rationalist tradition arises from the conception of politics as the field of the approximate and the provisional, and this too is grounded in the Rationalist view of human nature. Burke declared:

We must soften into a credulity below the milkiness of infancy, to think all men virtuous. We must be tainted with a malignity truly diabolical, to believe all the world to be equally wicked and corrupt. Men are in publick life as in private, some good, some evil. The elevation of the one, and the depression of the other, are the first objects of all true policy.[17]

Politics is the perpetual movement from one stage of the provisional to another. There are no complete solutions, only the constantly repeated approximation towards the embodiment of justice in concrete arrangements, which do as constantly dissolve with the passage of time. Thus to be a Rationalist politician is to exist in a state of moral tension between the actual and the desirable. Gladstone said: 'Men have no business to talk of disenchantment; ideals are never realised'; but that is no reason, he meant, why politicians should not persist and toil and hope. This moral tension is shown in the words of another Rationalist statesman, Smuts, on the eve of his departure from London to San Francisco, to attend the founding of the United Nations, 27 March 1945:

I myself should like to have a declaration of faith of the fundamentals wherein we believe. There are certain things which are our ten commandments, the basis of our whole Western outlook. I should like to see them solemnly affirmed. Even if some of these things are not carried out completely in practice it is right to affirm them and know when you are falling below your own standard.

Ideals are never realized, but should be striven for; the fundamentals wherein we believe will not be carried out, but it is necessary to affirm them: here is the moral tension within which Rationalist statecraft is conducted. (The mode of all statecraft and political action is compromise. Politics is the art of the possible; Talleyrand said the statesman has '*le tact des choses possibles*', and Bismarck '*Die Politik ist keine exakte Wissenschaft*'. Here the Rationalists and the Realists are agreed and the Revolutionists too in a way.)

For the Rationalist, the compromise inherent in political action is a compromise one makes with the total situation in which one has to act; it is an adjustment to one's political environment; and the principle governing the compromise is the choice of the lesser evil. 'Politics is a field where action is one long second-best and where the choice constantly lies between two blunders.'[18] The great exponent of the doctrine of the lesser evil in English political writing is Burke:

It is no inconsiderable part of wisdom, to know how much of an evil ought to be tolerated; lest, by attempting a degree of purity impracticable in degenerate times and manners, instead of cutting off the subsisting ill practices, new corruptions might be produced for the concealment and security of the old.[19]

---

17. Edmund Burke, *The Works of the Right Honourable Edmund Burke* (London: Samuel Holdsworth, 1842), vol. I, p. 134.
18. Quoted in *The Church and the Atom* (Westminster: Press and Publications Board of the Church Assembly, 1948), C.A. 875, p. 7.
19. Edmund Burke, 'Present Discontents', *The Works of the Right Honourable Edmund Burke*, vol. I, p. 148.

The most consistent exponent of the doctrine of the lesser evil in international history has been the Papacy. The policy of the Vatican always shows the greatest respect for time and place, and seeks what it is best to do under the given circumstances rather than trying to introduce ready-made solutions. 'To avoid greater evils' is the guiding rule. Pius XI, in his address of 14 May 1929 justifying the Lateran Treaty with Mussolini, in which the temporal states of the Church were at last signed away, said: 'When it is a question of saving souls or avoiding greater evils, we would find the courage to treat with the Devil in person.'[20] It was in almost exactly the same words that Pius VII defended the Concordat of 1801 with Napoleon, and that Pope Paul V used, two hundred years earlier, in describing his policy in the struggle between the Papacy and Venice of 1605–7. This was the first head-on collision between the Counter-Reformation Papacy and a modern Catholic power; it was the last occasion on which the Papacy claimed to exercise direct spiritual authority in a secular state, and the last on which it laid a state under an interdict. The papal claims were resoundingly repudiated. The characteristic Rationalist attitude towards political ethics is to hold that the only moral choice possible is between a bad solution and a worse one.

Choosing the lesser evil is a principle of political ethics which does not contain within itself the test of its own applicability. There is no verification principle in politics. How to apply the principle in a particular situation is a matter of political judgement, and judgements will vary. To decide which is the lesser evil requires an assessment of imponderables and contingencies, and such assessments will be different. Chamberlain defended the Munich Settlement in the House of Commons by reference to the principle of a lesser evil; and Roosevelt's apologists (especially Walter Lippmann) defended the Yalta Agreement similarly. Others have thought that the scales in which they weighed the evils were faulty.

Principles of political ethics are disquietingly protean. Like Proteus, the old man of the sea who changed into lion, snake, leopard and boar, flowing water and tree, when Menelaus seized him, so such principles shimmer and dissolve and reconstitute themselves in a slightly different shape even while they are being appealed to. Chamberlain also defended Munich by appealing to the doctrine of justification by necessity, and this was stating his ethical principle with a different focus and emphasis which made it a different one from that of the lesser evil. This protean quality is the fascination and difficulty of studying political ethics; it is worth having in mind when looking at the Realist principles.

---

20. D.A. Binchy, *Church and State in Fascist Italy* (London: Oxford University Press, 1941), p. 83.

Realists

For Realists, like Rationalists, there is clearly a difference in the standards of behaviour of private life and political life, but the Realist does not construe this difference in terms of a double standard of *morality*, a tension between personal and public morality; he sees it as a difference between the sphere of the moral and that of the non-moral. The validity of ethics is restricted to private relations, and politics is left as the domain of the non-ethical.[21]

This double standard of morality can be seen in Luther. The doctrine of justification by faith maintains the separation of religion from ethics. It was in the spirit of Lutheran thought to attribute totality of value to inward morality, and depreciate external morality, the moral issues involved in power, property, war or slavery, even though this morality was still stated in terms of natural law. Luther echoes Augustine's antinomy between the city of God and the earthly city. But Augustine reconciled the antinomy through the fundamental unity of Christian ethics: through the Church the virtues of the city of God flowed back into the organism of temporal society. In Luther's treatise on 'Temporal Authority' (1523), the reconcilement is subsequent and external, seeking in secular power both the moral order of society and the effective organization of the Church. Society is not a community but a power, a necessary evil to restrain the 'beastliness' of our inclinations. Luther's pessimism goes beyond that of Machiavelli. To govern according to the Gospel would be like letting loose savage beasts. It is therefore necessary to separate the two kingdoms: 'that [kingdom] where there is pardon from that where there is punishment; that [kingdom] where a man gives up his own right from that where he claims it.' According to Luther: 'Conscience has nothing to do with the laws, works and justice of the earth.' A prince may be a Christian, but must govern not as a Christian but as a prince. This was an attempt to spiritualize the Church, leaving the dirty work of history to the state. It was in effect an abdication of all moral and organizing activity into the hands of the state.[22]

In this intellectual and spiritual atmosphere, a doctrine of state sovereignty and the autonomy of politics develops. The mysterious theory of *raison d'état* takes shape. Pascal said: '*le coeur a ses raisons que la raison ne connaît point*';[23] *raison d'état* theory had already said: 'The state has its morality which morality knows nothing of.' Justus Lipsius, the first editor of Tacitus (1574), said that sovereigns should be moral, but that there were two moralities: a rigorous one for

---

21. See David Hume (as Realist), *Treaties on Nature* (London: Dent & Sons Co., 1949), vol. II, pp. 200, 228, 265-7.
22. Luigi Sturzo, *Church and State* (London: Geoffrey Bles, 1939), pp. 195-6.
23. Blaise Pascal, ed. Leon Brunschvicg, *Pensées* (Paris: Libraire Hachette, 1922), p. 458.

private persons, and a wider and freer one for sovereigns, who have heavy and dangerous responsibilities to discharge: 'He must sometimes evade and twist, mix prudence with justice, and, as they say, sew to the lion's skin if it is not enough, a fox's skin . . .'[24] This was a reference to Machiavelli:

A prince, therefore, being compelled knowingly to adopt the beast, ought to choose the fox and the lion; because the lion cannot defend himself against snares and the fox cannot defend himself against wolves. Therefore it is necessary to be a fox to discover the snares and a lion to terrify the wolves. Those who rely simply on the lion do not understand what they are about. Therefore a wise lord cannot, nor ought he to, keep faith when such observance may be turned against him . . . Endless modern examples could be given, showing how many treaties and engagements have been made void and of no effect through the faithlessness of princes; and he who has known best how to employ the fox has succeeded best.[25]

Notice how Machiavelli begins by recommending the character of the fox as one who can escape from snares, and unconsciously switches over to regarding the fox as one who sets snares. But he was adapting an old tag which is to be found in Plutarch and Pindar.[26] As Cicero said: 'While wrong may be done, then, in either of two ways, that is, by force or by fraud, both are bestial: fraud seems to belong to the cunning fox, force to the lion; both are wholly unworthy of man, but fraud is the more contemptible.'[27] The voice of ancient Rationalism speaks here. In Plutarchian and Machiavellian form this became a proverb in Renaissance political literature. (The Rationalist tradition survives in Lipsius too, who laid down three conditions before consenting to the 'wider scope' of political morality: public utility; legitimate defence; and a spirit of moderation.)[28]

Richelieu, that great exponent of *raison d'état*, not only tended in practice towards the separation of morality from politics, he also wrote in his *Maximes d'Etat* (LXXX): 'In state affairs it is not as in others; in the one case we must begin by elucidating where right lies; in the other by execution and possession.' That is, shoot first and litigate afterwards. Mazarin's thought is expressed by his librarian, Gabriel Naudé, in his *Considérations politiques sur les coups d'état*: there are two prudences, one ordinary and easy, the other extraordinary and difficult. From time to time, princes must abandon right in preference for the common good, or 'reason of state'. Thus,

24. Quoted in L. Sturzo, *Church and State*, p. 269.
25. Niccoló Machiavelli, *The Prince*, (London and Toronto: J.M. Dent, 1928), ch. XVIII, p. 142, see also p. 158.
26. Plutarch, 'Lysander', *Lives* (London: Heinemann, 1959), vol. IV, ch. 7, p. 251. 'Isthmian Odes IV' *The Odes of Pindar* (London: William Heinemann, 1919), verses 45–50, p. 465.
27. Cicero, *De Officiis* (London: Heinemann, 1947), bk. I, XIII, p. 45.
28. L. Sturzo, *Church and State*, pp. 268–9.

without secrecy, the massacre of St. Bartholomew's Eve would have failed of its purpose, as would the murder of the Guises.[29]

There is a further degree of sophistication when the double standard is enlarged to a triple standard: personal morality, which is moral; civic morality, which is quasi-moral; and international morality, which is non-moral. This makes a distinction between two kinds of political morality, which was suggested if not worked out by Hobbes, who taught that morality is derived from power: 'Before the names of just and unjust can have place, there must be some coercive power.'[30]

Hume expresses this also in *An Inquiry Concerning the Principles of Morals* (1751): human nature cannot subsist without the association of individuals, and that could never take place without regard to the law of equity and justice. But nations can subsist without intercourse: they even subsist during a general war.

The observance of justice, though useful among them, is not guarded by so strong a necessity as among individuals; and the *moral obligation* holds proportion with *the usefulness*. All politicians will allow, and most philosophers, that REASONS of STATE may, in particular emergencies, dispense with the rules of justice, and invalidate any treaty or alliance, where the strict observance of it would be prejudicial, in a considerable degree, to either of the contracting parties.[31]

Similarly, Creighton wrote to Acton (12 April 1887): 'The statesman always seems to me in a non-moral position, because he has to consider what is possible as well as what is best, and the compromise is necessarily pitiable.'[32]

To regard politics as the sphere of the non-moral is in effect to regard it as the sphere of the immoral. This is the implication of Cavour's famous saying: 'If we were to do for ourselves, what we are doing for Italy, we should be great rogues.'[33] It implies an antithesis, not between the morality of private life and that of public life, but between the morality of private life and the immorality of politics. It is how Mazzini saw it, or at least saw Cavour's career:

Partisans of opportunity, you have no right to invoke principles; worshippers of the *fait accompli*, you may not assume the garb of the priest of morality. Your science lives in the phenomenal world, in the event of the day — you have no ideal. Your alliances are not with the free, but with the strong; they

---

29. ibid., p. 268.
30. Thomas Hobbes, ed. M. Oakeshott, *Leviathan* (Oxford: Basil Blackwell, 1946), ch. XV, p. 94.
31. David Hume, *Essays and Treatises* (Edinburgh: Bell & Bradfute & Blackwood, 1825), vol. II, sect. IV, p. 243.
32. J.N. Figgis, ed., *Selections from the Correspondence of the First Lord Acton* (London: Longmans, Green & Co., 1917), vol. I, p. 310.
33. E.L. Woodward, *Three Studies in European Conservatism* (London: Constable & Co. Ltd., 1929), p. 297n.

rest not on notions of right and wrong, but on notions of immediate material utility. (From an open letter of June 1858 in *L'Italia del Popolo*)

Thus, if politics is the sphere of the non-moral, it is the sphere of expediency, governed not by considerations of right and wrong but only of immediate utility.[34] The chief criterion of action is results. This is Machiavellianism:

When the safety of one's country wholly depends on the decision to be taken, no attention should be paid either to justice or injustice, to kindness or cruelty, or to its being praiseworthy or ignominious. On the contrary, every other consideration being set aside, that alternative should be wholeheartedly adopted, which will save the life and preserve the freedom of one's country.[35]

Like Rationalists, Realists see politics as the field of the approximate and provisional and they see compromise as the characteristic mode of statecraft, but they tend to see compromise differently from Rationalists. The latter conceive of political compromise as being between the political agent, or statesman, and the totality of circumstances within which he has to act. Realists conceive of it more narrowly, as a compromise between the political agent and his opponent or enemy. Instead of being construed as an approximation of justice in intractable circumstances, compromise is construed as a bargain to be struck with your opposite number.

The pursuit of a compromise of this second kind, a bargain, is also governed by the principle of choosing the lesser evil, but the result of conceiving of political compromise in this manner is subtly to deflect one's interest and attention from the consideration of trying to secure some sort of justice for all parties concerned, to the consideration of the technical conditions for reaching an agreement. The emphasis is on the technique rather than the content of the bargain, on the sheer expertise, what Machiavelli called *virtù* (virtuosity).

The Realist will say that the Rationalist account of politics is unreal, and does not provide a true description of what happens. It is all very well to speak of politics as the sphere of justice (of, for example, the Anglo-Egyptian negotiations over Suez in 1954 as an assessment of the rights due to either party, and of Eden and General Neguib as trustees for their respective nations), but this is just a kind of political allegory. A university of moralists, theologians and jurists could not arrive at any useful conclusions about what, if any, the just rights of the British (for whom Eden was the supposed trustee) were in the Canal Zone, or whether the just rights of the Egyptian people were properly

34. See J.S. Mill, *Utilitarianism* (London: Dent, 1929), pp. 55ff.
35. Niccoló Machiavelli, tr. Leslie G. Walker, *The Discourses of Niccoló Machiavelli* (London: Routledge & Kegan Paul, 1950), vol. I, p. 573.

represented by General Neguib, a military dictator established by *coup d'état*. The negotiations, far from being an Aristotelian essay in giving to each that which is his due, were, rather, between two harassed statesmen, one trying to confirm his seizure of power by a diplomatic success, the other trying to confirm his position as heir-presumptive to the leadership of the Conservative Party; one trying to out-manoeuvre the dispossessed politicians of the Wafd and the street-mobs of Cairo and Alexandria, the other trying to outflank Tory backbenchers; one trying to revive and renovate the most corrupt, ramshackle and precarious state in the Middle East, the other the representative of a declining great power which was seeking (with as good a grace and as small a loss of prestige as possible) to liquidate a sphere of influence which it had become too weak to maintain. They were both striving, not for an assessment of rights but an accommodation of interests, with an awareness of the possible benefits from the United States if they pulled it off, and of the more concrete dangers from Russia if they did not.

To speak, again, of the four-power 'parley at the summit' in the summer of 1955 as an assessment of rights due to each party, and of Eden, Eisenhower, Bulganin and M. Fauré as trustees for their respective nations, is yet another example of political allegory. What were the rights of the United States in Western Europe, or of the Soviet Union in Eastern Europe? Was the USSR in any sense a trustee for the People's Republics and East Germany, Bulganin a true trustee of the Russian people, or the United States in any sense a trustee for NATO? This was not an Aristotelian essay in giving to each that which is his due, but a meeting of four harassed statesmen: Eisenhower looking over his shoulder at Congress and the Republican Party; Eden anxious to consolidate his election victory; Fauré expecting to be summoned home because his majority in the Chamber had collapsed before the conference ended; and Bulganin anxious to consolidate his position and overthrow Malenkov, with all that implied then of the new dependence of Russia on Mao. All four were aware of the armaments race and haunted by it, and haunted more by the dangers of relinquishing their positions of strength without tangible compensation. Again, they were striving, not for an assessment of rights but for an accommodation of interests.

The Cyprus problem in 1956 is a third example where to talk of Eden, Dulles, Makarios, Karamanlis and Menderes as trustees for their respective nations, is no more than a political allegory. Whether Britain had any just rights in Cyprus; whether her oil-cum-strategic interests in the Middle East created just rights; whether Greece's nationalist claims to Cyprus were just; whether it would have been more just for the Cypriots to have Enosis at the expense of the massacre or oppression of the Turkish minority (whatever promises were given) than for the Turks to be protected under British rule at the expense of the Greek Cypriots' not having self self-determination; or whether it was just for a NATO power to take over a base in Cyprus at the expense of the desires and claims Russia had for a share in the arrangement of the eastern Mediterranean and the Middle East are unanswerable questions. But these are not the terms in which politics are discussed (except for the benefit of politically illiterate electorates) or shaped. This was again a group of harassed statesmen, Eden wondering how far he could back out of an untenable position without provoking the lunatic Tory fringe into a break-away; Karamanlis preferring a moderate line but knowing that his government only held on to power by keeping in line with Greek public opinion on Cyprus; Menderes cursing the British for having used Turkey as an alibi for their own political incompetence and wondering how to save face if he abandoned the Cypriot Turks; and Dulles wondering how much Turkey would have to be offered in economic compensation for the abandonment of its intransigence over Cyprus. All of them were haunted by the apparent crumbling of NATO, and all were striving, not for an assessment of rights, but an accommodation of interests.

This is the true portrait of political action in international affairs, and it shifts the emphasis away from the moral tensions and pre-occupation with justice of the Rationalist view, to the actual conditions in which diplomatic agreements are brought off. It considers the political support negotiations can count on, the balance of forces in the region concerned, and the element of timing.

Appeasement, since the failure of Chamberlain's policy, has been the term of abuse Rationalists reserve for the Realists' kind of compromise: the 'bargain' compromise, accommodation-of-interests rather than assessment-of-rights compromise. Appeasement has come to mean compromise in which some party's rights are ignored or betrayed.

If political decisions are seen in these Realist terms, the idea of the lesser evil loses its central place as an ethical principle, and is replaced by two other criteria: necessity and success. Justification by necessity and justification by success are non-ethical principles. Justification by necessity obviously differs from the principle of choosing the lesser evil; it implies that there is not a choice of evil courses but one inescapable evil course which it is decided to adopt. There is almost certainly some degree of illusion or intellectual dishonesty in the appeal to this principle: is a government ever faced with a situation where there is no choice of evils? Going to war is usually adduced as the supreme example of a necessitous decision, when the principle of lesser evil has become inapplicable; but after all, a country need not go to war: it can give in. The Czechs did in 1938; the Danes in 1940. And it can lay down its arms after defeat, as the French did in 1940.

Chamberlain's defence of Munich, as already suggested, slid imperceptibly between the lesser evil and the necessity principles. In March 1939 (after Hitler's entry into Prague), he told the Birmingham Unionist Association: 'Really I have no need to defend my visits to

Germany last autumn, for what was the alternative?'[36] It was a question demanding the answer 'None'. But the truth was, of course, that there was an alternative, which Chamberlain (and his hearers also) regarded as the greater evil.

Dr Dalton appealed to the same principle of justification by necessity in the House of Commons debate on the American loan agreement in December 1945: 'But to those who are critical of these arrangements I put one blunt question: What is your alternative? What would happen if we reject this agreement?'[37] and Mussolini: 'When an event was fated to happen it was better to happen with one's consent than in spite of it.'[38]

The principle of justification by success goes even further than the necessity principle into the realm of the non-moral. The latter shows Realism, as it were, on the defensive: to justify a political decision on the grounds that it is unavoidable represents a last departing tribute to the validity of the ethical: the tribute of recognition but non-fulfilment. The principle of success shows Realism fully matured, and moral tensions finally replaced by considerations of technical accomplishment: politics for politics' sake. Thus Rationalists condemn the success principle very severely: Burke said, 'the only infallible criterion of wisdom to vulgar judgements is success', and Acton, 'there is not a more perilous or immoral habit of mind than the sanctifying of success'. But the principle cannot be dismissed quite so sweepingly. Hitler said: 'The test of greatness as applied to a political leader is the success of his plans and his enterprises, which means his ability to reach the goal for which he sets out',[39] and this expresses at least half the truth. Treitschke observed: '"War creates no right which was not already existing", as Niebuhr [Barthold Georg Niebuhr, great-grandfather of Reinhold] truly said, and, for this very reason isolated deeds of violence are justified by their successful accomplishment, witness the achievement of German and Italian unity.'[40] And Sumner Welles: 'The wisdom of any foreign policy can generally be determined only by its results.'[41]

It is characteristic of politics that actions which by themselves are ethically reprehensible can have consequences which are recognized by subsequent generations as beneficial: and '*die Weltgeschichte ist das Weltgericht*'[42] (the world's history is the world's judgement).

---

36. Neville Chamberlain, *The Struggle for Peace* (London: Hutchinson, 1939), p. 20.
37. *Hansard's Parliamentary Debates*, vol. 417, col. 440.
38. Benito Mussolini, *Scritti e discoursi* (Milan: Hoepli, 1938), vol. XI, p. 226.
39. Adolf Hitler, tr. James Murphy, *Mein Kampf* (London: Hurst & Blackett, 1939), p. 181.
40. Heinrich von Treitschke, *Politics* (London: Constable & Co., 1916), vol. II, p. 598.
41. Sumner Welles, *The Time for Decision* (London: Hamish Hamilton, 1944), p. 223.
42. Friedrich von Schiller, 'First lecture as Professor of History', Jena, 26 May 1789, *The Oxford Dictionary of Quotations* (Oxford: Geoffrey Cumberlege, 1953), p. 415.

Revolutionists

A look at the ethical principles behind Revolutionist political theory shows the same questions, but again with new emphases. Like Realists and Rationalists, Revolutionists see a double standard of ethics inherent in political life. However they see it not as tension between love and justice, nor a contradiction between private ethics and political amorality. The true Revolutionist knows no tension between private morality and political life; the former is subordinated to the latter, to the Revolutionary aim. But Lenin betrayed traces of this tension when listening with Gorki to Beethoven:

I know nothing that is greater than the 'Appassionata'. I'd like to listen to it every day. It is marvellous super human music. I always think with pride — perhaps it is naive of me — what marvellous things human beings can do! . . . but I cannot listen to music too often. It affects your nerves, makes you want to say stupid things and stroke the heads of people who could create such beauty while in this vile hell. And now you mustn't stroke anyone's head — you might get your hand bitten off. You have to hit them on the head, without any mercy, although our ideal is not to use force against anyone. Hm, Hm, our duty is infernally hard.[43]

It is the vestiges of this tension in Lenin that make him truly great. Kaganovich told Victor Kravchenko: 'A Bolshevik must be hard, brave and unbending, ready to sacrifice himself for the Party. Yes, ready to sacrifice not only his life but his self-respect and sensitivity';[44] and Danton: '*Que mon nom soit flétri et que la France soit libre*' (may my name be vilified, but let France be free). The Revolutionist must sacrifice himself and his private ethics for the cause, so there is no tension or dichotomy between private life and political aims. The political sphere swallows up the private. The conception of a double standard is transposed into the terms of political chronology: the contrast is between the political ethics by which the revolution is being brought to fulfilment, and those which will obtain when evolution has been achieved. Now: split skulls open; then: there will be no violence. 'Now' is the sphere of *Interimsethik*.

Revolutionists, again like Realists and Rationalists, see politics as the field of the approximate and provisional, and believe compromise to be the characteristic mode of statecraft. But they interpret these conceptions in a slightly different way from the other two traditions. They see politics as a field, not of perpetually repeated and unfulfilled approximation, but of steadily increasing approximation towards the fulfilment of political ends. This difference of view provides one of the specific marks of the Revolutionist. While the Rationalist conceives

---

43. Quoted in Edmund Wilson, *To the Finland Station* (London: Martin Secker & Warburg Ltd., 1941), p. 386.
44. V. Kravchenko, *I chose Freedom* (New York: Charles Scribner's Sons, 1946), p. 275.

of compromise as doing the best possible in the given situation, the totality of circumstances, the Revolutionist sees that every decision alters the given situation progressively and contributes to the direction of future events. Like the Realist, he will perhaps interpret compromise as striking a bargain with one's political opponent, but he will see this in the light of tactical manoeuvring within the terms of a comprehensive strategic plan. The Revolutionist can be expected to be as opportunist in his political ethics as the Realist.

After Yalta, Stalin professed indifference about the internal regime in the new Poland, provided only that it gave guarantees that Polish territory would never again be the avenue of a Western invasion against Russia. Then Manuilsky (a former chairman of the Komintern and Foreign Minister of the Ukrainian SSR from 1944−52) pronounced in a speech that the Soviet Union was safe only if Poland was sovietized. At the San Francisco Conference a Polish delegate asked Manuilsky to explain the inconsistency. His reply was memorable: 'We are political men, and at different times, on different questions, we put forward different statements.' The theory of political compromise as tactics governed by an *Interimsethik* recurs constantly in Marxist writings, and is highly developed. Vladimir Sorin wrote: 'Tactics permit manoeuvering, tacking, the transition from certain methods of struggle to others, alternate attacks and retreats on the basis of an exact calculation of forces.'[45] And Lenin declared: 'I want to support Henderson [leader of the British Labour Party from 1914 to 17] with my vote in the same way as a rope supports one who is hanged', and again:

It is necessary to combine the strictest loyalty to the ideas of communism with the ability to make all necessary practical compromises, to 'tack', to make agreements, zig-zags, retreats and so on, in order to accelerate the coming into political power of the Hendersons . . . and their loss of power.[46]

Such a conception of political tactics is not related to the principle of justification by necessity, and that of justification by success undergoes a protean change when Revolutionists appeal to it. It becomes more accurately described as the principle that the end justifies the means.

The fundamental principle of democracy is *salus populi suprema lex*. Translated into the language of revolutionaries this means the success of the Revolution is the supreme law. If for the success of the Revolution we were

---

45. 'Partiia i Oppozitsiia' (The Party and the Opposition), Moscow, 1925, p. 42, quoted in Raymond L. Garthoff, 'The Concept of the Balance of Power in Soviet Policy-Making', *World Politics*, vol. IV, October 1951 (Princeton: Princeton University Press), p. 91.
46. V.I. Lenin, 'Left Wing Communism: An Infantile Disorder', *A Handbook of Marxism* (London: Victor Gollancz, 1935), pp. 880, 887.

to find ourselves obliged temporarily to restrict the action of one or other of the democratic principles, it would be a crime to hesitate before such a restriction. (Lenin at the second Congress of the RSDLP (Russian Social-Democratic Labour Party) in Brussels, 1903.)

This recalls an earlier Revolutionist, Billaud Varennes, member of the Committee of Public Safety, when he declared:

We were *statesmen*; putting the safety of the cause entrusted to us above every other consideration. Do you reproach us with the means we used? But the means made that great cause to triumph. Our eyes were fixed too high to see that the ground on which we trod was covered with blood. Reproach us if you will but also say: 'They did not fail the Republic!'[47]

For Rationalists, the means ought to be morally consonant with, and appropriate to, the end; Realists tend to confound the end in means, losing sight of the end and emphasizing technical success alone; Revolutionists are those who assert the literal meaning of the principle, that the end justifies, and sanctions, the means. It is not irrelevant that the doctrine is first attributed to the Jesuits. The Rationalist principle of the lesser evil becomes transformed by Revolutionists into that of doing evil that good may come. They do not weigh unavoidable evils and choose the lesser with loathing, as Lincoln did, but boldly commit an evil with the assurance that good will result, as Lenin did. This is *politique du pire*, and gives another dimension to the principle of necessity, forming the criterion for the principle of success. Where the Realist muses 'If it comes off, I will be justified', the Revolutionist says, 'It is bound to come off, therefore I will do it'. Revolutionist ethics, and the moral tensions they give rise to, are most brilliantly expounded in Arthur Koestler's *Darkness at Noon*.[48]

Inverted Revolutionists

This survey of international ethics would not be complete without mention of another tradition, contrasted with these. It is that of inverted Revolutionists, of whom pacifists are the chief, although not the only, example. They assert that there is no double standard of morality. They say, in effect, that the Sermon on the Mount lays down an absolute standard of ethics which is valid in all circumstances. Bismarck said, 'you cannot govern with the Sermon on the Mount'; Luther, as we have noted, that to govern according to the Gospel would be the same as letting loose savage beasts; and Churchill: 'The

---

47. Quoted in C. Dawson, *Understanding Europe* (London: Sheed & Ward, 1952), pp. 197–8.
48. Arthur Koestler (Ivanov vs. Rubashov), *Darkness at Noon* (London: Jonathan Cape, 1941), pp. 149–54.

Sermon on the Mount is the last word in Christian ethics. Everyone respects the Quakers. Still, it is not on these terms that Ministers assume their responsibilities of guiding States.'[49] But the Quakers and Tolstoy and Gandhi assert the authority of the perfectionist ethic. They repudiate any valid distinction between love and justice; all human relationships must ultimately be based on love. Justice, properly understood, is the fulfilment of love, and not a separate and implicitly contradictory principle. If love and righteousness are aimed at, justice shall be established on the way; indeed it will be secured only if one aims primarily not at it, but at the love-relationship of which it is only an uncompleted part.[50] Thus there is not a double standard of morality but a single one, and political ethics ought to be assimilated to private ethics.

This doctrine is particularly associated with absolute pacifists, those who repudiate war in all circumstances, but similar language has been used by statesmen who are not pacifists. In his address to Congress on the declaration of war in 1917, Wilson said, in Grotian vein:

We are at the beginning of an age in which it will be insisted that the same standards of conduct and of responsibility for wrong shall be observed among nations and their governments that are observed among the individual citizens of civilised states.[51]

However, these statements express an approximation of public to private ethics without going so far as to assert an identity of the two; they could still be considered as declaring only that the ethical is valid in both domains.

For the inverted Revolutionist, politics is not the art of the possible. Adherence to an absolutist and uncompromising ethic means that there can be no compromise with evil. The opposite of compromise is to stand out in assertion of your perfectionist ethic. It is the Lutheran: 'Here I stand; I can do no other', or what the Quaker tradition calls 'testimony': 'All bloody Principles and Practices we . . . do utterly deny, with all outward Wars, and strife and fightings with outward Weapons, for any end or under any pretence whatsoever; and this is our Testimony to the whole World' (in 'Declaration from the Harmless and Innocent People of God called Quakers against all Plotters and Fighters in the World, 1660').[52]

Just as a perfectionist ethic replaces compromise by 'testimony', so it repudiates the principle of the lesser evil and asserts instead the

---

49. Winston S. Churchill, *The Second World War: The Gathering Storm* (London: Cassell & Co., 1954), vol. I, p. 265.
50. See G.H.C. MacGregor, *The Relevance of the Impossible* (London: The Fellowship of Reconciliation, 1941), p. 81.
51. E.H. Carr, *The Twenty Years' Crisis* (London: Macmillan & Co. Ltd., 1939), p. 195.
52. G.W. Knowles, intro. and notes, *Quakers and Peace* (London: Sweet & Maxwell Ltd., 1927), Grotius Soc. Publications No. 4, p. 21.

doctrine of *meliorism*: the doctrine that the world may be made better by human effort. Political action presents itself to the inverted Revolutionist not as a choice between evils, but as an upward striving towards good. Thus Isaac Pennington, an early Quaker (1616–79) wrote:

> I speak not . . . against any magistration or people's defending themselves against foreign invasion, or making use of the sword to suppress the violent and evil-doers within their borders (for this the *present estate* may and doth require . . .); but yet there is a *better state*, which the Lord hath already brought some into, and which nations are to expect and travel towards.[53]

There is a clear contrast in emphasis between this and the characteristically Rationalist statement of General Smuts, quoted earlier (p. 243). For Smuts, it is good to assert one's principles, although practice will almost certainly mean a revising downwards from that standard; for the Quaker, it is agreed that general practice is low, and it is all the more one's duty to revise practice up to principles.

But here difficulties start appearing. Adopting the perfectionist ethic (asserting that the way of testimony is greater than the way of compromise, and the principle of meliorism greater than that of choosing the lesser evil), in the hope of escaping from the ambiguities and cutting through the entanglements of political ethics, nevertheless leads speedily back again to the maze of the double standard. This is like Alice, in the garden of the house she reached through the Looking Glass, discovering that every path she followed twisted curiously, more like a corkscrew than a path, and bringing her slap into the door of the house again.[54] Lewis Carroll is no less convincing as a political allegorist than in illustrating Freudian theory. The way of testimony, the principle of meliorism, both admit and imply that there is a double standard: for the inverted Revolutionist it obtrudes itself in the distinction between the small minority governed by a perfectionist ethic, and the large majority within which the minority hopes to act like the leaven within the lump. It does not appear, as with the Rationalist, in the distinction between the ethic of love and that of justice; nor, as with the Realist, in the distinction between the ethic of private life and the non-morality of political life; nor as with the simple Revolutionist, in the distinction between the *Interimsethik* of ruthless expediency and opportunism and the ultimate ethic of love.

There are at least two levels on which the inverted Revolutionist's position tends to break down and become something different. The extreme of perfectionism is what is known as quietism. It is the total withdrawal into the sphere of the private ethic, and repudiation of the political sphere altogether. It involves a passive attitude towards life,

---

53. ibid., p. 23.
54. Lewis Carroll, *Through the Looking Glass* (London: Macmillan, 1921), p. 26.

devotional contemplation, and abandonment of the will. This has been a position adopted by many religious sects, before and since the Reformation, and it is very attractive to the intelligent and sensitive person today: the political sphere obviously offers nothing but insoluble predicaments; there is inevitably going to be a third world war which will destroy civilization; for political incompetence and buffoonery there is nothing to choose between the political parties so there is no point in exercising one's vote; all one can do is to retire within the sphere of private life and personal relationships and cultivate one's garden. (This is a position which is close, perhaps, to E.M. Forster's.)

It is a position, however, which is inverted, indeed, and introverted, but no longer Revolutionist. Revolutionism was defined at the outset as an approach to international politics which is governed by missionary zeal to renovate the international community. George Fox, in his 'Epistle to all Friends Everywhere', wrote: 'Live in love and peace with all men, keep out of all the bustlings of the world; meddle not with the powers of the Earth; but mind the Kingdom, the way of peace.'[55] We might interpret this in a quietist sense, but it would be wrong to do so. Quaker doctrine clearly sees the characteristically Quaker testimony, of non-resistance and absolute adherence to the ethic of love, as something that is intended to spread, evoking the latent power of love in all people, and transforming the world by the transformation of souls.

A second example of meliorism, and the repudiation of the lesser evil principle, is provided by Henry Wallace's speech at Chicago, 29 December 1947:

There is no real fight between Truman and a Republican. Both stand for a policy which opens the door to war in our lifetime and makes war certain for our children.
Let us stop saying 'I don't like it, but I am going to vote for the lesser of two evils.' Rather than accept either evil, come out boldly, stand upright and say, so loudly that all the world can hear — 'We are voting for peace and security for ourselves and our children's children'.[56]

Exactly this same doctrine was appealed to subsequently by the English Bevanites, continental neutralists, and Indian foreign policy. It is a doctrine which seems, to the external critic, to carry the impulse to revise one's practice upwards to the point where one's feet lose contact with the earth. The repudiation of the principle of lesser evil can become the pursuit of the illusory alternative; this is the danger it always runs, and at this point it loses the moral dignity of the quietist who recognizes that the political predicament is insoluble, and withdraws from politics altogether.

---

55. *Quakers and Peace*, p. 20.
56. See Peter Calvocoressi, Henry Wallace announcing himself as candidate for the Presidency, *Survey of International Affairs, 1947–48* (London: Oxford University Press, 1952), p. 43ff.

Conclusion

The character of political principles is elusive (it is an elusiveness which gives all study of ethics its fascination); they have a protean nature and one principle shades off imperceptibly into another. Here, more than in any of the paradigms offered before now, it is essential to emphasize that this has been an attempt to pin down and define the *central* principles and *characteristic* doctrines of each of the three traditions. Each blends with the others along the circumference. The principles of political ethics are a sliding-scale or spectrum. The single standard slips into implying a double standard; the stern conception of moralism, that the only ethic is to do our duty in politics, slides into doing our best in politics, which implies approximation and compromise. Doing your duty becomes choosing the lesser evil, but that is one form of doing evil that good may come, and appeals to the principle of justification by necessity. It enters on to the domain of the principle that the end justifies the means, which is opportunist in character, and appeals to the principle of justification by success.[57]

Statesmen act under various pressures, and appeal with varying degrees of sincerity to various principles. It is for those who study international relations to judge their actions, which means judging the validity of their ethical principles. This is not a process of scientific analysis; it is more akin to literary criticism. It involves developing a sensitive awareness of the intractibility of all political situations, and the moral quandary in which all statecraft operates. It requires a sympathetic perception which offers an insight into moral tensions, and it is to be obtained by cultivating the acquaintance of politicians and statesmen; by reading history (beginning with Thucydides, which is a record of Koestler's 'Antinomies of Applied Reasoning' concretely illustrated); and by reading Hardy's *Dynasts*, *Gulliver's Travels*, and political novels such as *War and Peace*, *Nostromo*, *Darkness at Noon*, *Nineteen Eighty-four* and others.[58]

---

57. See Arthur Koestler, 'Antinomies of Applied Reasoning', *The Yogi and The Commissar* (London: Jonathan Cape, 1945), pp. 11, 12.
58. Martin Wight mentions 'just a few' further names and titles: Warren Beck; Dostoevsky, *The Possessed* and *The Devils*; E.M. Forster, *A Passage to India*; A. Malraux; Thomas Mann, *The Magic Mountain*; Somerset Maugham, *Then and Now*; Dmitri Merejkowski, *December 14th*; Harold Nicolson, *Public Faces*; George Orwell, *Animal Farm*; Roger Peyrefitte; Ignazio Silone; Stendhal, *The Charterhouse of Parma* [Eds].

12: Conclusion: the balance of the three traditions

In this work I have aimed to establish the existence of the three traditions of international theory. At the same time I have provided certain provisional criteria for classifying any particular theory or assumption about international relations.

A view which emphasizes expertise, technique and *virtù* (virtuosity), which appeals implicitly to the principle of justification by success, asserts that war is natural to man and that it is no use waging it with kid gloves, and which implies a repetitive or cyclical theory of history, may be called Realist. A theory which stresses the moral tensions inherent in political action and the necessity and difficulty of justifying political power, which maintains that war may be waged only with economy of means, and that there are strict limits to what is permissible in war, and which appeals to the principle of the choice of the lesser evil, is in the Rationalist tradition. The Revolutionist view of international relations assumes the necessity of universal renovation. It divides the world into the kingdom of light and the kingdom of darkness, the former being in a state of latent or actual holy war with the latter. It is a view which postulates ideological uniformity between states as desirable and asserts an interim ethic until the kingdom of light is triumphant. It is one, moreover, in which all principles have an ideological limitation, and in which the end justifies the means; or which alternatively asserts that the kingdom of light will triumph only through identification of political with private ethics.

However, all this is merely classification and schematizing. In all political and historical studies the purpose of building pigeon-holes is to reassure oneself that the raw material does *not* fit into them. Classification becomes valuable, in humane studies, only at the point where it breaks down. The greatest political writers in international theory almost all straddle the frontiers dividing two of the traditions, and most of these writers transcend their own systems.

Machiavelli was inspired to write by a passion foreign to the principles of his theory — a passion which breaks out in the last chapter of *The Prince*. Hume's political theory, as expounded in *A Treatise of Human Nature* and in the *Essay on the Balance of Power* is Realist, yet it has affinities with the Rationalist tradition. Hamilton was a Rationalist who moved towards the Realist position. Rousseau provides an interesting contrast between his political theory (*Contrat Social*) and his international theory (*Paix Perpetuelle*). The theory of human nature in the latter work is Rationalist if not Realist — it is almost Hamiltonian; and the federal solution of the international problem which Rousseau proposed is much more along United Nations than League of Nations lines.[1] It was not Rousseau who transposed the doctrine of the general will into international terms; this was the achievement of Revolutionist theory after him.

Thus, the three traditions are not like three railroad tracks running parallel into infinity. They are not philosophically constant and pure like three stately, tranquil and independent streams flowing first from Vitoria and Suarez to J.L. Brierly, secondly from Machiavelli to E.H. Carr, and lastly from Ignatius Loyola to Eric Hobsbawm and Palme Dutt. They are streams, with eddies and cross-currents, sometimes interlacing and never for long confined to their own river bed. They are, to vary the metaphor, threads interwoven in the tapestry of Western civilization. They both influence and cross-fertilize one another, and they change, although without, I think, losing their inner identity. Some of these changes I want to discuss briefly under the suggested heading of 'tendencies', but the main theme might be called 'the erosion of Rationalism'.

It is possible to detect three tendencies at work in the last two centuries: Rationalism into Revolutionism, Rationalism into Realism, and Realism into Revolutionism.

Rationalism into Revolutionism

The tendency of Rationalism towards Revolutionism can be illustrated on the diplomatic level of Rationalist theory. In the discussion of the origins of the theory of the balance of power, it was suggested that there was occasion to notice the displacement of the principle of equilibrium.[2] It was first developed by Realist thought, as a mechanistic description of how international politics worked. It passed to the Rationalists, and was adopted by them as a prescription. This is the movement from analysis to policy, from pure international theory to applied international theory.

While Realism was developing a balance of power theory, the original Rationalist prescription was derived from the just war

---

1. F.M. Stawell, *The Growth of International Thought* (London: Thornton Butterworth Ltd., 1929), p. 165.
2. ibid., p. 161-2.

doctrine. In any war one side was fighting justly, the other not, or less so, and the business of other states was to judge on which side justice lay and aid that with passive benevolence, if not with action.[3]

Spinoza, himself a Realist, was among the first to advocate a balance of power on common-sense grounds.[4] By the end of the seventeenth century it was generally accepted as a central principle of public international policy. Eighteenth-century writers were highly conscious of the balance of power: Hume's *Essay* represents the balance of power as a piece of Realist description, it is an essay in international sociology. Rousseau's *Perpetual Peace* offers it both as Realist description and as policy. Its acceptance into Rationalist tradition may be dated from Vattel, the eighteenth-century naturalist jurist, who innovated on the traditional list of possible causes of a just war by adding the preservation of the balance of power. From then on Rationalism asserted the doctrine of preserving the balance of power (e.g. Burke versus the French Revolution, particularly in *Letters on a Regicide Peace*) down to 1914. At the end of the First World War, the adherence to the balance of power doctrine weakened, and the theory of collective security took its place.

There is an ambiguity about the theory of collective security. On the one hand, in the Realist's view it simply institutionalized the balance of power. Instead of attaining a grand alliance on an *ad hoc* basis painfully and against a disturber of the peace, as for example against Napoleon, the alliance would already be functioning before the event and thus might be a successful deterrent. 'If a League of Nations is a potential alliance, it is essentially an alliance against the *unknown* enemy.'[5] Perhaps indeterminacy of the enemy was the flaw in the Realist conception of collective security.

The alternative view is that collective security replaced the balance of power.[6] As mentioned before (p. 178), this certainly seems to have been the view held by President Wilson. In his Four Principles speech to Congress in February 1918, he says: 'Peoples and provinces are not to be bartered about from sovereignty to sovereignty as if they were mere chattels and pawns in a game, even the great game, now for ever discredited, of the balance of power';[7] and again, 'there must be, not a balance of power, but a community of power; not organised rivalries, but an organised common peace.'[8] In a speech at Guildhall on 28 December 1918, Woodrow Wilson continues the line of argument:

---

3. Sir Geoffrey Butler and Simon Maccoby, *The Development of International Law* (London: Longmans Green Co. Ltd., 1928), p. 229.
4. Stuart Hampshire, *Spinoza* (Harmondsworth: Penguin Books, 1951), pp. 187–202.
5. Sir Arthur Salter, *Security* (London: Macmillan, 1939), p. 155.
6. See chapter 8, pp. 166, 178.
7. Woodrow Wilson, Address to a Joint Session of Congress, 11 February 1918, 'Four Principles Speech', *The Papers of Woodrow Wilson* (Princeton, NJ: Princeton University Press, 1984), vol. 46, pp. 322–3.
8. ibid., vol. 40, p. 536.

They fought to do away with an old order and establish a new one, and the centre and characteristic of the old order was that unstable thing which we used to call 'the balance of power' — a thing in which the balance was determined by the sword which was thrown in on one side or the other; a balance which was determined by the unstable equilibrium of competitive interests; a balance which was maintained by jealous watchfulness and an antagonism of interests which, though it was generally latent, was always deep-seated.[9]

Here we see ideas of renovation and universality, which are characteristic of Revolutionism, and the suggestion that the balance of power might be determined by something other than the sword, which recalls inverted Revolutionism, even if in the pursuit of an illusory alternative.

The belief that the balance of power has become obsolete, that it has been replaced by collective security, has become prevalent in the Western World since then. Bevin voiced it in the House of Commons in 1945.[10] At the Preparatory Commission of the United Nations on the location of the United Nations headquarters, objections to having them in the territory of a great power were described as based on the premise of the balance of power, and therefore obsolete, since the concept underlying the United Nations was collective security (see above p. 179). This non-Realist doctrine of collective security has oscillated between inverted Revolutionism and pure Revolutionism. In inverted Revolutionism, its deterrent aspects are emphasized and it becomes fused with pacifism: the Kellogg Pact is the great monument to this confluence of two incompatible theories. In the pure Revolutionist sense, its punitive aspects are emphasized. If it does not deter an aggressor, it means waging war and this will be not war in defence of interests, like most wars, but war in assertion of a principle, which is ideological war. Thus, violence will be in defence of peace, which is inconsistent with violence in defence of security. Here the doctrine that the end justifies the means reappears, even 'doing evil that good may come'. This is the collective security doctrine which has been criticized as universalizing war:

The threat of universal war as a means of establishing universal peace is a peculiarly English conception that has crystallised in the doctrine of 'sanctions'. This doctrine is analogous to the doctrine of the proletarian dictatorship which would establish social peace by making class-war permanent and universal. 'Sanctions' are the counterpart of the revolutionary terror — the purpose of either is peace, but the effect of both is the consolidation, through war or the threat of war (whether between classes or nations), of power in the hands of those who hold it.[11]

---

9. ibid., vol. 53, p. 532.
10. See Ernest Bevin in the House of Commons, 23 August 1945, *House of Commons Debates* (1945), vol. 413.
11. F.A. Voigt, *Unto Caesar* (London: Constable & Co. Ltd., 1939), pp. 206–7.

It has been said that collective security makes local wars general.

After 1947, the year of the first major crisis of the United Nations, when great-power unanimity was shattered as a result of Russia's use of the veto for purposes of destruction,[12] the doctrine of collective security shifted still further in the direction of Revolutionism, and became associated with the conduct of the Cold War by the West against the Soviet Union. This conduct oscillated between containment and a crusade of liberation, both based on the premise of a holy war; while the conduct of the Cold War by the Soviet Union against the West was based on the doctrine of the balance of power. It was a curious reversal of doctrines.

The tendency of Rationalism into Revolutionism might also be illustrated by three concrete revolutions which happened almost simultaneously and impelled the process: the American, Industrial and French Revolutions.

The American Revolution itself was Rationalist and conservative. Thus it was supported by Burke and Gentz.[13] Its Revolutionist effects came later, in the nineteenth and twentieth centuries, and are seen in the idealism, utopianism, legalism and moralism which culminated in Wilson and Eisenhower. It is open to argument how far these effects were vestigially Rationalist.

The first or British phase of the Industrial Revolution dominated the first half of the nineteenth century. It was expressed in an international theory whose Karl Marx was Adam Smith, and Lenin, Cobden. This *laissez-faire* doctrine has many of the marks of Revolutionism. It proclaims the international solidarity of economic interest, repudiates the doctrine of the balance of power, and uses non-interventionism as a mode of intervention (as Palmerston did in the Italian War of Independence). Cobden and Bright had a passionate admiration for the United States. The international policy they looked forward to was fulfilled in President Wilson.

The French Revolution however is the fountain-head of modern Revolutionism. In political theory this means Rousseau; in international theory, Kant. Kant was the funnel through which the intoxicating alcohol of Rousseau was poured into the veins of international society. Kant saw this as his own function: for him Rousseau was 'the Newton of the moral world'.

Rationalism into Realism

Concrete historical forces are behind this tendency. They are in the

---

12. See Martin Wight, eds Hedley Bull and Carsten Holbraad, *Power Politics* (Leicester: Leicester University Press, 1978), p. 233.
13. See Friedrich von Gentz, tr. J.Q. Adams, *The French and American Revolutions Compared* (Chicago: Gateway editions, H. Regnery & Co., 1955).

nature of international life itself with its inherently anarchical aspects. It is best illustrated in the triumph of *Realpolitik* in the eighteenth century both in practice (Frederick II) and in theory (Vattel). Vattel paid lip-service to Grotius, but adapted the theory of the law of nations to absolute sovereignty and to the unfettered liberty of sovereigns. This trend continued in the nineteenth century with international positivism.

Burke and de Maistre were the two greatest opponents of the French Revolution. The frequent ambiguity in Burke's writing may illustrate the tendency of Rationalism into Revolutionism, or rather, counter-Revolutionism: 'He who fights against tigers must become the tiger himself.' De Maistre tends towards Realism. Sometimes his doctrine of war seems to come close to the Prussian militarism of Moltke and Treitschke but it is never an identity of view; what with them is the expression of a kind of barbarian instinct, with him is an inference drawn from a highly developed intellectual system.[14] One might ask whether de Maistre's theory of war was not more Revolutionist than Realist, a basis for the doctrine of the holy war? This may be so in his successors; during the Napoleonic Wars he himself had been a counter-Revolutionist and all for a holy war against the French Revolution and Napoleon. But his theory of war was written after the Restoration, when emotion could be recollected in tranquillity. He was then concerned, not to prescribe political action, but to explain political experience. He discusses the question of international society; all arguments (he says) to prove the formation of an effective international society are impossible: the Kantian international social contract is impossible. There are societies of individuals but there is not an international society, he says categorically, dissociating himself from Suarez. The argument is made *en passant*, his conclusion apparently being based on the 'great law of violent destruction of living beings'.[15]

Realism into Revolutionism

One might say that the concrete historical forces bound up with and behind this tendency are, primarily, technological developments unifying the world. The inherently anarchical character of international life always makes Realism an easy and attractive interpretation of things. But Realism changes its context as the world is unified economically. Small powers are swept up by great powers, and these for strategic as well as economic reasons have to expand themselves into *Grossräume*, spheres of influence; indeed, the only rational and realistic

---

14. See chapter 10, p. 216.
15. Joseph de Maistre, *Les Soirées de Saint-Pétersbourg* (Paris: Libraire Catholique Emmanuel Vitte, 1924), vol. II, p. 13.

(small 'Rs') organization of international life would be a world state. The technological drive itself creates revolutionary ardour.

Secondly, the democratization of domestic life has made *Realpolitik* fanatical. Increasingly since 1789 wars have been revolutionary wars inflicting revolution as well as defeat on the vanquished. In the field of international theory this tendency is best illustrated by German thinkers from Frederick II to Hitler.

Frederick was the classical calculating Realist. Hitler regarded him as his forebear (not Bismarck, who was Ribbentrop's hero). Frederick's bust stood on Hitler's table, his portrait on his bunker wall. But in Hitler, *Realpolitik* had become demonized into a Revolutionist nihilism. Fichte and Hegel were the great transformation points of Prussian Realism into German Revolutionism, as Kant was the transformation point of eighteenth-century pietistic Rationalism into idealistic Revolutionism.

This German sequence is the main example of the tendency of Realism moving towards Revolutionism. But Hegel's European influence extended to Britain and Italy (although not to France) and through the latter may have been responsible for a great deal of ambiguity in Fascist Revolutionism.

Confluence of the traditions

So there has been a confluence, a convergence, if not to say confusion of traditions. One reason for the revived interest in international theory today is an awareness of this confluence, and a desire to sort things out. Two observations could be made and one problem posed.

Take the theory of appeasement, especially in its classic form in Britain in the 1930s. This policy had its theoretical formulation, and books were written to justify it. It is difficult to characterize, because it blended many elements. We have seen soft as well as hard Revolutionism. Appeasement makes one wonder whether there might not also be a soft Rationalism and a soft Realism.

One could argue that the dominant strains in appeasement were, to begin with, sentimentality, optimism about human nature in politics, self-deception, even pacifism — which was soft Revolutionist. Secondly, there was a false adherence to justice and fairness towards Germany, a false conscience about the injustices of Versailles, a false adherence to the procedure of pacific settlement, false legalism, and false non-interventionism and respect for the rights of a Nazi revolutionary state to arrange its own affairs freely. It was false because it was tinged with the sentimentality referred to above, and it was largely based on sloth and complacence. It was soft Rationalist behaviour. And thirdly, there was national egotism, isolationism, and readiness to betray small allies and violate obligations, all of which led logically to great power deals like Munich. This was soft Realism because it was not nearly smart enough, and led to catastrophic unsuccess.

The second observation concerns the prescriptive rights of Revolutionism. The great difference between Burke's day and ours is that Revolutionist states have been admitted to international society, whence innumerable theoretical inconsistencies arise. A state erected on principles of hostility to other states is admitted to the rights of other states. Revolutionism has itself therefore acquired prescriptive rights.

Here is an example: in October 1950 the General Assembly debated whether United Nations forces should cross the 38th parallel and establish UN authority in North Korea, and so unify Korea. Yugoslavia argued against it: the purpose of the UN action was to check aggression, not to overthrow the regime of an aggressor, for this would be a precedent for intervention in any country's internal affairs. Here was a traditionalist Rationalist argument used to defend a Revolutionist state. It was an argument which in the end excused stalemate, a drawn battle, war with limited purposes.

Has a democratic domestic society the right to defend itself against Revolutionist subversion by suspending democratic rights? Has a Rationalist international society the right to defend itself against Revolutionist subversion and pressure by un-Rationalist methods? Was it not Rationalist to exclude China from the United Nations? Was it not Burkean? The principle had been forfeited, however, when the Soviet Union was admitted. The bar should not have been China's particular misdemeanours but her general construction on principles of hostility to the rest of international society.

The problem posed concerns Mr Dulles's foreign policy.[16] Was he wrong? If so, was he wrong in his principles or his practice? Morgenthau considered him wrong in principle.[17] But if you do not go all the way with Morgenthau you may enquire: How did Dulles's principles differ from those of Grotius or Gladstone? Perhaps the atrophy of Rationalism can be illustrated by the sequence Gladstone–Wilson–Dulles. But it needs to be shown that the deterioration of principle has actually taken place. Perhaps principles have not deteriorated, but their application is no longer appropriate; they have become less relevant.

Valedictory

Rationalism, which used to be an orthodox, traditional, and respectable school of international theory, has grown steadily weaker, steadily dissolved, shedding its strength and support to the schools on

---

16. John Foster Dulles was appointed by President Eisenhower as Secretary of State on 20 January 1953. He resigned on 15 April 1959 and died 24 May 1959.
17. See Hans J. Morgenthau, *Dilemmas of Politics* (Chicago: University of Chicago Press, 1958), pp. 298ff.

the flanks. Hence we have had the recent fashionable division of international theory into two schools: Realists and utopians (Carr), or realists and idealists (Morgenthau).

In this course of lectures I have not wanted to favour any particular international theory. I have had only two conscious aims. One has been to show that the two-schools analysis of international theory is not adequate. It was in fact the reflection of a diseased situation. The diseased situation in Britain in the 1930s inspired E.H. Carr to write. Another diseased situation in the United States during convalescence from isolationism inspired Kennan and Morgenthau to write.

The two-schools analysis may be a useful diagnosis for these diseased situations, but the more it is made the basis for a general international theory the more untrue it seems to become. Thinkers like Grotius or Lenin get crammed into pigeon-holes which were not made for them. Morgenthau implicitly admits that the two-schools scheme breaks down when he allows a category of statesmen with whom there is mysterious coincidence between what moral law demands and what national interest requires. This category includes Jefferson, John Quincy Adams, Gladstone, Cleveland, T. Roosevelt, Wilson as war-leader, Franklin Roosevelt.[18]

I have suggested a triple classification to cover all the phenomena (excluding inverted Revolutionists). But a good argument might be made for at least a quadruple one which would distinguish soft Revolutionists, from Kant to Nehru, from hard Revolutionists like the Jacobins and Marxists. And I have suggested that if Realism is defined by the classic Realists — Machiavelli, Richelieu, Hobbes, Hume, Frederick II, Hegel — then contemporary Realists appear as much Rationalist as Realist.

Kennan is really a Rationalist because he maintains that national interest should be guided by justice; he advocates a non-interventionist policy against the Soviet Union; and he argues that war is the breakdown of policy. Morgenthau is also, partially, a Rationalist. Of his six principles of Realism in the second edition of *Politics among Nations*, at least three are Rationalist: there are objective laws of politics (no. 1); there exists a tension between morals and politics, and prudence is the principle of the lesser evil (no. 4); the moral aspirations of one nation may not be identified with universal moral laws: there is an awareness of the danger of idolatry and respect for the interests of others (no. 5).[19] Nevertheless Morgenthau is fundamentally a Realist: he takes the Hobbesian position that power creates morality; he denies natural law; and he endorses justification by success.

---

18. Hans J. Morgenthau, *In Defense of the National Interest* (New York: Alfred A. Knopf, 1951), p. 19.
19. Hans J. Morgenthau, *Politics among Nations* (New York: Alfred A. Knopf, 1954), pp. 4–10.

If my first aim was to demonstrate the inadequacy of the 'two-schools' analysis, my second aim has been to try to bear out Tocqueville's point which I made at the outset that there is very little, if anything, new in political theory, that the great moral debates of the past are in essence our debates. So I have not wanted to offer any definite conclusions, apart from these: to delimit the scope of international theory, to mark out its boundaries, stake its circle. The reflective person will perhaps feel free to move round the circle and enter into any position without settling anywhere. Of course, if one is preoccupied with the need to impart advice to those who conduct foreign policy, one will have to know where one stands. But it is desirable, and certainly not impossible, to combine the urgency of the committed citizen with the philosophical detachment of a student of international politics.

I find my own position shifting round the circle. You will have guessed that my prejudices are Rationalist, but I find I have become more Rationalist and less Realist through rethinking this question during the course of giving these lectures. If I said Rationalism was a civilizing factor, Revolutionism a vitalizing factor, and Realism a controlling disciplinary factor in international politics, you might think I was playing with words, but I hope I have shown that there is more substance to international theory than that.

Bibliography I:
select bibliography on
international theory

1. General

C. van Vollenhoven, *The Three Stages in the Evolution of the Law of Nations* (The Hague: Nijhoff, 1919).

F. Melian Stawell, *The Growth of International Thought* (Home University Library, London: Thornton Butterworth Ltd., 1929).

Frank M. Russell, *Theories of International Relations* (Appleton Century, 1936).

Kenneth W. Thompson, 'Toward a Theory of International Politics', *American Political Science Review*, vol. xlix, pp. 733–46.

Kenneth W. Thompson, 'Mr. Toynbee and World Politics: War and National Security', *World Politics*, vol. viii, pp. 374–91.

2. The Kantian tradition

Dante, *De Monarchia*, tr. D. Nicholl (Weidenfeld & Nicolson, 1954).

Hubert Languet, *Vindiciae contra Tyrannos*, ed. H.J. Laski (Bell, 1924), part iv.

Kant, *Idea of a Cosmopolitical History* (1784).

Kant, *Perpetual Peace* (1796).

Kant, *Metaphysical Principles of Jurisprudence* (1797), sections 53–62.

Kant's Principles of Politics, ed. W. Hastie (Edinburgh: Clark, 1891).

Kant's Philosophy of Law, ed. W. Hastie (Edinburgh: Clark, 1887).

'The Act of the Holy Alliance', in W. Alison Phillips, *The Confederation of Europe*, (Longmans, 1920), appendix.

R. Cobden, *Russia* (1836), ch. iii, 'The Balance of Power' in *Political Writings* (1868), i. 253–83.

G. Mazzini, *Life and Writings*, 6 vols (Smith, Elder, 1890–1): 'Notes on the Organisation of Young Italy', i. 174ff. 'Pact of Fraternity of Young Europe', iii, 26ff. 'The Holy Alliance of the Peoples', v. 265ff. 'Non-Intervention', vi. 300.

John S. Curtiss, *An Appraisal of the Protocols of Zion* (Columbia University Press, 1942).

J.A. Hobson, *Imperialism* (new edn, Allen & Unwin, 1938).

Lenin, *Imperialism* (Moscow: Foreign Languages House).

History of the Communist Party of the Soviet Union, chapter 6, section 3: 'Theory and Tactics of the Bolshevik Party on the Questions of War, Peace and Revolution'.

G.A. Nasser, *The Philosophy of the Revolution* (Buffalo: Economica Books, 1959).
A. Camus, *The Rebel* (Hamilton, 1953).

Critical

R. Fueloep-Miller, *The Power and Secret of the Jesuits* (New York: Viking Press, 1930).
H. Heine, *Religion and Philosophy in Germany*, tr. John Snodgrass (London: Trübner and Co, 1882).
B. Croce, *History of Europe in the Nineteenth Century* (Allen & Unwin, 1934).
G. Santayana, *Egotism in Germany Philosophy* (2nd edn, Dent, 1939).
J. Dewey, *German Philosophy and Politics*, (2nd edn, Putnam, 1942).
A. Koestler, *The Yogi and the Commissar* (Macmillan, 1945).
C.J. Friedrich, *Inevitable Peace* (Harvard University Press, 1948).
D.W. Brogan, *The Price of Revolution* (Hamilton, 1951).
E. Voegelin, *The New Science of Politics* (Chicago University Press, 1952).
W. Schiffer, *The Legal Community of Mankind* (Columbia University Press, 1954).
Isaiah Berlin, *The Hedgehog and the Fox* (Weidenfeld, 1953).
A.J.P. Taylor, *The Trouble Makers* (Hamilton, 1957).
Gustav A. Wetter, *Dialectical Materialism* (Routledge, 1958).
Elliot R. Goodman, *The Soviet Design for a World State* (Columbia University Press, 1960).

3. The Grotian tradition

Grotius, *De Jure Belli ac Pacis*, prolegomena (1625).
C. van Vollenhoven, *The Framework of Grotius' Book De Jure Belli ac Pacis* (Amsterdam, 1931).
Locke, *Second Treatise of Civil Government*, chapters 2 and 3.
Montesquieu, *De l'Esprit des Lois*, books 9 and 10.
Rousseau, tr. C.E. Vaughan *A Lasting Peace* (London: Constable, 1917).
Bentham, *Plan for an Universal and Perpetual Peace*.
The Federalist, numbers i–xxv.
Burke, *Thoughts on French Affairs* (1791).
Burke, *Letters on a Regicide Peace* (1796–7).
Wordsworth, *Tract on the Convention of Cintra*, ed. Dicey (Milford, 1915).
A.E. Zimmern, *Spiritual Values and World Affairs* (Oxford University Press, 1939).
R.G. Collingwood, *The New Leviathan*, chapters 28–30 (Clarendon Press, 1942).
John H. Herz, *Political Realism and Political Idealism* (Chicago University Press, 1951).
Robert E. Osgood, *Ideals and Self-Interest in America's Foreign Relations* (Chicago University Press, 1953), introduction and conclusion.
George Kennan, *Realities of American Foreign Policy* (Princeton University Press, 1954).
H.H. Marshall, *Natural Justice* (Sweet & Maxwell, 1959).

Critical

A.P. D'Entrèves, *Natural Law* (Hutchinson's University Library, 1951).
Leo Strauss, *Natural Right and History* (Chicago University Press, 1949).
W. Lippman, *The Public Philosophy* (London: Hamilton, 1955).
J. Bryce, *Studies in History and Jurisprudence*, essay xi: 'The Law of Nature' (Oxford: Clarendon, 1901).
Ernst Troeltsch, 'The Ideas of Natural Law and Humanity in World Politics', in O. von Gierke, *Natural Law and the Theory of Society*, tr. E. Barker, appendix i (Cambridge: Cambridge University Press, 1934).
John Eppstein, *The Catholic Tradition of the Law of Nations* (London: 1935).
H. Lauterpacht, 'The Grotian Tradition in International Law', *British Year Book of International Law*, 1946.
J.L. Hammond, *Gladstone and the Irish Nation* (Longmans, 1938), chapter v: 'Gladstone's European Sense'.
H.J. Morgenthau, *Dilemmas of Politics* (Chicago University Press, 1958), chapter 14: 'The Military Displacement of Politics'.

4. The Machiavellian tradition

Machiavelli, *The Prince* (1513, 1532).
Machiavelli, *Discourses*, ed. L.J. Walker (Routledge, 1950), 2 vols.
Bacon, *Essays*: 'Of Empire', 'Of the True Greatness of Kingdoms'.
Hobbes, *Leviathan* (1651).
D. Hume, *A Treatise of Human Nature*, book iii, part ii: 'Of Justice and Injustice'.
Hegel, *Philosophy of Right*, tr. T.M. Knox (Clarendon Press, 1942).
W. Bagehot, *Physics and Politics* (London: Kegan Paul).
H. von Treitschke, *Politics*, tr. Dugdale and de Bille, vol. ii, chapters 27–28 (London: Constable and Co, 1916).
Hitler, *Mein Kampf*.
S. Freud, *Civilisation, War and Death* (Hogarth Press, 1939).
B. Russell, *Power, a new Social Analysis* (Allen & Unwin, 1938).
F.A. Voigt, *Unto Caesar* (Constable, 1938).
R. Niebuhr, *Moral Man and Immoral Society* (New York: Scribner, 1949).
R. Niebuhr, *Christianity and Power Politics* (New York: Scribner, 1940).
R. Niebuhr, *Christian Realism and Political Problems* (New York: Scribner, 1953).
E.H. Carr, *The Twenty Years' Crisis* (Macmillan, 1st edn, 1939).
H. Butterfield, *History and Human Relations* (Collins, 1951), chapter i.
H. Butterfield, *Christianity, Diplomacy and War* (Epworth, 1953).
H.J. Morgenthau, *Scientific Man versus Power Politics* (Chicago University Press, 1946).
H.J. Morgenthau, *In Defense of the National Interest*, (Knopf, 1951).

Critical

F. Meinecke, *Machiavellism* (Routledge, 1957).
R.W. Sterling, *Ethics in a World of Power* (Princeton University Press, 1958).
W.K. Hancock, 'Machiavelli in Modern Dress', in *Politics in Pitcairn* (Macmillan, 1947).
L. Woolf, *The War for Peace* (Routledge, 1940).

J. Burnham, *The Machiavellians* (Putnam, 1943).

G. Orwell, 'Second Thoughts on James Burnham', in *Shooting an Elephant and Other Essays* (1950).

R. Hofstadter, *Social Darwinism in American Thought* (Beacon, 1955), chapter 9.

H.J. Morgenthau, *Dilemmas of Politics* (Chicago University Press, 1958), chapter 21: 'E.H. Carr'.

5. The Gandhian tradition

Tolstoy, *The Kingdom of God and Peace Essays* (World's Classics).

A. Huxley, *Ends and Means* (Harper, 1937).

J.V. Bondurant, *Conquest of Violence: the Gandhian Philosophy of Conflict* (Oxford University Press, 1958).

M.W.
February, 1965

Bibliography II: supplementary reading list

The following books published more recently and presented in chronological order may prove useful to the reader. We are grateful to Peter Butler, Michael Donelan, Maurice Keens-Soper, James Mayall, N.J. Rengger and Hidemi Suganami for assistance in compiling this list (Eds.).

Herbert Butterfield and Martin Wight, eds., *Diplomatic Investigations* (London: George Allen and Unwin, 1966).

M.G. Forsyth, H.M.A. Keens-Soper and P. Savigear, *The Theory of International Relations: Selected Texts from Gentili to Treitschke* (London: George Allen and Unwin, 1970).

E.B.F. Midgley, *The Natural Law Tradition and the Theory of International Relations* (London: Paul Elek, 1975).

Hedley Bull, *The Anarchical Society* (London: Macmillan, 1977).

W.B. Gallie, *Philosophers of Peace and War* (Cambridge: Cambridge University Press, 1978).

Andrew Linklater, *Men and Citizens in the Theory of International Relations* (London: Macmillan, 1980, 2nd edn., 1990).

Howard Williams, *Kant's Political Philosophy* (Oxford: Basil Blackwell, 1983).

Hedley Bull and Adam Watson, eds., *The Expansion of International Society* (Oxford: Clarendon Press, 1984).

Vendulka Kubálková and Albert Cruickshank, *Marxism and International Relations* (Oxford: Clarendon Press, 1985, pbk. edn., with new Postscript, 1989).

John A. Vasquez, ed., *Classics of International Relations* (Englewood Cliffs, New Jersey: Prentice-Hall, 1986, 1990).

R.J. Vincent, *Human Rights and International Relations* (Cambridge: Cambridge University Press, 1986).

Martin Ceadel, *Thinking about Peace and War* (Oxford: Oxford University Press, 1987).

James Der Derian, *On Diplomacy: A Genealogy of Western Estrangement* (Oxford: Basil Blackwell, 1987).

Ian Clark, *The Hierarchy of States* (Cambridge: Cambridge University Press, revised edn., 1989).

Hedley Bull, Benedict Kingsbury and Adam Roberts, eds., *Hugo Grotius and International Relations* (Oxford: Clarendon Press, 1990).

J.D.B. Miller and R.J. Vincent, eds., *Order and Violence: Hedley Bull and International Relations* (Oxford: Clarendon Press, 1990).

M. Donelan, *Elements of International Political Theory* (Oxford: Clarendon Press, 1990).

June 1991

Paradigms of international theory

	Machiavellian	Grotian	Kantian	Quaker
1. Human Nature:	Pessimistic: Hobbesian paradox	'Men are in publick life as in private, some good, some evil. The elevation of the one, and the depression of the other, are the first objects of all true policy'. (Burke)	Optimistic: Rousseauite paradox	
History:	Cyclic and repetitive	'We are not to expect perfection in this world; but mankind, in modern times, have apparently made some progress in the science of government'. (Washington)	Linear: immanent progress	
Political Coercion:	'Thank God for Machiavelli and that kind of writer, who tell us not what men ought to do but what they in fact do'. (Bacon)	'The great task is to discover not what governments prescribe but what they ought to prescribe, for no prescription is valid against the conscience of mankind'. (Acton)	'Philosophers have only *interpreted* the world in various ways; the point however is to *change* it'. (Marx)	
	Power	Authority	Force	Love
	Politics for politics' sake	Politics for the sake of the good life	Politics for the sake of the doctrine	Repudiation of politics
	Primacy of foreign policy	Primacy of domestic policy	Primacy of ideological complexion	

	Machiavellian	Grotian	Kantian	Quaker
2. International Society:	'Bellum omnium contra omnes' (Hobbes)	'Societas quasi politica et moralis'. (Suarez)	'Civitas maxima' (Wolff)	Brotherhood of man
	Composed of perfect societies	Expressed in diplomatic institutions	Composed of men	
	Fewness and inequality of its members			
	Laws of power politics:		Laws of social progress:	
	Always divided into victors and vanquished		The commercial spirit	
	Chequer-board system of antagonisms and alliances		The spirit of Enlightenment: world public opinion	
3. Relations with Barbarians:	Civilisation has right to expand by conquest	Civilisation has rights only of peaceful trade and conversion	International society embraces all mankind	
	Barbarians have no rights	Barbarians have rights under natural law	Barbarians have right of reprisal against civilisation	
	Exploitation	Trusteeship	Assimilation	
	Aid for strategic motives	Conditional aid	Unconditional aid	
		Aid to promote stability and prosperity	Aid to secure ideological allies	

continued . . .

	Machiavellian	Grotian	Kantian	Quaker
4. National Interest:	Conflict of interests	Tension (contrived harmony) of interests	Solidarity (natural harmony) of interests	
	Sacro egoismo	'Our interest, guided by justice' (Washington)	Interest of mankind	
	Your security is my insecurity	Collective security		
	Presumption against Small Powers	Presumption in favour of Small Powers	Presumption in favour of doctrinal allies	
		Continuity in foreign policy	Discontinuity of foreign policy	
International Right:	Right of the stronger	Right of prescription	Right of ideology	
		Non-intervention the norm	Non-intervention as a mode of intervention	
5. Diplomacy:	Deterrent	Retributive	Reformatory	
	Political self-sufficiency	Political interdependence	Abolition of foreign policy	
	Outsider cannot judge	Outsider has valid judgment	Doctrinal orthodoxy gives valid judgment	
	Divide and rule	Unite and influence: Concert principle	Moral isolationism	
Balance of Power:	Existing distribution of power	Even distribution of power	'Exploding all balances' (Burke of the Jacobins)	
	Any possible distribution of power My side needs margin of strength	Principle that power ought to be evenly distributed		

	Machiavellian	Grotian	Kantian	Quaker
Holding the Balance:	Enjoying a special advantage Enjoying predominance	Having a special duty		
Negotiation:	Objective conditions: Political flux Fear and greed Negotiate from strength	Objective conditions: Dealing on equal terms Mutual confidence Reconcile interests	Objective goals: Reduce tension Open diplomacy Moral suasion: appeal to world public opinion	
Collective Security:	'A general invitation to all the other foxes to get their tails cut off' (Chamberlain) Conciliation Appeasement	Institutionalisation of the balance of power Sanctions Resistance	A kind of crusade	
Peaceful Change:	Yielding to threat of force	Order precedes justice	Justice precedes order	
Disarmament:	Impossible because it would upset existing balance of power Only to be imposed after defeat	Difficult because it would freeze existing balance of power Security (control) precedes disarmament	Necessary because demanded by world public opinion Disarmament precedes security	
Cold War:		Containment Neutrals deserve respect	Liberation Neutrals are enemies	

continued . . .

	Machiavellian	Grotian	Kantian	Quaker
6. Causes of War:	Conflicting interests of states	Natural passions of men	'The minds of men': Educate Institutional maladjustment: Economic inequality Racial inequality: } Improve	
Nature of War:	Continuation of policy Ultima ratio regum: Preventive war	Breakdown of policy Just War: war as litigation: Resist violation of rights or aggression	Instrument of history Holy War: Crusade: Liberation	Non-resistance
	Unlimited warfare Unconditional surrender	Limited warfare Negotiated peace	Genocide Revolution a condition of peace	
7. International Law:	Positivism	Natural law	Natural rights: international law is ideology of the status quo	
Obligation:	Rebus sic stantibus	Pacta sunt servanda	Obligation is provisional Cum haereticis fides non servanda	
Ethics:	Double standard: expediency vs. morality Raison d'etat: Justification by necessity Justification by success	Double standard: justice vs. charity Political morality: Choice of the lesser evil Not all means are permissible	Double standard: Interimsethik vs. millennium Do evil that good may come: politique du pire End justifies the means	Single standard love Do good regardless of consequences

Index